# 'Ali Shari'ati and the Shaping of Political Islam in Iran

**Middle East Today**

Series editors:

Mohammed Ayoob
University Distinguished Professor of
International Relations
Michigan State University

Fawaz A. Gerges
Professor and Chair of Middle Eastern
Politics and International Relations
Director of the Middle East Centre
London School of Economics

The Iranian Revolution of 1979 and the subsequent Gulf Wars, along with the overthrow of the Iraqi President Saddam Hussein, have dramatically altered the geopolitical landscape of the contemporary Middle East. This series puts forward a critical body of first-rate scholarship that reflects the current political and social realities of the region, focusing on original research about the Israeli-Palestine conflict; social movements, institutions, and the role played by nongovernmental organizations such as Hamas, Hezbollah, the Taliban, and the Muslim Brotherhood; Iran and Turkey as emerging preeminent powers in the region—the former an Islamic republic and the latter a democracy currently governed by a party with Islamic roots; the oil producing countries in the Persian Gulf and their petrol economies; the potential problems of nuclear proliferation in the region; and the challenges confronting the United States, Europe, and the United Nations in the greater Middle East. The focus of the series is on general topics such as social turmoil, war and revolution, occupation, radicalism, democracy, and Islam as a political force in the context of modern Middle East history.

*Religion and the State in Turkish Universities: The Headscarf Ban*
Fatma Nevra Seggie

*Turkish Foreign Policy: Islam, Nationalism, and Globalization*
Hasan Kösebalaban

*'Ali Shari'ati and the Shaping of Political Islam in Iran*
Kingshuk Chatterjee

# 'Ali Shari'ati and the Shaping of Political Islam in Iran

Kingshuk Chatterjee

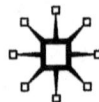

'ALI SHARI'ATI AND THE SHAPING OF POLITICAL ISLAM IN IRAN
Copyright © Kingshuk Chatterjee, 2011.
Softcover reprint of the hardcover 1st edition 2011 978-0-230-11333-6

All rights reserved.

First published in 2011 by
PALGRAVE MACMILLAN®
in the United States—a division of St. Martin's Press LLC,
175 Fifth Avenue, New York, NY 10010.

Where this book is distributed in the UK, Europe and the rest of the World,
this is by Palgrave Macmillan, a division of Macmillan Publishers Limited,
registered in England, company number 785998, of Houndmills,
Basingstoke, Hampshire RG21 6XS.

Palgrave Macmillan is the global academic imprint of the above
companies and has companies and representatives throughout the world.

Palgrave® and Macmillan® are registered trademarks in the United
States, the United Kingdom, Europe and other countries.

ISBN 978-1-349-29511-1   ISBN 978-0-230-11922-2 (eBook)
DOI 10.1057/9780230119222

This book is printed on paper suitable for recycling and made from fully
managed and sustained forest sources. Logging, pulping and manufacturing
processes are expected to conform to the environmental regulations of the
country of origin.

Library of Congress Cataloging-in-Publication Data

Chatterjee, Kingshuk.
  'Ali Shari'ati and the shaping of political Islam in
  Iran / Kingshuk Chatterjee.
      p. cm. — (Middle East today)

  1. Shari'ati, 'Ali.  2. Islam and politics—Iran.
  3. Muslim scholars—Iran.  4. Iran—Politics and government.
  I. Title.
  BP80.S517C43 2011
  320.5′570955—dc22                              2010049232

A catalogue record of the book is available from the British Library.

Design by Integra Software Services

First edition: June 2011

10 9 8 7 6 5 4 3 2 1

*To*
*My father, Manoj Kumar Chatterjee,*
*Who could not wait to see this book*
*And*
*My mother, Swapna Chatterjee,*
*Who did.*

# Contents

| | |
|---|---|
| Acknowledgments | ix |
| Note on Translation and Transliteration | xiii |
| Introduction | 1 |
| 1  The Languages of Power and Politics in Modern Iran | 21 |
| 2  Language of Opposition Politics in Late Pahlavi Iran | 47 |
| 3  The World as *Tauheed*: Envisaging an Islamic Alternative | 73 |
| 4  The Purpose of Political Order: The State or the People? | 99 |
| 5  Sovereignty as Responsibility: *Mazhab-e Aitraz* | 121 |
| 6  The Individual as an Agent of Change: *Khudsazi-ye Inqilabi* | 153 |
| 7  The Ripples of a Revolution | 175 |
| Conclusion | 197 |
| Appendix I    Shi'ism—A Brief Sketch of the Early Years | 203 |
| Appendix II   Selected Works/Lectures of 'Ali Shari'Ati | 209 |
| Glossary of Arabic and Persian Terms | 215 |
| Notes | 219 |
| Select Bibliography | 253 |
| Index | 269 |

# Acknowledgments

It is not an easy task for me to acknowledge appropriately all the assistance I received over the years that went into this work. I was given access to the resources of several libraries, institutions, organizations, and even personal collections without which this work would not have seen the light of day. I have also benefited immensely from interactions with innumerable people upon a range of subjects that have fed into my understanding of the protagonist of my work, my research area, a country and a culture that I have come to love. It may not be possible to mention all of them, but that does not in any way diminish the significance of the role they played in the making of this work.

I am deeply indebted to the Institute for Research and Development of Humanities in Tehran and the authorities of the *Hamaesh Jahani Hikmat-e Motahhari*, who were kind enough to invite me to Iran on two separate occasions. I am also grateful for the support I received from the National Library in Tehran, the libraries of the *Hosseiniyah-ye Ershad* and of the Islamic Encyclopaedia, and the Amir Kabir Institute in Tehran. A special word of appreciation goes to the authorities of the Constitution House, Tabriz.

My time in Iran would not have been nearly as productive as it actually was without the people I met there. I am deeply indebted to Nahid Tavassoli and her family, Reza 'Alijani, Taqi Rahmani, Muhammad Fayyaz Baksh, and Muhammad Muhammadi (who volunteered as an interpreter during my interview with Rahmani) for the long sessions that have helped me make much better sense of 'Ali Shari'ati. I would also like to express my gratitude toward Morhad Saghefi, Kaveh Bayat, and the whole of the *Guftogu* group, who agreed to have me crash in on one of their meetings. I owe a large part of the success of my field trip to Masood Pedram, whom I never met and spoke with only over the phone. But for him, I would probably never have managed to engage with Shari'ati's students and friends as meaningfully as I did. I deeply appreciate Dr. Abbas Manouchehri, who gave me quite a lot of his time, and even gave me a copy of his own doctoral thesis on Shari'ati. I am also particularly grateful to Asef Bayat for all his kindness, valuable advice, and support. Finally, my friends Fatemeh

Sadeghi and her husband, Muhammad Malijoo (aka Omid): my field tour of 2006 would not have been possible had it not been for Fatemeh, who secured me the affiliation I required in Iran. Seeing Iran through the eyes of Fatemeh, Omid, and their friends like Masood Soufi and Paran, I have come to develop a deep attachment for the country and its people.

I would like to express my gratitude for the Fulbright Foundation and the CIES, Washington, D.C., for giving me the opportunity of working for a couple of semesters in the U.S. Naval Academy (USNA) at Annapolis as a scholar-in-residence in 2006–07. My work would have been somewhat poorer without the regular access my stint gave me to the Library of Congress and that of the Naval Academy itself. I would like to specially mention the staff in the Middle East and North Africa section in general, and Ibrahim Pourhadi in particular, for making my time at the Library of Congress so productive. A special word of thanks also to the staff at the library of the Naval Academy, and Barbara Breeden in particular—but for whom I would have had to make so much more effort in laying my hands on useful resources. I would further like to express my appreciation for the staff at the Butler Library in New York for all their cooperation in the brief period that I worked there.

My stint at the Naval Academy was particularly productive in terms of sheer academic exchange. I learned a lot from my colleague Ambassador John Limbert, one of the hostages in the U.S. Embassy in 1979, over the periodic lunches that he would ask me to join him for. I benefited immensely from the experiences of my friends and colleagues Gale Mattox, William Garrett, Robert Kaplan, the academic-with-a-smile Deborah Wheeler, Captain McMahon, and especially, my friend Lt. David Wilcox. I would further like to put on record my gratitude for Ermin Sinanovic, my friend and colleague at the USNA, for his valuable comments and insights on my work. I am also deeply grateful to Prof. Misagh Parsa for his advice, support and encouragement, and to him and his wife, Susan, for the wonderful hospitality I received from them.

I would further like to thank the Iran Culture House, New Delhi and that at Bombay, for a steady supply of primary and secondary sources over the years, even before I had the opportunity to visit Iran. I am also thankful toward the Jawaharlal Nehru University (JNU) and the Institute for Defence Studies and Analyses (both in New Delhi) and the National Library at Calcutta for helping me maintain a steady momentum with my work during those early years.

I am indebted for the support I have always received from the Maulana Abul Kalam Azad Institute of Asian Studies. Having initially been the chief repository of secondary resources in Calcutta for my work, the Institute eventually provided me with a fellowship and then sponsored my field trip to Iran in 2006. This work would not have been possible without the support from MAKAIAS.

I value most highly my interactions with Habib Khalilee Shirazi, who continues to give me a flavor of Iran in Calcutta itself, recounting his personal experience of the country that I have learned to love in a way he would understand. I would further like to thank Professor Asad uz-Zaman, who went beyond the call of his duty in starting me off with Persian. I am equally appreciative of the support and kindness of Sayyid Akhtar Hussain of the Persian Studies Department at JNU. Without the two of them, I would not have made the little progress I have made with my Persian. I would also like to record here my appreciation for Sanaa Sadek, my colleague at the Naval Academy, who volunteered to start teaching me Arabic, and whom I nearly drove crazy.

I would like to thank Professor Gautam Bhadra for triggering my interest in Islam, and Professors Jayanta Kumar Roy and Suranjan Das for opening many doors for me. I am also greatly appreciative of the support and encouragement of Madhumita Majumdar, and my friends (who happened to have been my colleagues), Binoda Mishra, and Kaushik Bandopadhyay; a word of thanks also to Suchandana Chatterjee for always being a big help.

Professor Bhaskar Chakraborty warrants a special mention, for instilling in me a fascination for the history of ideas, especially of the Quentin Skinner variety. This work would not have been conceived of in this manner but for his influence on my thinking. I would also like to thank Subhas Ranjan Chakraborti, Lakshmi Subrahmanian, and Shireen Maswood for their constant support and encouragement; Basudeb Chattopadhyay for more than one reason and Dhruba Babu for just being there. Most of all, I am indebted to Professor Hari Shankar Vasudevan, my mentor and probably the person from whom I have learned the most. If I were able to follow a tenth of the ideas he has floated in my presence, this work would have been considerably more enriched than the way it stands now. His indulgence throughout the course of my research and pleasantly exacting disposition toward the end made it an absolute privilege to work with him.

A word of appreciation is in order for Farideh Koohi-Kamali and Robyn Curtis who made working with Palgrave Macmillan such a pleasure; a special mention is due to Flora Kenson for project management and to Sandhya Ghoshal for weeding out many of those bits that frequently clutter any text. I am also indebted to Ms. Kalpana Shukla for encouraging me to approach Palgrave Macmillan in the first place.

At a more personal level, my friends Anindya Chaudhuri, Anindya Sengupta and Atoorva Sinha provided major support in various ways all through the years. I would also love to acknowledge my friends Madhumita

Buddhiraja, Sutapa Rani Dasgupta, and above all my soul-mate Abeda Razeq for helping me retain my sanity over the years. Life seems to be a blessing having friends like these.

Last but not the least, I thank my parents for their patience, consideration, and support that has seen me through. My father, Manoj Kumar Chatterjee, could not live long enough to see the book in print. I am thankful that my mother, Swapna Chatterjee, did.

# Note on Translation and Transliteration

Despite various attempts at standardizing the mode and methods of transliterations of Arabic and Persian words in English, there is yet to be a simple, scientific, and at the same time, reader-friendly style. There are scholars who prefer each Arabic and Persian letter of the alphabet to be distinct from every other in transliteration, but this occasionally confuses the way a term is pronounced by someone who does not read the source language. There are others who prefer to transliterate a word the way it is pronounced; but even this can be a bit confusing if two words have very similar pronunciations, and are to be differentiated only by means of accents or stress.

Keeping in mind the strength of both the styles, the transliteration in this work by and large follows the way in which a word is spelled, particularly if the word is of Arabic origin (viz., *ummah*), but abjuring diacritical marks as far as possible for the sake of convenience of the reader. Thus, ع ('ain), requiring a lengthening of the vowel that it follows or precedes, is indicated with an apostrophe, that is ( ' ); ق (qaf) is spelled with a "q" rather than a "gh," which is the way it is pronounced in Tehran; و (wao) is generally spelled with an "o" and وّ (wao tashdeed) with a "w/vv", taking into account both the spelling and the pronunciation; ه (he) is spelled with an "eh" for Persian words but "ah"/"at" when the word is Arabic, in consonance with the standard variations in pronunciation. For the sake of simplicity, frequently used Persian words have been spelled the way people are more familiar with their usage. Thus, Persian has at least two variants of the soft sound "t," at least three of "s," and five of "z," with only subtle variations of pronunciation that are almost incomprehensible to someone who does not speak Arabic. No distinction is made in the way they are transliterated from Persian. Thus, Reza is spelled with a "z" and not a soft "d" the way it is done for Arabic (viz., Rashid Rida, which for a Persian speaker would be Rashid Reza). Also for the sake of familiarity, Fatemeh is used interchangeably with Fatima; " ا " (alif mud, pronounced "aa") is spelled properly in the case of *bazaar*, but not Aadam instead of Adam. Terms like *ummah* (Arabic) have been used in their original Arabic form, except when the original text, using its Persian variant *(ummat)*, is being quoted.

Translations from the Persian texts, unless otherwise mentioned, are my own.

# Introduction

Much of the academic debate on aspects of Islam and Muslim life during the last three decades has been dominated by concern with the rise of a militant brand of political Islam, supposedly aiming at the foundation of an Islamic order characterized by adherence to the *shari'ah*.[1] The Islamic Revolution that occurred in Iran in 1979 has often been identified by scholars as among the major milestones in this quest for an Islamic order, by virtue of the debate it generated among Muslims as much as among non-Muslims. More importantly, it is sometimes taken to be a catalyst for what has been identified as the "second generation" of political Islam.[2] Such a narrow identification of the Islamic order frequently distracts attention from the position that such an order is not simply about conforming to the corpus of Islamic laws, but also about the values, issues, and concerns of Muslim societies. In turn, the limited approach to the Islamic Revolution in Iran fails to examine the complexity that marked its political origins and the subtleties of the language of politics that has evolved in Iran, and indeed elsewhere in the Muslim world. Only an intellectual history of the Islamic Revolution—bearing in mind these issues—is capable of setting this record straight. And a firm contribution to such a history is the purpose of this book.

Here, I deal with some aspects of political thought in Pahlavi Iran (1925–79), explicating the ideas of one figure in particular on the eve of the 1979 revolution—'Ali Shari'ati Mazinani. My goal is to explore the development of a language of political Islam in the closing decades of the Pahlavi regime and to demonstrate the close connections between such a language and the origins and character of the Islamic Revolution.

Initially, I delineate crucial trends in pre-1979 politics: "the Pahlavi project of state building" and the terms that marked it, the constitutionalist opposition to that project, and the variety of Islamist oppositions. Thereafter, through a study of the speeches and publications of Shari'ati, I mean to chart the development of a new language of politics in late Pahlavi Iran that advocated resistance to injustice as a positive social, political, and moral virtue and to indicate the manner in which such virtue was equated with the essence of *being* a Muslim. Like other "reinterpretations"/"reinventions," the making of this political language relied on an "essentialization," in this case of Islam—as though arguing that what was being said was always there in the essence of Islam, and had been merely played down in the course of history. I argue that by his innovative use of a set of signs and symbols derived from the history and legends of Islam, Shari'ati was creating a new set of *signifiers* and *signified* for the *referent* of Islam.[3] This is not to argue that Shari'ati was changing the very meaning of Islam, because arguably Islam *does not* have any one *meaning*. This is only to make the case that Shari'ati was imparting a new meaning to what being "Islamic" *signified* by devising a new language of politics in modern Iran.

I chose Shari'ati as my point of entry into the study of the language of revolutionary politics in late Pahlavi Iran because of the impact he had as a radical figure in the broad swathe of opposition to the Shah. Even though Shari'ati died in exile in 1977, the enormous urban demonstrations opposing the Shah that characterized the Islamic Revolution carried posters of *both* Shari'ati and Khomeini. In the politically charged days of 1977–79 their message of uncompromising resistance to the Pahlavi regime (using terms of reference that were so visibly Islamic) seemed identical to many casual observers. After 1979, when Khomeini's followers (and those who supported him for the sake of political expediency) gained control of the levers of the state, Shari'ati fell out of favor somewhat because of the terrorist activities of a group inspired by him, the *Mojahedin-e Khalq*. In the 1980s, Shari'ati's memory was partially rehabilitated by the regime in order to accommodate a vocal leftist combination of clerics (the Society of Combatant Clergy) supportive of the establishment. In present day Iran, Shari'ati is deployed in defense of the current establishment as much as to assail it from the standpoint of political Islam.[4]

The accommodation of Shari'ati was, however, always a reluctant one at best, not least because one of his trademarks was vehement anticlericalism. Other thinkers, such as the communist-turned-Islamist author Jalal Al-e Ahmad, made their peace with the residual significance of the 'ulema in Iran's political life, and some were willing to allow the 'ulema some influence if not actual participation. Shari'ati issued almost a blanket denunciation of the 'ulema as an order for having successfully robbed Islam of its dynamism by confining it to a deadening legalist system. His vision of an Islamic order attached little significance to the 'ulema. In fact, a considerable part of his appeal to urban Iranians, especially the youth, is frequently attributed to this anticlericalism.[5] The problem in denying his credentials, however, as one of the architects of the intellectual opposition to the Shah, would have been still greater than the cost of accommodating him. At a time when the organized political opposition to the Shah had been ruthlessly suppressed, Shari'ati was among the few to have kept up the momentum of opposition by assailing what he understood as the essence of the Pahlavi order—*istibdad* (authoritarianism/despotism).

Most importantly, however, Shari'ati almost reinvented the possibilities of Islamic terms of reference to manufacture a thoroughly modern language of politics. This language was modern enough to win him considerable popularity among a generation of urban Iranians who grew up in a reasonably secularized milieu. Courtesy his immensely popular lectures at the *Hosseiniyeh-ye Ershad*, probably far more people in Tehran had heard and read 'Ali Shari'ati than had heard (or even heard of) Khomeini before 1977. In fact, Morteza Motahhari, the disciple of Khomeini who introduced Shari'ati as a speaker at the *Hosseiniyeh-ye Ershad* in 1967 later felt compelled to engage in a confrontational debate with Shari'ati in the early 1970s in order to defend the *'ulema*. Regardless of individual positions on the nature of political Islam, people had to frequently address issues in response to Shari'ati, as Motahhari, Bazargan, Taleqani, and other advocates of political Islam found out.

In this work I chart the manner in which Shari'ati contributed to the crafting of a language of political Islam, and plot some of its potential implications. To do this I have explored Shari'ati's politicization of a set of key concepts from Shi'i terminology (viz. *tauheed, ummah, imamat, jihad, shahadat, intezar*) and a set of figures from Shi'i legends (such as 'Ali, Fatima, Hossein) to weave the notion of a just society with an enlightened being, the *raushanfikr*, at the heart of it. I then go on to argue that although Shari'ati's works had no indication of any structuralist approach to the institution of democracy, he was nonetheless working toward *a* democratic ideal from a behavioralist standpoint. I mean to show that Shari'ati's approach to politics was aimed more at shaping individuals who could provide leadership to the people in the search for a just society, because he was not bothered with the institutional bases of such an order. The sort of persona that Shari'ati was defining to be the essence of a Muslim was remarkably similar to the essence of a model citizen in a democratic society, if there is such a thing.

My study of the evolution of the language of political Islam addresses an area that has seldom been touched upon with any seriousness till date. As with studies of most other revolutions, research on the Iranian revolution of 1979 has tended to focus either on its causes or on the character of the regime that followed. In either case, the ouster of the last Pahlavi ruler, Muhammad Reza Shah, and the declaration of the Islamic Republic feature as the pivotal points of the revolution. The actual shaping of the Islamic regime (first through the framing of the constitution and then by instituting it in the body politic) is treated merely as details following the revolution. The main reason for this is perhaps that while subsequent scholarly analysis of the revolution revealed deeper socioeconomic roots, the Islamic element in the shaping of the revolution appears by and large axiomatic.[6]

This tendency to accept the use of an unmistakably Islamic *rhetoric* as evidence of the Islamic *character* serves to confuse more issues than it resolves. A simple acceptance of the political *rhetoric* of the revolution as its manifest agenda fails to uncover the complexities latent in the various strands of ideas that made up the revolutionary language. Simply put, the general approach to the study of the revolution would argue that leadership by the Shi'i *'ulema*, their successful deployment of Islamic terms of reference to galvanize popular resistance to the Pahlavis, and the creation of a professedly Islamic state to respond to the iniquities of the previous regime are adequate markers of the Islamic character of the regime. Little attention is paid to uncovering what was being claimed as *Islamic* as against the *un-Islamic* regime of the Pahlavis—and by *whom*. The fairly rudimentary answer that is given to these questions is that the opposition ranged on a broad Islamist platform denouncing social iniquities as opposed to the essence of Islam. While the answer is broadly correct, it stops short of breaking down the various planks constituting the opposition platform. It does not bring out that all the revolutionaries did not speak of the same things as iniquities, neither does it indicate that different things were essentialized as Islamic by different groups.

Such a restricted perspective fails to provide a clear understanding of what precisely was *Islamic* or *revolutionary* in the revolution of 1979. One might identify the successful resistance to the authoritarianism of the Shah by means of a mass mobilization over a period of nearly two years (1977–79) cutting across Iranian society as the revolution, culminating in the abdication of the Shah on January 16, 1979. This implies that the revolutionary essence of 1979 lay in its opposition to despotism. The subsequent triumph of the Islamist revolutionaries led by Khomeini, virtually hijacking the revolution, it is often argued, was where the revolution went astray.[7] Alternatively (as has been done) one might stretch the story of the revolution beyond the Shah's abdication to Khomeini's return from exile and assumption of leadership of the country, signifying the triumph of the forces opposed to the Pahlavi modernization project.[8] One might also look upon the proclamation of the Islamic Republic (April 1979) as the culmination of the revolution, where the essence of the revolution lay in the termination of the monarchical principle in the Iranian body politic.[9] Again, the revolution might also be identified in the unequal compromise between the Islamist and democratic elements in the constitution that was drafted, and the way these two elements then shaped the regime.[10] All of these approaches, however, fail to elucidate the "Islamic" character of what took place.

## Observing an Islamic Revolution

The failure to engage with the Islamic nature of the revolution was largely because of a tendency that affected scholarly as well as popular perceptions—to equate Khomeini with the challenge of political Islam. This equation of Khomeini with political Islam was mostly an illusion that caught on quickly as much in the Islamic world as in the west. The Shah was dislodged by a resistance movement, which was supposed to be the same as the Islamic movement that came to power. That was not quite the case. The resistance also involved democrats and socialists of various shades, Islamic and secular—principally the *Nehzat-e Azadi*, and the Islamic Marxists like the *Sazman-e Mojahedin-e Khalq*. Between the spring and autumn of 1979 (i.e., proclamation of the Republic in April and promulgation of the constitution in November) a major struggle for power ensued between Islamic democrats like Bazargan and the revolutionary *'ulema*, a struggle that was manifested in the two drafts of the constitution. The constitution that was pushed through in the spring of 1979 established a compromise between the Islamic and democratic elements that *together* made the revolution. By the autumn of 1979, though, the hardliner *'ulema* had established a stranglehold on political institutions. As one spectrum of opinion managed to marginalize the democratic apparatus with the bluster of revolutionary Islamist fervor (viz. the attack on the U.S. embassy), the revolution was virtually hijacked, leaving the socialist and democratic forces high and dry.[11] For observers outside Iran, however, these tensions were not apparent. Accordingly, in both contemporary western and Muslim worlds the Islamic element in the making of the revolution was quickly associated with the regime that followed.

In course of the 1980s, a veritable crop of literature emerged professing to explore "the origins" or "roots" of the revolution. Most of the authors were mindful of the outcome of the revolution even before they had started digging out its roots. Many of them emphasized the adverse impact of modernization on the Iranian state, and the position taken by the *'ulema* establishment within that discourse of contested modernization. This would have been an acceptable approach if the *'ulema* responded at every stage of what occurred, or if they responded qua *'ulema*. But neither of these was true. Hence, historical literature on 1979 developed with a definite tilt. The principal concern was—how did Iran become a theocracy? How did the *'ulema* come to power in a twentieth-century setting?

Did the Pahlavi regime dig its own grave by trying to rapidly secularize a deeply religious society? Or was it undone by its iniquitous and heavy-handed treatment of the people? There was no dispute concerning whether the Islamic Republic was at all a theocracy.

The preoccupation with the ascendancy of the Shi'i *'ulema* gave the revolution a flavor distinct from any other phenomenon in the twentieth century, challenging some of the cardinal postulates of the social movement literature. Barrington Moore defined the structuralist orthodoxy for a long time, arguing social movements to be products of particular dispensations of class structures and class relations in agrarian states as they begin to modernize—completely discounting the role of ideology in social movements.[12] Such orthodoxy made little room for behavioralist theories highlighting the motivational dynamics behind social movements. Gurr's argument that social movements were motivated essentially by a sense of frustration at social change, leading to aggression toward the agents of change, or Johnson's stress on shifting value systems and ideologies as the key, or for that matter Tilly's emphasis on the role of organized group conflicts with well-defined aims—all of these raised substantive questions about social movements that the structuralist positions failed to address.[13] Nevertheless, these did little to deflect structuralist thinkers like Theda Skocpol, who insisted that social movements by victims of modernization flourish when social coalitions fracture in agrarian/semi-bureaucratic states during the course of modernization, crippling the instruments of coercion.[14] Skocpol's conjuncturalist variant of structuralism was unwilling to accommodate even William Sewell's suggestion for the incorporation of ideology/value-system/worldview in the conjuncturalist paradigm as an explanatory variable.[15] However, the role played by political Islam in the mobilization of the Iranian people behind the revolutionary banner in 1979 reopened the debate on the significance of ideologies behind social churning, thereby strengthening the hard revisionist positions in the study of social movements and revolutions.[16] Structuralist theoreticians like Skocpol were in a tight spot having to accommodate the potency of ideology in the generic sense as a causative factor for revolutions.[17] This urge to accommodate, however, remained largely confined to understanding the idioms of political Islam more as a factor of Islam as a religion rather than of political awareness. The Islamic character was taken as natural for a movement supposedly led in the main by the *'ulema*.

\* \* \*

A fair number of scholars look at 1979 from the structuralist standpoint, as a social revolution prompted by the social dislocation that accompanied

Iran's encounter with modernization in the twentieth century. They find the revolution virtually built into the trajectory of Iran's program for social and economic modernization in what was essentially a premodern polity. Advocates of this argument stress on the decisive character of the class alliance that made the revolution possible. The advocates of political Islam simply managed to harness this alliance better, thereby leaving their stamp on the revolution. They contend, therefore, that the revolution of 1979 was not made, it "came."

Such interventions pivoted around some important questions about modernization—the phenomenon that was widely considered inevitable for the Third World by the middle of the twentieth century—namely, what is modernization? Does it simply denote mechanization of the economy? Or does it involve larger reconfigurations of society and polity as much as the economy? Should attendant transformations in any modernizing society be unique to the society concerned, or should they follow any set pattern?

Nikkie Keddie, for instance, believed that the Pahlavis were undone by their modernization agenda because it came in the garb of westernization.[18] Iranians had misgivings about the west owing to their encounters with western powers in the nineteenth century. The social dislocation caused by rapid industrial development under the Pahlavis in their bid to emulate the west aggravated this misgiving. The attendant policy of secularization, Keddie maintained, alienated the *'ulema,* who were thus willing to provide leadership to the voices of opposition, with their formidable organizational network in a broad-based alliance embracing the entire nation. Hence, when the disruptive effects of modernization became unendurable, a groundswell of opposition swept the Shah away.

Ervand Abrahamian by contrast attributed the revolution to the incomplete character of the Pahlavi agenda: modernizing the economy and society but not the polity.[19] Abrahamian argued that the Pahlavis had disrupted the modernization of the Iranian polity that had started with the Constitutional Revolution of 1906. The protagonists of constitutional government (viz., that under Mosaddeq) failed to resist the Pahlavi regime owing to inadequate bonding between the various forces of the quasi-modern polity. By the 1970s, the disruptive effects of the Shah's modernization of the Iranian economy helped forge an opposition movement that ushered in a social revolution. Abrahamian argued that the revolution that dislodged the Shah was essentially modern and "progressive" in terms of its political agenda of contesting authoritarianism, but Khomeini's role in holding the opposition together allowed the *'ulema* to take over and put their stamp on it. Abrahamian later situated the role of ideology within his narrative of 1979 as a social revolution by pointing out that Khomeini's political positions were basically protests against the established order in the background of economic dislocation. *Khomeinism* worked, he seems to be arguing, not because it was professing an Islamic agenda, but because it was professing a radical revolutionary agenda.[20]

Homa Katouzian on the other hand argued the incomplete character of the Pahlavi program of modernization of Iran as the chief reason behind the social dislocation in Iran, which caused the revolution.[21] Ruling a rentier state with proceeds from the sale of petroleum, the Pahlavis were not quite mindful of social interests on a broad scale. Bankrolled by oil revenue and guided by the state, the frenzied pace of Iran's industrialization prevented modernization of the economy as a whole even as traditional sectors began to suffer from the dynamics of modernization. Once the oil prices dropped in the mid-1970s, the state could not sustain most of the limited developmental activities to which it was committed. As Iran faced an economic crisis of unprecedented magnitude, the "petrolic despotism" of the Shah was diagnosed as the malady, and a groundswell of popular discontent forced him out. Khomeini happened to emerge as a leader, says Katouzian, simply because of his uncompromising rejection of everything that the Shah stood for, not necessarily on account of anything he himself stood for.

While almost all the structural approaches to 1979 rested on the social dislocation caused by the Pahlavis, there was little by way of the role such dislocation played in the making of the revolution before Misagh Parsa.[22] He refuted the idea that the urban poor constituted the mainstay of the ascendancy of the *'ulema* during 1977–78. He showed instead that the "petty bourgeoisie" played a far more crucial role, as against the urban poor who barely participated in the resistance till after the Shah had actually left the country. Having benefited from Iran's rapid development and standing to lose everything once that development halted, the petty bourgeoisie constituted the left-wing revolutionaries (Islamist and Marxist) and the student community (Islamist and secular nationalist alike) at the forefront of the demonstrations against the Shah throughout 1978, increasing the pressure on the regime sufficiently for the Shah to eventually quit. Parsa accounted for the ascendancy of the *'ulema* as almost ascendancy by default. With all alternative structures capable of resisting the government dismantled by the Pahlavi, opponents of the regime used the religious space because it was the only one that remained available for deployment. When the Shah was finally ousted, the *'ulema*, as the custodians of the structures of religious institutions in Iranian life, were able to wrest leadership from the society at large.

Such structuralist approaches to 1979, however, left unresolved many other questions. If the dislocation brought about by the modernization of

Iran was indeed the determining factor, what pushed the discontent over the edge? Also, if social discontent was indeed the causative factor, then why did the leadership come to rest in the *'ulema* rather than the Iranian left? Why did the masses rally behind Khomeini in 1979, rather than Mosaddeq in 1953?

Accordingly, some scholars chose to assign some potency to political Islam in the making of the Islamic Revolution, closer to the behavioralist argument. They appreciate that without the objective conditions of general disquiet occasioned by the policies of the Pahlavi state such a revolution could not have taken place. Nevertheless, they contend that without the mobilization that took place during 1977–79, such disquiet would not necessarily have led to the revolution. That is to say, the revolution was "made."

Shahrough Akhavi, for instance, contended that the Shi'i *'ulema* constituted the main bastion of political Islam in the run-up to the revolution. The *'ulema*, he argued, were crucial to the administrative apparatus of the nineteenth-century Qajar state, and had wielded considerable influence over Iranian society for too long a period to remain unaffected by any major social reordering.[23] Pahlavi modernization confronted the *'ulema* with the need to either submit to state power or confront it. Although some of the *'ulema* opted to yield, once the material basis of *ulema's* autonomous existence was attacked, a large number of them decided to confront the regime. Akhavi argued that once the regime faced concerted opposition from all sections of the society, ability of the *'ulema* to mobilize resources and masses as well as their organizational activity proved decisive in capturing power by marginalizing the rest of the opposition.

Said Amir Arjomand argued along similar lines, stressing on the propensity of the *'ulema* toward political participation owing to the character of the clergy-state relations, which helped them organize themselves in the limited political space left behind by the Shah.[24] Arjomand also highlighted the reformulation of certain aspects of Shi'i tradition as well as its transformation into a political ideology acceptable to all Iranians (lay or clerical, religious or secular), appealing particularly to the classes that were most affected by the economic vicissitudes—namely, the urban poor. Confronted with resistance brought about by a combination of the two factors, Arjomand argues, the Shah was compelled to relinquish power.

Mansoor Moaddel took a far more nuanced position in his various works on the history of modern Iran. Situating Islamic modernism within a complex body of responses generated in the Muslim world, Moaddel spoke of "ideology as an episodic discourse," categorically dismissing the fairly popular notion of relentless opposition by the *'ulema*.[25] He identified the emergence of the discursive alternative of Islamic order as the decisive factor in undermining the Pahlavi regime in 1979, although he did not discuss the Islamic alternative at any great length.

## Locating Islam in the Islamic Revolution

Clearly, there was an assumption in much of this debate over 1979 that religion per se was *not* quite the driving force behind the phenomenon unlike what popular impressions had implied. This then prompted the question—what made the revolution *Islamic*? The mere fact that the *'ulema* enjoyed overwhelming powers in the new state proved insufficient to make the case for the revolution being Islamic. The discourse of political legitimacy deployed by the Islamic Republic was *not* derived from any of the traditionally accepted points of reference for Islam—neither the Qur'an, nor the *ahadith* (sing. *hadith*) or the *shari'ah*. Instead the Islamic Republic derived legitimacy from a body of political ideologies that used Islamic terms of reference, and used Islam as only one of the ingredients of that language of politics. Indeed, while the Republic deployed the revolutionary doctrine of *Vilayat-e Faqih* (Rule of the [Islamic] Jurisprudent), propounded by Ruhollah Khomeini, sanctioning the establishment of an Islamic order, the incidence of sovereignty (if not its exercise) remained for all practical purposes in the people—as it had remained theoretically ever since the *Mashruteh* revolution of 1906 that led to constitutionalist politics in Iran. To many observers, inside Iran as much as outside, the revolutionary regime seemed afflicted with a dilemma: whether to be a theocracy (as Khomeini and his followers are supposed to have wanted) or a democracy (as Bazargan and Bani-Sadr preferred). With time the dilemma is supposed to have changed into something more complicated: whether to be a theocratic democracy or a democratic theocracy.

Such assessments of the revolution, needless to add, are influenced by the way the Islamic Republic has moved on since 1979. The problem of reading backward into history is of course that what appears as a binary at one stage might not necessarily have been present at an earlier time. This problem of a clear binary is typical of some of the scholarly approaches to the study of Islamic ideology—as though to be "Islamic" is necessarily to be "theocratic," in which the *mashruteh* (constitutionalist) or democratic tradition cannot find any meaningful place. Some other scholars would argue that "Islamic democracy" is a tautology because to be "Islamic" necessarily means being democratic, but not vice versa—so once Islam is founded as the basis of an order, it cannot fail to be democratic in spirit.[26]

A more nuanced perspective reveals that the relationship between "Islam" and "democracy" in Iran was never very clear-cut—be it in the run-up to 1979, or since. The relationship between the two was mediated (as in so many other areas of West Asia) by modernity and the responses of different sections of Iranian society to that. Depending on one's location on the matrices of power in nineteenth- and twentieth-century Iran, one could choose to be "Islamic" and/or "democratic" to contest authoritarianism; one could opt for "Islam" to ensure social liberties of a minority confronted with "secular/liberal" majoritarianism; one might even be "democratic" in order to be "Islamic" or vice versa. An individual's profession of attachment to bodies of ideas was probably more of a negotiation strategy than an article of faith in a society that was modernizing very fast. Negotiations were as much between the individual and the state, as between the individual and the society or even the state and the society, but the rules underlying such negotiation remained to be spelled out clearly. That is not to say all those who put up a flag for relegating Islam to the private sphere of a Muslim's life were necessarily less pious (although, they might have been), nor indeed can it be argued that all those who favored incorporation of Islam in the public sphere were necessarily devout Muslims (which they may not have been). A large corpus of thought in twentieth-century Iran (as indeed in much of the Muslim world) was devoted to exploring not so much *whether* to be Islamic as *what is it to be Islamic*—and contrary to the way it occasionally seems, this point is far from resolved.

A growing segment of the literature on the Islamic Revolution seeks to address the role this creative dynamism played in the making of the revolution. The pioneering work in this respect was by Hamid Dabashi, who spoke of how the opposition to the Shah successfully undercut Pahlavi legitimacy to rule by weaving into shape a *Theology of Discontent*.[27] Using the works and pronouncements of four lay and four clerical intellectuals, Dabashi made the case that the revolutionary Islamic ideology proved extremely successful not simply because it was *Islamic*, but also because it was *revolutionary*. Almost extrapolating Chalmers Johnson, Dabashi argues that the social dislocation occasioned by the Pahlavi project of modernization created a large constituency that was discontented with the official "modernist" discourse. The discontent was conjured up as an alternative discourse that was then "theologized"; in order to dispute the claims of the Shah being an agent of Providence in Iranian society, Providence itself was invoked to decry the Shah as a subversive element.

Mehrzad Boroujerdi took the argument a step further and explored other figures that were not under international scrutiny like Khomeini. His point was that the discordance between the modernizing policies of the Pahlavi state and Iranian society was so great that Iran's intelligentsia frequently responded to modernity with nativism.[28] Boroujerdi contended that the version of modernity thrust upon Iran by the Pahlavis was so visibly alien to the prevalent culture of sociability that the society and the state seemed to be at cross-purposes. The Iranian intelligentsia responded by creating an alternative culture of sociability that would either domesticate this alien dispensation or else reject it altogether. He showed how a large number of intellectuals deployed a nativist discourse to accommodate (what they understood as) the core of modernity without succumbing to an all-encompassing *modernism*. The crux of the revolutionary ideology lay, Boroujerdi seems to believe, in the unequivocal expression of nativism.

Ali Mirsepassi, dealing with Iran's negotiation with modernity and how that negotiation fed into the resistance to the Pahlavis, criticized the predominant understanding of "modernity" and its attributes in terms of the European/western experience.[29] He contended that each society *negotiates* with the broader "modern" economic and technological dispensations in its own spatial and temporal context, and thus comes up with a particular form of modernity that need not necessarily conform to another form that evolved elsewhere. Mirsepassi argued that Iranian society, like any other modern society, used multiple strategies of negotiation with modernity. While the secular constitutionalists and the leftists ended up constricted by needs of ideological conformity, the Islamists deployed the most pragmatic negotiation skills. Hence, revolutionary Islam is a signifier of Iran's "modernity," rather than the lack of it.

Vanessa Martin's take on the Islamic element in the Islamic Revolution was substantially different from these positions. In her work *Creating an Islamic State*, Martin showed the idioms of Islamic politics came from more than one source (such as 'Ali Shari'ati and Khomeini) but they were converging in their aspirations for a less unequal social order.[30] Thus, the political language of an Islamist *'alim* inspired by the *'irfan* tradition was shown to potentially have much common ground with a Sorbonne-educated socialist. Their ideas were geared against the inequities of the modernist Pahlavi regime, and their quest for an authentic Islamist discourse of resistance to the alienating nature of "modernism" was as "modern" as the discourse they opposed.

It appears fairly clear from the range of works on the intellectual origins of the revolution that 1979 was not about the rise of a religion to power. Neither was the revolution necessarily about the rise of the Iranian *'ulema* to political power, although this was what happened in 1979. Inquiry into the intellectual origins of the Islamic Revolution clearly shows no one—not even Khomeini—*actually* spoke of a *takeover* of the government by the *'ulema* before 1979. Khomeini was the only major protagonist of the position that the *'ulema* would function effectively as the guardians of the Islamic state, but he did not specify the form such guardianship might take. Among the other major ideologues of the revolution only Jalal Al-e Ahmad spoke of *'ulema* stewardship, but that was not the same as the *'ulema* actually being involved with the quotidian task of ruling. Many, including 'Ali Shari'ati, actually brushed aside such an option altogether. Islamic revolutionary ideology in late Pahlavi Iran was not about *who ruled,* but *how to rule.* There was no one single Islamic prescription of rulership, but there *was* a language of political legitimacy that derived its terms of reference from what was claimed as an Islamic value-system.

## Reading the Language of Political Islam

Significantly, despite the interest in Islamic intellectual traditions manifest in this last kind of literature, overall, while the causation of the revolution, its socioeconomic roots, and its political character have all been elaborately commented upon, study of the intellectual character of the revolution remains considerably underworked. Scant attention is paid to what it is actually that made the revolution *Islamic* for the people who staged it. Why was it called *Inqilab-e Islami* (Islamic Revolution) or *Inqilab-e Islami-ye Irani* (Islamic Revolution of Iran), for instance, rather than simply *Inqilab-e Irani* (Iranian Revolution)? Was it called Islamic because its leadership was drawn from the *'ulema,* or because the opposition was overwhelmingly Muslim, individuals who were mobilized by an urge to defend their faith? If the latter, how did they seek to defend it, and from what? Was there any conceptual correspondence or contradiction between the identities of *Irani* and *Islami*? Could one be both *Islami* and *Irani* in equal proportions? And if not, then in which circumstances would one of these override the other? Did 1979 mark one such point when the *Islami* dimension overrode the *Irani*, or was it a case when the former subsumed the latter? And why, either way, did the opposition movement develop tensions over *what* the revolution signified after the Shah had been driven out? What, in other words, did Islam *signify* to the Iranians in the fateful run-up to 1979?

The simplest response that can be given to any query about the nature of Islam is that it is a "revealed religion" that was preached by the Prophet Muhammad and followed by millions of people around the world. Muslims are marked out not simply by the God they believe in, but also by the manner in which such belief is expressed through the five pillars of the faith—the *faradh al-'ain* (fivefold obligations).[31] Moreover, it is very widely believed by Muslims and non-Muslims alike that Islam lays down a very comprehensive body of religious laws, the *shari'ah*, to regulate almost every aspect of human life. The measure of a good Muslim is frequently taken to be the extent to which an individual conforms to such regulations. Indeed, as Muslims and scholars of Islam insist, Islam is not simply a religion that a large number of people follow; it is also a way of life for them. And being a way of life it is not simply a corpus of inflexible, immutable ideas transmitted and received without any modification—it stands for a vibrant intellectual, social, and cultural order. From such a nuanced standpoint, Islam stands for an entire civilization that nourishes that order with the "revealed religion" at its core. The term *Islamic* denotes any values, practices, or ideas that pertain to this civilization of Islam.

Such abstraction about the nature of Islam begs the question whether the values, practices, or ideas that bear the *signs* of belonging to the Islamic civilization are uniform through the ages and across diverse locations on the globe. For instance, the *shari'ah*, which is often assumed to signify the legal injunctions that are supposed to keep Muslims on "the straight path," differs considerably from one society to the next in the same age, and even in the same society from one age to another.[32] There is, in other words, no total uniformity in the requirements of conduct of a Muslim. Indeed, barring the Qur'an there is hardly anything that all Muslims have in common.[33]

It is reasonable, therefore, to argue that with changes in the societal and temporal context of a civilization, with different material and human conditions that obtain, the meaning of Islam, and being a Muslim, changes. If one sets aside the centrality of the Qur'an in the Islamic scheme of things, at the risk of being charged with blasphemy, it is possible to argue that there can be almost as many Islams as there are Muslims, where each interprets the social, cultural, and civilizational values that *signify* Islam. To borrow the terminology from a different discipline, Islam is not so much of a cathedral as a *bazaar*.

Eric S. Raymond's essay on software engineering methods, "The Cathedral and the Bazaar," was based on his observations of the Linux kernel development process and his experiences managing an open source project, "fetchmail." It was first presented by the author at the Linux Kongress on May 27, 1997, and was published as part of a book of the same name in 1999.[34] Commonly regarded as the manifesto of the open source movement, the essay contrasts two different free software development models. In the *Cathedral* model, source code is available with each software release, but the code developed between releases is restricted to an exclusive group of developers—which then defines the parameters within which the software has to operate. The *Bazaar* model, in which the code is developed over the internet in view of the public, is not restricted within a set of strict parameters—its users modify the package as they go along.

An important comment on the character of artificial intelligence and the way it evolves, this theory can be used to understand the history of ideas as well. In the *Cathedral* model, ideas are devised by their original proponents in the manner of an architect laying down the designs of a cathedral (hence the name). The finished structure of ideas bears a direct resemblance to the original design—just as the finished form of a cathedral bears a direct resemblance to the architect's plans. In this model, only the original body of ideas is "authentic," and all else that evolved afterward in modification or enhancement of the original is like a deviation, or corruption. The *Bazaar* model, by contrast, avoids any strict parameters and any fixed ideas. In this model, accordingly, there is no such thing as the "authentic" idea, and each of the ideas can be equally valid regardless of the stage at which it evolved.

Both the *Cathedral*-type and the *Bazaar*-type models have been applied to the study of Islam. Examples of application of the *Cathedral*-type model are those claims that suggest that the most defining attributes of Islam are to be found either in the Qur'an alone (a position adopted by, inter alia, the Wahhabis) or in that and only some of the *ahadith* (a position generally adopted by the much maligned category of thinkers, "fundamentalists"). Such "fundamentalists" hold that the "essence" of Islam lies embedded in the injunctions to be found in the Qur'an, and everything else that has been subsequently derived (including judge-made laws) are "deviations" from the "fundamentals" to which the Muslims should return. The model might also be said to apply to any understanding of Islam that is decidedly legalist—that is, the position that the "essence" of Islam is *signified* by the injunctions of religious law, the *shari'ah*, and any violation of, or nonconformity with, such law involves a deviation from that "essence."

By comparison, the *Bazaar*-type model can be said to have been applied whenever various aspects from the lives of Muslims—social, cultural, intellectual, political, et cetera—have been taken as *signifiers* of Islam. Hence emphasis on morality, ethicality, and a humane disposition, Sufi quietism, the duty to profess loyalty toward an oppressive ruler, as also the responsibility to resist an oppressive ruler, each of these has been understood to be crucial *signifiers* of the faith at various times and places. Application of this model assumes that Islam is a civilization, and not simply a religious order bound by a code of religious injunctions. It assumes that the symbols and *signifiers* of Islam are being constantly negotiated, new symbols are being regularly generated and accepted as completely legitimate *signifiers* of the faith. In other words, the model is premised upon the notion of "polyvalence" of Islam, where it can be *signified* as different things by different people using a set of *signs*.

In terms of the various studies on the intellectual origins of the revolution, it is possible to identify both the *Cathedral* and the *Bazaar* models at play. The *Cathedral* would denote the approach that suggests political ideas are devised by ideologues, and handed down for the people to adhere to, for better or for worse—the case made, clearly, by Dabashi or Abrahamian.[35] By contrast, the *Bazaar* would denote the approach that suggests much of the meanings associated with any ideology develop independently of what the originator of those ideas may have wished. This is the premise underlying Brumberg's work on Iranian politics in the 1990s, where he argued Iranians were *Reinventing Khomeini*.[36]

The advantage of the *Bazaar* model in analyzing Islamic political thought is that it allows a full flow to the possibilities that are latent in the multiple meanings of words without undermining the worth or legitimacy of the "Islamic" terms of reference. However, inadequate rigor in the use of this model can result in major fallacies. A regular feature of the application of the *Bazaar* model in social sciences in general and Islam in particular tends to be the temptation of every *Bazaar* to behave like a cathedral. While there are multiple *signifiers* for Islam, each *sign* on its own is claimed to signify the "essence" of Islam as the *referent*. A number of scholars have set about exploring a particular aspect of Muslim society or history, and have drawn their deductions of what Islam is, or is not.[37] There exists a corpus of literature that even claims to reveal "what Islam *really* means" (emphasis mine).[38] The problem that characterizes this genre of literature is that the works identify some element or the other in Muslim lives as the "essence," and deny the "essentiality" of any other element. This is almost as bad as the reverse case, where every protagonist claiming to be speaking on behalf of Islam or Muslims is accepted as doing so.[39]

There are some other fundamental methodological issues that vitiate both the *Cathedral* and the *Bazaar* approaches once they are applied to the study of the Islamic intellectual tradition. One of the pivotal concerns in this respect is, as Quentin Skinner suggests, the central dilemma of "reading" a particular text, that is, what constitutes the "meaning" of a text/speech?[40] Should one consider only what the author *said* in the text—that is, the *Cathedral* model? Or should one factor in the "intention" of the author in the *reading* of a text (shall we say, the blueprint of the cathedral)? Or indeed, as the *Bazaar* model assumes, should one accept that the author is dead, and explore instead how a particular text was "transmitted" and "received," that is, what was the text *understood to have said* rather than simply what it *appears* to have said?

Put simply, if while addressing his audience in Tehran in the late-1960s 'Ali Shari'ati spoke of "incidents" dating back to the seventh century, then should it be assumed that that was precisely what he meant to do? Since many of his works were lectures delivered in a *Hosseiniyeh* (where discussions on the "nature" and "meaning" of Shi'ism took place) or before an audience oriented toward Islam, this could quite eminently have been the case. However, given the differences in terms of tone and content between the addresses of Shari'ati and most of his contemporaries, a literal reading cannot account for the uniqueness of Shari'ati's addresses. So should one instead look for the intention behind what Shari'ati had to say? Should we recover the *act* behind the *speech*, the "illocutionary force" of his addresses, as John L. Austin's "speech-act" approach would urge us to do?[41] Thus, if Shari'ati praises the martyrdom of Imam Hossein at Karbala as an example for all Muslims, do we read this simply as a recounting of the valor of Imam Hossein? Or do we read this as an exhortation to resistance against tyranny? Also, if the latter, is it to be so read only if people realize the exhortation as such and respond to it? What if they do not?[42]

But as Jacques Derrida warns us, it may not even be possible to "read" the meaning of a text, because the terms of references used to signify meanings do not carry any meanings intrinsically. In deconstructing the "signs" that make up a text in terms of what they mean to the reader, the reader invariably loses the sense of what it might have meant to the author.[43] To continue with the given example, if Shari'ati's audience *thought* that he was exhorting them to violent resistance in talking about Karbala, does that necessarily mean Shari'ati was doing so? It is thus important to distinguish between the illocutionary force of a text (i.e., author's intention) and its perlocutionary effect (understanding by reader).[44]

Deconstructing the methodology argued for by Skinner, I have tried to locate as far as possible Shari'ati's ideas not only within the historical and intellectual context of his time, but also the precise stages of his life in which such ideas evolved—in the hope that the context might indicate why a particular text/speech said what it did.[45] Still more importantly, I assume, following Skinner's approach, that if the same protagonist has been engaging with a broad range of issues, then however sprawling the scope of such engagement might seem to us, for the protagonist it made a particular sense. Hence, I mean to try and establish a pattern in what Shari'ati said or wrote over a number of years, and account for shifts in emphases by locating them in the larger context of such shifts, as and when they occurred.

However, while it is easier to locate a written text with a reasonable accuracy, or even a lecture the content of which was pretty unique, it is often difficult to pin down the exact context of many ideas that Shari'ati played with in his speeches. This is largely because having to deliver well over 100 public lectures in about six years, Shari'ati tended to repeat himself a lot. Sometimes such repetition was expressly desired by the audience of one place who had heard of a lecture/course of lectures delivered elsewhere. But most of the repetition was owing to the fact that Shari'ati was trying to push forth a definite cluster of arguments to a huge audience across different places and at different times. In culling his lectures and writings, therefore, I have tried to maintain as best as possible the chronological sequence in which his ideas evolved. However, in a few cases I have chosen to set forth the arguments out of turn, especially when the clearest formulation of an argument came sometime after the argument was originally mooted. Consequently, a large number of his lectures, while they have played a pivotal role in the making of Shari'ati's stature as a demagogue, have been allowed to make way for others where the argument is more crisp and hard-hitting.

There is yet another area of concern while handling Shari'ati. Being a demagogue who believed in direct communication with his audience, Shari'ati presented his ideas almost entirely through around 100 public lectures in a period of six years. At present, of the 37 volumes of his works collected posthumously, except for some major works and a few handwritten pieces, the overwhelming majority of his ideas are to found as transcription of his lecture tapes or class notes of his students made available for publication. As a result it is quite a regular feature to trace subtle differences between two versions of the same text. The ideas of Shari'ati himself, therefore, might be said to evolve within the *Bazaar* model, where the listener actively intervenes in the process of "listening" and creates his own version of Shari'ati's persona. Hence, an attempt is made here to accommodate the possibility of such "active listening," unless there is compelling evidence that any particular interpretation involves a deliberate act of opinionated and politically motivated interpolation.

Using primarily the multivolume collected works of Shari'ati and the writings of some other of his contemporaries (like Jalal Al-e Ahmad and Ruhollah Khomeini) an attempt is made here to understand the terms of reference of the language of political Islam that evolved in the context of prerevolutionary Iran. Although most of such primary sources are accessed in Persian, I have chosen to rely on the English translation of Khomeini's works by Hamid Algar to understand the theological and juridical nuances better.

For biographical information on Shari'ati, I have relied largely on what is perhaps the most authentic biography yet of Shari'ati—*the Islamic Utopian*, by Ali Rahnema.[46] Rahnema's work explores the various stages of Shari'ati's life and the influences (both personal and intellectual) on him, making him according to Rahnema the visionary of a utopian order. I have also made use of Shari'ati's biography *Tarhi az ek Zindagi*, written by his wife, Puran Shari'at-Razavi, for purposes of corroboration.[47] Further, I have relied considerably on the works and personal insights of a young Iranian academic (although barely known outside), Reza 'Alijani, who is in the forefront of the study of Shari'ati in Iran, popularly known as the genre of *shari'atishenasi*.

Shari'ati is accessible to the English-speaking world through a series of translations that date back to the 1970s. The highly selective translations of Hamid Algar, those commissioned by the *Bonyad-e Farhangi-ye Doktor 'Ali Shari'ati* ('Ali Shari'ati Foundation, for short) and the Hamdami Foundation present a representative but extremely narrow sample of Shari'ati's thoughts. The range of secondary literature available in English is paltry, although contributions by Shahrough Akhavi, Abdulaziz Sachedina, Yann Richard, and Abbas Manouchehri constitute important digests of Shari'ati's thought. By contrast, a prodigious amount has been written about Shari'ati by his friends, followers, and critics alike in Persian, almost nothing of which has been translated so far. I have used some of these resources in trying to give an account of how Iranians have creatively engaged with the language of political Islam, not only to negotiate with the Islamic Republic but also to come to terms with the Islamic Revolution that brought the Republic into being.

## The Chapters

The first chapter deals with the languages of power and politics, and the emergence of the state-centric discourse that characterizes the history of modern Iran. It contends that the disjunction of the interests of the state from those of its people left the state vulnerable to attacks mounted in defense of the interests of the people, the role that was played by protagonists of political Islam.

The second chapter explores the three dominant strands of opposition to the regime (constitutionalism, Marxism, and clerical Islam) through three major protagonists—Mohammed Mossadeq, Jalal Al-e Ahmad, and Ayatollah Ruhollah Khomeini. The chapter indicates how varying usages of Islamic idioms mounted a challenge against the institutional, intellectual, and politico-social foundations of Pahlavi Iran, reclaiming the only discursive space in modern Iran that the state had not tried to occupy—religion. The chapter means to establish political Islam not as a political agenda driven by traditionalist religious considerations, rather by essentially modern political, economic, and societal considerations

The third chapter introduces 'Ali Shari'ati as the only major protagonist of political Islam to challenge the normative foundations of modern political orders in general and the Pahlavi order in particular. The chapter details the foundation of his political thinking upon an innovative interpretation of the concept of *tauheed,* suggesting that a political order that does not represent the interest of all of its component parts equitably is ipso facto un-Islamic.

The fourth chapter discusses Shari'ati's critique of political regimes throughout the history of man as an instrument of class rule. It then elaborates the manner in which Shari'ati introduced the Shi'i concept of *Imamat* as the means of attaining the Islamic ideal of *ummah*, which was premised upon the notions of equity and justice and argued the essence of an Islamic order to be the notion of popular sovereignty.

The fifth chapter involves the question of popular sovereignty in terms of assumption of responsibility by the component people, the argument that set Shari'ati apart from all of his contemporaries. The chapter suggests that Shari'ati emphasized on the need for opposition to the abuse of sovereignty as an assertion of sovereignty in itself—and that *jihad* and *shahadat* signified such assertion of sovereignty.

The sixth chapter develops the notion of the *raushanfikr* as a highly individualistic understanding of the concept of humanity from within the Islamic intellectual tradition as it had come into being in Iran. The chapter deals with Shari'ati's emphasis on the role of individuals (male and female) and human initiative as the real motor of historical progression.

The seventh chapter deals with the resonances of the prerevolutionary language of political Islam in the Islamic Republic. It argues that the revolutionary ideology that the Islamic Republic has projected came into being only after the revolution, and shows even that ideological construct has been challenged from within and outside the ruling establishment with terms of references drawn from the prerevolutionary language.

Finally, in the conclusion, it is argued that Shari'ati's critique is Islamic in character because he was devising a new set of *signifiers* and *signified* to refer to the *referent* of Islam. He was not suggesting the revival of any old order that claimed to be Islamic, rather he was laying down what he believed an *Islamic* order should be like, where *Islamic* was meant to be a *signifier* of an ideal that Shari'ati understood to be the "essence" of Islam.

# I

# The Languages of Power and Politics in Modern Iran

For many observers of the Islamic Republic of Iran, the political culture ushered in by the revolution of 1979 lies deeply rooted in the history of Iran in the twentieth century.[1] The dynamics of politics in the last two decades of the Qajar dynasty, the negotiation of power in the kingdom between the Qajar rulers and their subjects since the *Mashruteh* (Constitutional) revolution of 1906, helped evolve new languages of power and politics that, they believe, continue to be relevant in modern Iran, redefining the relationship between the state and the society, the state and the individual, and the society and the individual. The new political language assigned to the people a centrality in political discourse that was unthinkable in the kingdom of Persia until that time. However, the manner in which such centrality would become operational in political life was not fully worked out by the *Mashruteh* revolution, leaving Iran open to a prolonged conflict over the dilemma that has characterized the country's history since then: does the state belong to the people? Or, do the people belong to the state?

### The Mashruteh Connection: From Mulk to Mellat

The *Mashruteh* revolution of 1906 was the culmination of a series of struggles by various sections of the kingdom of Persia to rein in the arbitrary power of the weak Qajar Shah. In many ways it was a definitive experience that marked the transformation of the kingdom of Persia into a modern nation-state. The centre stage of politics shifted to the impersonal *watan* (country), embodying the *mellat* (people/nation); the Shah, after centuries of unbridled power, suddenly found himself reined in. Iran began to speak a very modern language of politics.

The need to restrain the powers of the Shah had emerged with particular urgency by the second half of the nineteenth century. The military weakness of the Qajar rulers facilitated the economic penetration of the kingdom of Persia by Czarist Russia and the Britain, and the kingdom became a major area of imperial rivalry between the two.[2] By the second half of the nineteenth century, Russia had established its sphere of influence in the regions adjacent to the Caspian Sea, and Britain in the regions adjacent to the Persian Gulf. Commercial concessions and economic privileges sold by the Qajar rulers to the foreigners threatened the merchants of the *bazaar* (market), that is, the *bazaaris* in the various urban conurbations of Tehran, Esfahan, Tabriz, Mashhad, Shiraz, et cetera. Since the competitive advantage enjoyed by the foreigners proved decisive, resentful of the loss of their *own* markets the *bazaaris* of Iran began to coordinate their resistance to such policies from the 1880s, their activities culminating in the tobacco protests of 1892–94.[3] Their objective of excluding the *khariji* (foreigner) from the economic space of Iran helped define the aggrieved "self" of the *Irani*, that is, the people inhabiting the *Sarzameen-e Iran* (Land of Iran).

The definition of the Iranian "self" was also facilitated by some initiatives undertaken by the Qajar state. Mindful of the dangers of military inferiority of the kingdom vis-à-vis the Russians and the British, some sections of the Qajar elite began to advocate modernization of the regime so that it became strong enough to stand its own ground against the foreigners.[4] Among the reforms initiated to this end, the introduction of secular "western" education gave birth to a secularist and modernist intelligentsia *(monavver al-fikr)* hailing from the professional middle class, heavily influenced by the "west."[5] This modernist intelligentsia believed that human progress was attainable only if the three chains of royal despotism *(istibdad)*, clerical dogmatism *(istihmar)*, and foreign (economic) imperialism *(isti'mar)* could be broken. As long as these three chains were strong, they held the people down, as in a sleep *(khwab)*. The modernists were determined to get the Iranians out of their sleep and usher in the *asr-e bidari* (age of awakening).

The professional middle class had begun to see the territoriality of the kingdom in terms of *wataniyyat* (national identity). Influenced by the dominant western category of "nation," this new professional class saw the people of the kingdom not in terms of their regional, linguistic, religious, or sectarian affiliations, nor indeed as simply subjects of the *mumalik/mamlikat* (kingdom). Instead they began to regard *mumalik/mamlikat* as one *mellat* (community of people) inhabiting one *watan* (homeland)—Iran.[6] Defense of the *mellat* and the *watan* became the driving concern of the professional middle class in general, and the secularist intelligentsia in particular.[7] The broad-ranging discussions carried out by the modernist intelligentsia through the budding crop of newspapers and journals, expressing avowed opposition to European economic penetration of the *watan,* not only helped raise awareness of material problems but also reinforced the notion of being a *hamwatani* (compatriot) as against a *khariji* (foreigner), which coincided very neatly with the experience of the *bazaaris.*[8]

In the last quarter of the nineteenth century, the nascent notion of *wataniyyat* moved to the centre stage of the public sphere in the realm.[9] Categories like *mellat* (nation), *qanun* (laws), and *showra* (consultation) began to feature in the political discourse of the time. Malkum Khan, a modernist, had begun to publicize such concepts in his London-based newspaper, *Qanun,* in the 1890s.[10] After the tobacco protests a fair number of the *bazaaris,* and their principal social ally, the *'ulema,* began to favor the notion of institutional checks on the Shah, reminding the Shah about his duties vis-à-vis *daulat wa mellat* (the state and the nation/people) as against the previous references to *daulat wa ri'aya* (the state and the subjects).[11] The sense of being a *mellat* united by its adversities reinforced the idea of the Iranian "self," sharply posited against the western, non-Islamic "other." This binary was given a more conveniently concrete form because of foreign economic penetration, where the *daulat* was not safeguarding the *mellat.* The reason why the *daulat* failed to protect the *mellat* was that the *hakim* (ruler) was arbitrary and not answerable to anyone. Hence, the need for *qanun* to regulate everyone in the kingdom including the *hakim,* and such laws could be arrived at only through *showra* of the *mellat.*

The desire to regulate the Shah's authority escalated into a mass movement by the *bazaaris* in the winter of 1905, demanding, among other things, the institution of an *'adalatkhaneh* (house of justice) to ensure the rule of law. By the summer of 1906, at the behest of the modernist intelligentsia, the stakes were raised in demanding a constituent *Majlis-e Melli* (National Assembly, hereafter, *Majlis*). When the reigning Qajar, Muzaffar al-din Shah (r. 1896–1907), relented and authorized the convening of a constituent assembly in 1906, the *Inqilab-e Mashruteh* (Constitutional Revolution) began, which after a vicious civil war (1908–09) heralded the end of arbitrary rule in Iran.[12]

However, the stakes of the *Mashruteh* Revolution were considerably higher than the mere weakening of the court. The revolution marked the establishment of the notion of popular sovereignty in the body politic of the kingdom of Persia. In the first major document of the revolution, the *Qanun-e Isasi* (Fundamental Laws), the *Majlis* was granted extensive powers as "the representative of the whole people"; it was further accorded the right "in all questions to propose any measure that it regards as conducive to the well-being of the government [*hokumat*] and the people [*mellat*]."¹³ In the finished document of the constitution (the Supplementary Laws), it was clearly enunciated that "The sovereignty is a trust confided (as a Divine Gift) by the People to the person of the King."¹⁴ The 1909 constitution would thus seem to indicate that God continued to be accepted as the ultimate point of origin for all political authority, and that the principle of divine delegation was retained (rather than arguing that human beings qua human beings created sovereign authority). The change lay in the idea of incidence of sovereignty in this world—in the people as a collective entity, the *mellat*, rather than in the office or the person of the Shah. Whatever authority the Shah enjoyed, he did so not because he was assigned by God to look after the temporal affairs of the *ummah* (community[of the faithful]) within the confines of that particular realm, but because the people had appointed him to look after the interests of the *mellat* that constituted that realm.¹⁵

There was, indeed, a major debate over the connotation of the *mellat*, and the nature of the *daulat* that came into being. A section of the *'ulema* was concerned that this new principle of popular sovereignty contradicted the notion that sovereignty belongs to God alone. Resolved to regulate arbitrary power, they believed that the fact of divine sovereignty had to be categorically emphasized by declaring the body of Islamic laws *(shari'ah)* to be the source of all regulation in the society. They demanded that the government be *mashru'eh* (in accordance with the law, i.e., *shari'ah*) rather than *mashruteh* (in accordance with the constitution). This would imply that the state would be defined as Islamic from a legalist standpoint (i.e., Islamic laws provide the regulatory parameters of the state), rather than from a societal standpoint (i.e., Islamic values and norms inform the majority of social practices in the state).¹⁶ The modernist intelligentsia, by contrast, were determined that the people would be defined in terms of territoriality of the state rather than any confessional character—that is, as *Mellat-e Irani* (the people of Iran) rather than *Mellat-e Islami* (Islamic people). This would imply that Iranian nationals would be entitled to the protection of laws not as Muslims (or people of other persuasions acknowledged by Islam), but as *Iranians*, regardless of their confessional type—hence the notion of equality before the law. A useful compromise was arrived at in the 1909 constitution: the *Ithna 'Ashari* (Twelver) variety of Shi'ism was acknowledged as the official religion of the state, and all legislations passed by the *Majlis* would have to be vetted by a committee of Shi'i *'ulema* as not being opposed to Islam. Further, a fair proportion of ecclesiastical and personal laws applicable on the Muslims would continue to be administered by the *'ulema*, so that the Islamic character of the state would remain undisturbed.¹⁷

Regardless of advocacy of *mashru'eh* or *mashruteh,* it was more or less resolved that sovereignty resided in the people rather than the ruler. It was also more or less resolved that in modern Iran, governance would have to be in accordance with laws, rather than arbitrary. Most importantly, the state was assigned with the direct responsibility of promoting the interests of the people, and the laws were meant to ensure that such responsibility was discharged—failure in doing this would render the regime concerned illegitimate. The Pahlavi regime, which ruled Iran for almost half of the twentieth century, stretched these principles to their limits before the regime collapsing.

### The Statist Discourse of Modernity: The Daulat in Search of a Mellat

By laying the foundations of popular sovereignty in Iranian politics, the *Mashruteh* Revolution also settled another major debate that had taken place during Qajar rule. The *nizam-e jadid* (new order), initiated under the Qajars to overcome technological backwardness and weak military organization, involved effecting a series of changes collectively categorized in later times as *tajaddud,* conveying vaguely the sense denoted by the term "modernity."[18] After the constitutionalist triumph, the decisive debates in the country were not concerned with *whether* there should be any *nizam-e jadid*, rather what would be the form of the modernization that the state should pursue.

In the second half of the nineteenth century, as British and Russian penetration of the economy betrayed Iran's technological inferiority, some observers had argued that Iranians should embrace advances made by the west in science and technology, that Islam was perfectly compatible with modernity (understood primarily as an outcome of modern science). The most powerful advocate of this viewpoint was Jamal al-din Asadabadi, alias al-Afghani.[19] Adoption of western science and technology, it was believed, would blend with Iran's rich Perso-Islamic sociocultural heritage to equip the country for a definitive place in the world.

However, the secular modernist intelligentsia believed that Persia's relative backwardness was made more pronounced by inefficient despotism, and the malaise could be remedied only by "modernization" of the state apparatus by broadening the social basis of political power and making the rulers accountable to the ruled—in a manner similar to the western experience. The *Mashruteh* revolution brought protagonists of this particular notion of modernity to positions of power.

The principal agenda before the *mashruteh-khwahis* (constitutionalists) was to transform the weak Qajar kingdom into a strong modern nation-state. The state apparatus began to be modernized almost as soon as the constitution was given shape, finances being among the first things that the *mashruteh-khwahis* tried to set right, because without sound finances the armed forces would continue to be ineffectual.[20] This became evident when the British and the Russians reoccupied their respective spheres of influence in 1911 in the background of regional and tribal disturbances in Azerbaijan, Khorasan. After nearly half a decade of Russian presence in the north and British presence in the south, collapse of the Russian presence after the Russian Revolution of 1917 gave the Iranians a major opportunity to put their house in order. Coinciding with uprisings in Gilan and Azerbaijan in the north and British attempts at turning Iran effectively into a vassal state,[21] a nationalist backlash began in 1919 that culminated in the rise of Reza Khan, and of a statist discourse of political legitimacy.

\* \* \*

The postwar nationalist backlash, however, was qualitatively different from the *Mashruteh* period because it sought to deploy the resources of the state into the service of the "nation" not only to defend it from external powers, but also to define the contours of the "nation" itself that had to be defended. Previously, being an *Irani* denoted simply to be a resident of the kingdom of Persia (whose component regions have tended to vary over centuries) at any specific point in time. It was probably only in the course of the first quarter of the twentieth century that the Iranian "self" developed the attributes associated with the modern category of "nation" under the guiding influence of the state. The state began to lay down what it *meant* politically, socially, and culturally to be an *Irani*. In this process of nation-building, although the "nation" began to be cast into a mold by the state, the people who constituted that "nation" were not consulted about the manner in which they were cast into the nation. Instead of the popular sovereignty for which the *mashruteh* struggle was waged, the people of Iran seemed to have attained only political sovereignty for their government. Iran in the half-century of Pahlavi rule, thus, presented the anomalous sight of a people appropriated by their government.

Before the rise of Reza Shah, while there was some agreement on the need for a *nizam-e jadid*, there was little agreement on what constituted the element of novelty in the order except that bare minimum agenda that held the constitutionalists together—namely, the need to establish a limited monarchy, to keep an elected legislative stronger than the executive, and to abolish commercial capitulations (to foreign entrepreneurs and concerns) in order to rid Iran of the evil of foreign capitalist exploitation. The constitutionalists were divided between modernist votaries of territorial nationalism (advocating political centralization, national unification, and communal integration) and the older social elite (opposed to centralization and jealously defending regional autonomy).[22]

After Reza Khan persuaded the last Qajar Shah to appoint him as the *Sardar Sepah* (Commander-in-Chief) in 1921 owing to the strength of his Russian-trained Cossack troops, he enhanced the military might of the state substantially, and suppressed most of the tribal and ethnic uprisings that plagued the country at that time. The prospect of a strong and centralized state swiftly won over for him a significant portion of Iran's articulate classes, cutting across the political spectrum.[23] Consequently, when Reza Khan ascended the throne in 1925 as Reza Shah, the founder of the Pahlavi dynasty, he received overt support from all the principal political formations.[24] A consensus seemed to have emerged on the necessity of a strong central authority, and Reza Shah was chosen as the instrument for the creation of that strong state. Reza Shah, though, had his own agenda to push.

\* \* \*

Reza Shah (r. 1925–41) never managed to systematically write about his vision of a modern Iran. A pattern emerges, nonetheless, from what he said and did in the course of three decades when he virtually presided over the destiny of his country. Confronted with the obvious weaknesses of the Qajar state, Reza Shah Pahlavi shared with many of his compatriots the desire to forge Iran into a powerful, integrated, and "modern" nation-state. Squabbles among the constitutionalists in the *Majlis* over the direction of modernization, however, apparently revealed the limitations of constitutionalism as an agent of rapid change in a traditional society. Reza Shah chose instead to follow the path to "modernity" laid down in post-Ottoman Turkey under the guiding influence of Kemal Atatürk, largely because post-Ottoman Turkey, too, evolved a varied discourse on the challenges of modernizing a traditional land.[25] Central to this discourse was a statist approach, where the executive authority was projected as pivotal, not only to the functioning of the body politic but also to the trajectory of "modernity." The government, as Reza Shah devised it, was purported to be the principal agent of "modernization" of the "traditional" land.

Centralization of authority was pivotal to Reza Shah's agenda of modernization. This was accomplished through a systemic reform of the state apparatus as it existed in 1925. To start with, Reza Shah refashioned and strengthened the armed forces in stages—first as *Sardar Sepah* (Commander-in-Chief), then as the Shah.[26] During 1925–41, the size of

Iran's standing army increased from 40,000 to 127,000 troops, with a small air force, 100 tanks, and a few gunboats.[27] Equally significant was the centralization of the bureaucracy. The haphazard collection of traditional *mustawfis* (accountants), hereditary Mirzas (descendants of military commanders of previous eras), and other government functionaries was gradually transformed into a body of 90,000 full-time civil servants operating under ten ministries at the provincial and central levels.[28] The local, provincial, and central authorities were organized in a hierarchical manner, which ensured that, for the first time in the history of the land, Tehran wielded direct command over the provincial towns and in the countryside.[29] Establishment of a central authority was made more effective by the simultaneous project of physical integration of the country, as an intricate network of railways and roadways left Iran more united as a country than ever before as early as the 1930s.[30]

The process of centralization undertaken by the Pahlavi state included the major task of subjugation of the various tribes of Iran. To ensure their permanent subjection Reza Shah extended army outposts in their territories, disarmed their warriors, conscripted their youth, stirred up their internal divisions, subverted their leadership, restricted their annual migrations, and pressed ahead with sedentarization of tribes.[31] Central authority thus managed to penetrate the networks of tribal power and wield substantial authority over the various tribal confederacies that had strengthened during centuries of weak central rule.

The Pahlavi state under Reza Shah was also determined to end the stranglehold of foreign capital over the Iranian economy. The nineteenth-century capitulations that granted Europeans extraterritorial jurisdictions were abolished, and foreign officials (such as Arthur Millspaugh, the Treasurer-General appointed by the *Majlis*) were removed from positions of influence.[32] Right to mint currency was transferred from the British-owned Imperial Bank to the National Bank of Iran *(Bank-e Melli Iran)*, and the administration of the telegraph system from the Indo-European Telegraph Company was nationalized. Reza Shah had noticeably less success in reducing the formidable influence of the Anglo-Iranian Oil Company (AIOC, formerly known as Anglo-Persian Oil Company, or APOC). Although in 1932 he cancelled a concession made out in 1912, he failed to increase the state's share of revenue from Iran's oil revenues substantially.[33] The Pahlavi state also started in earnest the industrialization of the country during the 1930s under the cover of high tariff walls, government monopolies, and state finance for modern plants with western technology. By 1941, Iran became the largest industrial economy in West Asia, employing over 50,000 wage earners in the industrial sector.[34]

Modernization of the state also necessarily involved an almost complete overhaul of the existing educational infrastructure. Previously western educational institutions were run by state officials, religious communities, and foreign missionaries mostly in the urban and suburban areas; education in the countryside remained primarily within the traditional *madraseh* system. Reforms undertaken by Reza Shah not only saw standardization under the Ministry of Education (which ran over 2,300 schools in 1941), a general secularization of education could also be seen as people began to prefer the state schools over the *madraseh* on account of better job prospects. In higher education, the Tehran University was founded in 1934, followed by several other universities in the various provinces over the next four decades. After 1929, the government sponsored higher education of at least 100 students each year in different parts of Europe. Graduates from this educational apparatus mostly joined government service as office workers, administrators, skilled technicians, lawyers, doctors, and academics. For the better part of the Pahlavi era, this urban educated professional middle class formed the bedrock of support that the government could count on.[35]

\* \* \*

The Pahlavi regime received widespread support in its bid to centralize authority by disarming and forcibly settling the various tribes, strengthening Iran's armed forces, pursuing railway construction, and to an extent, even in its attempts to eliminate all distinctive communitarian affiliation in public life. The regime focused on the creation of one nation out of Iran's multiple religious, linguistic, and ethnic groups by erasing their outward distinctions. In 1928, all traditional and ethnic headgear were outlawed, except in the case of registered clerics and clergymen; first the "Pahlavi hat" and then in 1936 the "international headgear" (felt hat) became the approved headgear for all Iranians, replacing the traditional Persian *kuleh* for Muslims, and ethnic and tribal headgear of all sorts. Communitarian education was equally vigorously attacked by the state— Baha'i schools lost their right to teach in 1934; the Armenians lost their right to teach European languages in that year, and their right to teach altogether in 1938; all linguistic minorities (Turkic, Arabs, and Kurds alike) were compelled to take up Persian as the primary language in schools, driving vernaculars into the confines of informal education in the privacy of homes. Communitarian, ethnic, and linguistic identities that had been the bedrock of social formations till the early twentieth century were being dismissed out of hand. Shi'i and Sunni, Muslims and Christians, Jews and Zoroastrians, Turks and Arabs were summarily asked to stop sporting any of these identities, and to become *Iranian* almost overnight.

However, Reza Shah never had a definite political outfit or social group that supported him consistently and continuously. Groups and social classes that supported him on one issue very often fell out over another. Lack of a steady support base never quite mattered because, once elected the monarch, Reza Shah did not need the *Majlis* to stay in power. The repressive police machinery and armed forces being at his disposal, any outfit or group likely to threaten him could be effectively smothered. Reza Shah's ability to manipulate elections to the *Majlis* almost without fail since the 1920s made his position still more secure. Nonetheless, the frequency with which groups that required exclusion through repression and electoral manipulation surfaced across the political spectrum indicates that the Pahlavi agenda neither represented any single social constituency, nor worked to the detriment of any single one.

The Pahlavi project of nation-building addressed major concerns emerging from the *mashruteh* period. Even as Reza Khan was becoming Reza Shah, an article in the reformist journal *Ayandeh* (the Future) seemed to anticipate the Pahlavi project:

> Our aim is to develop and strengthen national unity... We mean [to establish] cultural, social and political solidarity among all the people who live within the present borders of Iran... We will attain it by extending the Persian language throughout the provinces; eliminating regional costumes; destroying local and feudal authorities; and removing the traditional differences between Kurds, Lurs, Qashqayis, Arabs, Turks, Turkomans, and other communities that reside within Iran. Our nation will continue to live in danger as long as we have no schools to teach Persian and Iranian history to the masses; no railways to connect the various parts of the country; no books, journals, and newspapers to inform the people of their rich Iranian heritage; and no Persian equivalents to replace the many non-Persian names in Iran. Unless we achieve national unity, nothing will remain of Iran.[36]

Not only reformists in the political center, even the left was not altogether immune to the "progressive" credentials of the Pahlavi regime. As early as 1926, the Socialist Party (fiercely opposed to anything that undermined democracy in Iran) adopted as some of its goals "strengthening of the central government," equal justice for all citizens "irrespective of birth and nationality *(melliyat)*, and government projects to eliminate rural and urban unemployment."[37] Accordingly, in view of programs like establishment of strong central government, state-led industrialization, secularization of the public space, et cetera, even the socialists chose to support the Pahlavi regime occasionally.

Despite such broad congruence of the regime's agenda with the views of a large section of the intelligentsia, the Pahlavi state drew ambiguous responses from the nation it claimed to represent. As in Kemalist Turkey, Pahlavi modernization was not principally a societal process, unlike the western societies from where the baggage of "modernity" was borrowed. It was instead a policy goal set and pushed through by the ruling elite, formulated as a response to western challenges. Since Atatürk's Turkey had already shown how a Muslim society could modernize by westernizing certain aspects of its life, the Pahlavi regime found it convenient to follow that model, *mutatis mutandis*, for Iran.[38] However, despite the contributions of the Pahlavi regime in "modernizing" the state of Iran, there remained concerns as to whether governance could really be "modern" with a repressive regime at the helm; also the society was far from being "modernized." The discontent with Pahlavi modernization was largely due to its incomplete character—for some Iranians, "modernization" of the society was a more pressing task, which the regime not only did not facilitate but actually impeded; for others, the Pahlavi bid for modernization was an attack on the traditional way of life that had to be stopped.

Clear (if occasional) sources of opposition were groups associated with the *Mashruteh* movement. Numerically small among these were those modernist veterans of the movement who, inspired by western intellectual and political paradigms, were loath to see one kind of despotism replace another. Generally supportive of programs for national integration, sedentarization of nomadic tribes, and secularization of the public space, these modernist *mashruteh-khwahis* were uncomfortable with the rampant practice of electoral manipulation (which Reza Shah did almost as a rule from the 1924 *Majlis* elections). Rise in oil revenues subsequent to the renegotiation of the D'Arcy contract for oil exploration in 1933 reduced the Shah's dependence on the civilian population, and therefore the *Majlis*, even further. As the Shah reduced the *Majlis* to a virtual rubber stamp, muzzled the press and the judiciary, the modernist *mashruteh-khwahis* became further alienated. Yet, they failed to criticize the regime, partly because of repression and partly because they valued modernization of the nation almost as much as democratization of the polity. Probably the most significant figure among this lot was Ahmad Kasravi, who, in a series of articles published in 1942 in *Parcham,* summed up the ambivalent position of the *Mashruteh* generation after the removal of the Shah.[39] He scored the Shah high on centralizing the state, pacifying the tribes, disciplining the clergy, abolishing the veil, eliminating feudal relations of power, trying to unify the people, and establishing modern schools, cities, and industries; on the other hand, he scored the Shah poorly for trampling upon the constitution, favoring the military over the civilian administration, accumulating a private fortune, widening the gap between the haves and have-nots, and murdering "progressive intellectuals."[40]

A far larger segment among the *mashruteh-khwahis* who opposed Pahlavi hailed from the traditional middle class of the *bazaars*. Some of these individuals did not favor the western democratic model, but they generally preferred to have the ruler's authority subject to some sort of popular control. This preference turned into a necessity when Reza Shah's modernization program started to attack those aspects of Iranian social life that many among the traditional middle class cherished—namely, the symbols and customs associated with community living. This was true as much for the ethnic and linguistic minorities (viz., Turks, Azeris, Armenians, and Jews) as for the majority Shi'i community, but the secularization of the public space offended particularly the sensibilities of middle-class Muslims, who often had deep ties with the Shi'i *'ulema* establishment.[41] They found the ban on headgear, unveiling of women, restrictions on conventional religious practices, et cetera, to be an assault on their dignity and identity. Religious sensibilities were further offended by the repeated attacks on the clergy (considered the custodians of Shi'ism), by depriving them first of their sources of income, and then reducing their significance in the realm of Shi'i jurisprudence.[42]

The landed and *bazaar* elements were, moreover, directly affected by the Shah's economic reforms—that is, appropriation of landed property and its distribution between the Shah and his cronies, dismantling of age-old guilds of the *bazaar*, and support for modern industry over traditional manufacture. To their mind, the Shah's reliance on foreign models of social and economic institutions constituted evidence of his being a foreign agent; thus the *bazaar*, the old elite, and a section of the *'ulema* defended constitutionalism and representative democracy because only the entire nation together could fight "xenocracy." They were not opposed to "modernization" of the state structure. Their objection was against blind emulation of the west. A large part of Mosaddeq's National Front originated from this body of opinion.[43]

Probably the staunchest critics of the Pahlavi regime were the younger generation of western educated Iranians who came into public life after the *Mashruteh* revolution. Exposed to the western world to a greater extent than their predecessors, these individuals found Pahlavi reforms superficial, its patriotic credentials pretentious. In their opinion, Reza Shah was no patriot; rather, he was a self-seeking founder of a new dynasty, who enriched himself in whichever way possible. A Qajar trained by Tsarists, and helped to power by the British, the Shah was merely helping the foreign powers rule Iran by proxy. The reforms were dismissed as cosmetic, saying that instead of challenging the traditional forces these helped them consolidate their influence over society. In other words, the Pahlavis impeded the emergence of a "modern" society free of premodern inhibitive social structures and influences. Many of these critics were influenced by the moral and intellectual assumptions of socialism, and some were inclining even toward communism. Their program involved working toward the capture of the state machinery so that inequities of development could be addressed directly, and the pernicious influence of foreign capitalists could be contested. Needless to say, being less malleable to the Pahlavis the left-inclined political activists paid a much heavier price than most other opponents of the Shah. In 1926, the Socialist Party was dissolved and thereafter the brunt of the repression was directed toward the Communist Party. By 1931, the socialists had disturbed the regime adequately to bring in stringent press laws and resort to crackdown on anyone suspected of harboring "collectivist" sympathies.[44] After Reza Shah's abdication, these forces resurfaced as the *Hizb-e Tudeh-ye Iran* (Party of the Iranian Masses).

Amidst such a wide range of views, the aggregate political discourse that emerged during the Pahlavi era was undoubtedly statist in its persuasion, unlike the late Qajar discourse that had aimed at regulating the power of the state. For the better part of the Pahlavi era, almost no major political formation ever questioned the manner in which state power was being (or intended to be) let loose on the very people who constituted the *mellat*.

\* \* \*

This does not mean, however, that the *mellat* vanished from political discourse altogether; quite the opposite. Since the *Mashruteh* revolution, the *mellat* has survived as probably the only constant factor in the political life of modern Iran. One indicator of this centrality of the discourse of "nation" in modern Iran is the name of the various newspapers that were published. Of the 326 regular and irregular, national and regional newspapers and journals published in Iran that are listed with the Library of Congress for the period, 38 carry the term *Iran* or *Irani*, 17 carry *mellat*, and 13 carry *mardom* (people). In fact, the most significant feature of Iranian politics in the Pahlavi era was that political allegiance was neither sought for, nor given to, the person of the reigning monarch or the institution of monarchy. The Qajar dynasty was *voted out* by the people in a referendum, and replaced by the Pahlavi dynasty that was something like a "People's Monarchy."

Addressing the most pressing concerns in contemporary Iran, the Pahlavis had successfully appropriated the political category of the people and harnessed it to the state. Drastic and frequently unpopular reforms were undertaken in the name of the *mellat*. Thus, although Reza Shah took the constitution for a ride, systematically rigged *Majlis* elections, and used the *Majlis* like a rubber stamp for his personal authority, he refrained from dissolving it altogether—all the popular and unpopular reforms alike of the Reza Shah era were ratified by the *Majlis*, the one organization that represented, theoretically, the whole nation.

Nor was the Shah alone in trying to appropriate the *mellat* for himself. Almost every shade of opinion in modern Iran—modernists, traditionalists, socialists as much as royalists—chose to define the nation in its own way before claiming to represent it. The Pahlavi policy of secularization of the public space was defended as essential to the integration of the nation of Iran, while it was resisted as an assault on the dignity of the people; state-led industrialization was identified as essential to the advancement of the economy of the nation, even as the policy was criticized as promoting foreign capitalist interests and as unmindful of the true interests of the Iranian masses.

The most potent argument against Reza Shah (just like that against his son in the 1970s) was that his reign had seemed to benefit the nation less and himself (along with his cronies) more. Repression mounted in the late 1930s (and later in the late 1970s) precisely because the regime's claims to speak for the people appeared thin. When the Allied need to open up a line of supply into the Soviet Union prompted the British and the Soviets to invade Iran and persuade Reza Shah to abdicate in favor of his son in 1941, the BBC launched a propaganda blitz targeting Reza Shah's avarice and cruelty, stressing how these worked against the interests of the people. The popularity of the broadcasts took even the British by surprise.[45]

### The Making of 1979: The Struggle between the State and the People

Reza Shah's replacement on the throne in 1941 by his son, Muhammad Reza Shah, under Anglo-Soviet supervision triggered the debate about the significance of the *mellat* yet again. The new Shah began with a visible relaxation of his father's repressive order, restoring elementary civil and political liberties, which helped meaningful politics revive after remaining moribund for a decade and a half.[46] A multi-pronged contest broke out between Pahlavi loyalists (principally, beneficiaries of Reza Shah's policies), traditionalists (social and religious, opposed to the Shah, but favoring constitutional monarchy over democratic republic), liberals (favoring modernization of the state apparatus, but insistent on democracy), conservatives (social and religious, opposed to the Shah, but preferring a strong constitutional monarchy over democracy with a weak monarchy), and socialists (mostly outside the *Majlis*, especially in the Tudeh party, gradually speaking of class war and social revolution)—each claiming to represent the *mellat*.[47]

Once World War II was over, Britain ended its military occupation, but the Soviet Union began to encourage the rise of left-wing forces in the Iranian province of Azerbaijan. The Tudeh swiftly capitalized on this development to emerge as a major force to reckon with. This made Moscow hopeful of being able to detach the oil-rich Azeri region, and if possible, the whole of northern Iran that was a part of the Russian sphere of influence in the Great War and of the Soviet sphere in World War II.[48] Subsequent U.S. intervention not only forced Moscow out but also placed the Shah under the protective wing of the United States as the latter's global fight against communism extended to Iran. Socialists began to be persecuted across the country, precisely at a time when the Tudeh Party broke major grounds owing to its activities among the working class. Politicians of all other persuasions and the religious establishment were alarmed at the rapid rise of the Tudeh party, and treated with suspicion anything that even remotely resembled a socialist agenda.[49]

The most significant assertion of the *mellat* in Iran before 1979 developed around the *Jeb'eh-ye Melli* (National Front) in the context of the postwar economic crisis.[50] The National Front, led by Muhammad Mosaddeq, launched what became known as the "Oil Nationalism," culminating in the nationalization of the Anglo-Iranian Oil Company in 1951 by a government headed by Mosaddeq.[51] As the traditionalist *bazaaris*, liberal nationalists, and socialists alike were favoring the nationalization program, for a brief while it seemed that the nation had indeed claimed the state for itself. Although Mosaddeq was subsequently toppled by a military coup with the backing of the CIA, along with a large part of the Shi'i *'ulema* and even some liberals, who saw in his government something like a socialist "anarchy," the Mosaddeq era established one point beyond dispute. By nationalizing the petroleum resources of the country, Mosaddeq was staking the people's claim on a highly remunerative national resource that the previous ruler had failed to deploy in the service of the nation.

Even after Mosaddeq's ouster and the restoration of Muhammad Reza, the principle of oil wealth as a national resource had to be admitted by the British half of the AIOC.[52] Pahlavi despotism was reestablished on the foundation of this national wealth, and the Shah launched a period of economic liberalism coupled with virtually a political dictatorship, supported by the conservative and moderate elements, who found the monarchy to be the most formidable defense against communism.

Posturing as an opponent of communism, Muhammad Reza Shah positioned Iran in the vanguard of U.S. plans for containing communism in Asia, turning Iran into one of the most important U.S. allies in West Asia after Israel. The subsequent arms transfers worth $500 million (1953–63) made by Washington to Tehran strengthened the coercive machinery of the state considerably: the armed forces grew to over 200,000 personnel and the military budget rose from $80 million to $183 million (1953–63); the *Sazman-e Ittela'at wa Amniyyat-e Keshvar* (National Security and Information Organization, alias SAVAK, after the Persian acronym) was set up with assistance from the CIA and the Mossad. This machinery was deployed quite continually till 1977 to stamp out almost all effective opposition, particularly those with a socialist bent, and especially the Tudeh.[53]

The 1960s marked a second successful attempt by the *daulat* to regain the initiative lost to the *mellat*. The decade began with something like an economic crisis brought upon by the government's policy of deficit financing, prompting the Kennedy administration to call for liberalization of the regime and a thorough land reform lest Iran collapsed before communist advance. It was in this context that the White Revolution was launched by Prime Minister Ali Amini and Minister for Agriculture Hassan Arsanjani, and subsequently appropriated entirely by the Shah.[54]

The White Revolution had six principles: (i) distribution of arable land among the cultivators, (ii) nationalization of woods and forests, (iii) electoral reforms including enfranchisement of women, (iv) denationalization of state monopolies to finance land reform programs, (v) profit sharing between management and workers, (vi) creation of Literacy Corps (educated conscripts) to eradicate illiteracy from the countryside.[55] Adopting such a program, the Shah seemed to be jettisoning the broad coalition of moderate and hardliner conservative groups on which the regime rested apart from the military bureaucratic elements. Instead, he seemed to have opted for the more moderate segments among the liberals of the National Front, who accordingly changed their goal from democratic *(hokumat-e melli)* to constitutional *(hokumat-e qanuni)* government.[56]

By the late 1960s, when Iran's petroleum revenue began to rise dramatically, the second generation of Pahlavi modernization began to be given shape. In the early 1970s, as OPEC states engineered a price hike for crude from $1.79 per barrel in 1971 to $11.65 in December 1973, Iran's oil revenue shot up from $2,308 million (1972) to $20,488 million (1976).[57] The surge in the government's earnings was channeled into a frenzied program of industrialization.[58] Till the mid-1970s, Iran's economic indices could excite envy in any Third World country. Industrialization proceeded at a breakneck speed, principally in the heavy industrial sector. This went hand in hand with urbanization—prompted by the "pull factor" of industrialization and the "push factor" of uneconomic holdings due to land reform, causing a veritable demographic revolution.[59]

But the tale of Iran's modernization had a seamier side. Iranian industry under the Pahlavis developed few organic linkages with the rest of the economy. Thus, hardly any multiplier effects were generated beyond the transport, communication, and construction sectors. Still, while the oil revenue kept flowing in increasing amounts, there was plenty of wealth to be distributed through a variety of economic activities. When, however, the world oil market went into a crisis in the mid-1970s and revenue plummeted, state-run industrial ventures ground to a halt. In the absence of significant industrial ventures independent of the state, economic development failed to be sustained. Urbanization continued nonetheless, stretching urban infrastructure beyond endurable limits. Accordingly, social tensions intensified and, repression notwithstanding, dissidence began to be increasingly vocal since 1975.[60]

By 1977, the Pahlavi regime became a victim of the very modernization that it saw as its raison d'être. In 1977–78, even the closest allies of the Shah began to switch loyalties. With almost every section of the Iranian people opposed to the Shah's highhanded inefficiency, the Shah had only one hope of survival—total disunity among the forces of the opposition. Since some of the opposition forces advocated constitutionalism and others some sort of Islamic order, the possibility of persistent disunity was fairly high. Yet from mid-1977 to early 1979, the opposition held fast, forcing the Shah to abdicate on January 16, 1979—heralding the Iranian Revolution of 1979.

Quite apart from the success in ousting an apparently invincible ruler, the significance of the revolution lay in the *Islamic* color it had come to attain. This caused considerable surprise not only in the outside world, but also among a large segment of Iranians themselves. For, despite the continued and visible presence of the Shi'i *'ulema* in Iranian society, Pahlavi Iran had developed such a powerful drive for secularization that its Islamic component frequently receded from the radar of observers.

**The Politics of Secularism and the Challenge of Islam**

Ever since the *Mashruteh* revolution, as the idea of the country as a people bound by territory became central to the self-image of Iran, the agenda of development and progress proved crucial in the rhetoric of political legitimacy and governance. Premised upon the notion of a historical unity of the Iranian people stretching back a couple of millennia, the Pahlavi approach to the history of Iran suggested that the country did not belong to one ethnic, linguistic, or social group or the other, rather all the groups had contributed to the greatness of the Persian kingdom, and had benefited from an integrated state. The glory of the Persian civilization was projected in terms of achievements of the centralized state-systems, be it the Achaemenids, the Sassanids, the Abbasids, or the Safavids. That is to say, the country was great because the rulers were vested with greatness, and the Pahlavis claimed that their agenda of developing Iran into a modern nation-state would restore to Iran her lost aura of greatness. Indeed, for a dynasty that was founded on plebiscite, the urge to establish unquestioning allegiance from the people required the sanction of history: Pahlavi claim to that sanction lay in its self-image of a dynasty charged with the modernization of Iran.

There was, arguably, a second and a more fundamental agenda behind tracing the annals of Iran's glory back to the coming of Aryans and to the days of the Medes and Zoroaster. A whole generation of secularist intellectuals felt gratified when Reza Shah began to convey the impression that Iran's grandeur was not simply because of Islam; rather Islam gained more by way of grandeur than it imparted to Iran. The urge to distinguish the Iranian identity from that of Islam stemmed from a debate that had raged in Iran from the second half of the nineteenth century.[61]

Like elsewhere in the Muslim world, confronted with the "manifest" material superiority of the west, Iranians started to look for the cause of their own relative backwardness. As elsewhere in the Islamic world, some of them identified the "real cause" to be the fairly popular view that Islam endorses a kind of long-run fatalism.[62] Many Iranians came to believe that such fatalism impeded the search for new ideas and new experiences in their society, as the public space was so overwhelmingly swayed by Islamic considerations. Their preferred solution, as in other Muslim societies, was to reform the society in the light of advances in the realm of knowledge, made in the west but adaptable anywhere. With prominent thinkers like Mirza Fath 'Ali Akhundzadeh, Mirza Aqa Khan Kermani, and Mirza 'Abd al-Rahim Talebof in the nineteenth century and Ahmad Kasravi and 'Ali Akbar Dehkhoda in the twentieth among protagonists of this position, votaries of the secularist approach to modernity (hence, "secular modernists") tended to argue that it was the history and culture of the Persian civilization that made the people of the land distinctive, rather than Islam, which was merely a part of it.[63] If Islamic public discourse was to impede the progression of the civilization, then in the interests of the country such discourse had to be secularized in the manner of more advanced societies. Islam thus had to be banished from public life, and relegated to the personal sphere of the lives of Muslims, if that. The secular modernists attacked Iran's traditional culture because of its various religious practices, tribalism, ethnic divisions, and communal sectarianism. They sought the solution in the formation of a centralized state with an emphasis on pre-Islamic kingship and culture, the expansion of secular education, the spread of the Persian language among non-Persians, the adoption of western philosophy and technology, and the destruction of clerical influence.[64]

The Pahlavis in general and Reza Shah in particular championed the cause of secular modernity pretty aggressively. Although in the initial years Reza Shah treaded carefully in handling the *'ulema,* the agenda of secularization was never really in doubt. The most significant change came in the realm of laws. Since the days of the Abbasid Caliphate, Islamic laws had gradually become the foundational logic of state power in Persia. The Safavid dynasty had made *Ithna 'Ashari* Shi'ism the official religion of Persia, and in the process Ja'fari Shi'i *fiqh* was institutionalized in the kingdom. *Ithna 'Ashari* jurisprudence remained pivotal to the Persian judicial system till the *mashruteh* revolution began to talk of a constitution with a corpus of laws derived from various European juridical traditions. The Pahlavis undermined the traditional judiciary by insisting on the training of professional lawyers in centers of secular education, effectively derecognizing experts of Islamic law trained in traditional seminaries unless they followed up their seminary education with a stint at secular institutions.[65] As a consequence of such measures, the *'ulema* began to be robbed of their monopoly over state laws and the last real utility that Islamic laws potentially had (as a restrain on executive authority) effectively disappeared.[66]

Moreover, during the late Qajar days, disillusioned with a despotic state that claimed to be the defender of Islam, secular modernists had begun to rework the historical imagination of the country in a bid to undermine the legitimacy of the existing order. Previously, following the Islamic scheme of historiography, Islam was supposed to have heralded the beginning of civilization in Iran, while the pre-Islamic age supposedly exemplified the age of *jahiliya* (ignorance).[67] The secular modernists of the *mashruteh* period began to adopt the paradigm of classical western historiography of "classical age-dark age-renaissance," depicting the pre-Islamic era as an *'asr-e monavvar* (enlightened age); the Islamic era as that of *jahiliya*, misery, and despotism; and the late nineteenth century as the *asr-e bidari* (age of awakening).[68] Whether it was the publication of studies in the history and myths of ancient Persia by Hasan Pirniya, the research on Zoroastrianism and its sacred texts by Ebrahim Purdavud, or the monumental lexicon by 'Ali Akbar Dehkhoda—all were geared to highlighting pre-Islamic Persian culture.[69]

This fitted in quite neatly with the Pahlavi advocacy of Iranian nationalism. The name of the dynasty itself was chosen as a throwback to the pre-Islamic past.[70] The entire issue of renaming Persia as Iran was equally symptomatic of attempts to de-center Islam from the national life. At a time when Hitler was championing the notion of Aryan racial superiority over other races of Europe and the world, Reza Shah wanted to emphasize the Aryan roots of Iranian civilization in his bid to further distance the country from the Arab/Semitic people of the Muslim world. He encountered considerable opposition from people who pointed out that the name Persia itself preceded the coming of Islam, and could be traced back at least to the glorious Sassanid era, if not earlier.[71]

But of all Reza Shah's measures under the rubric of secularization, the decision to outlaw the *chador* was probably the most symbolic and controversial. Islam calls for men and women to dress and carry themselves modestly lest others be tempted. For women, modest dress is generally defined in terms of the notion of *hijab*, which involves covering up the hair on one's head. In Iran, the predominant form of *hijab* for centuries had been the *chador*, a single loose-flowing garment that covered the body from head to toe, but left the face exposed. Secularists believed that Iranian women should participate in the public sphere, and the *chador*, which to them symbolized the confinement of women within the private sphere, had to go. When the *chador* was outlawed in 1934, it was followed by directives to the police to remove the veil from women who came out in *chador* in public. The police harassment that followed made it very difficult to keep any kind of *hijab* in public. While many Iranian women (primarily from the wealthy or professional segments of Iranian society) welcomed these measures, many other women (from the traditional segments of the society) who otherwise moved around in public quite freely, decided to stay at home.[72]

\* \* \*

The secularist agenda, in many ways, had been the defining attribute of the Reza Shah era. Unlike his father, though, Muhammad Reza Shah was somewhat ambivalent toward secularization. In the 1940s, while Muhammad Reza was still very weak, he tried to reduce the harshness of some of his father's policies in a bid to court popularity among his subjects; this included a roll back of some components of the secularization agenda. After the Mosaddeq interlude, he went for a very public rapprochement with the *ulema*. By the 1960s, however, as his power grew, Muhammad Reza decided to revisit the politics of secularism.

The Shah's rapprochement with the *ulema* had an additional consideration as well. During the early years of his reign, Muhammad Reza Shah realized that Islam could provide a powerful counterpoint to the Tudeh ideology among the masses. He also appreciated that the support network provided by the mosques in the realm of poor relief and collective sociability made the 'ulema a powerful ally in this venture to resist the Tudeh. As the *bazaaris* proved to be a decisive factor in swinging the 'ulema either way, the Shah decided to humor the *bazaar* as well.[73] The 'ulema too were concerned about the steady ascendancy of the Tudeh among the urban underclass, the segment of the society where the secularization agenda had been least effective. Hence, despite supporting Mosaddeq in the first phase of his struggle against the Shah, once the Tudeh support for Mosaddeq became overt and resolute, the *'ulema* began to favor the Shah.[74]

In the post-Mosaddeq years, the Shah vowed to uphold religion, and continually denounced the Tudeh as "enemy of private property and Islam."[75] The Shah and the Shah Bano, Soraiya, made periodic pilgrimages to Mecca, Karbala, Qom, and Mashhad, and prominent religious leaders like Ayatollah Boroujerdi, Ayatollah Behbahani, and Imam Jom'eh of Tehran gained easy access to the court. During this period of bonhomie between the Shah and the *'ulema*, the *Ayatollah-ye Ozma* (the Grand Ayatollah), Boroujerdi, successfully carved out an autonomous space for the *'ulema* by restructuring the clerical establishment financially.[76]

The death of Boroujerdi in 1961 ended the cordial relationship between the Shah and the *'ulema*.[77] Indeed, a large section of the *'ulema* led by Imam Jom'eh of Tehran continued the official line in its entirety, which was that the *'ulema* stood guard over the timeless features of Islam and therefore should not intervene in temporal politics lest the clergy began to value material things more than the spiritual.[78] By this time, however, elements with a major reformist agenda argued that such a quietist interpretation of Shi'ism was in total contrast with its essence, and that such notions had come to dominate Iranian thinking because of defects in the theological establishment itself.[79] They argued that Islam embraced a more holistic worldview, eclipsed for long by the study of mere jurisprudence. Neglect of the philosophical aspects of Islam, they contended, lay at the root of the perceived redundancy of the *'ulema*. Whereas the *'ulema*, once freed from the trappings of jurisprudence, could interpret Islam in the light of the changed circumstances of the modern world. Among the more radical of these reformists was the minority of clerics led by Ayatollahs Ruhollah Khomeini and Sayyid Muhammad Taleqani, who believed that if a temporal ruler was not promoting Islamic governance, every true Muslim was obliged to remove him from power. Among the more moderate of these reformers were scholars like Allama Tabatabai and Morteza Motahhari, who concentrated more on reorganization of the *'ulema* establishment itself. Both these sections favored some sort of indirect participation by the *'ulema* in public life, preferably as a regulator of legislative and executive activities.[80]

The Shah had been wary of the more radical *'ulema* like Khomeini, but refrained from any direct measures because Boroujerdi successfully restrained them. Once Boroujerdi died, however, he was determined to not let the radicals gain in strength. Hence, letters of condolence on

Boroujerdi's death were sent to moderate Ayatollahs like Shari'atmadari and Golpayagani, but not radicals (and direct associates of Boroujerdi) like Khomeini. He also refrained from pronouncing anyone within the Qom establishment as the *Ayatollah-ye Ozma* (the supreme point of reference for the *Ithna 'Ashari* Shi'i) in Iran lest it posed a moral challenge to the authority of the Shah.[81] By this time, moreover, having launched the White Revolution, the Shah had gained support from the urban Iranians on the one hand and the landed magnates and peasantry on the other. Thus, he became bold enough to disregard the refractory *'ulema*.

The quite stunning success of the White Revolution in the 1960s, accompanied by steadily increasing oil revenue, made the Shah strong enough to return to the original Pahlavi project of secularization of the public space. Women, forced out of the *hijab* a generation earlier and given the benefit of public education, had begun to join the workforce to meet the needs of a fast expanding economy for educated personnel, to the great annoyance of the conservative *'ulema* and the *bazaaris*. Muhammad Reza aggravated the annoyance by extending to women the right to vote and be voted, and by appointing them to high ranks in the government.

In 1971, the Shah went to the extent of celebrating 2,500 years of Persian monarchy, in a grand demonstration of a return to the early Pahlavi agenda of a national identity that predated, was more glorious than anything associated with Islam in Iranian history. As the Aryamehr (Aryan Sun), the Shah was once again staking the claim to be the driving force in the life of *mellat-e Iran*, where all progress emanated from the state. In 1963, the *'ulema* were charged with being an obstacle to such progress when Khomeini began his opposition to the Shah.[82]

Significantly, the resistance of the *'ulema* to the White Revolution too was in the name of the *mellat*. The land reforms under the White Revolution had hit a large segment of the *'ulema* directly in their capacity of absentee landlords, and the *'ulema* considered women's franchise as "an invitation to prostitution."[83] Thus, when Khomeini called for resistance to the Shah in 1963, he struck an immediate cord among the *'ulema* but little else besides. However, in 1964 Khomeini's call to resistance was predicated upon a denunciation of the Shah's grant of extraterritorial rights to U.S. forces stationed in Iran (bringing back memories of capitulation to the foreigners under the Qajars), rather than any aspect of the White Revolution, which was rather popular in Iran at the time. It was almost as if the Shah was accused of undermining what his own father had accomplished by attempting to free the country of foreign domination.[84] Since then, till about 1977, the *'ulema* did not engage in any major overt opposition, although close disciples of Khomeini like Ayatollah Montazeri, Morteza Motahhari, 'Ali Khamenei, and Akbar Hashmi Rafsanjani clandestinely developed a network of *'ulema* devoted to Khomeini. It was this network of Khomeini supporters that subsequently led the popular demonstrations against the Shah during 1977–79, forced the Shah to abdicate in January, and eventually seized power in the autumn of 1979.[85]

During Khomeini's exile, the rise of a generation of lay Islamists strengthened the Islamic alternative. Protagonists like Mehdi Bazargan, Abolhasan Bani-Sadr, and above all 'Ali Shari'ati argued that over previous centuries the *zahiri* (manifest, exoteric) elements of the *faradh al-'ain* (the five principal obligations of the faith) had eclipsed the relative importance of *iman* (genuine belief, consisting of unflinching faith in Allah), since belief was not easy to gauge but enforcement of external conditions and regulations was easy. Thus, even though the Iranian society continued to adhere to Islam over the ages, it was merely Muslim by practice, not a community of true believers *(momin)*. One reason behind this decline in *iman* was indeed the restriction of *'ilm* (learning) to archaic studies associated with the early days of Islam, without accounting for the changing world. The lay Islamists meant to use *'ilm* from all quarters and apply it to the precepts of Islam in a bid to understand Allah and his creation better.[86] In other words, they favored a conscious choice in favor of a modernity that was mindful of the identity of the *mellat* that was being modernized, and opposed any transformation of that identity simply in a blind urge to be modern. They wanted, as they saw it, modern Iran to be both *modern* and *Iranian,* and Islam was integral to that identity. Hence, secularization in the sense of a conscious de-Islamization of Iran ran contrary to the interests of the *mellat.* After the ouster of Muhammad Reza Shah in 1979, these lay Islamists fought hard against the clerical Islamists to keep Iran on the path of constitutionalism—asserting that sovereignty belongs not to those who hold power in the *daulat,* rather to the *mellat* in whose name the *daulat* is constituted.[87]

## Popular Sovereignty or Political Sovereignty?

Clearly, therefore, the discourse of politics in modern Iran had come to center on the pivotal category of *mellat,* or nation/people. All concerns pertaining to the public space tended to be articulated with reference to the national self, and all other concerns (viz. progress, modernity, state, Islam, etc.) had to accommodate this core concern in order to be taken seriously. Here lay a major contradiction: the category of *mellat* had emerged to contest the despotism that was carried out in the name of Perso-Islamic political tradition, but after the *mashruteh* interlude, Qajar despotism was replaced by that of the *daulat* representing the *mellat.* Popular sovereignty, once achieved, was revealed for all practical purposes to be merely political sovereignty of the state from most external influences—and even that was not always above dispute.

A major problem that confronted the people of Iran was that even though the Iranian body politic was supposed to be structured around the *mellat,* the people who were supposed to comprise the *mellat* had no say in determining how the category of the national self was to be defined. For instance, early on in pursuit of the nation-building project, it was decided that Persian (spoken at most by one in every two Iranians) would be considered as the official language and the principal cementing factor for Iranian nationalism, because it had been the official language of the kingdom for centuries. Making Persian the official language won support from ethnic Persian-speaking people as well as those who did not speak Persian (both Reza Shah and Ahmad Kasravi, who supported the idea, were ethnically Turkic). But the despotic manner in which the state stopped public schools from teaching other languages violated the very sort of rights that the state was purported to safeguard. In this case, the Pahlavis followed the predominant logic associated with nationalism that forces that might compromise the unity of a people should be contested vigorously for the sake of that unity itself.

Similarly, on the issue of veiling, the state following a socially progressive agenda violated a basic right that it should have upheld. Use of the *hijab,* and especially its more extreme variant, the *chador,* was undoubtedly of religious significance to traditional Muslims. This was taken by the Pahlavi state to be a crucial obstacle to its agenda of secularization. Yet, instead of simply encouraging women to appear in public without the *hijab,* the Pahlavis declared the *hijab* to be illegal, hoping this would help women in breaking out of the seclusion of their *andarun* (inner quarters of the Iranian household). Indeed, a large number of women from urban middle-class educated families seized this opportunity and came out in the *birun* (the outside world) and even began to follow professional careers. However, it is equally true that a large number of women from traditional families were outraged when women in *hijab* were forcibly unveiled; many of them refrained from appearing in public, which previously they had no problem in doing from behind the veil. Apart from the fact that this made the measures for bringing women out into the public space partially counterproductive, a more fundamental point was at stake. The Pahlavi regime, having set itself the "modernist" task of emancipating women, was determined to force the *hijabi* women to be free. Thus, socioreligious imposition was to be replaced by that of the state; once again the private persona of the people was being interfered with in the name of the public persona.

These concerns were symptomatic of some of the major problems that characterized the onset of the "modern" state/society from the nineteenth century. If the state is purported to represent the concerns of the constituent people, how would such concerns be formulated and represented? Would the category of "people" denote a collective entity, comprising individuals but greater than the sum of all individuals? Or would it denote the individual in a generic sense, thus theoretically according the individual as much significance (if not more) as the collective entity itself?

Several related questions emerged repeatedly in the discursive space of modern Iran—namely, what constitutes progress for a nation? Should the agenda of state modernization alone guide the question of national identity, or should the former be guided by the latter? Should the state be allowed to dictate what constitutes the national identity, or should it set its agenda of governance within parameters laid down by the society on that matter? What role, if any, does Islam play in the making of the modern Iranian identity? Should Islam limit itself merely to the role of a private subculture with minimal presence in public life, or should Islamic values be allowed to commingle with the national identity? Above all, how does the individual relate to both the state and the society? The language of politics of resistance that was developed in late Pahlavi Iran was formulated within the parameters set by this discourse, and all who chose to engage in this debate—including 'Ali Shari'ati—had to work within these parameters.

# 2

# Language of Opposition Politics in Late Pahlavi Iran

The discourse of opposition in Pahlavi Iran essentially pivoted around contemporary concerns pertaining to modernization and progress that provided the Pahlavi regime its legitimacy. The manner in which the regime under both Reza Shah and Muhammad Reza progressively manipulated and established control over the entire apparatus and the institutional space of the state made it very difficult to challenge the regime directly. Hence, the opposition slowly began to adopt a language and moved into a discursive space that the regime had vacated. It decided to confront the Pahlavi vision of *Iran as a modern state* with the counter-vision of *Iran as a just state*. The features of "justice" were understood and enunciated differently by different protagonists, but the underlying principle that defined such superiority had a common strand. Almost every opponent of the regime charged the state with being at odds with the people it was supposed to *represent*.

This was significant because the Pahlavi dynasty came into being as a result of a plebiscite in 1925—it derived its authority, technically, directly from the people. Despite ruling in the name of the people, however, the Pahlavi rulers went to great lengths to manufacture a "popular consent" suited to their own dynastic agenda and did their best to delegitimize any other opinions that might be thrown up from outside the ruling establishment. Indeed, *manufacturing consent* for the convenience of governments was a fairly well-established practice,[1] and the Pahlavis were neither the pathfinders nor the most impressive of its protagonists; yet the general reservations about the impact of such a policy on governance can be well borne out by looking at Pahlavi Iran. Pursuing the self-assumed task of establishing a "modern" nation-state modeled upon (what was believed to be) the "western" political experience, Pahlavi determination to forge Iranian national identity as the bedrock of a powerful state prompted them to reject the other supposed outcome of modernization—that is, the creation of a democratic polity by broadening the social basis of political power and developing the institutional apparatus of democracy. The constitutionalist element in Iranian politics gradually tended to become moribund from around 1930 as the Pahlavis weakened the institutional checks on executive authority. The state having successfully appropriated the central position in the discourse on (popular) sovereignty, any effective challenge to the ruling establishment had to rely on something that could question not simply Pahlavi rule but the claim of popular sovereignty underpinning it.

In course of the 1930s, the Pahlavis became so powerful that opposition of any kind was neither organized nor sustained. The secularist statist ideology that dominated much of the discourse of Pahlavi Iran since the late 1920s tried to delegitimize all inherited identities (such as religion, ethnicity, and language) apart from territorial nationalism. As a result, in the aftermath of the fall of Reza Shah, when a discourse of the opposition began to emerge, the more radical of its components concentrated on the 'Other-ing' of the *rentier* state by challenging not only the regime, but also the entire intellectual baggage that sustained the representative credentials of an increasingly unrepresentative state. The outcome was a progressive strengthening of a propensity toward intellectual nativism, which changed the character of the intellectual climate of Iran in the twentieth century to an extent.[2]

In this intellectual challenge to secularist étatism, the option to engage with the issue of the role of Islam in the life of Iran was particularly tempting. Such engagement varied from the "godless communism" of the Tudeh party (which rejected the validity of any role for Islam) to the theories of *hokumat-e Islami* (Islamic government, of which *Vilayat-e faqih,* or Rule of the Jurist, is one variety) by Ruhollah Khomeini. By the 1960s, as cumulative industrialization and urbanization accorded greater significance to mass politics, more and more people were willing and able to be mobilized in order to voice their grievances against and expectations from the state. Hence, the political discourse broadened beyond the middle-class concerns with nation-building to engage with issues of entitlements of the people vis-à-vis the state. As in many other parts of the world, communism provided a powerful ideological alternative to Pahlavi étatism. However, many Iranians proved immune to it because communism was too closely associated with the Russian state, which they had learned to distrust. Instead, several ideational positions emerged using Islamic terms of reference. Use of Islamic idioms had the advantage of intelligibility; aspirations couched in a familiar language proved more comprehensible to people who did not have access to the lofty discourse of secular modernism.

However, as elsewhere in the Islamic world, use of Islamic idioms did not completely desecularize the language of politics in modern Iran.[3] The structures of the modern state as much as the socioeconomic concerns that it generated, in a way, prevented a return to the premodern political language. Islamic idioms were deployed not to ensure obedience to the ruler but to uphold the principle of popular sovereignty against the manifest arbitrariness of the ruler.

Among the large number of Iranians who resorted to various Islamic terms of reference, three major intellectual protagonists of twentieth-century Iran stand out because of their distinctive contributions to the making of the Iranian discourse of resistance to the Pahlavis: Muhammad Mosaddeq (1882–1967), who emphasized primarily on the institutional bases of constitutional political authority; Jalal Al-e Ahmad (1923–72), whose powerful conceptualization of *gharbzadegi* made intellectual nativism respectable in Iran for more than a generation; and Ruhollah Khomeini (1902–89), who blended institutional politics with the normative categories of Islam. The Islamic idioms deployed by each of the three was distinct from the rest, being inspired by three different traditions: Mosaddeq tried to reconcile the political tradition of *mashrutiyat* (constitutionalism) with the social tradition of Islam in Iran; Al-e Ahmad was a Marxist who saw Islam as an instrument for attaining Marxist objectives; Khomeini essentially understood Islam as a juridical order where executive authority was held in check by a body of laws. Between them, they represented three powerful strands of opposition in late Pahlavi Iran (constitutionalism, Marxism, and Islamic clericalism) that tried, and failed, to mobilize the masses.

## Mosaddeq: From Constitutionalism to Populism

For many Iranians of his generation, Mosaddeq was the pivot of the discourse of nationalist opposition to the Pahlavi regime. Seen by his contemporaries as either the Rostam of the age or a wretched communist, this veteran academic-turned-politician was probably the only major voice that consistently spoke of institutionalization of political power in the *mashruteh* tradition. His resistance to the Pahlavi regime in defense of a rule of law prompted Reza Shah to keep him interned most of the time between 1925 and 1941. What made him more respectable than Reza Shah or any other of his contemporaries was his determination to situate "the people/nation" at the heart of the discourse of power. Despite defining the people and institutions of the country primarily in terms of the *Ithna 'Ashari* Shi'i order (like many of the other political opponents of the Pahlavis who toyed with the role of Islam in public), Mosaddeq's vision of the institutional apparatus of sovereignty was largely free of any religious or sectarian intonations. Mosaddeq and his brand of popular nationalism, accordingly, occupy a major position in the political imagination of modern Iranians on either side of the religious-secular divide.

Mosaddeq was born to a high Qajar bureaucrat and a great-granddaughter of the Qajar king Fath 'Ali Shah in 1882.[4] Among the earliest students of the School of Political Sciences in Tehran aiming at becoming an auditor, Mosaddeq appreciated quite early the significance of accountability in public finance in particular and in governance in general. He soon became an ardent supporter of constitutional rule, and in 1909 he went first to Ecole des Sciences Politiques in Paris (which he abandoned because of bad health) and then to study law in Swiss Neuchatel. In 1914, he secured his doctorate in law and was admitted to the bar—thenceforth he became known as Dr. Mosaddeq.[5]

One of the cardinal assumptions in Mosaddeq's approach to law as revealed in his thesis was his heavy reliance on "reason" and social custom.[6] While generally the *fuqaha* saw *aql* (reason) as only one potential means of deriving legislation, Mosaddeq declared the weight of reason to be superior to all other sources of law.[7] Aware that he was running against Shi'i jurisprudential tradition in asserting the supremacy of reason over the other sources of law, Mosaddeq developed a historical scheme that vindicated his position. He argued that, from the time of the Prophet to 938 was "the epoch of revelation and inspiration"—a period when the Prophet received direct guidance from God, and a period of infallible interpretation by the Prophet and the Imams, till the Twelfth Imam disappeared at the end of this period. From 938 to 1906, the Shi'i witnessed "the formalist epoch," during which the *fuqaha* kept themselves within the restraints of the law as elaborated up to 938, that is, the law remained stationary. Mosaddeq then went on to argue that the *Mashruteh* revolution heralded the onset of "the positivist epoch" in which laws could be "made" once again, so long as they conformed to the Shi'i legal tradition.[8]

The idea that legislators "made" laws was largely alien in the Shi'i legal tradition—the *fuqaha*, either individually or collectively, could at best "discover" the law by weighing proofs *(ayat)* as to the intention of the Divine Legislator, downplaying conjunctural factors. By contrast, Mosaddeq argued that the Iranian parliament could pick and choose whichever was considered the most appropriate among the sources of law *to address the interests of the people* at particular historical conjunctures. Persuaded by the *mashruteh* discourse on state and power, especially the autonomy of state laws from the universalistic realm of religion, Mosaddeq concerned himself only with the nature of laws that would be the most appropriate in the historical conjuncture of modern Iran.[9]

The emphasis on particular conjunctures had an interesting bearing on Mosaddeq's political thinking. He believed that if laws were adapted to the needs of Iran, they would conform to religion, reason, and customary practice. In a series of his works published during this period, he explicated his position on what should be the relationship between the state and the people in Iran.[10] He admitted that the equality of all people before the law, as laid down in the constitution, was not based on any categorical injunction in any of the sources of Islam, but on reason, since all who assume equal burden under the law must have an equal standing before the law. As none of the categorical injunctions of Islam regarding social organization and dispensation of political power contradicted the principle of equality before the law, the principle was not potentially un-Islamic. He was more concerned about legislators being mindful about specific "habits" and "resources" of Iranians, rather than a search for a reading of God's mind detached from cultural and social circumstances. He saw Shi'i Islam as one of the most important components of the Iranian social and cultural world.[11] This regard for the particular context also explains why Iranian laws "must conform to the true interests of the country," and not be "set aside on the pretext of imitating Europe."

Mosaddeq's approach to the relationship between law and religion in public life was pragmatic. Iranians needed Iranian solutions to form an effective polity—hence, Iranian laws had to take heed of Shi'ism not because Shi'i beliefs are in themselves capable of generating the best laws, but because conformity to Shi'ism would address the problem of acceptability of a new body of laws and regulations in Iran. He went on to contend, though, that while Shi'ism was a natural part of the sociocultural landscape in Iran, it would be effective in public life only to the extent that it was flexible. Thus, as early as 1914, in terms of the nature of the state and the role of religion in it, Mosaddeq took an instrumentalist view of Shi'ism to help institutionalize the rule of law as envisaged by the *mashruteh* movement.

Mosaddeq's politics rested on the twin foundations of the *mashruteh* era—constitutionalism and nationalism. In 1919 he opposed the Anglo-Iranian treaty that would have reduced Iran to a British satellite. In 1925 he was one of the five who voted against the elevation of Reza Shah to the throne and cautioned about its impact on the mechanism of constitutional government. Mosaddeq's opposition cost him his liberty as he was first arrested and then exiled to Birjand, where he was held in solitary confinement for several months.[12] For the next 15 years little was heard of the exiled Mosaddeq as Reza Shah gained in stature. But once Reza

Shah fell from power, Mosaddeq was immediately hailed as a hero. Having earned political capital by his refusal to compromise with the Shah, he immediately resorted to push his nationalist-constitutionalist agenda into the center-ground of Iranian politics in the 1940s.

Mosaddeq's agenda in the 1940s, up to his deposition in 1953, essentially related to the democratic system. Arguing that Reza Shah's dictatorship was built on military foundations, he took the position that the armed forces had to be brought under civilian/parliamentary control if Iran was to be democratic. He further contended that so long as the traditional nondemocratic centers of power in the countryside remained strong, democracy would remain weak, and therefore vulnerable to authoritarianism. A strong democratic apparatus required thorough social reforms, which were impossible to attain as long as landed families packed the parliament. Hence, Mosaddeq began pushing for electoral reforms to increase the representation of the educated and marginalize the illiterate masses, popularly reckoned to be the bastion of conservatism.[13]

The second item on Mosaddeq's agenda was assertion of Iran's national sovereignty. He was sternly critical of the prevalent practice of trying to balance the "northern neighbor" (the Soviet Union) with the "southern neighbor" (Britain), and occasionally inviting a third force (Germany, France, the United States) to offset both. This policy of "positive equilibrium" worked on the principle of distribution of concessions, which turned Iran into a free-for-all. He favored instead a forward-looking neutralist policy, called "negative equilibrium," whereby all concessions would cease, and Iran would strictly pursue a nonaligned course. This gained particular relevance from the mid-1940s as cold war tensions between the capitalist and communist blocs gave a new dimension to traditional western ambitions in the region.

These goals constituted the twin pillars of the *Jeb'eh-ye Melli*, or the National Front, the most formidable political challenge that the Pahlavi dynasty faced before 1979. Indeed, Muhammad Reza Pahlavi had only a tenuous hold on power in the 1940s, and almost all political formations took advantage of this to reinforce constitutional checks on the Shah's authority. But the drive that Mosaddeq brought to this enterprise soon projected him to national leadership. True to his *mashruteh* credentials, Mosaddeq used the question of Iran's foreign relations to galvanize the debate on the constitutionalist issue. Reza Shah's gradual alignment with Berlin had occasioned his forced abdication under Allied pressure in 1941. Mosaddeq argued this was possible because Reza Shah's policies toward foreign powers had reduced him to such dependence that foreigners would want to take the subservience of Iran for granted and could interfere at will in Iran's internal affairs. Mosaddeq's solution was, on the one hand, to conduct foreign relations in such a manner that Iran *would* not be taken for granted; on the other hand, he sought to restructure the political apparatus so that Iran *could* not be taken for granted. Both these solutions came to revolve around Iran's most crucial natural resource cum export—oil.

From the closing stages of World War II, Iran's petroleum reserves were deemed crucial enough for Britain, the Soviet Union, and increasingly even the United States to take interest in controlling them. With British and Soviet troops actually present on the ground during the duration of World War II, many political forces in Iran proved willing to court foreign powers using oil as the bait in order to advance their own political ambitions. While people like Premier Muhammad Sa'id favored opening up resources to the British and the Americans, the Soviet reaction prompted others like Premier Ahmad Qavam and the Tudeh party to solicit sweeping concessions to Moscow. Mosaddeq opposed both of these to argue that Iran should not commit itself to any country to such an extent that it became influential in Iran's domestic politics—hence, the policy of "negative equilibrium."[14] As he put it in the course of a debate in the *Majlis:*

> For us a foreigner is a foreigner. Whether he is northern or southern makes no difference. Balancing ourselves between them is the only means of ensuring our freedom . . . I am an Iranian and a Muslim, and I shall fight as long as I am alive, against anything that threatens Islam and Iran.[15]

At this stage the newly installed Shah, Muhammad Reza, was keen to strengthen his own authority. Accordingly, he encouraged the royalists to argue that the *Majlis* was contributing to the problem of foreign domination by keeping the military weak and proposing to curb the powers of the Shah as the Commander-in-Chief and cut down the military budget. Mosaddeq countered this by advocating the principle of parliamentary control over the military, reducing the Shah to the position of titular monarch, as in the United Kingdom.

In 1949, capitalizing on a sympathy wave prompted by the specter of communism following a failed attempt on his life by a youngster with communist linkages, Muhammad Reza persuaded a nominated Constituent Assembly to amend the constitution. Among other changes, the amendments increased the size and functions of the military and restored to the Shah powers that were whittled away after the ouster of Reza Shah. Many Iranians were deeply suspicious of what was clearly a throwback to the previous ruler, and came together to form the National Front *(Jeb'eh-ye Melli)*, a small but vocal minority of deputies in the sixteenth *Majlis.*[16]

Constituted with an agenda to establish the *Majlis*'s supremacy in the apparatus of governance, the National Front eventually gravitated toward the question of national control over Iran's oil industry. Mosaddeq and his fellow deputies from the Front challenged the constitutionality of the 1949 amendments and demanded abrogation of those powers accorded to the Shah, which he had been denied since the fall of Reza Shah. They advocated freedom of the press and opinion, free and fair elections, social equality, and the rule of law buttressed by the constitution and the *shari'ah* as a guarantee against incipient despotism. Mosaddeq emphasized: "The country belongs to the people and people have the inalienable right to choose their representatives. If they do not exercise that right, a small minority can gain control and work not for the interests of the majority but for its own selfish profit. The Shah must stand above politics but remain in touch with the needs and feelings of the people."[17]

The focus of the crisis shifted from the domestic to the external setting when after years of secret negotiation with the AIOC, Premier 'Ali Mansur, nominated by the Shah the year before, came up with a bill proposing revision of the 1933 deal on revenue-sharing. There were misgivings all around about the exploitative character of the deal with the British-controlled Anglo-Persian Oil Company. Mosaddeq's policy of negative equilibrium initially favored a renegotiation of the deal such that Tehran gained a bigger and fairer share of oil revenues, depriving the British of any undue leverage against either Iran or any other power.[18] The National Front accused the government of a sell-out and demanded nationalization of the oil industry. Mansur was replaced by General Razmara, whose heavy-handed attempts to force the deal through cost him his life. Razmara's assassination scared the more conservative deputies to accommodate the National Front rather than confront it. At this stage, the Tudeh also threw in its support behind Mosaddeq, hoping Moscow would gain from the British weakening, and the party would stand to benefit accordingly. Thus, in 1951, the Shah had no option but to appoint Mosaddeq as the Premier, with his agenda of nationalization of the oil industry.[19]

One of Mosaddeq's first acts as Prime Minister was to appoint a parliamentary committee to implement the policy of nationalization. This was followed swiftly by a British embargo on Iranian oil by the end of 1951, which embroiled Mosaddeq in a major diplomatic incident as much as a financial crisis, as the AIOC pulled out all its technicians from the country and Iran shut down all British consulates accusing London of interference in its internal affairs.

Mosaddeq simultaneously tried, unsuccessfully, to push through an electoral reform that would increase representation of the urban constituencies against the traditionalist bastions of the countryside. Fierce resistance followed from the landed aristocracy of the various regions of the country, denouncing centralist bias and undemocratic conduct of Premier

Mosaddeq—a charge often difficult to deny.[20] To counter such allegations, Mosaddeq resorted to attacking the social privileges of the landed upper class as detrimental to social harmony, therefore harming national interest. He then stepped up the ante, by asserting the premier's constitutional right to appoint his own cabinet. He resigned when the Shah denied him his choice of Minister for War.

The subsequent mass demonstrations in favor of Mosaddeq and the bloodshed that followed state crackdown on demonstrators forced the Shah to relent and invite him to form a cabinet of his own choice. Having won hands down, Mosaddeq pushed ahead to strip the crown of all the powers it had regained since 1941, including effective command over the armed forces.

Having won this victory for the constitutionalist cause through popular pressure, however, Mosaddeq tended to slide toward populism at the expense of constitutionalism. He used martial law to silence opponents of his social reform program and exacted from the *Majlis* special powers not only to maintain financial solvency (in the light of the oil embargo) but also to implement electoral, judicial, and educational reforms. When the Senate objected to several of these populist reforms, its term of office was reduced from six years to two; when the opposition in the *Majlis* resisted, the National Front deputies resigned, taking the numbers below quorum, therefore effectively dissolving the seventeenth *Majlis*. Backed by the Tudeh party, the National Front called for a referendum. Out of nearly 2.05 million votes cast, the National Front won around 2.03 million. In August 1953, Mosaddeq appeared as good as invincible.[21]

This invincibility, however, turned out to be deceptive. By 1952, Mosaddeq had alienated the military completely and was beginning to lose some of his supporters among the *bazaaris* by soliciting radical social and economic reforms. Many *bazaaris* had supported Mosaddeq fully with his nationalization of the oil industry. Once the financial consequences of the oil embargo prompted the government to propose nationalization of other industries/services, however, some of the *bazaaris* began to lose their enthusiasm. Suspecting a gradual onset of communism, Kashani and the clerics associated with the National Front began to drift away.[22] Once the proposals for enfranchisement of women and for judicial reforms under the leadership of a secular jurist (sympathizing with the Tudeh) came in, the fear gained ground that Islamic values were being subordinated to godless communism. The National Front was premised upon challenge to foreign domination and the Shah's arbitrary authority. The very success of the nationalization of the oil industry and the curtailment of the Shah's authority had removed the common objective that had held the radical secular and traditional religious forces together. Thus, by 1953, the social coalition that held the Front together lay in ruins. In July 1952, when Mosaddeq asked the *Majlis* for an extension of his emergency powers, Kashani denounced the latent "dictatorial" streak and spoke of Mosaddeq's secular ministers as "Kremlin-controlled atheists." Accordingly, as the disgruntled military began to plot against Mosaddeq with CIA backing, it felt secure enough to contact the clergy by playing up the "communist threat." The conspirators fomented tension in the regions, and when the Tudeh party vigorously rallied to the defense of the center, Mosaddeq was lured into inviting military intervention to quell the disturbances. The military seized the opportunity to remove Mosaddeq himself from power and handed the reins back to the Shah in August 1953. The National Front was dismantled—several of its top leaders, including Mosaddeq, were either imprisoned or put under house arrest.[23]

Mosaddeq's downfall marked the defeat of the only organized opposition to the Shah that tried to institutionalize checks on the Pahlavi crown. Interestingly, though, the defeat came precisely when the constitutionalist, having won, decided to abjure constitutionalism. Addressing the concerns of a large component of the middle class and then some of the economic concerns of the underclass, Mosaddeq persuaded himself that he was speaking for the whole Iranian nation. This was ironic, in the sense that Mosaddeq had dedicated his entire career to contesting appropriation of the category of the "people" by the ruler. Indeed, his assertion of Iran's national sovereignty on the world stage was more effective than the Pahlavis were ever to achieve, but the constitutionalist language of opposition that he had started out with could have proved a more enduring legacy for Iran, had he himself not ceased to speak that language.

Mosaddeq championed a brand of Iranian nationalism that resisted western domination of the country, but it did not essentially challenge any fundamental category within the western intellectual tradition. Hence, Mosaddeq was not so much disputing what the Shah wanted to do (casting Iran somewhat in the image of the west) as how this was being done. A more fundamental challenge to the Pahlavi regime came from one of the most political protagonists of twentieth-century Persian prose, Jalal Al-e Ahmad.

## Jalal Al-e Ahmad: The West as the Other

Jalal Al-e Ahmad represented in his person the twin facets of the binary that can be said to characterize modern Iran. On the one hand was his strong association with the anti-imperialist and socialist causes, which underpinned his nationalist credentials; on the other, was his take on Islam as an instrumental religion in the age of the masses. The nationalist in Al-e Ahmad made him a resolute opponent of the Pahlavi scheme of modernization, but resort to nationalism proved an ineffective device in resisting the Pahlavis. By depicting Iranians' preoccupation with modernizing Iran in accordance with the western paradigm as a veritable disease, Al-e Ahmad helped open up the debate on the very meaning of modernity, and if it indeed were desirable.

Al-e Ahmad was born in 1920 to a religious family from northern Iran. He was initially a student of Dar al-Fanun, one of the bastions of modern education in Iran to work toward a high school diploma. But in 1943, Al-e Ahmad's father, Ahmad Taleqani, a deeply religious cleric, persuaded him to enroll as a *talib* (student) at Najaf in Iraq, the most renowned center of Shi'i jurisprudence in the contemporary world. However, Al-e Ahmad decided to return within a few months to complete his high school diploma at the Dar al-Fanun. Al-e Ahmad's decision to receive his diploma from a secular high school in Iran, rather than his certificate as a jurist from Najaf indicated his break with the traditional understanding of Shi'ism as touted by his father. During his final year at the Dar al-Fanun, he was temporarily attracted to the radically anticlerical views of the secular modernist Ahmad Kasravi.[24]

In 1943, marking the completeness of his shift away from his clerical origins, Al-e Ahmad joined the Tudeh party. Al-e Ahmad rose very swiftly within the party, and was assigned the responsibility of promoting the cause of socialism and organizing workers in the industrial city of Abadan in 1945. Al-e Ahmad earnestly believed in the hope of delivering masses from their exploiters as part of a universal struggle on the side of the oppressed, till about the time of the Pishehvari incident of 1945.

At the close of World War II, Moscow began to support an Azeri communist, Sayyid Ja'far Pishehvari, in his policy of establishing a Soviet satellite state in his home province. In September 1945, the Tudeh provincial committee in Azerbaijan called for an insurrection and the establishment of an "autonomous state." By November, the Red Army helped the movement gain control over Iranian garrisons stationed in the province of Azerbaijan; in December, elections were held for the newly formed Azeri parliament. As secessionist tendencies gained weight in Iranian Azerbaijan, the central committee of the Tudeh party in Tehran supported the movement unconditionally.

This decision militated against the nationalist sensibilities of people like Khalil Maleki and Al-e Ahmad.[25] Soon it became clear that Pishehvari incident was not one-off case, because the Tudeh, under the protection of the Red Army, even campaigned for Moscow to be given a favorable oil concession. Al-e Ahmad felt great shame in having organized demonstrations against his own government to give an oil concession to a foreign state.²⁶ Accordingly, Maleki and Al-e Ahmad left the party with a group of their followers in 1948. Indeed, there may have been other reasons for Maleki and Al-e Ahmad to leave the Tudeh party with many of its members. Hamid Dabashi suspects Maleki and Al-e Ahmad, like so many other second- and third-tier leaders of the Tudeh party, left it because the central committee successfully frustrated their ambitions.²⁷ However, there is no doubt that the Pishehvari incident and the oil concessions issue served for many as the principle (foreign influence on the party) on which to break. Despite his break with the Tudeh party, Al-e Ahmad did not break with socialism: in 1951 he joined Maleki to found the *Hizb-e Zehmatkashan* (Party of the Toilers), and the year after, they set up the *Niru-ye Sevvom* (Third Force). A year later, both of these were to be part of the National Front led by Mosaddeq.

The splinter parties that Al-e Ahmad associated with, and the National Front as a whole, proved considerably ineffective in terms of mass politics by comparison with the Tudeh. But while the organization of the Tudeh was impressive, its policy of currying favor with Moscow ensured that a nationalist like Al-e Ahmad could not be associated with it. He was convinced that substantive resistance to the Pahlavis could be possible only by means of mass mobilization, but he also recognized that socialism/communism would never succeed in mobilizing Iranians beyond a narrow class base, and sometimes not even those within the ranks of the proletariat. Socialism, the way he saw it, was an ideology suited to mass mobilization in a different context; it had no resonance for the Iranian masses. Iran needed some other banner for mass mobilization, and only someone capable of understanding the essence of the people could shape that body of ideas. Thus, after the fall of Mosaddeq, Al-e Ahmad more or less withdrew from active politics and instead set about on a search for the "*ruh-e Iran*" (soul of Iran).

Al-e Ahmad's quest took him down a fairly tortuous path. He began by translating works of existentialist thinkers, which he thought had a bearing on Iran's predicament.²⁸ His translations of Gidé's *Return from the Soviet Union*, Dostoyevsky's *The Gambler* (1948), Camus's *The Stranger* (1949), Sartre's *Dirty Hands* (1952), and Eugene Ionesco's *Rhinoceros* (1966) seem to indicate almost a desperate urge of a thinking man to reclaim his autonomy from an ideology that sought to impose intellectual constraints on its adherents. However, his affinity for the existential mode of thinking was less driven by what it stood for, than by what it spoke out against. He shared with the existentialists their deep reservations against *masheen wa tamaddun-e masheen* (machine and civilization of the machine, i.e., industrial civilization), which was his personal shorthand for the west.

Contrary to what Boroujerdi and Dabashi seem to believe, Al-e Ahmad's perception of the "west" was not of a monolithic whole. Having been to France, the United States, and the Soviet Union, he was aware of the differences within the western civilization. However, he seems to have used the term to signify the one component of that western civilization, a particular variation of the industrial society, which became the dominant impression of the "west" in the mind of the developing world. Al-e Ahmad's use of western critiques of the industrial civilization has been depicted as a contradiction, as his own dependence on western intellect. This is misreading him completely. Al-e Ahmad painted the "west" using this broad brush, and set out to discover the "soul of Iran," in such a manner that the "west" could emerge as the ultimate "other." This strategy was of momentous significance because the Pahlavis had sought to make the "west" the measure of success for the project of modernization, raison d'être of the regime. By questioning the suitability of the paradigm for Iran, Al-e Ahmad tried to undermine the very basis on which Pahlavi legitimacy rested.

Al-e Ahmad's search for the soul of Iran confronted him with those realities of his homeland that the Tudeh had left untouched. In a series of ethnographical studies, Al-e Ahmad began to explore the lives of rural Iranians in the most far-flung parts of the country, to measure and analyze the duality of impact of *tamaddun-e masheen:* how it destroys the rhythms of some local lives even as others remain completely impervious to such destruction. For instance, writing about the small village of *Urazan,* whence his own ancestors hailed, Al-e Ahmad highlighted how the advances made by Iran passed it by: there were no schools, no hospitals, no police. The villagers there had not seen even so much as a matchbox.[29] This was to be contrasted with his findings near Qazvin and then Kharg, an island on the Persian Gulf for exiled criminals and political activists. Written after his 1958 trip to the island, *Kharg: Dorr-e Yateem-e Khalij* spoke about the island's transformation to meet the needs of an oil installation. Documenting the local culture of the island on the verge of destruction by "westernization," Al-e Ahmad compared Iran to the weak and exhausted body of a sick man with an unnaturally big head (i.e., the oil industry), forcefully dragging itself the country just to feed the "west." More than the mere economic consequences, Al-e Ahmad resented the cultural alienation ushered in by this subordination to western interests: "the entire local and cultural identity and existence will be swept away. And why? So that a factory can operate in the 'west,' or that workers in Iceland or Newfoundland are not jobless."[30]

In his most renowned work, *Gharbzadegi,* Al-e Ahmad made a full exposition of all his reservations about the evils of industrial civilization in the Iranian context.[31] *Gharbzadegi* he defined as a malaise in the Iranian society, "the aggregate of events in life, culture, civilization, and mode of thinking of a people without a supporting tradition, no historical continuity, no scale of transformation."[32] The malaise was in what he likened to a state of intoxication with the "west" *(gharb)*.[33] The idea played primarily with the Marxian concept of "alienation," but Al-e Ahmad gave it a sociocultural dimension that proved more resonant than the economic one. He argued that a large number of Iranians (meaning primarily the secular modernists) were so "struck" *(zadeh)* by the material culture and industrial civilization of the west that they wanted to emulate the western societies in all respects. As he observed:

> We have failed to preserve our own historical and cultural character in the face of the onslaught of the machine. Indeed, we have been defeated. We have failed to take a resolute stand against this contemporary monster. Until we comprehend the essence, basis and philosophy of the western civilization, by only emulating the west outwardly and formally (embracing its machines) we shall be like the ass going about in a lion's skin.[34]

Contrary to a belief generally held by commentators on Al-e Ahmad's works,[35] he was not opposed to industrial technology per se. He admitted that "[w]e need take certain things from the west. But not everything. From the west...we are looking for technology. Technology we have to import. We will also learn the science that goes with it. That in itself is not western; it is universal."[36] His concern was that collective preoccupation of Iranians with western military might was being translated into a moral hegemony of the west. The country was physically as much as temperamentally being turned into an image of the west, anything that did not have a counterpart in the "west" was being discarded as an obstacle to becoming like the "west." In this manner, Al-e Ahmad contended, the "west" was depriving Iran of its identity, and the country was succumbing to the evils of colonialism.

> We no longer consider ourselves as deserving any right... Indeed, even if we want to justify an aspect of our belief about this world or the next, we evaluate these on their principles, following the injunctions of their advisers and counselors. We follow them in our studies, carry out census, and pursue research like them. But even that is all right, because science has developed a kind of universal methodology. Scientific methods have no sign of any specific country. But curiously we get married like they do in the west; imitate their liberalism; evaluate the world, dress, and write like them.... [From among] two old rivals finally one has ended up cleaning up after the circus; the other one runs the show. And what a show! A pornographic scandal that robs us of our minds. So that they can plunder the oil.[37]

For anyone who chose to read it, *Gharbzadegi* was a clear denunciation of the Pahlavi agenda of westernization projected as modernization, not of modernization per se. But Al-e Ahmad did not charge only the rulers of "westoxication"; attacking all those contemporary intellectuals who supported the westernization agenda, he tried to undermine the intellectual edifice that lent legitimacy to the regime. He denounced the secular intellectuals as "a spineless bunch of self-centered hypocrites ... [having] no root in the soil of this land."[38] This included even the most steadfast opponents of the Pahlavis, members of the Tudeh party. Citing the pro-Soviet position adopted by the party, he lamented that the party "could not give itself local and national form, and thus solve people's problems; it grew its roots on waves, not in the social depth."[39] He believed that no effective resistance to the exploitative force of colonialism was possible with imported ideas:

> If the Tudeh party was defeated, as was the National Front ... it is because ... all these people have ventured into the battlefield of politics with imported ideas: boasting of communism and socialism ... and not even trying to adapt those "-isms" to the local conditions.... The pretense of defending the benefits of a working class in the absence of a large proletariat, and complete neglect of the concerns of the peasantry despite the existence of a large majority of peasants, [these contributed to the defeat of the Tudeh party].[40]

Al-e Ahmad rejected imported ideologies not because these were imported, but because these failed to mobilize the people in defense of their own interests. As he was to shrewdly observe:

> [Y]ou can be effective in politics, or in the affairs of a society, if you measure the extent of receptivity or tolerance of that society towards your ideas. And in order to achieve this measure, you have to know that society, its traditions, history, the factors instrumental in shaping its collective belief, and the forces that mobilize its masses in the streets.[41]

Hence, at the expense of being repeatedly accused by fellow-secular intellectuals of being an *akhund* (cleric) true to *his* personal roots, Al-e Ahmad dared suggest the use of religion as a mobilizing strategy in Iran. Commenting on the tendency of communist parties to consider religion as the opium of the masses, he highlighted the successful deployment of religious symbols in the Gandhian movements in India, Buddhist symbols in the case of Viet Cong, and even the Shi'i tropes during the Tobacco protests in Iran of the 1890s. He praised the National Front experiment of the Mosaddeq era, where "the leaders were shrewd enough to lead the struggle in such a way that through collaboration with the religious leaders every uneducated common person would identify the government as the instrument of tyranny which gave the oil to the [British] company and then treated its own subjects harshly."[42]

Perhaps most interestingly for a secular intellectual, Al-e Ahmad began to advocate the role of the Shi'i *ulema* in political mobilization. For all practical purposes, in the secularized milieu of Pahlavi Iran, the *ulema* were almost never included among the category of intellectuals, hence they were rarely thought of as components of the intellectual edifice on which the legitimacy of the regime rested. Al-e Ahmad, though, argued that because of reasons of "social readership" the *ulema* would necessarily be integral to the intellectual map of the Iranian society—that is, ideas of the *ulema* were derived from, and enjoyed a readership in, the society to such an extent that paralleled, or even exceeded, that of the secular intellectuals. To substantiate his claim of the *ulema*'s ability to exercise social leadership, he pointed out that while the people paid their religious taxes voluntarily, the government's taxes had to be extracted.[43] He believed that religious authority institutionalized in the *ulema* in twentieth-century Iran left them in a crucial position of social leadership, being directly connected to the society; moreover, because of the doctrinal possibilities latent in Shi'ism, such social leadership could be transformed into political leadership in the name of the "vanished Imam."[44] After Khomeini's 1963 uprising against the White Revolution, Al-e Ahmad witnessed a powerful vindication of his postulates. In 1964, therefore, he went for *Hajj*, and produced an almost day-by-day record in *Khasi dar Miqat* (Lost in the Crowd). There he waxed lyrical about how he recovered his religiosity from the ruins of secular modernity, how he felt at one with other people using similar terms of reference and looking at the world with similar prisms: how, that is, he "got lost" in the crowd to find his way back to his roots at the age of 40, roots that he had abandoned in Najaf when he was 20.[45]

There is little agreement on whether Al-e Ahmad ever really recovered his faith, even as he advocated the use of religion as a mobilization strategy. Ayatollah Taleqani believed that his cousin Al-e Ahmad had initially lost faith because of his father's dogmatism, but after "the demise of the Tudeh gang" and as his erudition grew, "he almost returned to our own people, to our own habits and customs, and became attracted to religion."[46] Dabashi, Boroujerdi, Mirsepassi, and Mottahedeh alike believe "he was out in the sun too long" to have made a genuine return. Regardless of whether he recovered his faith or not, the central element of his political language was the idea of Islam as an instrumentalist religion. His focal aim was to counter and roll back the evils of the "west," meaning "industrial civilization." Whatever served to achieve this was welcome to Al-e

Ahmad. The best evidence of this lies in his verdict on Israel, which he visited in 1963:

> For me as an easterner, Israel is a model, better than any other, of how to deal with the West. How to extract from its industries... how to take ammunition from it and spend the capital thus obtained to advance the country, and how with the price of a brief span of political dependency give permanence to our newly established enterprise.[47]

To the great dismay of his Islamist readers, like 'Ali Khamenei, his praise of Israel came precisely at a time when he was advocating an active role for the *'ulema* in the politics of Iran. Even in his account of his trip to Mecca, Al-e Ahmad seemed more attuned to the popular dimension of the life of a Muslim than the doctrinal aspects of Islam. Further, after the 1963 uprising of a section of the *'ulema* led by Khomeini, in his public defense of Khomeini, Al-e Ahmad showed greater understanding of the historical reasons behind the significance of the Shi'i *'ulema* in Iran rather than the doctrinal positions on the matter. He chose to associate Islam with politics not because it was the word of God, but because people could be mobilized in its defense against a political authority that was plunging Iran headlong into a disaster.

\* \* \*

Jalal Al-e Ahmad's value as a thinker lay in his notion of *gharbzadegi*, which ranks among the more sophisticated pronouncements of intellectual nativism in Iran. Enjoying a readership that spanned across the spectrum of educated Iranians, religious and secular, Al-e Ahmad was, and remains, one of the most prominent critics of the modernism that characterized twentieth-century urban Iran. By attacking the very definition of Pahlavi modernization as a rootless phenomenon inspired by foreign ideas promoting foreign exploitative interests, Al-e Ahmad undermined the moral legitimacy that the Pahlavis claimed as architects of this new Iran. Before his critique of *gharbzadegi*, resistance to modernization/westernization was ipso facto a signifier of obscurantism. Al-e Ahmad's critique made resistance look not obscurantist, but actually respectable. The Pahlavis had established their nationalist credentials by advocating modernization; *gharbzadegi* made it possible for resistance to the modernization agenda look equally nationalist.

For a lay thinker, Al-e Ahmad was quite rare in having recommended *'ulema* leadership in Iranian politics; for this he was as much praised by his readers (lay and clerical) as he was criticized by secular and lay Islamist thinkers. His arguments in favor of *'ulema* participation in politics were motivated by the role they played in the society. However, there were doctrinal and institutional factors that supposedly inhibited the *'ulema* from playing such a role. Al-e Ahmad was so occupied in attacking the Pahlavi order that he had no doctrinal and institutional remedies to prescribe to this problem. It was left to Ruhollah Khomeini, a highly political *'alim*, to address these issues, and in the process revolutionize the world of political Islam.

### Ruhollah Khomeini: Envisaging Islamic Governance

Until the twentieth century, the predominant position among the Shi'i *'ulema* regarding politics was by and large quietist, determined to avoid confrontation with the state. When the *'ulema* intervened in politics, it was either when they had to provide leadership to their social constituency (viz. during the tobacco protests of 1892–93, the *Mashruteh* revolution of 1906) or when they were stung into action by the state (viz. during land reforms under the White Revolution). Even though Iran occasionally witnessed the emergence of politically proactive *'ulema* like Sayyid Hasan Modarres (during the early years of Reza Shah) or Ayatollah Kashani (during the Mosaddeq years), the *'ulema* as a body tended to avoid political confrontations with the state as late as the 1960s. The theory of a relentless struggle by the *'ulema* for "ten decades" is mostly a myth.[48] Ayatollah Ruhollah Mussavi al-Khomeini replaced this quietist orthodoxy with a dynamic one, enunciating a doctrine of activist Islam where one has to constantly "enjoin the good and forbid evil." He came up with a vision of Islamic governance, which (despite its potentially universalistic interpretation) had an institutional dimension that made it applicable almost uniquely to Iran. Here lay the basis of a large part of the institutional framework that was brought into being after the revolution of 1979.

\* \* \*

Ruhollah Mussavi was born in 1902 in the small town of Khomein in the province of Esfahan. Son of a minor cleric, Ruhollah finished his basic education in a local religious institution at the age of 19 and went to Arak for his higher education under (inter alia) Sheikh 'Abd al-Karim Hai'ri Yazdi, one of the most prominent clerics of his time. In 1922, following an invitation from the people of Qom, Hai'ri Yazdi settled down there to set up a seminary. Ruhollah followed Hai'ri Yazdi to Qom, studied under a variety of experts, and upon completing his education began his career as an *'alim* at that seminary, with which he remained associated to the end of his life (barring the years in exile).⁴⁹ It was at this stage that he used his place of origin as the eponym for his last name, and began to call himself Khomeini.

After receiving his *ijazeh* (permission to act as a *mujtahid* capable of *ijtihad,* that is, independent legal reasoning) at the remarkably early age of 34, Khomeini was known for his specialization in *'irfan* (Gnosticism).⁵⁰ The lectures on *'irfan* soon became very popular among his students because he used contemporary political and national events as his points of entry.⁵¹

The 1940s proved crucial for politicizing Khomeini. He was convinced by this time that westernized elites of the Muslim world were ultimately aiding the cause of the western imperialists and only Islam could prevent their success. In 1944, in response to Ahmad Kasravi's stinging attack on Shi'ism and the *'ulema* as the principal cause of Iran's backwardness (in the book *Asrar-e Hazaar Saleh,* i.e., Secrets of a Millennium), Khomeini wrote his first overtly political treatise—*Kashf al-Asrar* (Revelation of Secrets). Here, Khomeini was not yet the inveterate opponent of monarchy that he became since 1963, but his principal preoccupations about xenocracy and westernization contributing to the decline of the Islamic way of life were already in place.⁵² In a position similar to the *mashru'eh,* he pronounced himself in favor of the state consulting the *fuqaha* before policies were made. He fell foul of the Pahlavi establishment because of his sympathy for the radical Islamist cleric Ayatollah Kashani and the militant movement *Fedayan-e Khalq.* Thus, in 1961, upon the death of *Ayatollah-e Ozma* Sayyid Hasan Boroujerdi, the Shah sent his condolences to all prominent Ayatollahs barring Khomeini. Moreover, reversing his policy of noninterference in the matters of the *'ulema,* he refused to recognize anyone in Iran as Boroujerdi's successor as the *Ayatollah-ye Ozma.*⁵³

Khomeini considered the decision to bypass him for the succession as manifestation of the intent of secularization, and promptly went on the warpath. The virulence of his opposition nearly won him a death sentence, from which he was saved upon condition of going into exile (first in Turkey, then Iraq, and finally France) which ended only in 1979. Being out of the Shah's reach, Khomeini took the position of uncompromising opposition for over a decade and a half, unlike most other political forces in Iran, which compromised themselves by occasionally collaborating with the regime. This helped him establish himself as the embodiment of opposition to the Shah.⁵⁴ During his period of exile in Iraq, Khomeini delivered a set of lectures on *Hokumat-e Islami* (Islamic Governance) that form the most coherent formulation in favor of participation by the *'ulema* in governance.

\* \* \*

Emerging from the world of the *howzeh* (seminary), almost all of Khomeini's terms of references originated from the hermeneutical tradition of *Ithna 'Ashari* Shi'ism. His point of entry into the discussion on good governance was essentially similar to that of other *'ulema*—that is, governance in order to be good has to be in accordance with the *Shari'ah*. The more conservative elements among the *'ulema* had attacked the idea of *mashrutiyyat* (constitutionalism) as being opposed to that of *mashru'eh* (rule in accordance with the *Shari'ah*), because Allah is the sole sovereign legislator, and his laws are eternally valid. Hence, any popularly elected body could contain the executive authority within the bounds of law, but could not legislate by itself. Liberal *'ulema* believed that there was nothing intrinsically opposed between *mashru'eh* and *mashruteh*. The people could make laws in elected assemblies, but these had to be endorsed by a body of *'ulema* as being in conformity with the *Shari'ah*, that is, the *Shari'ah* enjoyed automatic ascendancy over popular will expressed through representative assemblies.

In the Islamic conception of state, temporal authorities are charged with the responsibility of creating conditions conducive to staying on *sabil al-mustaqim* (the straight path). Temporal authority is conceived of as a *visayat* (trust) held by political authorities on behalf of Allah. Theoretically, a ruler of any Islamic state enjoys his authority subject to his faithful execution of that "trust," thereby upholding Islam. In *Ithna 'Ashari* political tradition, the Imams were delegated the *Visayat*, and after the twelfth Imam went into *ghaibat* (occultation) no temporal authority was legitimate.[55] Muslims had to endure temporal authority only for the sake of averting *fasad al-zaman* (troubles of the age), because during the period of *Ghaibat al-Akbar* (Greater Occultation) the duty of Muslims was to ensure that the cardinal facets of Islam, especially the five pillars of faith, survived.[56] The *Ithna 'Ashari* Shi'i maintain, the *'ulema* were responsible for helping the temporal authorities to uphold law and order, and to enforce the cardinal facets of Islamic law in a period of general degradation. Those who did not succumb to the *fasad al-zaman* would be redeemed by the Imam Mahdi at the end of days *(Qayamat)*. Those steadfast in their faith would then enjoy eternal happiness. To enable laypersons to attain this the *'ulema* advised acceptance of the rule even of an oppressor *(zalim)*, lest disobedience caused general mayhem and disturbed the bare essentials of the Islamic way of life.

In his understanding of the nature of *Visayat*, Khomeini was quite categorical. True Muslims, he argued, were those who had no desire for material wealth, which sets man apart from man. A good Muslim would seek God all around him, and no earthly thing should distract him in his quest for Allah. Hence, the Prophet and the Imams all strove to establish an

Islamic order, which was first and foremost a *just* order. In 1971, when the Pahlavi dynasty declared its intention to celebrate 2,500 years of Persian monarchy, Khomeini set forth his own understanding of why the rule of Imam 'Ali was the regime in Islamic history that embodied the essence of "Islam as it truly is." 'Ali, he argued, was such a person that when he came to power, his life remained more meager than even those of the austere *'ulema,* or even the most frugal of greengrocers. The piece of barley bread that 'Ali would have for his meal tended to be so hard that "towards the end of his blessed life he could not break it with his hand. He would break it with his knee and would eat it [moistened] with water."[57] He then went on to argue that "Justice, that no ruler should go to bed with a full stomach while his subjects are awake hungry, is the basis of legitimacy."[58] This was to be contrasted, he implied, with a ruler (Muhammad Reza Pahlavi) who spent millions of dollars on "flagrant pomposity" when millions of his subjects lived in destitution.

Trained within a tradition that relied both intellectually and materially on laws, Khomeini stressed on the necessary connection between laws and justice. Law, he argued, is an instrument for the establishment of justice in society. "Law exists to be implemented for the sake of establishing a just society that will morally and spiritually nourish refined human beings."[59] He contended that the mere existence of all embracing regulations clearly presupposed the existence of some executive authority to uphold the regime. He argued that the Prophet performed executive and judicial functions that characterize any political authority. After the Prophet, those functions were to be discharged by the *vali amr* ("those who hold authority").[60] In *Ithna 'Ashari* Shi'ism, the 12 Imams were the *vali amr* after the Prophet, but thereafter no authority was legitimate. Unlike orthodox Shi'i position on this question, Khomeini argued that in the absence of the Imam, the designation of *vali amr* passed on to those versed best in the various regulations of Islam, that is, the *fuqaha* (jurists), not temporal rulers.

Khomeini was not the first one ever to speak of executive authority for the *fuqaha*. Mullah Ahmad Naraqi and Sheikh Morteza Ansari had spoken of the executive responsibilities of the *fuqaha*.[61] Khomeini built on their principles but substantially broadened the scope of their application by resorting to inferential reasoning. He argued that it was necessary to form an Islamic government to implement the regulations to ensure their continuance after the time of the Prophet, for God could not have willed his laws to fall into disuse within two centuries of their promulgation (i.e., with the disappearance of the twelfth Imam of the Shi'i).[62] Such an Islamic government was to be "a government of law" where "sovereignty belongs to God alone and law is His decree and command."[63] Everyone, the Prophet included, was subject to the divine law, which alone "rules over society."

Rule of divine law being the foundational premise of Islamic governance, Khomeini contended, knowledge of law and (the ability to dispense) justice were two essential attributes of a ruler. While intelligence and administrative ability were general qualifications desirable in a ruler, even a superlative command over any natural or theological sciences would not entitle one to be a ruler unless he was just and knew the law. If a ruler did not resort to those who knew the law, he would be unable to implement the regulations of Islam. Such rule would cease to be Islamic, hence would lose legitimacy. In *Kashf al-Asrar,* Khomeini had suggested that if a ruler was unacquainted with the niceties of Islamic law, it was his duty to depend on those who knew the law, namely, the *fuqaha*. In *Hokumat-e Islami* he revised his original position to argue that if the ruler were to depend on anyone else his power to govern would be impaired. Therefore, Khomeini submitted, "the true rulers are the *fuqaha* themselves, and rulership ought to be given officially to them, not to those who because of their ignorance of the law have to obey the jurists."[64]

In a truly radical interpretation, Khomeini then went on to argue that in terms of political authority there was no difference between that of the Prophet and the Imams on the one hand and the *fuqaha* on the other. Careful not to cross any unwritten laws of permissibility in interpretation, he did not suggest that the spiritual virtues of the *fuqaha* were as great as those of the Prophet or even the Imams; instead, he suggested that spiritual virtues had no bearing on the political authority wielded by the *fuqaha*. Authority in this context did not relate to the human origin of power at the disposal of the *fuqaha* (as against the divine origin in the case of the Prophet and the Imams), rather to the function of governance that they had to perform—that is, administration and execution of the law. In these respects, there could be no distinctions between the activities of the Prophet and the *fuqaha*, since the same law bound both, and both were enjoined by Allah to establish social justice on earth.[65]

Khomeini's dynamic understanding of the concept of *visayat* led on to an equally dynamic view of what Islam entailed. He insisted that the parochial legalism that characterized Shi'ism in Iran for ages was not in accordance with the essence of the faith. He identified Islam as a religion of people "committed to truth and justice...religion of those who desire freedom and independence...the school of those who struggle against imperialism."[66] He charged first the Jews (used almost as a shorthand for capitalists) and then the western imperialists with subverting and destroying Islam. Khomeini believed the western imperialists were more satanic than the Jews: the imperialists alienated people from Islam not to convert them to Christianity but because they found in Islam the only formidable obstacle before their materialist ambitions. These imperialists, he maintained, planted preachers in religious teaching institutions, teachers in universities, employees and agents in universities and the administrative apparatus, and even orientalist scholars in order to distort the revolutionary principles of Islam, "and to prevent Muslims from arousing themselves in order to gain freedom."[67]

Khomeini argued that neglect of Islamic laws pertaining to government (*hokumat*) made Iran vulnerable to foreign penetration. He contended that during the *mashruteh* movement, reforms of the legal system to remove the deficiencies in Iran owing to Islam actually aimed at subversion of the country. Hence, commercial codes detailing laws on usury, bypassing the *Shari'ah* ban on the matter, fomented inequity in society as the rich got richer and the poor became poorer; secularization of the judiciary served to delay justice and to make it expensive. His diagnosis was pretty categorical: "Their [western imperialists'] plan is to keep us backward, to keep us in our present miserable state so they can exploit our riches, our underground wealth, our lands and our human resources."[68]

For Khomeini, the way out of this materialist trap was to restore to Iran the Islamic values that gave humankind some dignity—where rulers were "men of God, not materialistic creatures" accumulating worldly wealth. Rulers who deviated from these high standards of governance were ipso facto unjust by nature, and were therefore *taghut* (illegitimate).

The most revolutionary dimension in Khomeini's thought related to the duties of a Muslim vis-à-vis a ruler who was *taghut*. To undermine the legitimacy of un-Islamic governments, Khomeini urged total noncooperation with *taghut* rulers. Citing Imam Sadiq's proscription on all recourse to illegitimate governments, including their executive and judicial branches, he urged avoidance of ruling apparatuses of kings and tyrannical rulers. This would ensure that "non-Islamic and oppressive regimes may fall and the top-heavy judicial systems that produce nothing for the people but trouble may be abolished."[69] According to Khomeini, Shi'ism was premised upon resistance against illegitimate rulers, as evinced by 'Ali's struggle against Mu'awiya and Hossein's struggle against Yazid. Invoking the examples of the two Imams, Khomeini exhorted the believers to *al-amr bi'l-ma'ruf wa'l-nahy 'an al-munkar* (commanding right and forbidding wrong) in a bid to contest illegitimate authority.

In this respect, he assigned special responsibility to the *'ulema*. He said, if one interpreted God's laws in a manner displeasing to Him, or executes laws that are anti-Islamic while claiming to conform to the requirements of Islamic justice, resistance by the *'ulema* becomes essential. Opposition by the *'ulema* would bring about public pressure on the ruler and force him back to the path of Islam. If oppressive and deviant rulers persisted in their un-Islamic ways, and tried to silence resistance by force of arms, then that would amount to armed aggression against Muslims. This would turn the ruler into a rebel *(baghiya)*, against whom Muslims had to wage *jihad* in order to restore Islamic norms to the realm of policymaking.[70]

Khomeini's notion of Islamic governance was not simply an ideology of resistance; it also carried within itself the blueprint of an alternative system, a system of governance unlike any that was known. He suggested a vague principle for the institutionalization of the role of the *'ulema* once an Islamic government was established. Khomeini submitted that the *fuqaha* had to continue engaging with the *ummah*, instruct Muslims about the essence of the faith, and guide them along the path of righteous dignity while waiting for the return of the Imam Mahdi during *Qayamat*. Islamic governance should, thus, ideally be a *Vilayat-e Faqih* (Rule of the Jurist), where the executive organ may or may not be run by the *fuqaha*, but superintendence by the *fuqaha* was mandatory. The Qur'an would be the source of all laws in such a state, and the role of the legislative organ of the government should be to apply such laws through specific measures; the *fuqaha* would watch over this activity so that the essence of Islam was not violated. This principle was eventually adopted into the Constitution of the Islamic Republic of Iran, when the office of the *Rahbar* (popularly known as Supreme Leader) was created, and the *'ulema*-dominated institution of *Showra-e Negahban* (Guardian's Council) was devised to impose a check on the elected representatives of the *Majlis*.

\* \* \*

Hamid Dabashi calls Khomeini the "theologian of discontent,"[71] a theorist who wove his political theory around the discontent of the *mustadhafin* (oppressed) and derived his inspiration from theology, from his understanding of how man should relate to God. Islam, as Khomeini seems to have understood it, was a program for social justice, and Islamic government was the means by which that agenda could be fulfilled. A roughly similar argument was later showcased by Abrahamian in his full-length monograph on Khomeini.[72]

There were several perceptible shifts in Khomeini's thought from the period when he wrote *Kashf al-Asrar*, through the period when he wrote *Hokumat-e Islami*, to public pronouncements in the 1970s that were mostly political and barely theoretical. Vanessa Martin contends that although Khomeini was saying nearly the same things all through the three decades of Muhammad Shah Pahlavi's reign, the element of continuity is not readily apparent because of Khomeini's phenomenal flexibility in matters of practical politics. This flexibility made all his particular responses appropriate for their immediate contexts and, Martin suggests, it was possible for him to be so flexible because he did not have one vision of an Islamic state but several. He advocated whichever variant was suitable at a particular juncture.[73] Hence, while observers dispute whether Khomeini ever really wanted to institute the Islamic state in the manner it was done, Martin would seem to argue that all Khomeini had to do was to settle for one of the many theoretical variants he had toyed with beforehand, depending on the occasion when he had to make his call once the Shah had left.[74]

Khomeini indeed had several visions of an Islamic state in terms of its form, but there was also an underlying unity holding these visions together. In all stages of his thinking, Khomeini never wavered from his notion of the fundamental aim of an Islamic state—establishing a just society. He also never wavered from his position that only the *'ulema* could properly guide the people to attain this goal . Thus, he was no believer in the absolute sovereignty of the people, even though he might approve popular involvement in politics. Throughout the different stages of his intellectual evolution he was unwavering in his commitment to the principle of *rahbariyyat* (leadership), inspired by the Platonist notion of Philosopher King.[75]

During 1967–79, the doctrine of *Vilayat-e Faqih* proved valuable in energizing Khomeini's disciples and galvanized the resistance to the Shah by a section of the *'ulema*. His teachings, sermons, and messages in exile were copied by hand, machine or made into cassettes and smuggled into Iran from Iraq, and then distributed through the network of his clerical disciples in mosques and institutions all across the country. His views were readily accessible to the *'ulema*, and through them to only a few lay followers, generally influential patrons of the *'ulema* in the *bazaars*. Nonetheless, despite the best efforts of Khomeini's disciple Morteza Motahhari, as late as 1977–78, lay Iranians opposed to the idea of clerical leadership in politics had barely taken notice of Khomeini, let alone either reading his works or hearing him in person. Even those who had heard of him did not necessarily agree, or believe, that ideas such as Khomeini's would gain any currency whatsoever in a society as thoroughly secularized as Pahlavi Iran.

\* \* \*

Mosaddeq, Al-e Ahmad, and Khomeini constituted the three most formidable challenges to the legitimacy of the Pahlavi establishment from three different directions. Mosaddeq challenged the constitutionality of the Pahlavi regime in the 1940s and 1950s; Al-e Ahmad questioned the nationalist credentials of the regime in the 1950s and 1960s by highlighting its abject intellectual and material dependence on the "west"; Khomeini challenged the regime in the 1960s and 1970s for deviating from the path of

Islam by manifestly promoting social disharmony and injustice. While each of these challenges contributed to the gradual erosion of the legitimacy of Pahlavi rule, none proved powerful enough to finish off the Pahlavis by itself, because each in its own turn failed to mobilize the masses on a sustained basis. Khomeini succeeded only when the secular and Islamic democrats, left-wing revolutionaries and Islamic socialists, urban professionals, *bazaaris* and the working class, university students, and the unemployed from all the cities of Iran decided to make common cause with the seminary students during the mourning ceremonies in Qom in the fateful summer, fall, and winter of 1978 and ushered in a veritable social revolution to topple the Pahlavis.

The Iranian revolution of 1979 was perhaps among the most urban of social revolutions ever. And because of the character of the country that the Pahlavis had built, one city—Tehran—enjoyed overweening influence first in the making and then in the breaking of the regime, playing almost as much a role as Paris played in 1789. The crowds that demonstrated in the streets of Tehran, and to an extent in other cities and small towns of Iran, were made up mostly of students from the "modern" educational institutions as well as workers from various industrial and service sectors. The regime fell foul of these sections of the population as repression peaked off at a time when the economic prosperity the regime had promised began to "melt into air" by the mid-1970s. In a country where the monarchy and the *'ulema* alike had taught the people to hate socialism, the students and the workers turned out onto the streets to demand an end to the iniquitous and unjust rule of the Pahlavis and their crony capitalists, demanding equality of economic opportunities and state support for the *mustadhafin*, an agenda that could have done the Tudeh proud. Such demands, however, were raised not to establish a socialist state, rather an *Islamic* state where popular sovereignty entitled the people to claim the resources of the state for their welfare. The principal architect of this most radical component of the discourse of resistance in late Pahlavi Iran that provided the impetus behind the highly charged revolutionary milieu of 1978 was 'Ali Shari'ati Mazinani.

# 3

# The World as *Tauheed*: Envisaging an Islamic Alternative

For better or for worse, the Pahlavi regime in Iran had become identified in the twentieth century with the country's agenda of modernization. For a considerable part of the time, almost none of the major voices that could be heard in the country were opposed to the centrality acquired by the state in this scheme of modernization. All that was at issue for them was who/what should wield that state power. Thus, constitutionalists like Mosaddeq and Bazargan wanted a popularly elected representative body to be at the helm of the state,[1] some traditionalist forces (such as the *'ulema* and the *bazaar*) preferred a system where the *'ulema* (and through them, the *bazaar*) would be able to exercise some restraint over state power, and radicals of the Tudeh party would prefer radical progressive elements to be in charge of that state apparatus in the Bolshevik fashion. But apart from Shari'ati, almost no one disputed that state power should be the principal agency of progress in the society.

The Pahlavis were, in a way, working to build Iran along the lines of the principle of the corporate state, where the country is imagined as being one single body/"corpus," and the direction for movement of the country as a whole would come from those who wield positions of power in the state apparatus. The ruling elite would identify what serves the best interests of the "corpus"; any cluster of particular interests outside the general cluster of national interests would ipso facto be understood to be at cross-purposes with the state, hence their lack of legitimacy of purpose in the discourse of governance.[2] This posture rested on two crucial assumptions: one, that the state, as represented by the ruling establishment, was the best judge of all that constituted well-being for the people, and two, that the state could be relied upon to enable the people attain that well-being. The Pahlavi regime in Iran ran along similar assumptions. Legitimacy of governance was established in terms of the regime's desire to promote the interests of the *watan* as an embodiment of the people; criticism of the regime came primarily in terms of its (in)ability to promote such interests. Few serious challenges were ever really mounted that contested that very definition of "national interests"—that is, who really were denoted as the "nation"? Was it simply a majority of individual Iranian nationals? If so, would national interests denote a majority of particular interests? If not, what else would pass for national interests, and how would these be identified and defined?

'Ali Shari'ati Mazinani engaged with these questions in a refreshingly different way. Unlike many of his renowned contemporaries, Shari'ati was a normative thinker. His opposition to the Pahlavi regime was not the result of disagreement with one or another of the regime's policies, nor indeed because the regime contributed to an incremental secularization of the public space. Shari'ati mounted a comprehensive challenge to the very idea of order that the Pahlavis had erected. Indeed, even as he accepted territorial national identities as the foundation of modern state systems, he refused to accept state structures as the essence underlying the organization of such national identities. In his way of thinking, nations represented civilizations (*tamaddun-ha*), shaped by the people by means of social and cultural values within a territorial frame across time. Shari'ati would argue that the people constitute the core around which the notion of "nation" has to evolve. He accepted, prima facie, that the nation constituted a unit *(wahd)*, but his elaboration of the connotation of that unity set him apart from many of his contemporaries. Absorbing a diverse range of intellectual influences encountered in the course of an interesting life, Shari'ati defined the crucial concept of *tauheed-e Islami* (loosely translated as "Islamic unity") not as uniting Muslims under one dispensation, but as unifying a people around some shared values derived from Islam.

## The Making of an Islamic Socialist

'Ali Shari'ati was born in 1933 at Kahak, near Sabzevar, in the northeastern province of Khorasan. His father, Muhammad Taqi Shari'ati, began his training in theology at the Mashhad seminary to become an *'alim* in the family seat of Mazinan near Mashhad. However, in the wake of Reza Shah's policy of secularization, Muhammad Taqi decided against it and began to teach at secular schools.[3] Taqi's association as a teacher of Arabic literature and religious sciences ensured for 'Ali Shari'ati a quality quite rare for a family that experienced considerable financial hardship. 'Ali had his primary schooling at Ibn Yamin school before moving on to Firdausi High School (the two most reputed private secular schools for boys in Mashhad those days), in both of which Taqi Shari'ati had taught at different stages.

At a time when the general milieu favored secularization, Muhammad Taqi introduced his students to an understanding of Islam that was compatible with the conditions of modern life. He sympathized with Ahmed Kasravi's critique of contemporary Shi'ism as primarily a preoccupation with certain rituals and practices that had crept into the faith under the Safavids, and also approved of the Tudeh party's stand on social justice, equality, and resistance to exploitation as compatible with his understanding of Islam. However, in course of the 1940s, he became concerned about the manner in which Tudeh sympathizers were vigorously disseminating antireligious propaganda among students.[4] Determined to contest this, he became instrumental in founding *Kanun-e Nashr-e Haqayeq-e Islami* (the Centre for the Propagation of Islamic Truths, hereafter the Centre) where he presented his understanding of Islam. Here, at the age of 14, 'Ali Shari'ati took the introductory and intermediary cycles of his father's courses on religious education and had his first exposure to the reformist Shi'i discourse in Iran.

Never an outstanding student, Shari'ati nonetheless quickly mastered Arabic and religious sciences even while at school. Because of financial circumstances, he was persuaded by his father to enroll at the *Tarbiat-e Modarres* (Primary Teachers Training Institute) even before he had finished his high school diploma, so that he could start teaching professionally. In 1952, after graduating from the *Tarbiat-e Modarres,* he was employed by the Ministry of Education to teach at the Ketabpour Primary School at Ahmadabad.[5] Even before being formally employed as a teacher, though, he was already lecturing at the Centre for some time—this was the context in which Shari'ati began to be politicized.

From the 1920s, the northern provinces of Iran developed a strong inclination toward socialism and communism, being open to influences from across the frontier; by the 1940s socialism had grown roots deep enough for even Islam-oriented thinkers to embrace its cardinal features like social justice and equality. In Khorasan, the Pahlavi policy against regional autonomy and tribal confederations there had caused a great deal of antagonism. Therefore, in Khorasan as in Azerbaijan, socialism was as much a gesture of defiance against the centralized state as a real political option.

The speakers at the Centre in Mashhad reflected this affinity toward socialism in the form of a moral philosophy based on the Qur'an, making Islam socially, philosophically, and politically relevant, concerned more with the temporal world than with the hereafter. During the charged times of the Mosaddeq years, after the regular religious discussions were over, younger members of the audience often stayed back to discuss politics. In 1951, many of the youngsters of the Centre gravitated toward the *Nehzat-e khudaparastan-e sosialist* (Movement of the God-Worshipping Socialists, or MGWS), which was to briefly merge with the secular Iran Party.[6] Once the MGWS split from the Iran Party to form *Jami'yat-e Azadi-ye Mardom-e Iran* (the League for the Freedom of Freedom of Iranian People, hereafter the League), Shari'ati joined it and became an active member in the pro-Mosaddeq platform in Mashhad.[7] By 1953, the League's position was radicalized as antimonarchist, antifeudalist, and anticapitalist views gained 1953, as the rift between Mosaddeq and Kashani became obvious, Shari'ati emerged at the head of a small group of 50–100 people supporting Mosaddeq. The vehemently antimonarchist content of at least one of his lectures was later (1957) to have Shari'ati arrested, along with his father. Shari'ati's involvement with the pro-Mosaddeq activity continued with the formation of the *Nehzat-e Moqavvemat-e Melli* (National Resistance Movement, or NRM), which the League members decided to join.[8] In 1954, the League decided to transform itself into a political party, the *Hezb-e Mardom-e Iran*. Shari'ati remained with the party till 1955, when he left active politics dismayed by the lack of solidarity among the nationalist forces.[9]

In 1955, Shari'ati enrolled as one of the first in the incoming class at the newly opened Faculty of Literature at the University of Mashhad.[10] The university authorities discouraged him from retaining his job as a primary school teacher, but Shari'ati disregarded the advice—as a result he ended up as a teacher and a student who was almost perpetually late for his classes. Despite his irregularity in attending his classes, his familiarity with Arabic and French since his days at Firdausi High School and his passion for literature helped him put up a good show at examinations, and eventually helped him top the class in 1958.

Shari'ati's days at the University of Mashhad were of great significance for his personal life as well, for it was here that he met Bibi-Fatemeh, alias Puran Shari'at-Razvi, as she was known after her marriage with Shari'ati.[11] Puran came from the family of a Khorasani merchant, Hajji 'Ali Akbar Shari'at-Razvi, who even after moving his business to Tehran retained his family house at Mashhad. Puran, who had most of her schooling in Tehran, returned to Mashhad for finishing school; she then went back to Tehran to study French at the Teachers' Training College *(Tarbiat-e Modarres)* till the Faculty of Literature was opened in Mashhad and her father brought her back to Mashhad once again. Shari'ati and Puran met each other in the course of their French classes. Puran recalled him as a lean, reasonably tall young man with a fast receding hairline who could switch very swiftly between somber academic discussions and witticism and jest. Shari'ati in turn was impressed by Puran's free-thinking and independent spirit, and particularly, by her political by her political consciousness manifested in her conviction of the evils of the Pahlavi regime.[12] Shari'ati began courting her from 1957, but Puran kept turning him down because she wanted to finish her graduation first. The marriage took place in July 1958, after they graduated.[13]

Soon after the examinations in 1958, the Shah announced that university graduates ranking first in their class would be sent overseas for higher studies. Shari'ati's fluency in French made Paris virtually an automatic choice for him. Several legends have grown up surrounding Shari'ati's stint at Sorbonne.[14] Unlike the claims of some of Shari'ati's adherents, his work was not on sociology but on medieval Iranian literature. Initially he wanted to work on philosophy of history, but a fellow Iranian student, Nasser Pakdaman, suggested that he take up sociology instead. Shari'ati, however, was firmly told by the authorities back home that his higher studies higher studies had to be in the discipline in which he had graduated, that is, literature.[15] Shari'ati, therefore, devoted directions—the dreary pursuit of his doctorate and the passionate pursuit of the subjects that interested him, namely, sociology, and sociology, and to an extent, philosophy.[16]

Subsequent claims by Shari'ati's adherents of his familiarity with people like Frantz Fanon and Jean-Paul Sartre seem more to be exaggerations of casual acquaintances than facts, but the impact that the intellectual ambience of Paris in the 1960s had on Shari'ati was undeniable. Upon his return to Iran, Shari'ati referred back and forth to his masters Louis Massignon, George Gurvitch, and Jacques Berque and mentors like Fanon and Sartre. A prominent scholar on Islam of his time, Massignon's (1883–1962) conception of Judaism, Christianity, and Islam as three strands of the same Abrahamic monotheistic tradition deeply influenced Shari'ati's understanding of Islam. Gurvitch (1896–1965), a Russian-Jewish émigré sociologist, contributed to Shari'ati's understanding about the western intellectual tradition. From Berque (1910–95), another prominent scholar of Islam, Shari'ati acknowledges having learnt about *degree de signification,* which showed how words that had been taken to signify something at a particular space and time could be taken to denote something else at another place and time—a lesson that Shari'ati learnt really well. Shari'ati's intellectual positions were shaped and honed to a large extent by these three scholars in the backdrop of what was probably the most significant event in the French political life of the 1960s—the Algerian War of Independence. Massignon, Gurvitch, and Berque alike were resolute supporters of the Algerian cause, and from them Shari'ati developed his initial understanding of the Third World problem. But he probably benefited as much, if not more, from his fellow students from Algeria, Morocco, Tunisia, or

Congo at the university's *Restaurant Musulman,* where he learned about the sociopolitical condition of African countries first hand.

While in Paris, Shari'ati had engaged in anti-Shah demonstrations along with other Iranians.[17] Accordingly, upon his return to Iran, he was promptly arrested and jailed for six months. After release, he joined a school near his home, followed by an appointment at the University of Mashhad. There he introduced a course on the sociology of Islam, the popularity of which among his students aroused suspicions of the regime and eventually cost him his job.[18]

The appearance of a western-trained professor using the language and jargon of western philosophers and social scientists couched in an Islamic terminology proved a novelty. In his lectures, traditional religious concepts were cast in a new mould that was no longer obscure, prosaic, and stale. His entire lectures began to be taped, transcribed and duplicated, and distributed by his students. During 1964–69, he held various teaching posts temporarily, but his association since 1965 with a group of Islamic reformists (clerical—like Motahhari—and lay—such as Nasir Minachi) proved more sustained once he became involved with the *Hosseiniyeh-ye Ershad* around 1967.[19] *Ershad* had many eminent protagonists like Mehdi Bazargan and Morteza Motahhari, but owing to his tremendously tremendously popular lectures beginning in 1968, Shari'ati soon emerged as its leading light.[20] In 1972 upon trenchant criticisms of the Shah from all quarters, the Pahlavi regime cracked down on all bodies that voiced opposition. *Ershad* was among these; Shari'ati was put in prison. In 1975, upon outcry from intellectuals associated with the Algerian freedom movement and with the Third World movements, Shari'ati was put under house arrest and subsequently in 1977 he left Iran in secret.[21] Shari'ati went to England via Belgium, where he died a natural death the same year.

In 1978, when the agitation against the Shah began to escalate, in cities like Tehran, Esfahan, Tabriz, Mashhad, Shiraz, et cetera, educated urban youth who had passed through the "modern" colleges and universities made common cause with their counterparts from the "traditional" seminaries, the first time since the fall of Mosaddeq. The radical students of the universities in Tehran and Mashhad particularly, but also others who had been students earlier in the 1970s, swelled the ranks of the opposition rallying behind posters of Shari'ati as much as Khomeini. After 1979, the more radical of Shari'ati's professed followers, the *Mojahedin-e Khalq,* fell foul of the establishment with their opposition to clerical control institutionalized in the Republic and the principle of the *Vilayat-e Faqih.* After a sustained militant campaign in Iran, the organization had to seek refuge in Iraq in the 1980s. Many others kept quiet or made their peace with the establishment, which they hoped would usher in the kind of Islamic society that Shari'ati had envisaged. A group of clerics, *Jama'-e Rowhaniyat-e Mobarez* (Association of the Combatant Clergy), inspired to an extent by the socialist agenda pushed by Shari'ati, constituted the minority socially liberal leftist component in the Iranian *Majlis* through the 1980s, and the principal support base of lay Islamist Prime Minister Hossein Mussavi.

It is ironic, though, that despite counting Shari'ati among its mentors, the *Jama'* developed a statist streak. In the 1990s, the socially and politically liberal elements of the *Jama'* left the platform to set up the *Ma'jma-ye Rowhaniyun-e Mobarez* (Society of the Combatant Clergy) and created the liberal wave of the *Dovvom-e Khordad* movement that brought the reformist President Khatami to power, one of its agenda being the creation of a liberal and open society.[22] In an interesting outcome of this development, there are at least two versions of Shari'ati's writings and lectures that are available in the market, with subtle differences of emphasis and also by way of interpolations or deletions between various texts. Those who support the status quo in favor of the state choose to highlight Shari'ati's role as an ideologue of the Islamic Revolution, and expunge much of Shari'ati's critiques of the clergy; those who seek to reform the establishment in a more liberal direction highlight his opposition to authoritarianism and clerical predominance in Islamic society.[23]

Clearly, therefore, Shari'ati continues to have his utility in terms of the language of politics that is spoken in the Islamic Republic. Admittedly, because of the manner in which the institutions of the Islamic Republic were devised around the person of Ayatollah Khomeini and his principle of *Vilayat-e faqih,* the works and opinions of Khomeini continue to be resorted frequently by both votaries and opponents of the establishment.[24] Nevertheless, the process of emergence of an Islamist social constituency among the urban laity in prerevolutionary Iran can be associated much more immediately with people like Shari'ati rather than Khomeini.

## Devising an Islamist Constituency

The Islamist constituency that 'Ali Shari'ati had helped shape along with other protagonists was altogether new in the history of modern Iran. As late as the nineteenth century, while Islam was believed to underpin almost everything in public life, there was barely a constituency that was pushing an identifiably "Islamist" agenda beyond perhaps the *'ulema*. Almost all the social constituencies in Iran tended to be functional—namely, *bazaari,* soldiery, peasantry, the urban working class, et cetera. Even the *'ulema,* in a sense, were defined more in terms of a functional constituency rather than a religious one, because the predominance of Islam in public life was taken for granted.²⁵ It was only with the tussle between *mashru'eh* and *mashruteh* after the 1906 revolution, as the predominance of Islam began to be challenged, that the *'ulema* began to define themselves in relation to the religion they practiced rather than the function they discharged in Iranian society.

An Islamist social constituency beyond the circles of the *'ulema* began to emerge in the early 1940s, around the time Shari'ati was beginning to go to school, partly in response to the secularization of the public space under Reza Shah. Between 1934 and 1941, the number of state-run schools of the western type increased from a few hundreds to over 2,300 with over 287,000 students. Over the same period, the number of *madraseh* fell from 389 to 250; the number of *tullab* (students) in *madraseh*s fell from over 4,000 to around 1,000; the number of students enrolled for traditional primary education in the *maktabs* rose slightly from around 29,000 to over 37,000.²⁶ This generated an impression that awareness of the faith was on the decline—an impression reinforced particularly because of the popularity of authors like Ahmad Kasravi, 'Ali Akbar Dehkhoda, Sadeq Hedayat among students of the "modern" education system. Just as important was Reza Shah's decision to outlaw popular manifestations of faith, especially the especially the *ta'aziyeh* processions on the *'ashura* and *rowzehkhvani*.²⁷ All of this created a degree of unease among a large number of Iranians who had some attachment with Shi'ism.

After the Shah's abdication in 1941, Muhammad Reza Shah relaxed controls on the Shi'i *'ulema*, eventually paving the road for the structural reforms of the Shi'i establishment by Ayatollah Boroujerdi that freed the *'ulema* from financial dependence on the state. This, *inter alia*, caused the number of *tullab* to nearly double between 1945 and 1959–60, even as the number of *madrasehs* rose by only a third. The proscription on *rowzehkhwani*, *Hosseiniyeh*s, and *hijab* ceased to be rigorously implemented. Despite the doubling of the number of *tullab* in the traditional educational institutions, however, the predominance of the *madraseh* and *maktab* in Iran's education system had been firmly dented. In 1961, the year Boroujerdi died and when Shari'ati was in France, more than a million students were enrolled at the state-run primary schools, over 350,000 in the secondary schools, and over 14,000 in vocational, technical, and teacher training institutes—as against the 13,000 enrolled at the *madrasehs*.²⁸

For 'Ali Shari'ati's generation, although the charm of "modern" education proved undeniable with its better prospects of employment in a modernizing economy, yet the concerns about secularization of the public space remained pressing among lay Iranians. The growing influence of the Tudeh party and communist ideology particularly was believed to be directly connected with the decline of Islamic sensibilities, especially as a large number of Tudeh sympathizers were found to be products of the "modern" educational system.[29] Accordingly, the relaxation of authoritarianism in the 1940s occasioned a spate of developments where the initiative rested with the laity. The bulk of such initiatives began from among the traditional middle class, especially the *bazaaris*. Several private schools of the western type that had been founded earlier by *bazaari* philanthropists in the major cities of Iran, and many others that came into being around the 1940s, made special provision for instructions pertaining to religion, especially Shi'i Islam. Ibn Yamin and Firdausi were two such highly prestigious private schools in Mashhad where Muhammad Taqi used to "defend Taqi used to "defend and revive" Islamic sensibilities in the classrooms, and where 'Ali had his education.[30] Apart from schools and colleges discussion centers and study groups began to emerge. In Tehran, for instance, Sayyed Mahmud Taleqani set up the *Kanun-e Islam* (Islamic Club) at the Hedayat mosque, where Mehdi Bazargan made his first public appearance as an Islamist thinker; both Taqi Shari'ati and the teenager 'Ali were closely associated with the Centre for Propagation of Islamic Truths in Mashhad. These and similar other attempts at reclaiming the public arena for Islam proved crucial to the emergence of organizations such as the MGWS of which Shari'ati was a member. Mosaddeq's sensitivity to the growth of such Islamic sensibilities among the "modern" urban and suburban youth like Shari'ati ensured their continued support for him, even when in 1953 his nationalist coalition began to dissolve because of defection of his clerical sympathizers on the one hand and pressures from the Tudeh on the other.

By the mid-1960s when Shari'ati returned from France, the second generation of Iranians groomed under the secularized educational apparatus of the Pahlavis made up the sizeable portion of Iran's youth. Secular laws being the norm of the state, Islamic governance defined by an agenda to enforce Islamic laws was not likely to have much support. On the other hand, the negative economic and social repercussions of the White Revolution caused discontent with the regime's activities to snowball. Organized opposition to the regime at this stage was not much pronounced, for the Shah had skillfully appropriated most of the developmental agenda advocated by the various political platforms, and effectively neutralized all institutions through which a challenge could be mounted. Thus, while reasons to mount opposition against the Shah were not altogether absent, no channels were able to enunciate a powerful critique of the government. The only available critique of the regime, Jalal Al-e Ahmad's *gharbzadegi*, being generally misunderstood as a condemnation of the whole phenomenon of modernity itself, did not hold much attraction for a youth educated along western lines. The subcutaneous anticlericalism of urban Iran, reinforced by western secularist assumptions, virtually guaranteed that no critique either challenging modernization or soliciting clerical rule would have any resonance among educated Iranians.[31]

On the other hand, despite the attempted secularization of the public space, the private space in Iranian society remained deeply attached to the traditional form of *Ithna 'Ashari* Shi'ism. Leaving aside the higher echelons of Iranian society, secularization occasionally went no deeper than the superficial level. Thus, while *ta'aziyeh* on *'ashura* could be banned by state fiat, no alternative could be found by the secular state to meet the popular need for sociability. When the Pahlavi state tried to impose non-Islamic Persian culture (festivals commemorating great milestones from pre-Islamic Persian history), such impositions were occasionally reduced to irrelevancies of courtly culture—the most extravagant being the celebration of 2,500 years of Persian monarchy, in 1971.[32]

By contrast, the resumption of private performance of *rowzehkhwani* and proliferation of *Hosseiniyehs* (principally under the patronage of men from the *bazaars*) during the reign of Muhammad Reza Shah kept Shi'ism vibrant and alive in the realm of popular culture. The graduates of Pahlavi secular education hailing from urban middling and lower-middle classes (and especially those coming from the traditional families of the *bazaars*) learnt to respect their faith because of their exposure to the vibrancy of such a tradition-minded popular culture. Besides, in a regime that was notorious for the denial of political freedom to its citizens, the only arena of public life where the freedom granted after the fall of Reza Shah was not completely repealed pertained to Shi'ism and the *'ulema* establishment. Thus, *rowzehkhwani*, passion-plays, *Hosseiniyehs* emerged to be the only arena in the public sphere where some degree of sociability was possible without government intervention.[33] The consequence was not that only religiously inspired critiques of the regime could come from such platforms; it was also the case that it was occasionally convenient to use religious idioms in order to make a political point without immediately having the SAVAK knocking on the door.

This social constituency of Iran's urban middle and lower-middle classes educated in the state education system was politicized by a number of people—'Ali Shari'ati was the most prominent among them. In the course of his career as a professional teacher at the school and university levels alike, 'Ali Shari'ati was never the most systematic of teachers. He almost never finished any curriculum set for him, and hated examining students as much as he hated appearing at any examination as a student. Yet, from his days at the University of Mashhad to his stint at *Hosseiniyeh-ye Ershad*, he enjoyed an enviable reputation. At a time when classes occasionally tended to go somewhat underpopulated, Shari'ati's classes were frequently overcrowded as even those who had not subscribed for his course would turn up. Quite apart from the particularly evocative manner of his speech, the content of what he had to say had a resonance among the youth of urban Iran. He used his classrooms and lectures to introduce a discourse of politics that was distinctly modern with the manner of its emphasis on accountability (*jawabgo'i*), deploying terms of reference that were identifiably Islamic. Confronted with a regime that laid claim to representing the people of Iran, Shari'ati questioned the very meaning of "representation" using intellectual categories that were derived as much from the Muslim world as from the world outside it.

### Redefining *Tauheed*

At the core of Shari'ati's political thinking lay the notion of *tauheed*. Conventionally understood, the idea of *tauheed* (unification/making something one or asserting uniqueness, viz., monotheism) is, arguably, the core of Islamic theology and religion. The concept of *tauheed* generally refers to the cardinal belief that there is no God but God *(la ilaha illa al-lah)*, and there is none other to share in his divinity *(la sharika lahu)*.[34] In the annals of Islamic philosophy, however, a whole discourse has evolved around this concept that requires a more nuanced understanding of the possibilities of the term.

The discourse on *tauheed* came into being presumably to address the question of relationship between the *khaliq* (Creator) and *khalq* (Creation)—whether the two are related, and if so, how? How is the latter to understand the former—whether attributes of the Creator can be understood by those who were created, and if so, how? One of the outcomes of the debate was the rise of the notions of *wujud* (loosely translated as "being" or "existence") and *mahiyyah* (appearance or form taken by *wujud*).[35] While the nuances varied widely among various schools of Islamic philosophy, the general frame of intellectual debate suggested that God is the only *wujud* that does not have a *mahiyyah* distinct from the *wujud* itself. This implied that one could aspire to understand God only through a study of his attributes, but even then not entirely comprehend the divine altogether. God was understood as a unity *(wahd)* comprising of all the 99 component superlative attributes, but was more than the sum of these; also, no other being in the universe shared this characteristic. *Tauheed* thus referred to the subsuming of all the divine attributes in the one, all-embracing *wujud* of God, the ultimate reality.

A powerful turn in the debate came with the rise of the transcendentalist doctrine of *wahdat al-wujud* (unity of Being) in the sixteenth century. In this respect, the rigorous logical discussions of al-Farabi and Ibn Sina, the critiques of al-Ghazzali and Fakhr al-din al-Razi, the illuminative doctrine of Shihab al-din Suhrawardi, and the experiential knowledge of Sufis like Ibn 'Arabi and Sadr al-din Qunyawi were unified in a vast synthesis by Sadr al-din Shirazi, of what was known as the School of Esfahan. "If correctly understood, it stands at the heart of the basic message of Islam, which is that of unity *(al-tawhid)* [sic] and which is found expressed in the purest form in the testimony of Islam, La ilaha illa'allah [sic]."[36] The doctrine rested on the idea that the reality of *wujud* belonged ultimately to God alone, and that he was the source of everything that appeared to possess *wujud*. For sure, not all Sufi thinkers accepted this understanding—Taqi al-din Taymiyyah and Shaikh Ahmad Sirhindi being two of the most prominent opponents. Nor did all protagonists of the doctrine agree on the nature of the transcendental unity: Ibn 'Arabi believed that only God has *wujud*, all else have only *mahiyyah*, so that the question of relation between the *wujud* of a particular existent and the Absolute Being does not even arise. For the sixteenth-century Iranian thinker, Mullah Sadra, however, the Absolute Being bestowed the effusion of *wujud* upon all *mahiyyat* in such a manner that all beings have it as though issued from that ultimate *wujud*.[37] It follows from this reading of the doctrine of *tauheed* that the ultimate reality is of a unity that is not disrupted despite the manifestation of a world of multiplicity.

In the twentieth century, the concept of *tauheed* was occasionally politicized to address the issue of social order. Making his case for Islamic modernism, Muhammd Abduh opened the first salvo by depicting *tauheed* as the harmonious unity between human Free Will and obedience to the Will of God.[38] Arguing that there is no conflict between reason and revelation, he exhorted Muslims to engage in *ijtihad* (legal reasoning) rather than *taqlid* (blind emulation of tradition) in order to adapt Muslim society to the modern world. Subsequently, from the standpoint of victims of authoritarian rule, Sayyid Qutb essentially argued the opposite case, suggesting *tauheed* represents the unity of God's purpose in creation, which can be attained only by complete submission to the will of God as manifested in Islamic law.[39]

'Ali Shari'ati was probably the first to place *tauheed* at the heart of political discourse by removing it from concerns of social order, and approaching it instead from the Sufi standpoint of concern about the human condition.

\* \* \*

It is a moot point whether 'Ali Shari'ati was of a Sufi bent of mind. Some of his friends like Nahid Tavassoli and her husband, Agha Mehdi, and disciples like Taqi Rehmani believe that Shari'ati was indeed inclined toward Sufism; by contrast, some of his students like Muhammad Faiyyaz Bakhsh doubt whether there was much in Shari'ati that was religious in the conventional sense, Sufi or otherwise.[40] There, however, seems little doubt that during and immediately after his stay in Paris (if not earlier), Shari'ati was deeply interested in, if not influenced by, the Sufi tradition. His mentor Louis Massignon particularly influenced him, which prompted Shari'ati to translate Massignon's monograph on Salman-e Pak or Salman Farsi soon after his return from France. Either way, in the first couple of years upon his return from France, Shari'ati was deeply engrossed in Sufi literature. The Sufi mystical imprint on Shari'ati is particularly clear in his works of this period (1964–68)—*Guftoguha-ye tanha'i* (Lonesome Conversations) and *Hobut dar Kavir* (Descent in Kavir), together referred to by Shari'ati as *Kaviriyat*.[41] These works came at a time when upon his return from the highly political ambience of France in the mid-1960s, Shari'ati was dismayed by the lack of a meaningful intellectual environment, and the endless preoccupation of his fellow Iranians with the trivial and superficial concerns of the day-to-day existence.[42] Shari'ati's disenchantment with the politics of opposition fed into his own distinctive (and eventually highly politicized) understanding of *tauheed*.

In *Kaviriyat*, Shari'ati told the story of Man's *judai* (separation) from God and his descent to earth, where he realizes his state of *hasti* (being) and finally speaks of the possibility of escape from this *jindan* (prison) by uniting with God.[43] The metaphysical concept of *judai* that Shari'ati played with was a tricky one: the *ruh* (soul, spirit) of man was "separated" from God and imprisoned in the earthly body made of *khak* (clay) as creation had come to an end. He explained that man's happiness in Paradise was in fact a grinding and painful joy because he was *tanha* (lonely). God then created Eve to cure his pain of being alone; yet happiness proved elusive because the real cause of unhappiness was not *tanhai* (loneliness) but *judai* (separation) from God.[44] The fall from Paradise was occasioned by man's having succumbed to materiality, and failing to see through the veil of matter, thus failing to reach out for God. For man to escape the agony of the material world and to secure the freedom provided by *ma'refat* (inner knowledge), a second act of *tafkik* (separation) had to be performed—liberating the spiritual (soul) from the prison of the material (body) so that man could reclaim the Heavens from which he was once expelled. Man seeks God in everything that he encounters in this world, but cannot find Him so long as he is trapped by the materiality of the *Zahiri* (external) world—"I search for my essence and cannot find it, I am his shadow but where is He? ... His absence made strangers out of all the present faces. His absence rendered all beings absence rendered all beings futile."[45] Man has to look inward to begin what Shari'ati calls the "Sufi dialectic," a transcendental transformation at the end of which the *ma'shuq* (Beloved) embraces the *a'shiq* (lover), who has shed his own essence *(wujud-e khudesh)*. When this reunion between man and God occurs, "I [i.e., man] will retrieve the heaven that I left behind. There, I, Love and God will conspire to recreate the world and recommence the act of creation. In this eternal past [*azal*] God will no longer [*azal*] God will no longer be alone and in this world I will no longer be a stranger."[46] Thus, man would cease to have his own existence and would be subsumed by the ultimate reality of God, the plurality of the temporal world would become a unity in the real world—this process of "making one" was the key to *tauheed,* as Shari'ati understood it.

Shari'ati developed his doctrine of *tauheed* further in the series of lectures entitled *Islam che ast?* (What is Islam?) as a part of his course called *Islamshenasi* (lit. Knowing Islam or Islamology) offered at the University of Mashhad during 1966–67.[47] The central argument around which the course developed was that the essence of Islam had been lost behind centuries of accretion, and hence needed to be known anew. The course was meant to identify *(shenakhtan)* the various signifiers of that essence. Shari'ati argued that Islam was not the first expression of *tauheed* in the sense of monotheism, but *tauheed* acquired a different connotation with the emergence of Islam. Unlike other monotheistic traditions, Islam's emphasis on the unity of God (therefore having only one worthy pursuit in life) had a centrality that was missing in the previous monotheistic traditions. "*Tauheed,*" as Shari'ati said, "was the basis of all the principles, not a belief alongside many others. *Tauheed* is the foundation of individual and social life, material and ideal, in other words, the base and the direction of the all phases of life of human beings, their thoughts, and their feelings."[48]

Shari'ati's elaboration on *tauheed* relied on the application of principles of Mullah Sadra with idioms drawn from Heideggerian phenomenology, which Shari'ati had picked up from Berque in Paris. He argued that the Qur'an designated all objects and occurrences as "signs" or "appearances" of the phenomenon of God.

> *Tauheed,* then, is to be interpreted in the sense of the unity of nature with what is larger than nature, of man with nature, of man with man, of God with the world and with man. It depicts all of these as constituting a total, harmonious, living and self-aware system. The Light Verse (Qur'an, 24:35) illustrates... [t]he whole of existence is like a burning lamp; this is neither *"wahdat al-wujud"* (unity of being ) nor multiplicity of being, rather unification (*tauheed*) of being.
>
> ... [T]he very structure of *tauheed* cannot accept contradiction or disharmony in the world. According to the worldview of *tauheed,* therefore, there is no contradiction in all of existence; no contradiction between man and nature, spirit and body, this world and the hereafter, matter and meaning.[49]

Shari'ati then applied this phenomenological interpretation of *tauheed* on to the human condition. He argued that *tauheed* being the norm, the normal condition of human society, as much as everything else, has no room for any essential difference. Any difference between man and man that is considered as a difference in essence in some form or the other is contrary to the principle of *tauheed*.

> Contradiction between nature and that which is larger, matter and meaning, ... spirit and body, intellect and illumination, science and religion, metaphysics and nature, working for men and working for God, politics and religion, ... life and eternity, landlord and peasant, ruler and the ruled, black and white, noble and vile, clergy and laity, eastern and western, blessed and wretched, ... inherent virtue and inherent evil, ... Arab and non-Arab, Persian and non-Persian, capitalist and proletarian, elite and mass, learned and illiterate—all these forms of contradiction are reconcilable only with the worldview of *shirk*—*thanaiyyah* (dualism), *thalathiyyat* (trinitarinism) or *chand-khudai* (polytheism)—but not with *tauheed* (monotheism). It is for this reason that the worldview of *shirk* has always formed the basis for *shirk* in society, with its discrimination among classes and races. Belief in a plurality of creators justifies and sanctifies a plurality of creatures, presenting it as something eternal and everlasting. Similarly, a belief in contradiction among the gods presents as natural and divine the contradictions existing among men. *Tauheed*, by contrast, which negates all forms of *shirk* regards all the particles, processes and phenomena of existence as being engaged in harmonious movement toward a single goal.[50]

Addressing a gathering comprising overwhelmingly of Muslims, Shari'ati's lectures were appreciated mostly at the primary level of establishing the superiority of Islam over other confessional varieties. However, the message was susceptible of a second and deeper reading. Shari'ati was saying that there could be no *essential* difference between one human being and another, because they are both "human beings." Apart from this essence of *bashariyat* (humanity), every other category of identity (presumably, religion included) was secondary. Accepting any of these secondary identities as fundamental was analogous to the sin/fallacy of *shirk*. The argument had a resonance that was lacking not only in Heidegger, whose idioms Shari'ati freely borrowed, but also Mullah Sadra, whose distinctions between *wujud* and *mahiyyah* informed Shari'ati's argument on *tauheed*.

But how does *tauheed* bear upon the essence of humanity? As Shari'ati put it in the course of his lectures at the Mashhad University, he saw the Qur'an as "the most profound and advanced expression of humanism."[51] Adam, according to Shari'ati, represented that very essence of humanity in its philosophical sense—made of *hama' masnun* (putrid clay) and *ruh-e khuda* (spirit of God). The constitution of this essence, he believed, was indicative of human destiny: *hama' masnun* implies all that is negative in the human essence—baseness, stagnation, and passivity; *ruh-e khuda* suggests an endless movement toward perfection and infinite exaltation. Comparing this Qur'anic binary with Pascal's statement in his book *Two Infinites* that man is an intermediate between lowliness and greatness, Shari'ati argued that man is a free and responsible will occupying a station intermediate between two poles—God and Iblis.

> The combination of these two opposites, the thesis and anti-thesis, which exist both in man's nature and in his fate, create motion in him, a dialectic, inevitable and evolutionary movement, and a constant struggle between two opposite poles in man's life.
>
> ... God or the spirit of God, which represents absolute and infinite purity, beauty, splendor, power, creativity, awareness, vision, knowledge, love, mercy, will, freedom, independence, sovereignty and eternity, is present in man as a potentiality, an attraction that draws him ... to the glory of the heavens; as an ascension towards the sphere of God's sovereignty and being nurtured with the attributes and characteristics of God, as afar as knowledge would reach. Aware of all the secrets of nature, man becomes a power enjoying lordship over the world; in front of him bow all material and spiritual forces, earth and heaven, the sun and the moon, and even God's angels, including the highest among them. Man is thus a creature and a creator, a servant and a master; he is a conscious, seeing, creative, decisive, knowing, wise, purposeful, pure and exalted will, the bearer of God's trust, and His vice-regent on earth, an eternal creature of paradise.[52]

The natural corollary of this argument pertained to the worth of human beings—and here Shari'ati made a claim seldom voiced before him. "*Tauheed* bestows upon man independence and dignity. Submission to Him alone—the supreme norm of all being—impels man to revolt against all lying powers, all the humiliating fetters of fear and greed."[53] This implied that any order that robbed human beings of their independence and dignity, and forced them to submit to anything temporal, was guilty of a breach of *tauheed*. Reasserting and restoring the lost dignity would then be the only way of reestablishing *tauheed*. Here lay the roots of Shari'ati's politicization of Islam.

### Politicizing *Tauheed*: The Dialectics of Islam

One of the reasons for Shari'ati's phenomenal popularity as a lecturer at the Mashhad University, and then as a veritable demagogue in Tehran, was the manner in which he approached the study of Islam. The compilations of his talks in Mashhad, Tehran et al. subsequently published as *Islamshenasi* (Islamology) and *Ravish-e Shenakht-e Islami* (Approaches to the Study of Islam) spoke of an Islam that was essentially far more dynamic than the secularist state institutions and the traditional *'ulema* establishment had seemed to convey. In contrast with the hidebound legalist interpretations and preoccupations of a traditional Islam, or even with the lachrymose evocation of Shi'i passion for injustices committed 13 centuries ago, Shari'ati's interpretation of Islam engaged with, appropriated, and contested all the major intellectual concepts that were circulating around the world in that era. Perhaps the most innovative among such appropriation and engagement was Shari'ati's view of history founded upon the idea of dialectics.

"History," Shari'ati argued, "represents an unbroken flow of events... dominated by a dialectical contradiction, a constant warfare between two hostile and contradictory elements that began with the creation of humanity and has been waged everywhere and all times."[54] History was not simply a narration of the evolution of man from one stage to another, nor simply the cause of transition from one stage to the other. Instead, history was primarily a record of the purpose behind such evolution—that, it involved contradictions and struggles between opposing forces. Such dialectical contradiction was the motor behind history: as Shari'ati put it, through the conflict of the two mutually opposed forces of good, that is, *tauheed* and evil, that is, *shirk*, locked in an endless combat, history moves on. In this conflict, only piecemeal victories are won marking the milestones of history until a final and total triumph of *tauheed* and the extinction of *shirk*.

Shari'ati's familiarity with the principles of dialectics came primarily from his study of Marx at an early date, followed by that of Hegel. Growing up in a society where socialism and communism proved to be powerful currents, thanks to the Tudeh party, inter alia, Shari'ati had absorbed the language and ethos of socialism even while he was a youngster with the *Nehzat-e Khodaparast-e Sosialist*. The Hegelian principle of dialectics and the Marxian principle of historical materialism made quite a deep impression on Shari'ati—*Islamshenasi* and *Ravish-e Shenakht-e Islami* are laced with references to dialectics, and a considerable number of his works and lectures refer directly or indirectly to Marx and Marxism. This certainly accounted for Shari'ati's sustained popularity within Iran's socialist circles.

But it would be incorrect to understand the binary nature of Shari'ati's historical analysis solely upon the principle of dialectics. Binary constitutes a major part of the theoretical paradigm of Persian cultural and literary tradition. The teachings of Zoroaster and Mani were both predicated upon the duality of cosmic forces. Even Islam was not immune to the influence of this powerful effect of the binary. *Ithna 'Ashari* Shi'ism is premised upon the notion that the house of 'Ali was on the right, while anyone not associated with the house was in truck with the enemies of Islam. While considerably different from the standard position taken in the Shi'i tradition, Shari'ati's theory of history was not premised upon a simple value-free Hegelian binary of thesis and antithesis leading to a synthesis, which in its own turn becomes a thesis by itself, and therefore is the precondition of a further antithesis; the Zoroastrian/Persian element in the conceptualization of the binary was fairly obvious. He couched the notions of thesis and antithesis in the Islamic terms of *tauheed* and *shirk*, where the dialectical relationship between the two did not necessarily lead to a synthesis of the two, rather the result was the triumph of one over the other, and this conflict would cease (and with it, history) only when *tauheed* inevitably triumphed over *shirk*.

The highlight of Shari'ati's use of the dialectical principle as a motor of history lay in the identification of the nature of *tauheed* and *shirk*, rather than the nature of conflict between the two. He did not approach history from that standpoint of history *per se*, rather from the standpoint of historical sociology and, to an extent, the philosophy of history—a remnant of his fascination with the two disciplines while he was at Sorbonne. Using the standard tools of analysis of the disciplines and Berque's *degree de signification*, Shari'ati read all history as a parable through the prism of the Qur'an. Adam was the essence of humanity, struggling between Good and Evil; Cain and Abel were read not as the first killer and his victim, rather as symbolic of the struggle for power, domination, and possession that occasion all conflicts between man and man, that is, the foundational premise behind all *shirk*.

In Shari'ati's reckoning, history began not with Adam, rather with his sons, Cain and Abel. Shari'ati argued that the dialectics that operated in Adam's life signified only the human condition; it was an internal existential struggle between the good and the bad within his own person. The struggle between Cain and Abel was, by contrast, "objective" in that it took place in "outer life," symbolizing a phenomenon that had actually taken place in history. "The story of Cain and Abel is the story of our philosophy of history, just as that of Adam is the source of our philosophy of man."[55] When asked to make a sacrifice, Cain had offered a handful of dry and withered corn—Shari'ati used this to deduce that Cain represented the system of agriculture and individual or monopoly ownership; Abel, by contrast, sacrificed a young and valuable red-haired camel, hence he represented the age of pastoral economy and primitive socialism.[56]

[A] permanent war began so that the whole of history became the stage for a struggle between the party of Cain the killer, and Abel, his victim, or in other words, Abel the pastoralist was killed by Cain the landowner. The period of common ownership of the sources of production, the age of animal husbandry, hunting and fishing, the spirit of brotherhood and true faith, came to an end. It was replaced by the age of agriculture and the establishment of the system of private ownership together with religious trickery and violation of the rights of others. Abel disappeared, and Cain came to the forefront of history, and there he still lives.[57]

In an interpretation of history clearly influenced by Marx's historical materialism, Shari'ati argued that during the stage of pastoral economy, individual ownership of the sources of production (water, land, etc.) or the tools of production (cows, ploughs, etc.) was absent, and everything was at the disposal of everyone. "The spirit and the norms of society, paternal respect, steadfastness in fulfilling moral obligations, absolute... obedience to the limitations of collective life, innate purity and sincerity of the religious conscience, a pacific spirit of love and forbearance"—these were the features of pastoral society as evident in the figure of Abel.[58] People worked to the point their *needs* were satisfied. When human society became agricultural, however, the need to restrict the factors of production and arrogate a part of the produce for oneself gave birth to private property. "It was a revolution that produced a new man, a powerful and evil man, as well as the age of civilization and discrimination."[59] People were no longer willing to confine themselves to the extent of their needs; everyone wanted to acquire to the point of satisfaction of their desires. Human society became divided into two rival and warring camps. "*Tabaqeh-ye Habeel* (Class of Abel) is that of the subject and the oppressed, i.e. the people, those who throughout history have been slaughtered and enslaved by the *tabaqeh-ye Qabeel* (Class of Cain)"[60]—a distinctly Marxian categorization of the relations of production between the haves and have-nots.

Shari'ati's philosophy of history, using the Cain-Abel paradigm, went farther to argue that the war between the systems of Cain and Abel is the perennial war waged by every generation. The banner of Cain, he argues, has always been held high by the ruling classes, whereas the subjected people have fought for justice, freedom, and true faith in a struggle that has continued, one way or another, in every age. In this struggle, both sides have made use of religion, which tended to perpetuate the struggle of one religion against another.

On the one hand is the religion of *shirk*, assigning partners to God, a religion that furnishes the justification for *shirk* in society and class discrimination. On the other hand is the religion of *tauheed*, of the oneness of God, *which furnishes the justification for the unity of all classes and races.* The struggle across history between Abel and Cain is also the *struggle between tauheed and shirk, between justice and human unity on the one hand, and social discrimination on the other.* There has existed throughout human history, and will continue to exist until the last day, *a struggle between the religion of deceit, stupefaction and justification of the status quo and religion of awareness, activism and revolution* [emphases mine].[61]

It is interesting to note that by speaking of *tauheed* and *shirk* in this manner, Shari'ati was introducing a usage that was almost entirely unfamiliar in the history of the modern era, let alone previously. He deliberately deviated from the standard connotations of monotheism and polytheism that these words carried, and played with the literal meanings of the terms. *Shirk*, or rather its near equivalent, *chand-khudai* (literally, polytheism), denotes imputation of divinity upon more than one; since the imputation of divinity implies devotion to, and being constantly mindful of, something or things, Shari'ati's implication had to do less with devotion to God, rather it had more to do with devotion per se. In an argument that has reasonable currency among the Sufis, Shari'ati was implying that devotion is all there is to religion; hence, when man devotes himself to wealth and power, he loses sight of the unwavering devotion to God.[62] No matter whether such an individual be a practicing monotheist or not, any alternate focus of devotion inevitably leads to *shirk*. By contrast, those struggling for justice and redresser of social inequality are in effect trying to restore the conditions to the point where there is no such alternate focus.

This point is borne out by what Shari'ati has to say with respect to other religions. He contended that all the founders and other protagonists of the great religions around the world—Zoroaster, Buddha, Confucius, Lao Tse, Jesus, Muhammad—were each sent with a mission to stand by the common people *(al-nas)*, and help them overcome the basic contradiction set in motion by the Cain-Abel paradigm. Although he went on to say (probably mindful of his audience accustomed to being spoken about the superiority of Islam) that only Muhammad and the Imams remained true to the divine mandate of working for the people, his initial submission that all religious protagonists had a similar divine mandate was revealing enough. If one leaves aside the consideration of which God to worship (if at all), Shari'ati seemed to be arguing that all religions are effectively programs for *restoring tauheed*. These programs may have failed, as he suggested in his lectures on *Tarikh wa shenakht-e adian* (History and the Understanding of Religions), yet the crucial thing was that the agenda was there in the first place to work against the inequalities of the material world.

Moreover, unlike Marx, who saw acquisition of political power as a factor of economic strength, Shari'ati concluded that the need to restrict the use of some means, tools, or fruits of production from the rest of the people in itself did not inevitably lead to private ownership; rather the ability to enforce such restriction was a more crucial determinant in the emergence of private property. Power, in other words, was a factor of force, not mere wealth. Indeed, as in the Marxian mode of understanding, wealth certainly worked on an exclusionary logic, but the exclusionary principle needed coercive support, lest those being excluded tried to stop the exclusion. Here Shari'ati seemed to agree with Marx that state *is* an instrument of class rule, but he emphasized less on the state as *the* organ of class rule and highlighted more the triad of *zor, zar,* and *tazveer* that made class-rule possible. The *tabaqeh-ye Qabeel,* that is, privileged classes comprised *zor* (force, i.e., political power), *zar* (gold, i.e., force of economic exploitation), and *tazveer* (deception, i.e., force of religious exploitation). In Qur'anic terminology, the *malik* (ruler, king) employed *zor* derived from *tegh* (sword), the *mutrif* (merchant) employed *zar* that came from *tala* (gold), and the *rahib* (lit. monk, ascetic, meaning man of religion) employed *tazveer* behind the guile of *tasbeh* (rosary beads). These three forces of oppression could be classified respectively into *istibdad* (despotism), *istismar* (exploitation), and *istihmar* (deception by clergy). Together these three forces of *shirk* subvert the order of *tauheed*.[63]

Shari'ati's detailing of the mechanism of the *tabaqeh-ye Qabeel* was simply an analysis of the nature of power that had become generally accepted as a result of classical Marxist historiography by the middle of the twentieth century. *Istibdad* (despotism) involved the ruling classes using political and military power to establish control over economic resources, enforcing the logic of exclusion that concentrated the benefits of resources among a handful at the expense of the majority, who originally had no less entitlement to the resources. The protagonists of *zor* used the state apparatus and misused the state machinery: making laws supporting economic exploitation of the majority, deploying the military to subdue dissent, using the judiciary to punish any transgression, and monopolizing all legitimate exercises of authority to promote a manifestly iniquitous agenda. So doing, authority itself earned disrepute because of its abuse by those who wielded it. *Istismar* (economic exploitation) denoted the power of wealth that operated on a similar principle of exclusion of the majority of people. Resources generally available were used in conjunction with human labor to create wealth, but the fruits of such economic activity were reserved for the privileged few. *Istihmar* (deception by the religious classes) was an important component in both *istibdad* and *istismar*. Many from the religious classes subjected the people to a dual deception: on the one hand, they advocated otherworldliness, suggesting nothing material in this world was of any significance, which implied exploitation was not worth resisting; on the other hand, the religious classes also advocated complete and unquestioning obedience to the ruler, however unjust the rule, for the sake of maintenance of order, thus helping the despotic ruling classes enjoy a legitimacy they did not deserve. Hence, the combined forces of *istibdad, istismar, and istihmar*—the forces associated with *shirk*—subverted the natural order of equity and justice that constituted the essence of *tauheed*.

The most crucial component of Shari'ati's philosophy of history, however, was what he called "tomorrow's history," when all contradiction ends with the death of Cain and a reestablishment of the "system of Abel, of equity and justice." And for that apocalyptic victory of *tauheed* over *shirk* to happen

> [i]t is the responsibility of every individual in every age to determine his stance in the constant struggle between the two forces... and not to remain a spectator... [H]istory advances on the basis of a universal and scientifically demonstrable process of determinism, but I as an individual human being must choose whether to move forward with history and accelerate its determined course with the force of knowledge and science, or to stand with ignorance, egoism and opportunism in the face of history and be crushed.[64]

Tomorrow's history, Shari'ati seems to suggest, will be written by people who *choose* to write their own history, not those who resign to the status quo. Man fell from God's grace because of something he did, that is, it was his actions that occasioned a breach in *tauheed*; by his action alone would he redeem his lost status as the Vice-regent of God, and restore the world to its original unity. Virtually all of his teachings at Mashhad and later at Tehran argued in this vein.

Unlike many other contemporary major advocates of political Islam, 'Ali Shari'ati refrained from speaking about an Islamic state and Islamic laws as the be-all-and-end-all of political life. At a time when Khomeini in Iran, Sayyid Qutb in Egypt, and Maududi in Pakistan were emphatic about the need for the enforcement of Islamic laws as an essential feature of (a mostly vaguely defined) Islamic governance, Shari'ati began to explore why Islamic governance was important in the first place. He spoke a language that was easily intelligible to western-educated Iranian youth, voicing concerns about how a society should be governed in accordance with certain *universal* values *championed* by Islam. He also projected an alternative vision of society where the underlying normative principles were Islamic enough to be acceptable and universal enough to be desirable.

The aim of advocates of Islamic politics worldwide has tended to be expressed by the term *ummah* (community), denoting the body of the faithful living under the dispensation of Islam.[65] Ever since the disintegration of the *Khilafat* (Caliphate) in the thirteenth century, the term was used more in the sense of a sociocultural signifier rather than a political entity; thus, there were component individual kingdoms *(mulk, saltanat)* within the Islamic *ummah*. Despite a brief resurgence of the idea of a *Khilafat* toward the close of the Ottoman rule in West Asia, Muslim reconciliation with the fragmented nature of political authority within the *ummah* was more or less final. In a world being fast compartmentalized into nations and nation-states, very few Muslim thinkers of any substance ever entertained any realistic vision of a political integration of the Muslim world. Indeed, some Pan-Arabist thinkers of the Arab world certainly thought of a closer coordination of Muslim Arab interests as a potential reintegration of the *ummah*, but it was more an assertion of regional Arab identity than of an Islamic *ummah*.[66]

In the modern era, therefore, the political connotation of the word *ummah* tended to be at the level of dispensation of societal order, rather than political structure of the state. Major thinkers of modern Islam, such as Muhammad Abduh, Rashid Rida,[67] and Sayyid Qutb of Egypt; Muhammad Iqbal in South Asia;[68] Mawlana Abu'l Ala Mawdudi of Pakistan;[69] and Ruhollah Khomeini, have each spoken of the *ummah* as the *ummat al-mominin* (community of faithful) living with the territorial confines of the nations *(umam, qaum, melal)* of the world, yet living under the social dispensation of Islam. Almost all the major Muslim thinkers of the modern era had to contend with the possibility of such arbitrary or unwelcome regulations framed by regimes of the states they lived in, and most of them resorted to the tried and tested demand for legalism ensured by the *shari'ah*. Advocacy of the *shari'ah* was not necessarily an obscurantist position, because, in the context of colonial and authoritarian rule in large parts of the Muslim world, the *shari'ah* was the only body of laws that the ruler could not tamper with; nor did it mean remaining hidebound to medieval laws as many Muslims all over the Islamic world appreciated the need for changes in tune with time. In fact, jurists like Muhammad Abduh denounced the juridical orthodoxy of the *'ulema,* ignoring the boundless possibilities of juridical renovation, as the reason behind importation of western laws and institutions. Rashid Rida's comparison of the legal system of every society to its language, however, was the most cogent defense of the *shari'ah*. He maintained that just as no language could allow grammatical rules of some other language to be appropriated indiscriminately, nor could any society allow to be governed by imported laws. Advocacy of the *shari'ah* was to resist imposition of laws and institutions inspired by the west, and introduced by secular governments desiring to impose arbitrary or unwelcome regulations. Almost all the major thinkers were appreciative of the fact that in practice, application of the *shari'ah* of one society was different from all others, and each was equally legitimate. Hence, in their call for the *shari'ah* to be made the basis for all laws, none of the thinkers were looking at identical laws being enforced all across the Muslim world. What they were looking for was that a similar set of legislative principles be accepted for Muslim peoples all over the world, quite like the prevalence of Christian values all over Christendom. Islamic *ummah*, therefore, much like the term *Christendom* in the western world, denotes certain standards in public and private life, and the *shari'ah* is supposed to be *a* (and some would argue, the most important) model of such standards for people who have faith in *tauheed-e ilahi* (unity of God).

'Ali Shari'ati deviated considerably from this mould of thinking. He argued that *ummah* was an ideational category, taking the place of all the similar concepts that in different languages and cultures designated a human agglomeration—namely, society, nation, race, people, tribe, clan—the *ummah* subsumed all of these categories, and was more than a sum of all of these. It was not, according to Shari'ati, simply an aggregate of human beings bound by a set of legislative principles; it was a possible (and the desirable) trajectory of human development.

> The word *ummah* derives from the root *amm*, which has the sense of path (*tariqeh*) and intention (*iradeh*). The *ummah* is therefore a society in which a number of individuals, possessing a common faith and goal, come together in harmony with the intention of advancing toward their common goal.
>
> While other expressions denoting human agglomerations have taken unity of blood or soil and the sharing of material benefit as the criterion of society, Islam, by choosing the word *ummah* has made intellectual responsibility and shared movement toward a common goal the basis of its social philosophy.[70]

This common goal was toward the establishment of a social system, based on "equity and justice and ownership by the people, on the revival of the 'system of Abel,' the society of human equality and thus also of brotherhood—the classless society *(ijtema'i be-tabaqeh)*."[71] Unlike socialism, Shari'ati argued, *ijtema'i be-tabaqeh* was not the aim of political activities, rather their fundamental principle—that is, short of a classless society, there could be no *ummah*.

\* \* \*

Shari'ati's biographer Ali Rahnema considers Shari'ati to have been a Utopian, primarily because of his notions of the *ummah*. In common parlance, *Utopia* is an ideal dispensation of sociopolitical order—which is the sense in which Rahnema probably used it. Significantly, the very name

*Utopia* (meaning, nowhere) is somewhat ambiguous. Is it supposed to imply that such a model *does not* exist anywhere? Or does it mean such a model *cannot* exist anywhere? Shari'ati's views have no such ambiguity. He was quite emphatic that the *ummah* as he understands it does not and did not exist (except briefly under Prophet Muhammad and Imam 'Ali), but he was equally emphatic that it can and would be brought about by determined and mindful people waging a relentless struggle; that *tauheed* would once again be restored to the world through the realization of the *ummah*. It was with that aim in mind that Shari'ati developed his theories of state and its responsibility as a resounding critique of the Pahlavi state.

# 4

# The Purpose of Political Order: The State or the People?

The discourse on power and authority in the late Qajar and Pahlavi eras was preoccupied predominantly with the conduct of the state: what should its form be in order to be most effective? To what extent should power and authority be focused in the person of a ruler? How far should checks and balances be institutionalized to prevent the temptations of despotism? Many of the key players in the public life of Iran—statesmen, politicians, bureaucrats, journalists, thinkers, et cetera—took their positions on the manner in which political order should take shape. The urge to think in terms of institutions became especially meaningful after the *mashruteh* movement, as the possibilities of restricting or regulating executive authority began to be realized. During the Pahlavi era, Reza Shah and his son alike explored an additional dimension within this discursive tradition. By testing the limits of executive authority staying within the bounds of the institutional logic of constitutionalism, the Pahlavis subverted the *mashruteh* tradition quite successfully, reducing the restrictions on executive authority effectively to a notional level.

The responses to such subversion of the *mashruteh* tradition tended, in turn, to be fairly divergent. While protagonists like Mosaddeq and Bazargan remained committed to the institutional complex envisaged in the 1906 constitution, thinkers like Khomeini and (to an extent) Motahhari considered the prevalent checks direly insufficient precisely because they could be bypassed with such ease. Khomeini's principle of *Vilayat-e Faqih* was not originally intended to take the form of an activist *Rahbar* that it has come to acquire in the Islamic Republic. It was intended to be an additional check on the executive authority that, being rooted in the *immutable* precepts of Islam, could not be easily manipulated or subverted by a despotic authority. In other words, the Islamist alternative envisaged by Khomeini and his disciples involved an imposition of a set of Islamic institutions atop the institutional complex created by the *mashruteh* revolution.

'Ali Shari'ati's approach to the issue of negotiating political dispensations was altogether different. Having once been a part of Mosaddeq's movement, disappointment with Mosaddeq's failure and disenchantment with his compatriots had turned Shari'ati away from institutional politics for the rest of his life.[1] He was dismayed by the manner in which the Pahlavi regime in the post-Mosaddeq era managed to subvert the institutional logic of constitutionalism, and by the manner in which his compatriots fell in line with the changes. Accordingly, the possibilities of institutional politics almost never appeared again on the map of Shari'ati's political thinking.

Moreover, when he resumed his teaching career, joining the Mashhad University upon his return from France, Shari'ati was repeatedly hauled up by the SAVAK, which wanted to keep a tab on him in the light of his anti-regime activities in France.[2] The Mashhad chapter of the SAVAK continued to keep an eye on him, but was generally satisfied with his protestations of innocence. However, the bureau in Tehran was always more suspicious of what he had to say, and required the Mashhad chapter to keep informing upon the lectures he was delivering. At one stage Shari'ati was even required to have his proposed lectures vetted before their delivery.[3] Thus, Shari'ati always had the possibility of losing his job hanging over his head, which, given his financial condition, made him behave with caution.

Shari'ati, thus, was neither willing nor able to come up with any direct criticism of the Pahlavi regime that could jeopardize his career as a teacher. In the courses he offered at Mashhad University, and in the lectures he began to deliver in cities like Abadan, Tehran, and Tabriz as his popularity grew, Shari'ati adopted an indirect approach instead. He developed a critique not of the Pahlavi regime, but of political order as a normative category. He refrained from even entering the debate regarding the nature of the state and its institutions that was then raging in Iran. He emphasized instead the human element and seemed to argue that whether a government is good or bad depends on the intentions and conduct of the people who drive it forward, not the institutional parameters they work within. This fed into his general understanding of *tauheed*, implying that regardless of the *form* of government involved, the direction and intentions of the government would determine the character of governance. If the rulers promote justice and equity, the order promotes *tauheed*; if the rulers hinder these, they promote *shirk*.

Adopting a normative approach, the questions Shari'ati raised and sought to address were quite different from those addressed by many of his contemporaries. His concern was *what* should governments do, not *how* should they do it. In this, Shari'ati broke with the predominantly state-centric thinking about politics that characterized modern Iran, and prima facie returned to the emphases that dominated the premodern Islamic approach in political thinking. But, despite this shift in emphasis, the nature of concerns addressed by Shari'ati makes his political thinking distinctively modern.

## The Vision of an Islamic Order: *Ummah* and *Imamat*

Shari'ati's lectures at the University of Mashhad and later at the *Hosseiniyeh-ye Ershad* were purposefully not devised as overtly political in their content, to elude the watchful eyes of the SAVAK. In the course of his lectures at *Ershad,* Shari'ati's discussions about *ummah* and *Imamat* (Imamate, lit. leadership) began to challenge many of the core elements of the standard assumptions of Shi'i political theorists. The hostile repercussion such discussions began to elicit from the *'ulema* made the SAVAK see Shari'ati as a stick with which to beat the *'ulema*. Hence, the growing popularity of Shari'ati's lectures did not immediately bring the Shah's forces down on to *Ershad*. Given the elbow room, however, Shari'ati successfully devised a vision of an Islamic order around the notions of *ummah* and *Imamat,* which, while at variance with the traditional understanding of these terms explicated by the *'ulema,* also ended up feeding into the critique of the Pahlavi regime.

Belief in *Imamat* is supposed to be one of the cardinal features of the faith *(usul al-din)* in *Ithna 'Ashari* Shi'ism. This involves the belief that the Prophet's political authority was meant to be delegated to the Prophet's cousin 'Ali ibn Abi Talib and his descendants through the line of his wife and the daughter of the Prophet, Fatima. Although the Qur'an does not accept the notion of Original sin, several of its verses describe man as sinful, oppressive, and ignorant. In *Surat al-Ahzab* it says that man accepted trusteeship of Creation because he is unjust and ignorant.[4] Shi'i hermeneutics take this to denote that man is essentially fallible, therefore incapable of handling the trusteeship of Creation on his own.[5] While man is engaged in a "ceaseless struggle to develop and advance towards perfection," "unbridled and unholy desires" too exist in man that prevent him from attaining it.[6] Thus, to redeem itself from its own dark and wicked side, mankind needs a personage who, because of his spiritual superiority, has realized the essence of all laws, one who while fully engaged in the struggle has never once succumbed to deviation or temptation. Such individuals are *masoum* (infallible/impeccable) and they alone are worthy and capable of leading men on the *sabil al-mustaqim* (the straight path) leading to God/Truth.

The *Ithna 'Ashari* Shi'i believe that the Prophet, his daughter Fatima, and the 12 Imams are the *Chahardah-ye Masoum* (the Impeccable Fourteen), whose intervention on behalf of the fallible humanity was meant to be the instrument of mankind's redemption.[7]

As with every other aspect of Islam that he chose to comment upon, Shari'ati refused to settle for a literalist reading of either *ummah* or *Imamat*. In one of his earlier lectures at *Ershad* in early 1969, Shari'ati expounded in detail what he believed the two notions signified. Instead of the standard understanding of *ummah* as being the Muslim community in general, he argued *ummah* was not any real order that exists, rather the standard of a societal and political order that Muslims have to attain. He took the *Ithna 'Ashari* Shi'i contention of mankind's relentless struggle with its own baser side, and used it to argue that only by succeeding in this struggle would Muslims be able to attain *ummah*. For him the aim was simple, even though very difficult to attain:

> [T]he object of the human individual is not *budan* (to be), it is *shudan* (to become); *ummat* is not to live free and happy, but to speed in the right direction, not being well rather being [which itself] is great; economy is not the end, it is [merely] the means; freedom is not the ideal, it is the necessary means for the attainment of the ideal. *Ummat* is a society that requires no terrestrial location; *ummat* is a society that is not founded on the impermanent foundations of blood and soil... *Ummat* is the expression [denoting] a society where individuals, under a great leadership, feel with their blood, faith and their lives about the issues of progress and evolution of the society and the individual.[8]

Shari'ati argued that the very meaning of *Imamat* is latent within the connotation of *ummah*, for *Imamat* is an expression denoting the direction of *ummah*—"there can be no *ummah* without *Imamat*."[9] However, while this conformed to the Shi'i requirement of belief in *Imamat*, the subtle nuances of Shari'ati's arguments were clear for anyone who chose to read him carefully. Shari'ati was suggesting that *Imamat* is necessary to attain the level of *ummah*; hence, the *Imamat* is a means to another end. Also, Shari'ati somehow avoided addressing the concept of *masoumiyyat* (infallibility) directly, leaving behind only an indication that infallibility would have to measure up to the requirements of *ummah*—that is, if a leadership does not help the attainment of the ideal of *ummah*, then such leadership is not intrinsically infallible by virtue of descent from a particular family.

It was in this context that Shari'ati took one of his rarest stands on representative politics, which he seldom clarified in any greater detail. Responding to a query of some of his students at *Ershad* in 1969 regarding the Sunni principle of *showra* (election) of rulers as against the Shi'i principle of *visayat* (trusteeship), Shari'ati subtly expressed his support for the former in modern times. He argued that in the early days of Islam, when the meaning of Islam was not clear to most Muslims, they needed guidance from those entrusted with preserving the faith and its values—hence, the Shi'i concept of *visayat*. However, once Muslims become more aware of their faith and its values, the trusteeship of the faith devolves upon the community as a whole. The *ummah* then has the responsibility to elect its own leaders to execute that trust—hence, the Sunni principle of *showra*.[10]

The implication of this argument was reasonably clear. *Ummah* being the ideal form of order in Islam, any order that fell short of that ideal was un-Islamic to the degree it fell short. Since *ummah* under the guidance of the *Imamat* denoted the only legitimate order, any community that had not reached the standards of the *ummah* was ipso facto devoid of the guidance of the *Imamat*, and hence was illegitimate. Thus, a ruling order *(nizamiyyat)* that relied on power *(zor)*, wealth *(zar)*, and religious deception *(tazveer)* was fundamentally devoid of any shred of legitimacy, because not only did it not promote the evolution of the community toward the level of *ummah*, it was actually leading the people in the opposite direction.

### Critique of Political Order: *Nizamiyyat* and *'adalat*

By talking about the history of Islam, Islamic civilization, and the history of human civilization seen through the prism of Islam, Shari'ati was able to develop a powerful critique of political order as it actually existed. The critique he developed was heavily influenced by two different political theories that emerged in two completely different historical settings—the predominant discourse on authority in *Ithna 'Ashari* Shi'ism, and the "orthodox" Marxist position on state, both of which had considerable currency in modern Iran.

Shari'ati's critique was an innovative blend of some cardinal aspects of Islamic political thought, the Shi'i notion of illegitimacy of the state, and Marxian assumptions regarding the state as an instrument of class rule.[11] In the course of his lectures delivered at Mashhad, Tehran, Shiraz, Abadan, Tabriz, et cetera, Shari'ati almost never referred to the category of *daulat* (state) as an embodiment of the dispensation of power in a society; his entire political critique revolved around the notions of *nizamiyyat* (order), *hokumat* (government), and *regime* as counterpoints to what he highlighted as the Islamic categories of *ummah* and *Imamat*. This avoidance of the category of the state implied an assumption that the structural dimension of political systems was less important than the relational dimension, similar to the Marxian position that production relations in every stage of society determine the corresponding form of state. Shari'ati's critique of political order was premised upon the assumption that the only determinant of legitimacy is *'adalat* (justice), which he took to mean equity and dignity of the human individual.

Shari'ati's critique of political order was generally in the form of parables overwhelmingly derived from the cultural world of Islam and the history of Iran. His division of mankind into the *tabaqeh-ye Qabeel* (class of Cain) and the *tabaqeh-ye Habeel* (class of Abel) in order to explain the origin of political order was highly symbolic. Cain's struggle with Abel was over property, but it was not *defense* of a right that was in the natural order of things. Rather, it was waged in order to *violate* the natural scheme by *creating* a new right that was underwritten by violence. Cain's subjugation of Abel was, therefore, a subversion of the natural order. Additionally, the argument was that Cain was not simply appropriating the fruits of his labor as his own (which is the standard defense of the right to private property). His labor had to make use of natural resources to be productive. Since natural resources belong to everyone, the principle of exclusion of such resources from general use was unjust. Thus, the order that came into being with Cain's subjugation of Abel, Shari'ati would argue, was illegitimate *because* it was unjust.

Shari'ati's characterization of the *tabaqeh-ye Qabeel* as a combination of the three forces of *zor, zar,* and *tazveer* was an equally symbolic characterization of the forces of order. Extending the parable into a general philosophy of history, Shari'ati depicted all the ruling orders in historical times as a combination of the three. Unlike the Marxian treatment of economics as the base on which the superstructure of politics is built, Shari'ati saw the three forces of *zor, zar,* and *tazveer* working too closely together for them to be distinguished into base and superstructure; yet, his analysis of the three was somewhat influenced by the Marxian approach.

*Zor* denotes political authority in the form of *nizamiyyat* (order) or *hokumat* (government) that rested on violence—hence the term, which means violence, and its symbol *tegh* (sword). The significance of the use of the term was to underline the factor of compulsion that is intrinsic to the notion of political power. Although Shari'ati never made this argument in as many words, yet his conceptualization of oppression seemed to revolve around the use of violence for the subversion of the natural order. Whenever, therefore, Shari'ati spoke of political power, he almost invariably brought in the category of *istibdad* (despotism/oppression), and cited examples from Iranian regimes known for their brutality and repression—namely, the Turks under Mahmud Ghaznavi and Seljuqs; the Mongols under Chenghiz, Timur, and Hulagu; the Afghans under Nadir

Shah, et cetera. Even when he spoke of rulers who were favorably rated in Iranian history, such as the Safavids, Shari'ati emphasized the fact that their authority was underpinned by violence.[12]

*Zar* denotes the illegitimate power of wealth that divides human society into *tabaqeh* (class), on the basis of possession of wealth—hence its symbol *tala* (gold). In Shari'ati's scheme of things, *zar* did not result in *zor,* rather it flourished only with the patronage of *zor*. Rulers resorted to oppression primarily because only by violation of the natural order of equity could their domination be ensured. *Zar* is, thus, as much the cause as the effect of *zor* because despotism can be sustained only if a small class is willing and able to benefit from such oppression by economically exploiting the rest of the people. Using Islamic terms of reference, Shari'ati spoke of the Umayyads as the archetypal proponents of this connection between political authority derived from violence and supportive of injustice. He indicated that the house of Mu'awiya formed the kernel of a cluster of propertied interests that felt threatened by the egalitarian message of Islam. Accordingly, the propertied interests (i.e., *zar*) made common cause with the forces of violence (i.e., *zor*) and challenged the rule of 'Ali.[13] The manifestation of *zar* took the form of *istismar* (economic exploitation) of one by another—individual, class, people, et cetera. According to Shari'ati, no exploitation could continue unless there was some threat of violence behind it.

*Tazveer* denotes the deception that is carried out in the name of religious authority—hence its symbol *tasbeh* (prayer beads). It relates effectively to the intellectual and ideational legitimacy that a ruling order requires. Shari'ati believed various societies had their own religions and every religion its own messenger(s), and each religion was intended to guide the society concerned to be a just order. But repeatedly in the history of mankind, messengers bearing God's message have chosen to associate with the forces of *zor* and *zar,* thereby subverting an order based on *'adalat* (justice) and legitimating *istibdad*—messengers such as Zoroaster, Mani, Buddha, Confucius, Lao Tse.[14] In the context of Islam and Iran, of the three forms of subversion that the natural order is subjected to, *istihmar* (religious exploitation) invited most of Shari'ati's wrath, because it "enchants" the people to the extent that "a *'rezim-e irteja'i*" (reactionary regime) gets to be founded on the principles of Islam, the *maktab-e inqilabi* (revolutionary school of thought), and political despotism and class exploitation come to ride on the twin legs of *Imamat* (i.e., ideal political order) and *'adalat* (justice).[15]

On the other hand lay the victims of such oppression and exploitation— the masses of people who make up a society, the *tabaqeh-ye Habeel* (class of Abel). The sword of the executioner (symbolizing *istibdad*/despotism) creates the conditions of oppression in which the owners of resources (symbolizing *istismar*/exploitation) compel the masses to create wealth and plenty. The masses are discouraged by the *rouhaniyat* (spiritual classes/clergy, symbolizing *istihmar* / deception) from resisting such oppression as God is supposed to have ordained all the powers that be, and besides nothing in this world is of any value, therefore oppression is not worth resisting.

In almost all societies around the world down the course of history, Shari'ati argued, order tended to be understood in terms of property *(isti'dad, darayi)* that creates a class hierarchy buttressed by violence carried out by a power with some claims to legitimacy. Civilization is founded on this notion of order. The ruling classes, representing the community as a whole, fashion into being an orderly mode of collective existence that is called *tamaddun* (civilization). Even the cradles of humanity, the classical civilizations of Greece, Persia, Egypt, China, India were all products of such hierarchical societies. Those great civilizations of the past were "huge mountains that man has carved with his own hands and fingers... These were, in my mind, the greatest heritage of my beloved humanity."[16]

But, Shari'ati stops to inquire, whose achievements were these? What did such civilizations achieve? Using the particular example of the pyramids, Shari'ati raised the question, were these achievements of the Pharaohs who lay buried underneath, in their hope of defeating their own mortality? Or, of the "thirty thousand slaves who worked for thirty years," carrying "eight hundred million stones" from a distance of nearly 1,000 kilometers and died in the process?[17] Shari'ati was convinced that "[a]ll of the great monuments which civilizations have built throughout history have been built upon the bones of [the masses]."[18] It is therefore the masses *(tudeha)* that are the architects of human civilization in all its splendor, not the ruling classes. Yet, ruling classes manage to exclude them from politics, depriving the *tudeh-ye siyasatzidayi* (depoliticized masses) of justice. Hence, Shari'ati argues, an order that is based on *hokumat-e zor* (rule by force) and *hakimiyyat-e zar* (power of wealth) is by its very nature unjust.[19]

In a world characterized by unjust political orders, Shari'ati argued, Islam had once aspired to establish justice.

> Today we define the principle of *'adalat* (justice) by saying "God is just, and the oppressor is not," and then let it pass, whereas *'adalat* is one of the features of God, and for that very reason one of the features of His creation, and Islam, founded on the principle of justice, has a special worldview.
>
> When I say *'adalat* is one of the features of God, it means that *'adalat* is one of the foundational principles of existence, and one of the fundamental

features of human life, hence it must be one of the basic premises of our society....

Islam is the school dealing with social issues that gives indication for the accomplishment of aims and rules that we call faith, and for the gradual evolution of mankind and achieving justice in human society.[20]

Shari'ati argued that the Qur'an was addressed primarily to the poor and the oppressed.[21] Influenced by his mentor Massignon's argument about the essential continuities between the Judean, Christian, and Islamic traditions, unlike any other of the prominent Islamic thinkers of modern times Shari'ati emphasized that "Islam is not a new religion because, in fact, throughout history, there has only been one religion."[22] The Prophet himself had proclaimed that while every prophet was appointed to establish this universal religion with reference to the particular contexts, its cardinal principle was simply *submission* (i.e., Islam) to the will of Allah. The Islamic movement was related to other movements that were "fought to free people." "The prophets stood up against the powerful, the wealthy, and the deceivers. In this way they demonstrated their unity of vision: one spiritual struggle, one religion, and one slogan throughout the whole of human history in all domains, for all times and all generations."[23]

Shari'ati pointed out that the group that gathered around Muhammad in Mecca was among the "most debased elements of the society," "the slaves, the tortured, hungry and belittled," who had been convinced by religion, science, philosophy, poetry, and art that "their fate was to serve their masters. They believed that they existed solely to experience suffering, to carry heavy loads, and to go hungry so that others might enjoy themselves."[24] The exploited and the oppressed, Shari'ati argued, found in Islam the only beacon of hope.

The Prophet of Islam was appointed to complete the movement which has existed throughout history in opposition to deception, falsehood, polytheism, discord, hypocrisy, aristocracy and class differences. This was made a goal of the struggle by the announcement that *all humanity is of one race, one source, one nature and of one God.* Equality was declared for all; and with philosophical disputation as well fighting against the economically powerful regime, *social equity* was upheld [emphasis mine].[25]

The order that the Prophet founded at Medina was an embodiment of this sense of equity and justice. It did not distinguish between the rich and the poor, aristocrat and slave—hence, the first *muadhdhin / muezzin* was an Abyssinian slave called Bilal.[26] The Prophet instructed Muslims to shorten their long-flowing robes and to trim their beards—the two signs marking the status of aristocrats. The Prophet even frequently rode a donkey bareback, instead of a properly saddled horse, in order to break down the symbols of class in Arab society. Subsequently, when Imam 'Ali assumed leadership of the *ummah,* he ordered all existing pay scales to be cancelled, and began paying equal salaries to everyone, whether the highest ranking military officer or his slave, since both were waging the same war in the defense of the faith.[27] Most importantly, as Shari'ati said, an ideal order is one where poverty is inexistent. As Shari'ati tells us, once, while talking about the essence of Islam, Abu Dhar is supposed to have said: "When poverty enters a home, religion exits through the window."[28]

The emphasis on equity was central to Shari'ati's notion of the ideal order, the *ummah.* It is one of the cardinal principles of the Islamic faith that the order the Prophet established was exemplary. Some Muslim theorists have subsequently argued that the political order set up by the Prophet means the prophetic mission was wedded to the political mission of Islam; hence religion and state are inseparable. Others argue that the Prophet had no political mandate; hence the fledgling state had no necessary bearing on the faith itself. Either way, theorists of political Islam have chosen to accept the exemplary value of the *ummah* that was set up at Medina. Shari'ati contended that the *ummah* of Medina under the Prophet and later Imam 'Ali, symbolized opposition to the creation or maintenance of economic, social, and political hierarchies of previously accumulated wealth. The Islamic *ummah* considers every individual at his/her true worth, as a creation of God. In an order thus based on *dad-girasti* (equity), political oppression *(istibdad)* and economic exploitation *(istismar)* would neither have any place nor any need.

The equitable character of the *ummah* made it an embodiment of *'adalat* (justice), thus fulfilling the principal purpose of political life by providing for an orderly conduct of human sociability. Shari'ati would seem to argue that the *ummah* founded by the Prophet was an example for Muslims to follow, not because it was founded by the Prophet, but because it was founded on the principle of *'adalat.* From this position premised upon the principles of politics, Shari'ati reworked the idea of political order not only in terms of Islamic politics as a whole, but also the notions of *ummah* and *Imamat* that had greater resonance in the Shi'i political milieu of Iran.

At a subtler level, Shari'ati was arguing toward a rationale for the purpose of negotiation with order, which was at odds with the logic pursued by the Pahlavi establishment. The Pahlavis had begun by setting forth the notion of the state as the primary agency for the development of the country, and they defined development almost exclusively in terms of industrial development with extensive foreign involvement. Shari'ati questioned the assumption that the state, or the ruling classes that direct its activities, automatically works for the well-being of the people. He argued that an ideal political order emphasizes on the promotion of equity in society. Thus, when an economy develops without benefiting its people, the state can be said to have failed in its primary objective.

**The Critique of Legitimacy: *Tazveer* in a Modern Context**

Shari'ati's critique of political authority had a particular resonance in the late 1960s. During 1963–70, by virtue of a revision of electoral laws associated with the White Revolution, a generation of younger and less experienced technocrats succeeded in replacing older statesmen. The government of Hasan 'Ali Mansur was made up of western educated technocrats who had just returned from America or Europe, and were generally considered to be unfamiliar and out of touch with their own country, with no respect for local culture or traditions. The Mansur government won considerable notoriety by supporting decisions upholding imperialist interests—especially the grant of extraterritoriality to U.S. military personnel in Iran in 1963, providing the immediate issue against which Khomeini raised the banner of rebellion. From the mid-1960s, therefore, concerns about Pahlavi proximity to the United States began to change into concern for the growing influence of imperialist and colonialist forces in Iran once again.

Mindful of SAVAK surveillance, Shari'ati refrained from directly criticizing Pahlavi proximity to the imperialist forces of the west. Instead, from reasonably early on he began to assault the very notion of legitimacy that the Pahlavis had tried to build as the architects of modern Iran. He put the regime to a simple but exacting test. In the Pahlavi march toward progress in the direction of a strong modern state, was Iran coming any nearer to becoming an *ummah*?

Shari'ati presented his critique in an innocuous manner, conveying the impression that he meant to address a dilemma that he seemed to share with many of his compatriots. On the one hand Iranian society was being materially transformed at a rapid pace by its encounter with the modern world. On the other hand was the manner in which the meaning of *being* an Iranian was changing so fast that none of the traditionally cherished values seemed immune to the process of change. The dilemma was whether to be modern or traditional in the circumstances. As in many other developing societies, in Iran this particular dilemma elicited positions on either extreme as much as those that sought to blend some aspects of modernity with some of tradition. Being a normative thinker, though,

Shari'ati abjured any discussion of the "conflicting" forms of tradition and modernity, and tackled instead the question of what really constituted modernity and tradition, and whether there was any substantive conflict between the two.

Shari'ati began with the predominant assumptions about the tradition-modernity binary. One the one hand he ranged the features generally associated with the forces of "tradition"—religious orthodoxy, social conservatism, asceticism, piety, mysticism; on the other he took stock of the signifiers of "modernity"—irreligion, social liberalism, industrialism, consumerism, materialism, nationalism. Then, in a very innovative manner he raised the question—what makes these ideas fundamental to human life? Shari'ati's answer was rather straightforward: issues or ideas were not fundamental in themselves; it was their context of space and time that *made* the issues fundamental. As he put it:

> For theories on social issues... logical consistency does not suffice. The context of the argument has to be taken into account. A valid and true statement expressed at an improper time and place will be futile. Conversely, an unsubstantiated argument may be of significance in a particular atmosphere.[29]

Shari'ati argued that an issue, an idea, or an approach could be extremely dynamic and progressive in one setting, and completely enervating in another. His preferred example to highlight this value-free character of ideas was central to the notion of modernity in Pahlavi Iran—nationalism. He argued that toward the end of the so-called Middle Ages in Europe, nationalism helped emancipate European society from the yoke of the Popes, who had used Christianity to dominate Europe—hence nationalism had performed a dynamic and progressive function at that conjuncture. But he cautioned that

> [n]ationalism is like a dagger which in the face of colonialism, carves up ... a continent which faces a common destiny and thus should be united.

> In Algeria in the 1950s, in order to divide the people and in turn to inflict a greater disaster in North Africa, the colonial powers propagated the progressive views of thinkers such as Rousseau, Voltaire and Morris Dubarre, which are scientific and emphasize nationalism. The central thesis of nationalism that each nation should have its own state was used to divide the Arabs and Berbers, who were united until then by their belief in Islam—thus they became victims of French colonialism. Now, in place of fighting the common enemy, Arab and Berber nationalists were fighting one another.[30]

This does not mean, Shari'ati pointed out, that nationalism is necessarily pernicious in the context of the developing or colonial world. It can also be used meaningfully in the context of the colonial world to refute what he calls "false bonds" and "fake common denominators" such as humanism, and develop anticolonial fronts, as in Asia, Africa, and Latin America. Nationalism in the Third World, Shari'ati argued, was "even more progressive than Marxism. It has taken the leadership away from official Marxism in the struggle for independence."[31]

Similarly, Shari'ati addressed the issue of industrialism in a backhanded manner. He traced the origin of industrialism back to the dawn of the scientific attitude in Europe, using Francis Bacon as his point of entry. Praising Bacon highly for his advocacy of doing away with superstition and his promotion of science as a means of understanding nature and improving the condition of human lives, Shari'ati made the case that scientific knowledge was a superior form of knowledge not because it was *scientific,* but because it had significance and a resonance in human lives. He argued that Bacon served the people of his era by liberating science, reason, and the masses from the restrictions of the Church. "If Bacon were alive today, however, he would have to say almost the opposite of what he said then."[32] Contemporary Europe, he argued, was wrong in believing it was stepping into Bacon's shoes by suggesting that science should focus solely on economic and material production, and that human potential should be used to promote consumerism. Such mindless consumerism results in a situation where "all human dimensions and potentials have become restricted and limited by the production of goods, excess in consumption, and the freedom of sex," and society is in need of a savior like Sartre.[33]

The principal argument that Shari'ati seemed to make was that approaching the tradition-modernity binary was a case of *awadi-ye geraftanha* (confusing the issues). Neither the concerns of traditionalism nor those of modernity had any intrinsic worth devoid of the context in which such concerns were raised. As a case in point Shari'ati cited the issue of sexual freedom, an issue that had dominated Iran since the laws on veiling of women during the Reza Shah period, and that had gained a new resonance with the extension of suffrage rights to women under the White Revolution.

> [T]oday, there are thinkers and authors who try to convince parents and youngsters that the cause of the misery in Muslim societies lies in sexual restrictions. If these barriers are removed and men and women interact freely, they argue, Eastern societies will be free from all miseries... While parents resist and the young generation insists on this issue, the society is gripped by war over sex. Parents consider sexual freedom the root of all

misery, while their sons and daughters consider it as a cause of salvation, progress, civilization, and freedom... In reality, the war of sexual freedom, which suddenly has become significant in Africa, Asia, and especially in the Islamic societies, is a sham to prevent the war that ought to be taking place, the anti-colonialist war. This war of sexual freedom is waged in order to prevent the waging of a struggle which would be dangerous to the powers that be in the world. Sexual freedom is used to... discourage [the youth] from thinking and pursuing economic and political freedom.[34]

What is interesting in all these instances highlighting the modern versus the traditional is that Shari'ati did not state his own position. His sole concern was to highlight that the nature of preoccupation with the tradition-modernity binary in contemporary Iran was essentially superfluous because it did not address the really serious issues that affected the people. He identified the triad of *zor-zar-tazveer* as the root cause for this confounding of issues, and emphasized heavily on the element of *tazveer*.

\* \* \*

According to Shari'ati *zor*, *zar*, and *tazveer* are symbolic of the roles performed in a society, rather than of the forces that perform them. Hence, *zor* denotes not simply the ruler, but any power that can physically coerce other people to do something; *zar* denotes not simply the exploitative merchants, but any agent of economic exploitation ranging from the slave owner right down to the colonial order; most importantly, *tazveer* denotes not simply the religious clergy but any class of intellectuals—religious or otherwise—that engages with the work of legitimating any hegemony—political, economic, social, ideational—that goes against the interests of the people.

Looking at the context of his own times, instead of attacking the Pahlavi regime directly, Shari'ati situated the transformation of Iran within its larger global context in order to formulate his critique. Growing up in a country where history made the people deeply resentful of foreign economic hegemony, Shari'ati's audience found a ready appeal in his attack on colonialism. Shari'ati's familiarity with the anticolonial and liberation struggles of the Third World from his days in France convinced him that economic exploitation of the Third World by the developed *gharb* (west) was the real cause of misery for millions of Africans, Asians, and Latin Americans. This fitted in neatly with his primary diagnosis of *istismar* (economic exploitation). Accordingly, he identified colonialism and imperialism as the two dominant forms of *istismar* in the modern world—an analytical motif that appears in Shari'ati's lectures time and again. He repeatedly referred to Iran as a colonized society because it was subject to systematic economic penetration by foreign powers—even though it was never colonized, strictly speaking.

Shari'ati argued that Iran, quite like any other economically backward society of the Third World, had been inveigled into the trap of "modernity" to "confuse the issues," in order to facilitate the process of *istismar*. The modernity that the west exported was the front for an exploitative order along with a base materialistic spirit and a philosophy of consumerism. "Equipped with the power of science, philosophy, technology, art, literature, sociology, history and psychology, and armed with every means of making war, peace, and politics," the west utilizes "every possible trick and inhuman plan to transform countries the world over into market places for goods and products. To that end, all human beings must become consumer animals, and all nations must be stripped of their authenticity."[35] The cultural baggage of modernity was exported by the west because "historical, scientific, psychological and sociological experience has taught the colonialists that before a society becomes incapable of 'economic productivity' and before it becomes a complete and permanent consumer of materials produced by others, it must cease its own intellectual activity."[36] The colonialists, he argued, had early on "identified religion as the biggest barrier in the way of cultural and political penetration among other nations" because religion frequently tends to impede such a reduction of man from the status of "god's creatures" to an economic animal.

> Colonial powers, particularly at their early stages, under the guise of "attacking fanaticism" attacked history, and using the pretext of "hacking away at superstition and old beliefs," assaulted tradition in order to produce a people without history, without tradition, without culture, without religion, and without any form of identity. In the face of colonialism, people have become like apes. They take pride in practicing "extreme modernism in the form of new consumerism" and deny their own cultural tradition by displaying exuberant imitation and assimilation. . . .
>
> It was for this purpose that as soon as the bourgeoisie established its foothold in Europe . . . in the sixteenth and seventeenth centuries, in the name of open-mindedness and scientism, it began opposing religion. When it set foot in the colonization phase and set foot in the East, its first aim was to attack the great religions under the guise of nationalism, liberalism, modernism and humanism.[37]

For anyone who chose to notice, here was a clear denunciation of the agenda of mindless modernization that was being pursued in Iran for the previous 100 years. The forces of *zor* and *zar* came together facilitating colonialist exploitation. But a far more serious charge was leveled against the force of *tazveer* that collaborated in this enterprise within the Iranian society. He believed that the western bourgeoisie wanted to eliminate religion from among the colonized elite simultaneously with encouraging the most corrupt possible form of religion among the colonized masses "so as to narcotize and benumb them with illusions, imaginary thoughts and foolish superstitions." Thus, colonial society became the battleground for a "sham war" in which two sides within that society—the westernized elite and the traditional clergy—fought each other in a battle that ultimately aided the cause of the colonizers.

The elite, enamored of the west, "assume the role of the enlightened *(monavver al-fikr)*" and advocate modernization of the traditional society along the lines of the west.

> Their function is to dispense hand-picked and selected European thoughts and ideas, and disseminate the western lifestyle, social relations and behavioral patterns. [They] are supposed to make people "modern" and assimilate the elites and the progressive and educated youth of non-European societies into European culture inside their own traditional societies, and hence establish a base for western penetration and arrival...
>
> The colonial movement of "assimilation" which was set under the phony titles such as enlightenment, modernism and progress, started by stipulating that the primary condition of industrialization, or becoming progressive like Europe and acquiring the new scientific outlook, was to rebel against one's own history and culture...
>
> The main function of this pseudo-European generation was... to act as a guide for those thieves who have stopped killing people so as to have a free hand to rob them.[38]

For a casual listener, Shari'ati's assessment of the intellectual encounter with modernity seemed to be taking a leaf out of Jalal Al-e Ahmad's *gharbzadegi*. However, Shari'ati's understanding of the west was more sophisticated than that of Al-e Ahmad. Shari'ati was aware that the traditional societies came to know of the west only through the mediation of the pseudo-Europeans, or the *gharbzadeh*s, but what they learnt about "was a vulgar modernism and civilization that did not exist even in Europe." That is to say, the people were so "struck by the west" that they did not even realize that they were not transplanting what they thought was a superior civilization, rather they were simply being tricked with a façade that left them poorer, materially as much as spiritually.

Unlike Al-e Ahmad, moreover, Shari'ati also looked at the other protagonist of *tazveer* in a society like Iran. He found arraigned on the other side of "the sham war" the forces of conventional religion where "all the faces are of the saints, all the costumes are religious costumes, and the conversations are centered around God, the hereafter, heaven, hell, good deeds, sin, revelation, the prophet, the Qur'an, *Imamat,* holiness, spirituality, piety, morality, asceticism ... and turning away from this world's material allurements." Shari'ati argued that the role of these forces of conventional religion, the traditional clergy, was to convince the people that this world is nothing compared with the other world that will come at the *akhir-e zaman* (End of Days). By preparing the people for the "eventuality" of the next world, they encouraged the people to disregard the "unpleasant" realities of this world. Of the traditional clergy, he said:

> Theirs is a dialectical role. These actors must destroy religion by propagating it! Under the guise of observing and honoring religious rites, in the name of glorifying great religious personalities, and behind the façade of seeking blessings and sanctification from the Holy Qur'an, these actors hide the true essence of the Qur'an and the true teachings of the leaders of Islam by preventing the people from understanding them. While maintaining the form and the content, they want to eliminate religion by turning it face to face against itself with the help of imported anti-religious thought.[39]

In thus criticizing the traditional clergy, Shari'ati pitched his critique of *tazveer* at a higher notch than Al-e Ahmad's *gharbzadegi*. Shari'ati accounted for the success of colonial penetration and *gharbzadegi* not simply through the fact that some people were dazzled by the material superiority of "western modernity," but also because others who were not dazzled by the west were benumbed by "oriental traditionalism." Thus, the binary of tradition and modernity that characterized the discourse of modern Iran, Shari'ati seemed to argue, was a typical example of "confusing the issues." The discourse was in effect a handmaiden of western capitalist exploitation, where "modernity" served to allure the people toward material comfort, and "tradition" consoled those who failed to attain such comfort with the promise of the next world. Torn between the two, the people were unable to comprehend the basic inequity inherent in the system thus brought into being.

Shari'ati was careful to avoid any direct allusion to the Pahlavi establishment, hence while speaking of contemporary Iran he spoke of *tazveer* as the discourse on development and *zar* as colonial and capitalist exploitation, but there was no mention of *zor* in the modern context. Nevertheless, it is possible to reconstruct for oneself the factor of *zor* from Shari'ati's analysis of *zar* and *tazveer*. The treatment of *tazveer* as simply the apparatus providing intellectual legitimacy to a political order was certainly suggestive enough. If both "traditionalism" and "modernism" were essentially contributing to economic exploitation, then a political order could not be working against such exploitation if it sought its intellectual legitimacy from either or both of such body of ideas. Hence—and this Shari'ati left unsaid in his earlier lectures—regimes that derived their legitimacy from either the traditionalist standpoint (such as the Qajars) or the modernist one (such as the Pahlavis) were equally illegitimate, because neither addressed the real needs and interests of the people.

### The Response to Shari'ati's Critique of Political Order

Shari'ati deliberately floated his critique of political order to provoke response from a youth that was either apathetic or cowering before the state machinery. In order to do this, accordingly, he spoke in a language that was innovative enough to appeal to the youth to come out of their apathy, and yet not alien enough to fail to strike a chord among his audience.

The student bodies that Shari'ati addressed in Mashhad, and then later in Tehran and elsewhere, had roughly similar profiles. His audience at Mashhad University (and then other centers of higher learning in other parts of Iran) consisted primarily of students from the state-run modern educational system in the province of Khorasan (and other provinces, as the case may be in accordance with the venue), mostly urban in origin but not exclusively so. First and foremost were those students who were working hard for a career, for whom religion was essentially a private affair, prompting them to refrain from political activism. A fair number of such students came from a background similar to Shari'ati's—that is, people who grew up with a deep attachment to the social and religious values strongly reinforced within the devoutly religious familial circle. There were also people from *bazaari* families, which for historical reasons remained closely connected to the societal network of the *'ulema* and thus resented the agenda of secularization of the public space. A reasonably large number of the urban students were also inspired by the socialist ideology, especially in its Tudeh variety, and had come to share a pronounced disrespect for religion and the religious establishment. In Tehran University, particularly, Shari'ati's constituency changed somewhat with the inclusion of a large number of people, western educated and attuned to western modes of thinking to the extent that they set correspondence with western standards as the touchstone for anything, people who were suspicious of religion and had converted to the Pahlavi agenda of modernity.

To such a diverse audience, Shari'ati's persona proved reasonably acceptable. For the modernized, urban component of his audience, he was a Sorbonne educated academic, always clad in western attire, smoking heavily and talking of sociology and the philosophy of history, Marxism, and existentialism. Shari'ati was a world removed from the traditional *'ulema* with their ostensible religiosity. For the more traditional audience, his usage of Islamic idioms and terms of reference made his arguments more acceptable as against others affiliated with the "godless" Tudeh. Shari'ati intended to, and did, bridge the social divide between the more traditional and modern segments of Iran's youth. This was also the reason why Shari'ati elicited severe responses from both leftist and Islamist ideologues, who believed he was trespassing in their respective territories.

The leftist criticism of Shari'ati was primarily in terms of his deviation from the doctrinaire brand of Marxism-Leninism. Among the earliest of responses was that of an anti-Tudeh Marxist and a close friend of Shari'ati, Ali Akbar Akbari, who wrote an article in the monthly *Hirmand* in 1968, followed by another in the leftist literary magazine *Faslaha-ye Sabz,* and finally a book in 1969. Evoking standard Marxist-Leninist arguments on the origin of classes, class struggle, historical materialism, the development of imperialism, the deterministic role of productive forces in explaining sociohistorical developments, Akbari sought to expose Shari'ati's methodological and theoretical shortcomings.[40] Shari'ati accessed Marxist ideas largely in the form of Persian translations of Marxist literature (fairly easily available in Iran from the mid-1920s) and those in French that he had used both while he was in France and upon his return to Iran; works of Iranian Marxists also constituted an important medium for his understanding of Marxism. It is doubtful, though, whether he ever accessed either Marx or Engels directly in either French or Persian translation, and he may or may not have come across some of Lenin's writings in their Persian translation.[41] It was as a student at the Centre of Propagation of Islamic Truths and at Mashhad University, while engaging with students inspired by Marx and/or associated with the Tudeh, that Shari'ati probably learnt the most about Marxism. The Tudeh, like socialists in most other Third World societies, found the positions of the Third International, calling for a social revolution akin to the Bolshevik Revolution of 1917, more relevant to their contexts. Accordingly, Shari'ati's understanding of Marxism was characterized by a doctrinaire position premised upon class conflict and the necessity of class struggle that seemed largely ignorant or unmindful of revisionist tendencies in Marxism. Hence, from the standpoint of a well-read Marxist, Shari'ati's theoretical and methodological basis could really not have been very sound. Yet if Shari'ati disappointed orthodox Marxists by "failing to understand" Marxism-Leninism, the Marxists disappointed Shari'ati no less in the initial stages by completely missing the areas of convergence between their mode of thinking and his. Hence, the Tudeh and its sympathizers initially branded Shari'ati as "an agent of the US, the CIA and the Pahlavi regime," and accused him of obstructing the imminent communist revolution in Iran by advocating the cause of the Islamists.[42] By 1971–72, as the revolutionary socialist character of Shari'ati's teachings became clear, his critics from the hard-left chose to revise their initial impression, and Marxist antipathy toward Shari'ati declined markedly.

The 'ulema were slow in responding at the initial stages, but their response was much more vicious when it came.[43] Shari'ati's initial clerical interlocutor was Ansari-ye Zanjani, who set the tone of the stand taken by later interlocutors as well (such as Morteza Motahhari), questioning Shari'ati's grasp over Islamic issues by attacking many of his unconventional readings of Islamic legends. He rejected Shari'ati's accusation that the 'ulema were hidebound and narrow-minded and reminded him that the clergy were defenders of the faith and acted according to the dictates of Islam. Zanjani accused Shari'ati of being "both ignorant and irreligious," and subverting Shi'ism by importing Sunni and socialist ideas. Shari'ati was even accused of being in the service of the Saudi Wahhabis, regurgitating old and deviant ideas (although Zanjani never specified which these were). The real thrust of clerical opposition to Shari'ati, however, came with Motahhari in the early 1970s.

The response of the state in 1967–69 was considerably less vicious than it was to become later. Because of the antipathy Shari'ati seemed to generate among the Marxists and the 'ulema, the SAVAK in Mashhad considered Shari'ati a useful counterpoint to the development of anti-regime ideology, and Shari'ati successfully assuaged all their suspicions initially, till the SAVAK in Tehran looked into his lectures closely and decided in 1969 to impose a ban on his public lectures.[44] The ban was subsequently revoked, but Shari'ati was asked to have his lectures vetted beforehand by the SAVAK. His standing with the regime, however, changed significantly after 1971 as he became more openly critical of it.

\* \* \*

Shari'ati's critique of political orders was developed at a time when the general condition of Iran did not seem altogether bad. The White Revolution had more-or-less effected the changes that the regime wanted, expanding the scope of state intervention in the economy; the burgeoning oil receipts enhanced the regime's independence from the people in the fashion of an archetypal rentier state.

The high level of state intervention, however, limited the operation of market forces. Contrary to the claims made by the regime, state development policies served particular rather than general interests—resulting in increasingly widening economic inequality and burgeoning inflation. Government policies toward industry, agriculture, and commerce consistently favored the upper classes over the working classes, urban over rural, and large modern ventures over smaller traditional ones. As government policies enriched only a minority of the people, the number of people who were discontented with the Pahlavis increased steadily all through the late 1960s.[45]

By the time Shari'ati began lecturing at the University of Mashhad and then at the *Hosseiniyeh-ye Ershad,* the frenzied pace of state-led changes in Iran's economy had begun to generate a broader set of social repercussions. Iran's population had grown from roughly 19 million in 1956 to about 25.8 million in 1966; by 1976 the figure was past 33.6 million. The population living in cities grew proportionately faster: Iran's urban population grew from 31 percent in 1956 to about 39 percent in 1966, climbing all the way up to 47 percent by 1976. In the 1970s, Tehran alone accounted for approximately a fifth of the total urban population in the country, growing at a rate of around 4.2 percent per year since 1966 to reach a figure of 4.5 million by 1976.[46] This upswing in the urban population was due in part to migration from the countryside in the wake of the White Revolution, and in part owing to the expansion of economic horizons in the urban areas as a result of state-led industrialization. The size of the urban working class grew rapidly, and the number of white-collar working population also increased proportionately. The government's efforts to accommodate this sort of rapid urbanization proved utterly inadequate. Health care, housing, and basic hygiene facilities put urban infrastructure under a major strain. Thus, notwithstanding western images of Iran's phenomenal development, the country was gradually moving into a crisis zone as early as the late 1960s.

It was in this context that Shari'ati's critique of political order began to draw attention. As some of his associates recall, initially his lectures at the University of Mashhad were attended by students who opted for his course; then other students from the university followed, impressed by what they heard from their fellow students, and finally, by what they read. As these students began to move back and forth between Mashhad, Tehran, and other cities of the country, Shari'ati's fame began to spread and invitations started pouring in for lectures to be delivered at various sorts of venues. By 1969–70 Shari'ati became a regular feature in the intellectual landscape of Tehran, appealing as much to Islamists as to socialists owing to his critique of political authority. This was also the time when Shari'ati became more openly radical in his opinions, inviting opposition from the clerical community and the orthodox Marxists and eventually being subjected to repression by the state itself as the revolutionary repercussions of his ideas began to be fully comprehended in the early 1970s.

# 5

# Sovereignty as Responsibility: *Mazhab-e Aitraz*

Shari'ati's critique of political authority revolved primarily around the issues of responsibility and sovereignty whenever such political authority was constituted. His standpoint, that the purpose of political community was to promote the well-being of the people inevitably carried a corollary with it—any order that failed to perform that crucial function of ensuring general well-being is ipso facto illegitimate. But, he argued, one of the general experiences of history (as indeed one of the basic assumptions of Islamic politics) happens to be that people prefer an unjust order to absolute disorder, hence the large majority of people seldom venture forth to assume the responsibility of ushering in change. Shari'ati believed that the benefits of any order were intrinsically deceptive in absence of justice; hence regardless of the intoxicating nature of material prosperity under an unjust regime, such material prosperity did not really serve the interests of the people.

Shari'ati's intervention about the responsibility of the people in the making of a just order had a resonance by the onset of the decade of the 1970s as the rise in Iran's earnings from her oil exports and the subsequent acceleration of state-led industrialization accentuated the social and economic volatility generated by the White Revolution of 1961. While prosperity increased quite visibly among a section of the people (hence increasing the number of people with stakes in the regime), the growing economic disparities generated a high level of discontent. The volatility in Iran's social life generated ambiguous responses from the body politic. On the one hand a fair number of Iranians favored the continued transformation of Iran into a strong and modern state; on the other hand many were apprehensive that the regime was becoming too powerful to be mindful of the people. Thus, in the course of the 1960s and 1970s, almost every segment of Iranian society wavered between support for, and opposition to, the Shah—depending on which policies he pursued at particular points in time. There was almost no significant section of the population that had not supported the Shah at one point or the other in those two decades—including the *'ulema,* regardless of their subsequent claims of relentless struggle.[1]

The vacillation between support and opposition was particularly chronic among the intelligentsia—lay and clerical. The *'ashura* uprising of 1963 in Qom led by Khomeini, ostensibly against the grant of extraterritorial privileges to U.S. military personnel stationed in Iran, received little support from either the *'ulema* or the secular intelligentsia. Khalil Maleki, Al-e Ahmad's friend and mentor, called it a *jariyan ertaja'i mazhabi* (reactionary religious episode) that should not be condoned by progressive Iranians. In an anticipation of this stand, a couple of months before the uprising, Nader Saleh, a member of the second National Front even informed the U.S. embassy that "since the ultimate aims of the Front were diametrically opposed to those of the Mullahs, the Front would never combine forces against the government."[2] Secular intellectuals, by and large remained aloof from the uprising because it represented primarily "a religious affair."

Yet only 15 years later, when Khomeini called for massive demonstrations by the clerical establishment and seminary students, various sections of society began to show their solidarity with the *'ulema* culminating in the ouster of the Shah, although each section joined because of its own grievances against the Pahlavi regime. Several commentators on 1979 explain this as a rediscovery by Iran of its "roots," ignoring the fact that many of the lay intelligentsia (religious and secular) who celebrated the fall of the Shah in January 1979 were opposed to the institutionalization of the principle of *Vilayat-e Faqih.*

A set of developments occurred in the interim period that might account for this change in attitude. On the one hand, lay intellectuals like the religious-minded Mehdi Bazargan and the secular Al-e Ahmad alike felt alarmed by the divide between lay and clerical intellectuals.[3] On the other hand, prominent (and mostly younger) clerics like Morteza Motahhari realized the need to change many of the hidebound approaches of a large section of the *'ulema,* lest the secularist perception of the outmoded nature of Islam gets justified.[4] Both lay and clerical intelligentsia, accordingly, tried to bridge the divide between secular needs and religious values, creating in the process a number of new organizations that were independent of both the state and the established seminaries (dominated by the traditional *'ulema*). Structured mostly for the purpose of religious discussions, the crop of such new organizations like the *Hosseiniyeh-ye Ershad* created the much-required public space where religious discussions could take place off the beaten path.

No less important was a new sensibility that emerged around the mid-1960s about the role of intellectuals in the development of a society. Previously the terms of *monavvar al-fikr* and *raushanfikr* connoted simply individuals or group of individuals who held "enlightened" ideas about the problems facing the society, and helped spread awareness about such problems and their possible solutions. In the mid-1960s, though, as the works of Jean-Paul Sartre and other French intellectuals began to be available in Persian translations, Sartre's ideas of *engagement* were directly adapted into the notions of *mas'uliyat* (responsibility) and *vazifeh* (duty), and above all in the notion of *ta'ahhod* (commitment) which became pivotal to the notion of being a *raushanfikr* (intellectual).[5] Sartre had challenged the classic theory of literature being beyond politics and contended that writing was an action that should have practical consequences. At a time when Muhammad Reza was able to muzzle all kinds of dissent, the lay intelligentsia of Iran began to argue that social "commitment" was to be measured by "the rebellious nature of all forms of expression," and that intellectuals should have a morally superior motive.[6] After the eventful summer of 1968 in Europe, where intellectuals came out resolutely in favor of the disgruntled youth who raised questions about state power, the debate about responsibility of intellectuals assumed a new dimension as the intellectual was required to be an activist.

'Ali Shari'ati's was a persona in which these two unrelated phenomena converged in the late 1960s and early 1970s. In a political context when any direct criticism of the Pahlavi regime was certain to be harshly dealt with, Shari'ati invoked the debate on the social role of intellectuals to assault the edifice of intellectual legitimacy that the Pahlavis had so carefully built up. In the course of his association with the *Hosseiniyeh-ye Ershad*, Shari'ati did more than any other protagonist to champion the cause of Islam as a solution to the challenges of the modern world. Moreover, by emphasizing the idea of *ta'ahhod* (commitment) and *mas'uliyat* (responsibility) to society as the cornerstone of Islam, he argued that activism was the essential component that could establish popular sovereignty. The radicalization of the urban youth of Iran in the 1970s would probably not have been possible without such crucial interventions in the contemporary debates.

## Shari'ati at Hosseiniyeh-ye Ershad: of intellectuals and raushanfikr

The *Hosseiniyeh-ye Ershad*, which began its activities from the autumn of 1963, was intended to be an unconventional religious institution, where the professional tear-jerking *rowzehkhwani* was replaced by lectures on social, political, and economic aspects of religion and its relevance to modern life.[7] A group of Islamic modernists, lay and clerical, were instrumental in the foundation of *Ershad*. These included Mohammad Homayun, a pious merchant and philanthropist; Naser Minachi Moqadam, a lawyer with close links with the *bazaar* and a close associate of Bazargan in the *Nehzat-e Azadi*; and a group of progressive clerics including Morteza Motahhari.[8] The governing body of the institution had more lay members than it had clerics, and the institution invited both lay and clerical members to address the students and researchers who enrolled for courses designed to familiarize students with a modernist interpretation of Islam. Among the earliest and fairly popular speakers were laypersons like Muhammad Taqi Shari'ati and the firebrand Fakhreddin Hejazi, and clerics like Motahhari. *Ershad* soon became popular enough for Motahhari to try to control it, causing him to have Hejazi dismissed and have Shari'ati introduced instead.[9] Motahhari recognized that a charismatic orator like Hejazi and Shari'ati was needed to win over and attract the youth; hence despite the resentment of his clerical colleagues for losing the edge to the modernist nonclerical preachers he invited Shari'ati to speak at the *Ershad*.

As in the University of Mashhad, Shari'ati's lectures at *Ershad* were immensely popular. 'Ali Davani, a clerical speaker at *Ershad* recalled that Shari'ati's first lecture attracted far bigger crowds than his own or Motahhari's.[10] This was largely because his fame had preceded him partly by means of those who had heard him elsewhere, but more significantly by means of the books he had written (such as *Hobut dar Kavir*), or those which had been compiled from his lectures at the University of Mashhad. Nahid Tavassoli, an admirer and friend of Shari'ati and one of the first women to attend lectures delivered at *Hosseiniyeh-ye Ershad*, remembers having an overwhelming urge to meet the author after reading Shari'ati's works on *Kaviriyyat*—she became one of the regulars at Shari'ati's talks. Her husband, Mehdi Agha, one of the earliest students to enroll for Shari'ati's lectures at the *Ershad*, recollects how the radically inclined youth of Tehran, especially those from professional middle class or *bazaari* origins and with a University or college background, found the Sorbonne educated Islamist to be as radical as he was profound.[11] Responding to the radical inclination of the students Shari'ati too set forth a slightly bolder discourse than he did at the University of Mashhad, and after the brief ban on his lectures in 1969, his position became increasingly revolutionary in its implications.

\* \* \*

At the *Hosseiniyeh-ye Ershad*, Shari'ati was addressing a group of people who had the benefit of some of the best higher education that the country had to offer. Even as education increased opportunities of material prosperity among the professional classes, the number of people who suffered as a result of Pahlavi policies grew disproportionately. Accordingly, in the late 1960s the educated youth of Tehran were trying to come to terms with a society, and especially a city, that was being transformed very fast. The issue of the splendor and affluence of northern Tehran coexisting with the filth and squalor of the new settlements of migrants from other parts of Iran was one that created a lot of concerns, both administrative and intellectual. In this background, Shari'ati's emphasis on equity had struck a favorable chord among the Tehran youth, especially because he did not ask what the government could do; he asked instead what they, the educated people, could do about their own society.

Like so many other Iranians in the twentieth century, Shari'ati's principal diagnosis of the problems of modern Iran was linked to the idea of "modernity" and how it was conveyed to the people. His reservation about the Pahlavi modernization project was not that it was transforming "traditional" Iranian society into a hybrid civilization where Iranian values were lost (for he had much to say against what many, including Jalal Al-e Ahmad, had argued in the idyllic depictions of Iran in the pre-Pahlavi times). His problem instead lay with how "modernity" was conveyed as a panacea for all kinds of problems, universally valid and true for all times, as if human society and behavior were bound by laws like the natural world. He appreciated the material achievements of "modernity" as a technology-regime that had advanced science, facilitating an understanding of "the general laws which govern man as well as nature, and whoever learns these can be useful and effective in any setting or environment."[12] This principle of universality, however, did not apply to human society and behavior as "[m]an is far from the age when the earth will be one human society [*ijtima*'] or one nation [*mellat*] with common language, culture, ideals and common problems."[13]

Shari'ati was concerned with the knowledge regime that "modernity" ushered in the traditional, especially Muslim, societies, characterized by a lack of communication between the masses and the educated class. In the industrial countries of the west the broad expanse of the media, literacy, and education ensured that the masses and the intellectuals share a reasonably similar outlook—as a result, the intelligentsia in the west respond to the needs of the people, and is thus able to better communicate with the masses. This, however, was not true for "traditional societies," such as Iran.

> Unfortunately, under the modern culture and educational system, our young people are educated and trained inside invincible ... fortresses. Once they re-enter the society, they are placed in certain occupational and social positions completely isolated from the masses ... As a result, on the one hand, the

intelligentsia pursue life in an ivory tower without having any understanding of their own society, and on the other hand, the uneducated masses are deprived of the wisdom and knowledge of the very same intellectuals whom the masses have sponsored (albeit indirectly) and for whose flourishing they have provided.[14]

The point latent in this observation is so subtle that its nuances may be easily lost. Shari'ati was not attacking modernity per se, rather he was charging the purveyors of modernity in Iran with having completely misunderstood the social dimension of modernity. The west had embarked on the path of "modernity" *because* the traditional paradigm was not serving the interests of the people any more. Shari'ati believed, an essential component of modernity was a sense of social accountability *(mas'uliyat-e ijtema'i)* which compelled a measure of social relevance among the elite. In a critique resonant with the cultural paradigm of *gharbzadegi*, Shari'ati argued that modernists in Iran refused to appreciate that in the name of "modernization" they were importing from the west a set of economic, social, political, and cultural solutions that were devised in the western context, and could not be transplanted to Iran in toto. Such insistence on westernization without reference to the needs of the people, Shari'ati seemed to argue, reflected either an unwillingness or inability to understand the factor of responsibility in social life.

He used the context of his critique of "modernists" (but not modernity) to enter into the debate about the role of intellectuals in a society, only to shift the emphasis from "educated" people to those who were socially conscious. Shari'ati rejected the equation of the two terms "intellectual" and *raushanfikr* (enlightened soul) that characterized much of the debate on the role of intellectuals in twentieth-century Iran. He understood "intellectual" to refer to "a person who does mental (as opposed to physical) work." A *raushanfikr* (pl. *raushanfikran*) by contrast is a person "who is *khud-agah* [self-conscious] of the 'human condition' in his time and space, and whose awareness inevitably and necessarily gives him a sense of *mas'uliyat-e ijtema'i* [social responsibility]."[15] Shari'ati denied any necessary linkage between the two for an intellectual may or may not be a *raushanfikr*—a person may work in the factory and yet be enlightened while an academic despite being an intellectual may not be enlightened, and very few can be both.[16] He was clear that "if [the *raushanfikr*] happens to be educated he may be more effective and if not perhaps less so," but acknowledged that even an uneducated individual may play an important role.

Shari'ati was equally clear that *khud-agahi* (self-consciousness) was not enough to define the social responsibility of a *raushanfikr*. "The greatest responsibility of those who wish to rebuild their society and bring together disparate, and at times, antagonistic elements of the society into a harmonious whole is to bridge the gap between... the pole of theory and the pole of practice—and to fill this great abyss of alienation between the masses and the intellectuals."[17] The task of the *raushanfikr* was, then, "to generate responsibility and awareness, and give intellectual and social direction to the masses," because "[o]nly *khud-agahi* [self awareness] transforms static and corrupt masses into a dynamic and creative centre."[18]

In arguing this, Shari'ati was using terms of references that the Iranians were already familiar with. Iranian intellectuals since the *mashruteh* era had invariably spoken of "spreading awareness" among the masses of people who were *bekhabr* (unaware), and the need to wake them up from their torpor *(bidar kardan)*. The latent assumption behind both the *mashruteh* and the Pahlavi argument in this case was that "traditional" learning had kept the people ignorant of the possibilities of "modern" education; hence the issue had to be solved first and foremost at a pedagogic level by discarding the entire "traditional" learning system in favor of the "modern" one. Promotion of scientific knowledge was deemed essential not simply to turn Iran into a powerful modern state, but also to overcome the obscurantism bred by the traditionalist system.

Shari'ati did not undermine the need for scientific knowledge by attacking it. However, he refused to accept scientific knowledge as the yardstick of *agahi* (awareness). According to him "scientists, technicians and artists provide scientific assistance to their nations, or to the human race, in order to help them to improve their lot and be better at what 'they are.'" The *raushanfikran,* by contrast, "teach their society how to 'change' and toward what direction. They foster a mission of 'becoming' *(shudan),* and pave the way by providing an answer to the question, '*che bayied shudeem*' (What should we become)?" In suggesting that it is the responsibility of *raushanfikran* to promote change in their society, Shari'ati was underlining the need for change, but at the same time disputed that scientific knowledge by itself either should, or need, determine the direction of the change.

> At most, [a scientist] discovers the "facts," whereas an enlightened person identifies the "truth." A scientist produces light, which may be utilized either for right or wrong objectives; an enlightened person, analogous to a "tribal guide" (*ra'id*) and as the vanguard of the caravan humanity, shows us the right path, invites us to initiate a journey, and leads us to our final destination. Since science is power and enlightenment light, from time to time, the scientist serves the interests of oppression and ignorance; but the enlightened person of necessity and by definition, opposes tyranny and darkness.[19]

Thus in Shari'ati's understanding, an erudite man who lives by his intellect despite all his learning and worth as an intellectual is of little significance unless he engages with the society and its problems. This willingness to commit oneself to the task of providing guidance to society, helping it move toward a higher and better stage, was a sufficient condition of being a *raushanfikr*. But it was also necessary for a *raushanfikr* to be "situated" in his historical context to be socially relevant. Here lay Shari'ati's point of entry into need for an Islamic renaissance in modern Iran.

**The Calling of raushanfikr in Iran: The Need for an Islamic Renaissance**

Shari'ati was categorical in his assertion that the needs and requirements of societies vary with space and time; hence there can be "no universal prototype for being enlightened." Each society at a particular historical conjuncture deals with a specific set of problems, and the responses cannot be broadcast to any other society where similar conditions do not prevail. Thus what an enlightened soul thinks appropriate for "Black Africa" would be inapplicable in the Muslim world; if Sartre's disenchantment with consumerism were transplanted in a society like India, where even the minimum standards of material life are not always available, the results would not be particularly encouraging.[20] Shari'ati argued, when the problems diagnosed in one society are understood to be universally valid quite silly conclusions tend to be drawn, leading to *awadi-ye geraftanha* (confusion of issues).[21]

While thus arguing, Shari'ati did not spare even the people he is known to have respected. Citing the case of Ahmad Kasravi, he argued, it was not of much significance whether Kasravi's critique in the late 1940s of Shi'ism, of Islam, its history and poetry was correct (he was even ready to assume these were correct); he raised instead the question whether these were the fundamental issues of that time—so important that they had to be raised instead of taking a position on an issue like that of oil nationalization. Shari'ati's position was simple—a raushanfikr had to be socially relevant and historically situated. A *raushanfikr* does not ask *az kuja aghaaz kuneem* (Where do we begin)? He asks instead, *az kuja aghaaz kuneem dar in jame'* (Where do we begin *in this society*)? The nature of the answer depends on where the observer identifies the real problems in a society. Since in Shari'ati's scheme of things the root of all social problems lay in inequity and injustice, his natural point of entry lay in engaging with the triad of *zor-zar-tazveer*.

With respect to modern Iran, Shari'ati believed Iran (as also the Muslim world in general) was roughly in the position that Europe was in the time of the Renaissance. Economically the dominant system of production was linked firmly to commercial agriculture with the predominance of "intermediate bourgeoisie"—as distinct from bourgeois capitalism that characterizes the European system. The Iranian bourgeoisie, he maintained, comprise primarily of the *bazaaris,* rather than industrial and financial bourgeoisie; and the *bazaaris,* being a commercial bourgeoisie mediating between the agricultural sector and the urban consumer, lack the dynamism of the modern [meaning, professional] bourgeoisie. Shari'ati acknowledged the emergence of a new bourgeoisie but noted that these had comparatively less significance in the Iranian society, because these were simply the middlemen in spreading western culture in these traditional societies. "Unlike its counterpart in eighteenth century Europe, which prompted urban production at the expense of rural production, the Iranian bourgeoisie has only enhanced urban consumption without contributing to urban production. Of course, there are individuals who have begun urban production, but they are simply scattered enterprises which cannot be called a national modern bourgeoisie."[22]

Does that mean Shari'ati was arguing that Iran was not *yet* at a stage of social evolution analogous to Europe but *might* be there someday? Was he moving with some kind of historical determinism of a Marxian vintage, where the emergence of what he calls a "national modern bourgeoisie" inevitably follows the trajectory set by developments in the west? It is difficult to conclude categorically on this point because Shari'ati never explored these possibilities directly. But it might be fair to suggest two points. First, if Shari'ati's lectures on *Tarikh-e Tamaddun* (history of civilizations) delivered in Mashhad in 1967 are anything to go by, then in all possibility he did not subscribe to any simple theory of linear progression toward any historically inevitable stage theory of social development. Second, while he probably did not believe in the historical inevitability of any particular outcome, he was firm in his belief that the conflict between the oppressors and the oppressed was inevitable, and the measure of a *raushanfikr* lay in his support for the latter.

Shari'ati's argument was principally that since the trajectory of the developments of west and Iran were so widely different, that to change the society along the lines laid down by the west, i.e. westernize it, would be to aid the process of *istismar* (economic exploitation)—such an endeavor can have no relevance for the society. A socially relevant stand in modern Iran thus had to range itself in opposition to the prevalent *gharbzadegi.*

The need for social relevance in Shari'ati's schema stemmed from what he spoke of as the "cultural taxonomy" of a people—that is, the prevalent spirit that governs the body of knowledge, characteristics, feelings, traditions, outlooks, and ideals of the people of any given society. "The common spirit which connects the said characteristics of society and gives meaning to them is culture, by which people breathe, get nourishment and grow."[23] For Muslim societies like Iran, Shari'ati argued, this very naturally had to be Islam and the *raushanfikr* had to resort to Islam as a social strategy, not ideology.[24]

Interestingly, therefore, in making his case for Islam as the pivot of Iran's cultural taxonomy, unlike the clerical Islamists as Khomeini or Motahhari, or even lay Islamists as Bazargan, Shari'ati did not simply say that Islam was the *sabil al-mustaqim* (the straight path), hence all Muslims had to follow it. Shari'ati was nearer Jalal Al-e Ahmad in thinking of Islam in terms of a social religion. Shari'ati cited the success of Gandhi to suggest that for any *raushanfikr* to succeed in India, he had to know about the Indian psyche and Indian philosophy. "A Gandhi," he observed, "because he knew his society and the mind of his fellow Indians, could move the society far greater than others."[25] Clearly, the value of the understanding lay in the *fact of being able to communicate* with the people, rather than simply the *message that was being communicated*.

> The same is true of an enlightened Muslim. He must know that the Islamic spirit dominates his culture and that the historical processes of his society, as well as its moral codes, have all been shaped by Islam.[26]

In so arguing, Shari'ati broke with the predominant tradition of the Third World movement that tended to blend nationalism with nativism or Marxism, but seldom religion. Opposing Franz Fanon's emphasis on the emancipating nature of secularism against the repressive nature of Christianity, Shari'ati argued that one cannot equate the role played by all religions under a blanket category: while Christianity in Europe played a repressive role, in Latin America it turned into the theology of salvation.[27] The role played by religion was thus determined by the historical context and the purpose it serves.

> For a historian or a philosopher to see all religions in the same light is tolerable, but not for a *raushanfikr*. He has to identify the kind of society in which he lives, understand its people, and at the same time, *appreciate the historical condition they are in*. A *raushanfikr* in the Islamic world can commit great error by *mistaking* the religious feeling that exists among the Muslim masses today as their *true* historical and cultural religion, thus fighting it as a source of calamities. He may then invite his society to accept an ideology compatible with nineteenth century German industrial society, thereby playing a deviant role in his society. *Such an "intellectual" will frighten the masses by alienating them from the educated class, which in turn will force them to take*

*refuge with the reactionary, deviant and colonial element in order to escape the anti-religious educated group.*[28] [Emphasis mine]

The distinction that Shari'ati makes here between what *true* religion was, and what it was *mistaken* to be was fundamental to his understanding of Islam—as already indicated in the previous chapter. Shari'ati believed Islam was not what it was presented to be by the forces of *tazveer,* rather what it could be *made to do*. He argued that the word *hikmat* (wisdom) is used in the Qur'an and the Islamic intellectual tradition to convey the same meaning as does "enlightenment." "The kind of *'ilm* (knowledge) which is emphasized in Islam is the awareness unique to man, a divine light and a source of consciousness of the social conscience."[29]

Here lies the significance of *tazveer*. Shari'ati argued that if the irreligious and pseudo-intellectuals succeeded in rubbishing Islam as an antiquated religion and misled the youth, they owe their entire success to the "pseudo-religious leaders" who have dispersed the youth by distorting Islam. They "bewitch the people and mesmerize them with fabricated and politically expedient sentiments," "meaningless and lifeless actions, habits, traditions and rituals." "The masses are kept busy with something called religion, certain useless abstractions such as love, hope, hatred, dislike and with weeping and incidents that they know very little about."[30] In their infatuation with the idea of the hereafter, the people are persuaded to forget their present condition, as well as their enemies. The argument was almost as if, Shari'ati says, "not to be in need of a shirt, one should ignore one's body."[31] *Tazveer*, thus, turns religion into "a philosophy of absurdity," and put the people to sleep.

The solution, according to Shari'ati, was "an intellectual revolution and an Islamic renaissance." Such a renaissance could not be led by western educated intellectuals who came out of universities that "not only were born and grew outside of and alienated from our traditional education system, but in opposition to it." Nor could the products of the traditional Islamic universities or the *hawzat* effect such a change as, "they have kept their doors tightly shut without even having one window open in the direction of the new intellectual and scientific waves."[32] The architects of the Islamic renaissance had to be people who had a foot in either camp. They would have to be cognizant of the advances in the realm of scientific and temporal knowledge made in the west and familiar with the contemporary outlook, and yet have the intellectual maturity to use such learning in order to understand their own culture, not undermine it—performing the role Jamal al-din Asadabadi, Muhammad Abduh and Allameh Muhammad Iqbal had done in their own societies. In the course of such Islamic renaissance the *raushanfikran* would combat the forces of *tazveer*, and herald the *bazgusht beh khishtan* (return to the "self"):

> Islam is what we must return to, not only because it is the religion of our society, it gives shape to our society, the spirit of our culture... and the foundation of our morality and spirituality, but also because it is the human "self" of our people... Islam has... a populist and progressive social outlook which believes in the fundamental values of justice, equality and committed leadership. It believes in the inevitable conflict between the two social poles of truth versus usurpation, in originality versus ownership and in society versus the individual... It also believes in man's everlasting and infinite evolution, and thus invites him to ascension to God through nature and reality, and through dominion over matter as well as through employing the forces of nature.[33]

The Islamic "self" is thus identified not in terms simply of professing faith in God, but a range of other features—morality, progressive social outlook, justice, equality, social cohesiveness—that were originally there, but were lost since then. Shari'ati identified the primary responsibility of the *raushanfikran* to stage a return to the "self."

## The Inversion of the Self: Tashai'yo 'Alavi wa Tashai'yo Safavi

On February 9, 1971, Iranian newspapers reported a guerilla attack on the gendarmerie outpost in the village of Siahkal. On March 17, 1971, 13 members of a left-wing group charged with the Siahkal insurgency were executed, whereupon the remaining members joined another group of leftist urban guerillas to form the *Fedayian-e Khalq-e Iran*. Although the Siahkal operation was a military failure, it brought to an end the period of apparent political stability since the uprising of 1963. It galvanized the youth of Iran and suggested that in conditions of repressive political condition, revolutionary struggle was the only way ahead. Shari'ati, as much as many of his listeners, felt highly stimulated. In that sense Siahkal probably marks the point from which Shari'ati decided to play out the full force of the radicalism of his ideas. Thus, in October 1971, when the Shah embarked on the extravagant celebration of 2,500 years of Iranian monarchy, Shari'ati mounted his severest attack on the state yet by highlighting how true Islam and the Islamic "self" were inverted to meet the needs of the state. The underlying argument was not lost on anyone: the celebrations of the institution of monarchy were tantamount to a celebration of the inversion of the "self."

Shari'ati considered it necessary to explicate the manner in which the "self" was inverted. The metaphor he used for this inversion was *shirk*, a term Islam uses for polytheism. But Shari'ati's treatment of the metaphor of *shirk* by relating it with *zor, zar,* and *tazveer* was quite unlike the prevalent usage of the term, among the Sunnis and Shi'i alike.

In his fiery lecture called *Che Bayied Kard* delivered at Mecca in 1969, Shari'ati had developed the tropes of *shirk* and *munafiq* (pl. *munafiqun*). About the *munafiq,* Shari'ati was to say:

> Anyone who is familiar with the Prophet and the Qur'an knows well that they foresaw the most important danger to Islam and Muslims as being neither *mushrik* (polytheist) nor *kafir* (unbeliever) nor *but-parast* (idolater), nor atheist, nor naturalist but *munafiq* (hypocrite)[34]

The first of the *munafiqun* he identified in the history of Islam were the Umayyads, who had once fought the forces of Islam and lost, but later joined the ranks of the faithful and subvert it from within.[35] The Shi'i consider Umayyad rule to be the beginning of consolidation of illegitimate authority because it was founded upon the denial of the claims of 'Ali and the Imams for the divinely-sanctioned leadership of Muslims. The Sunnis do not consider the origins of Umayyad rule to have been illegitimate, but many of them acknowledge that Umayyad era was an era of social and moral corruption, profligacy, opulence, oppression and injustice. Here, Shari'ati's tirade was apparently in accordance with the Shi'i denunciation of the Umayyads, but a careful reading indicates that Shari'ati's position rested on a different rationale. He considered Mu'awiyah and Yazid as guilty of *shirk* not simply because they had once "held the idols of Lat and Hubal in their hand," but because their resistance to 'Ali was in defense of inequity and injustice which were the essence of Meccan order in the age of *jahiliya* (the age of ignorance);[36] they were guilty of *shirk* because upon usurping political power they tried to restore the same inequity and injustice that prevailed before the onset of Islam, thereby subverting *tauheed*. Moreover, the Umayyads were *munafiqun* because they re-established *shirk* in the name of Islam, embarking on the practice of *tazveer* (deception) in defense of *zor* (oppression) and *zar* (exploitation). As Shari'ati had put it:

> The most dangerous enemy is the oppressor who is *clad in the attire of Islamic justice*, an idol worshipper, *human worshipper, money worshipper and power worshipper* whose slogans are those of *tauheed* ... an individual who is the guardian of ignorance and narcotizing, the propagator of superstition, lies, and illusion, the agent of social stagnation, and baseness, *one who deceives*

> *people and, in the name of Islam, asks people to forget their destiny, poverty and wretchedness*, and to ignore the danger of their enemies' conspiracy; one who in order to please the deities of the earth, in the phony attire of piety for the pleasure of Allah persuades people to accept the status quo. A *munafiq* is a person who portrays the God of Islam as a phenomenon that rewards only *toleration of ignorance, oppression, weakness, poverty, backwardness, disease*.... The *munafiq* does all this so that he himself will be rewarded by those who have always benefited from the ignorance, poverty, backwardness and superstition of the Muslims.[37] [Emphasis mine]

Even though prima facie this charge was leveled against the Umayyads, Shari'ati referred to them as not the sole practitioner of *tazveer*, but as its initiators. And the people he considers the most blameworthy were, clearly, the custodians of the faith, the *'ulema*. As he went on to argue:

> It is common knowledge that the *true Islam* was turned into the mockery we have today, not by the philosophical or military opponents of Islam, but by its supporters... Muslim jurisconsults, speculative theologians, interpreters of the Qur'an, religious judges, rulers, preachers, theosophists and the Caliphs. *These guardians of Islam*, who were responsible for the glorification of the Islamic rites and rituals for propagating the traditions of Islam, who were entrusted with enhancing its power, and who attempted to expand and inseminate its civilization, sciences, culture and mysticism—and not the infidels and materialists—*destroyed Islam from within* and made it lifeless, directionless and motionless.[38] [Emphasis mine]

When Shari'ati spoke of Islam being destroyed *(kharab kardan)* from within, he never used the term deviation *(bargashtan)*, because deviation involves starting from a point of origin and then moving away from it. Speaking of the particular case of Islam, Shari'ati preferred to the quote Imam 'Ali's observation that "the garment of Islam is like a sheepskin coat worn inside out."[39] The term sheepskin coat is used because this is a type of garment where "the difference between the inside and the outside is from extreme ugliness to extreme beauty." In other words, Shari'ati was not suggesting that after a great beginning, Islam gradually moved away from its original principles. He argued that the transformation from "what was" to "what is" was like an inversion, where that which had to be opposed becomes the objective, and the real objective is downplayed.

Islam as much as Shi'ism, Shari'ati argued, began with a negation—a negation of *shirk*, the religion of *ashrafiyat* (the aristocracy) and *maslihat* (prudence).[40] The Prophet waged a *jihad* (struggle) to destroy *shirk*, which was primarily a metaphor for inequity and injustice, and establish Islam, a metaphor for equity and justice. The *ummah* that thus came into being was founded on the principle of *'adalat*. Shi'ism too began with a "negation"—it rested upon the refusal of 'Ali to accept the election of Abd al-Rahman Abu Bakr ("personification of Islam of *ashrafiyat* and *maslihat*") to *khulafat*. This implied that 'Ali was opposed to the election of Abu Bakr not because 'Ali was being deprived of the right to the mantle of the Prophet, nor simply because this was in violation of an express wish of the Prophet on the matter of succession (which is the standard Shi'i position), but because such an election went against the interests of the *ummah*. 'Ali opposed the election of Abu Bakr because he was the personification of the religion of the privileged few that the Prophet was determined to root out. Hence, the Shi'i—partisans of 'Ali—were partisans committed to equity and justice.

Even after the death of Imam 'Ali, when power was usurped by Mu'awiyah, the refusal of Imam Hassan to legitimize the Umayyads made it possible for resistance to develop against a repressive and exploitative order that was virtually the embodiment of *shirk*. By the time Imam Hossein came into the picture, the positions gained by the *Muhajirun* and *Ansar* had been usurped, and the seductive nature of affluence corrupted the Islamic *ummah*. At this stage, Hossein decided to stand up and resist this subversion, fought and died at the battle of Karbala, continuing with the tradition of negation. Thus, Shi'ism, as Shari'ati put it

> was begun with a negation, negation of the course chosen by history. It was a rebellion against history, a history that in the name of Qur'an, followed the track of ignorance of Kasra [Sassanid] and Kaiser [Caesar], and in the name of Sunnah sacrificed the house that nourished the Qur'an and the traditions before everything.[41]

Shi'ism thus was the true inheritor of the tradition of Islam because of its opposition to oppression and injustice. It was indicative "of a social agenda, class and a political block ... [a] party whose foundation lay on the Quran and the *Sunnah*, but not the Qur'an and the *Sunnah* which came from the Umayyids, the Abbasids, the Ghaznavis, the Seljuq, Changez, Timur, and Hulagu—rather [from] the family of Muhammad."[42]

From the very beginning, Shari'ati asserts, Shi'ism was a *mazhab-e aitraz* (religion of protest).

> The Shi'i do not accept history, and the leadership and rule of those that have dominated history and deceitfully negated the succession of the Messenger in the society, the defense of Islam and the struggle against *kufr* [unbelief] of the majority of the world ... The Shi'i are representatives of the persecuted and justice-seeking in the Caliphate regime ... For this [reason], Fatima, heir of the Messenger, asserting the "rights of the oppressed" and [lodging]

the first "protest" in the eyes of the present, personifies the powerful and categorical "demand for justice."[43]

Shari'ati argued that all through the first millennium of Islamic rule, the Shi'i stood for opposition to all those who ruled in the name of Islam only to oppress and exploit them—the Caliphate of the Umayyads and the Abbasids, Sultanates of the Ghaznavids, Seljuqs, Mughals, Timurids, Ilkhanids, et cetera. These rulers, who had turned their own customary practices into the religion of the Sunni state were Muslim only in name. In all that they did, they strengthened *shirk*:

> In this manner, in the course of history... as aristocratic rule, class opposition, stifling of thought became more coarse and more obscene, stronger the sectarian prejudice and the linkages of religious learning with worldly rule and the more obscene the gap between the poverty and hardship of the masses and power and wealth of the ruler have become, the more powerful has the frontline of Shi'ism become... from being a school of thought and a special religion of the intellectuals and the wealthy, standing on the ground of correct understanding of Islam and the culture of the Muslims, against Greek philosophy and eastern Sufism, Shi'ism had developed into a profound and revolutionary political and social movement among the masses.[44]

In a very interesting explanation of Sunni persecution of the Shi'i, Shari'ati argued that the Caliphs and Sultans, who had accorded even the Jews, Christians and the Magi freedom, respect and influence, and even gave the atheists freedom of expression like intellectuals and free-thinkers, never relented in their oppression of the Shi'i. "The Shi'i they remembered with such indignation and enmity that their general massacre alone could not satisfy them: they were skinned alive and blinded, tongues cut off and set alight." To justify such conduct, all kinds of false worship were denounced as Shi'i practices. The Ghaznavids, Seljuqs and Mongols alike championed the most parochial ideas as traditional religion.

> It was then that Shi'ism, in different forms, moderate or extremist, manifested itself as... resistance by the plundered and repressed masses... ranged against crude partisanship, and the dry strangulated spirit and the ossified organization of the jurists and the pious people related with the ruling establishment. And finally the school of learning, moderate and resourceful—Imamate (leadership)—as the greatest current of intellectual and cultural resistance against the religion and culture of governance, which makes people aware of the call and gives lessons in this school in order to establish the twin principles of *Imamat* and *'adalat* (justice),

and the revolutionary slogan of *'ashura*, and mobilization of the opposing masses against the existing condition. With call to wait for the Imam Mehdi... keeping alive the hope of "deliverance after existence" and the thought of revenge and revolution and the final downfall of tyrannous repression and condemnation/denunciation of oppression of the governing powers.[45]

All of this, Shari'ati argued, changed completely with Safavid rule in Iran. The relentless campaign against oppression and class-based exploitation—that is, *zor* and *zar*—had made Turkish and Mongol rulers resort in vain to *tazveer*. The Safavids however achieved this aim with great success. Arising at a time when Persia was locked into a conflict for survival with Ottoman Turkish Empire, the Safavids needed an ideology that could bind their subjects to the throne, disregarding the call of the Ottomans who claimed loyalty of all Muslims as the inheritors of the mantle of the Caliphs. The Safavids accordingly picked on the one ideology that had denied all legitimacy altogether to the Caliphs—that is, Shi'ism. However, as Shari'ati reminds us, that *tashai'yo 'Alavi* (Shi'ism of 'Ali), which rested on the negation of oppression, could not have served the Safavids. The Safavids, therefore, devised their own form of Shi'ism by reviving Shu'ubite thinking and then blending the two—this Shari'ati spoke of as *tashai'yo safavi* (Safavid Shi'ism).[46] In the beginning the Shu'ubites propagated equality of all races, Arab or Ajami.[47] But gradually they turned to define superiority of the Ajami by emphasizing the Sassanid heritage to counter Umayyad glory. Shari'ati acknowledged that by forging a national consensus *(azahi-ye melli)* it helped redress the humiliation inflicted by Arabism.

> To ensure that *nasionalism*-e *safaviyya* (Safavid nationalism) might not prove to be rootless and ineffective in the manner of Shu'ubite nationalism, they mixed it up with the religion of the people. They made it *shu'ubi-ye Shi'i* (Shi'ite Shu'ubism) so that... the revitalized *Shu'ubigari* (Shu'ubism)... gave it religious sanctity. The Prophet and 'Ali were made racists (*nazadparast*)... the result was a new born *Paighambar-Padshah*, who was the marriage of nationalism and religion (*qaumiat-mazhab*).[48]

Shari'ati argued that the *'ulema* associated with Safavid Shi'ism had joined the ruling class by underwriting the monarchy in return for being associated with it. To provide an Islamic rationale for monarchies and to whitewash their unjust practices they falsified reports, words and deeds of Shi'i Imams. Referring to a *hadith* cited in Muhammad-Baqer Majlesi's *Bahar al-Anwar* on the marriage between Imam Hossein and Shahrbanu, the daughter of the last Sassanid king Yazdegard, Shari'ati argued that the Safavid clergy invented the account to fuse the concept of monarchy with Imamate. Disregarding Majlesi and another tradition that speaks of the marriage, he questioned the credentials of the sources of the hadith, and pointed out several discrepancies in the evidence as evidence of falsification.[49]

Shari'ati argued that the Safavid *'ulema* carried out the task of *tazveer* at two levels. On the one hand, they whipped up antipathy toward the Sunni by inducing fanatical love or idolization of Imams, and vilifying the Caliphs as enemies of the House of 'Ali. So long as the people believed that the Imams were capable of doing miracles, and that the Sunnis were responsible for denying them the mantle of the Prophet, it was possible to canalize the pent up emotions and energy of the people to fighting the Sunni instead of the oppressive rulers.[50] On the other hand, by emphasizing on issues of personal and specific ritualistic aspects of the faith the Safavid *'ulema* effectively and intentionally relinquished the social aspects of Islam.

> Instead of becoming involved in politics, Safavid *fuqaha* focused on writing about menstruation, ejaculation, the rituals of going to the toilet, ordinances concerning slavery and the responsibilities of the slave to the slave owner.[51]

By thus keeping the people away from the true spirit of Ali's Shi'ism, subservience to political oppression and exploitation was guaranteed by the Safavid clerics.

According to Shari'ati, it was in this setting that the Safavid *'ulema* came up with the ideational triad of *taqiyeh* (dissimulation), *taqlid* (emulation), and *intezar* (waiting).[52] *Taqiyeh* was defined as concealing one's beliefs in order to ensure self-preservation, so that when the Imam Mahdi returns, the believer would be available to follow the Imam.[53] *Taqlid* implied the obligation to offer unswerving and unquestioning allegiance to the ruling of the *'ulema*, because the *'ulema* were entrusted with the responsibility of guiding the faithful in absence of the Imams.[54] *Intezar* was defined as waiting for the return of the Vanished Imam, implying total acceptance of prevailing sociopolitical and economic conditions until social degradation necessitated the Imam to return; since the end of occultation was divinely determined, the Safavid *'ulema* considered action and struggle to establish a just society completely futile.[55] Shari'ati agued, the *jado-ye siah* (black magic) of Safavid clerics was of an order that they first distorted the concepts of *taqlid*, *taqiyeh* and *intezar*, and then elevated these warped interpretations to the level of indisputable principles of Shi'ism.[56] Here lay the foundations of quietist attitude in Shi'ism from which, Shari'ati argued, the true Shi'i had to "return."

## Return to the Self: Redefining intezar

The metaphor of *bazgusht* (return) dominated much of Shari'ati's thinking about Islam. The understanding that feeds this metaphor is derived from the Messianic streak in the Judeo-Christian-Islamic tradition that Massignon had introduced Shari'ati to, holding out the promise that on the Day of Judgement/*Qayamat* God would send a Savior to hold mankind to account, and the righteous would prevail and the sinful would be punished. Much of the ritualism and observance of fasts and penances in Judaism, Christianity and Islam is taken to be indicative of righteousness with the anticipation of the return of the "Savior" in mind. This anticipation is, in fact, one of the cardinal features of *Ithna 'Ashari* Shi'ism. The use of such a metaphor in political thinking, especially in Islamic thinking, generally takes the form of a return to the fundamentals of the faith, that is, the directives of the revealed text. Shari'ati's use of this metaphor, however had a distinctive flavor, because his usage had not one but two different roots—one *Ithna 'Ashari* Shi'i, the other Sufi.

The Shi'i metaphor of "return," which Shari'ati had in common with many other contemporary Iranian thinkers, pertained to the Vanished Imam. The *Ithna 'Ashari* Shi'i believe that the twelfth Imam, Muhammad ibn Hasan—usually referred to by his titles *Imam-e 'Asr* (Imam of the Period) and *Sahib al-Zaman* (Lord of the Age)—went into hiding by Divine command in 872 at the age of four, maintaining contact with the faithful through his deputies *(na'ib)*. The period between 872 and 939, when he maintained indirect contact with his people through four deputies consecutively, is known as *ghaibat-i sughra* (Lesser Occultation). Upon the death of the fourth of his deputies, the Imam passed into *ghaibat-i kubra* (Greater Occultation) which will continue till God grants the Imam the permission to manifest himself. *Ithna 'Ashari* Shi'i exegesis suggests that man is endowed with the power of receiving revelation through prophecy, which directs him toward the perfection of human norm and well-being of the human species—and if such perfection were not attainable, God would not have indicated its possibility. "Therefore, by reason of inner necessity and determination, the future will see a day when human society will live in peace and tranquility, when human beings will be fully possessed of virtue and perfection. The establishment of such a condition will occur through human hands but with Divine succor. And the leader of such a society, who will be the savior of man, is called . . . the Mahdi."[57]

A dominant position in the *Ithna 'Ashari* tradition since the Safavid era argues that even though all political authority till the coming of the Imam Mahdi is ipso facto illegitimate, it is not desirable for the Shi'i to resist existing temporal authorities lest there be social anarchy and chaos which makes it difficult for Muslims to carry on with their daily lives. During the *ghaibat*, therefore, the *'ulema* were assigned the *walayah* (authority) to guide the faithful regarding proper conduct (classifying all activity under the fivefold classification of *wajib* [proper], *mandub* [recommended], *murakkas* [neither recommended nor proscribed], *makruh* [discouraged] and *haraam*[proscribed]) so that the *usul al-din* (fundamental obligations of the faith) can continue to be fulfilled in preparation for the return of the Mahdi.[58] Till the return of the Mahdi, the Shi'i have to practice *taqiyya* (dissimulation, concealment of beliefs) so that the illegitimate political authorities cannot persecute them—that is, the Shi'i would have to resort to *intezar* (waiting).[59] The doctrine of *intezar* therefore is pivotal to Ithna 'Ashari Shi'ism, as "return" of the Vanished Imam signifies the ultimate realization of God's will on earth.

The Sufi metaphor of "return" was completely different from the Shi'i. The story of creation as given in the *Surah al-Baraqah* says when God expelled Adam and Huwwa (Eve) from the Garden of Eden for disobedience, He also assured that one day mankind would "return" to God if it follows His injunctions that God vouchsafed to man.[60] In Sufi exegesis following the principle of *wahdat al-wujud* (unity of being), disobedience is treated as a metaphor of losing faith in God, and is thus the same as losing track of oneself. Thus expulsion from Eden is a metaphor for the waywardness of man who has lost his way, and Islam (submission, to the will of God) is "the straight path" leading back to God, in whom the self has to be subsumed *(fanaa)*. Thus the "return" of man to Eden is also a metaphor, indicating man's return to his own self.[61]

Shari'ati blended both these metaphors of "return" to argue that as a result of *tazveer* Muslims had lost sight of the real essence of Islam. He argued that the mindless ritualism and superstition that was practiced as Islam was so completely removed from the original faith that an Islamic renaissance was absolutely necessary to "reawaken" the people to the faith. In order to bring such a renaissance about, Shari'ati set about challenging some widely prevalent ideas of Shi'ism, and ended by turning the cardinal precept of *intezar*, as it was held by the *'ulema*, on its head.

\* \* \*

The "return" that Shari'ati spoke of in the course of his discussion on 'Alavid and Safavid Shi'ism was predicated on an attempt to liberate Islam from the clutches of the *'ulema*. As early as 1967 in Mashhad, in a series of lectures on *Rawish-e Shenakht-e Islami* (approaches to the understanding of Islam), Shari'ati had asserted that the *'ulema* were versed only in the laws of Islam, but that Islam was not simply a compendium of laws.

In order to understand Islam, Shari'ati believed, it had to be approached from the standpoints of sociology, economics, ethics, history, et cetera, and the *'ulema* were not qualified to attend to any of these. As the *'ulema* were not familiar with the social, economic, political, and historical contexts in which particular laws were made, they were invariably confined to the letter of the law and missed its spirit altogether. In 1971, therefore, as he assaulted the *'ulema* establishment for its sustained legitimization of the Pahlavi regime, Shari'ati gave an unequivocal call for *ijtihad*.

*Ijtihad* (independent legal reasoning) is one of the five principle sources of Islamic law. There is a controversy among the Sunni as to whether *ijtihad* is at all permissible, but the Shi'i accepted this application of human reason to deduce new laws provided *ijtihad* is exercised by the *'ulema*. Shari'ati attacked this limitation of *ijtihad* to the *'ulema* by exploring the rationale behind such a suggestion. He argued that the original condition set for *ijtihad* was that only those who had knowledge *('ilm)* of the essence of the faith are capable of exercising it. Having already argued that the *'ulema* approached Islam through a literalist prism, ignorant/evasive of the essence of the faith, Shari'ati went on to argue that any "responsible" Muslim who understands the essence of the faith, and is aware of the requirements of a particular historical context, has the credentials required to be a *mujtahid* (a person capable of *ijtihad*). Shari'ati argued that the application of *ijtihad* in legal, economic and social domains guaranteed the concurrent evolution and modernization of religion.[62] It follows, therefore, that a *raushanfikr* could be a *mujtahid* despite not being an *'alim*.

In a very radical lecture on *Intezar Mazhhab-e Aitraz* (Awaiting the Religion of Protest) delivered at *Ershad* in 1971, Shari'ati deliberated upon the theory of *intezar*. Shari'ati began by talking of the prevalent positions on *intezar* in contemporary Iran, identifying three ideological *(eiteqadi)* strands. The nonreligious educated *(tehsilkardeh-ye ghairmazhhabi)* refuse to subscribe to the "return" of a Messiah who had disappeared a thousand years ago, because such longevity of any human being is opposed to biology, physiology, scientific logic and nature. Moreover, from the social viewpoint, messianic belief undermines progress and downplays human responsibility—because if deliverance would come from a Deliverer sent by God, man need not strive against injustice and oppression.[63] By contrast the religious masses *(tudeh-ha-ye mazhhabi)* believe in the inevitable return of the Vanished Imam "because they are told he would." They do not concern themselves with the point whether the Imam has an unnaturally long life or not; nor are they mindful of the basic contradiction this might entail for the Qur'anic injunctions on attaining justice and truth. "They just believe."[64] The third strand is that of religious modernists *(mazhabi-ha-ye mutajaddad)* who are concerned with proving not that Messianic belief conforms to the notion of human responsibility, rather that it is scientifically and logically possible for the Imam to live hundreds or thousands of years.[65]

Instead of passing a verdict on either of these strands, Shari'ati asked, what is the impact of belief in either of these three? He offered a simple test for discerning a good idea from bad:

> Our differences arise from our different interpretations of such fundamental beliefs. I understand them in one way, you in another, and someone else may have a third interpretation. Is my understanding of this Islamic issue right? Or is it yours? Is he right? Or is it that none of us is right?... But... one can easily determine who is right. If you see my interpretation and understanding, for example, of the principle of the Imamate has a positive effect on my life as an individual and on the society that believes in it, then it is correct.[66]

Shari'ati then proceeded to argue that there are two Islams. One is Islam as an ideology, "a body of beliefs, practices and ceremonies—all of which aim at spiritual, social, moral, and intellectual development of man. And the other where Islam is reduced simply to culture; where Islam is "a collection of information, knowledge, and sciences... as philosophy, theology, jurisprudence, etc."[67] Then he adds:

> What bestows responsibility, awareness and direction is Islamic belief; while Islamic studies is a field on learning available to an orientalist as well, just as it may be mastered by a misguided reactionary or an ill-intentioned enemy. That is why an uneducated man or woman may have a better understanding of Islam, may think and live more in line with the teachings of Islam, and may have a better grasp of the responsibilities he or she has towards Islam than a philosopher, scholar, mystic. A person, for example, who reads a few books of jurisprudence would have a grasp of the Islamic legal system, while he who studies the life of the Prophet understands the meaning of Islam.[68]

Thus, Shari'ati was arguing, that the understanding of Islam primarily as a body of regulations was flawed, and because they engaged only with the letter of the law, jurists and scholars frequently miss the activist essence of Islam. The result of such flawed understanding, he argued, was the complete "inversion" of an idea like that of *intezar*. Shari'ati differed with those that consider *intezar* primarily as a justification for defending the status quo, or those "who have usurped the authority vested in the Imam by Allah and Islam... these impostors who have enslaved the people mentally and exploit them materially" (i.e., the *'ulema*). In fact, Shari'ati argued the true significance of the doctrine is the very opposite:

> [T]he contradiction between the unrighteous prevalent reality and the suppressed liberating truth can be resolved only through the concept of *intezar* for the inevitable and certain victory of truth, unless we are prepared to abandon any hope of ever attaining freedom and justice, to deny the truth entirely and reconcile ourselves to what has happened.
>
> ... [*I*]*ntezar* is a blow against the realities which have up to the present dominated the world, history and Islam. "*Intezar*" is a way of saying "no" to the prevalent reality. The very fact that someone is waiting is a protest against the present conditions....
>
> *Intezar* is faith in the future and, by necessity, denial of the present. He who is content with the present is not waiting. On the contrary he is conservative. He is afraid of the future ... he likes the status quo and wants to preserve it.[69]

In Shari'ati's notion of *intezar* there was nothing passive. Nor, as he points out, was this waiting for the sake of waiting itself—as in Beckett's *Waiting for Godot*. Shari'ati's notion of *intezar* was a gesture of disapproval of the existing reality, a protest, and a willingness to do something about the reality. If the people would "wait" passively for the Vanished Imam to return by accepting *zulm* (oppression) and *be'adalati* (injustice), not challenging existing injustices, the Imam might never be able to return.

Shari'ati's position on *intezar* was revolutionary. The suggestion that for the Imam to return people have to be ready to resist injustice signifies that the return would not be a return in person, rather a return in the essence. Which implies, that *ghaibat* (occultation) in Shari'ati's thinking was a metaphor for the disappearance of justice from the world. *Imamat*, as Shari'ati had reiterated countless times was the form of leadership exercised by the Imams—working toward the establishment and maintenance of *nizamat-e 'adalati* (just order) and *'adalat-e ijtema'i* (social justice). And unless society was prepared to fight for it, justice would never prevail—that is, conditions that the Imam stood for would never be able to "return." This "return" of the Imam, therefore, was essentially a "return" in the metaphorical sense of the term. The return of the Vanished Imam was *bazgusht be khistan-e Islami* (return to the Islamic self) that would bring about the ultimate goal of all human activity—the state of *tauheed* when man would have "realized" his mission on earth and fulfilled God's design for man, and would once again be at one with God.

Shari'ati was therefore suggesting an agenda of very active resistance in order to attain *tauheed*. For the forces of *zor, zar,* and *tazveer* to be overturned, an incessant struggle *(jihad)* had to be waged of necessity.

By 1972, Shari'ati engaged directly with this issue against a highly volatile political backdrop.

### Islam as Assumption of Responsibility: Jihad and Shahadat

The galvanization of urban Iranian youth around radical ideas had accelerated with the Siahkal incident. Shortly after the *Fedayan-e Khalq-e Iran* came under the spotlight, the *Sazman-e Mojahedin-e Khalq* (Organization of the People's Warriors) initiated armed struggle against the regime.[70] They carried out a number of successful raids beginning in August 1971, but were soon paralyzed by repression as the government successfully neutralized most of its leadership.[71] The organization used *Ershad* as a base for its propaganda and even recruited members from there. Many of the members of the organization were initially among Shari'ati's students, and although there is no proof of any direct contact between Shari'ati and the Mojahedin, Shari'ati's sympathy for the armed revolutionaries of the Fedayan and then later the Mojahedin was quite manifest.

As the militant struggle against the regime began to escalate, Shari'ati was concomitantly pitching the tone of his radicalism fairly high. His attack on the legitimacy of existing political institutions coincided with increased activities of the Mojahedin to such an extent that the SAVAK began to entertain strong suspicions of collusion between the fiery oratory of Shari'ati and incremental disenchantment with the regime among the youth. In October-November 1971, Shari'ati delivered a set of highly charged lectures under the title *Shi'i, yek hezb-e tamam*. But the more emotional, and possibly the most political and most insurrectionary lecture—*Shahadat*—was delivered upon the revolutionary suicide of Ahmed Rezai and the passage of death sentence upon the Mojahedin founders in February 25, 1972.[72]

In this memorable lecture Shari'ati encapsulated almost all those issues that he had raised in his politically charged talks since his days at the University of Mashhad—namely, *tauheed, ummah, imamat, shirk, zor-zar-tazveer,* and *ma'suliyat*—before he delivered the *coup de grace* with a discussion of *al-amr bi'l-ma'ruf wa'l-nahi 'an al-munkar* (Commanding Right and Forbidding Wrong) and linking it with *jihad* and *shahadat*.

\* \* \*

*Al-amr bi'l-ma'ruf wa'l-nahi 'an al-munkar* (lit. Commanding what is Known [to be Right] and Prohibiting [what is known to be] Abominable) is often accepted as one of the cardinal principles in Islam. The Imami/*Ithna 'Ashari* Shi'i have one of the longest documented traditions of Commanding Right and Forbidding Wrong as a juridical problem.[73] While this doctrine has been interpreted variously in different jurisprudential traditions, among the *Ithna 'Ashari* Shi'i the predominant strain was quietist in its disposition: according to the sixth Imam, Jafar al-Sadiq, the founder of Shi'i jurisprudence, it was enough for the common man to nurse disapproval of something at heart (thus letting God know of his position), without expressing it lest it jeopardizes one's existence. Later, Classical Imami scholars believed that while it was incumbent upon the strong to enjoin upon others what is good and forbidding what is evil, no rewards were promised in this world and the next for those who perish trying to resist evil. The underlying assumption was, since the Vanished Imam would come at a time chosen by God when the world was replete with evil, there was not much point in resisting evil or enjoining good openly. So a good Muslim would confine oneself to doing what is good and refrain from what is bad in the private sphere of one's life.[74]

Having already questioned the foundational Shi'i premise for such quietist disposition by attacking the traditionalist notion of *intezar,* Shari'ati refuted the quietist logic with the doctrine of "free will." He said that *insan* (human being) was made of clay into which the breath of God generated life. Clay, the lowliest of all matter, denoted the worst attributes in *insan*; God's breath (carrying His spirit) the noblest ones. God thus gave *insan* the best and worst elements of creation and then gave him Free Will to go whichever way he chose—toward clay (i.e., evil) or toward God (good).[75] *Insan's* soul thus is contested over by good and evil in which *insan* chooses whether he will seek God or not. *Insan* is thus the maker of his own destiny—to seek God, he has to wage a struggle *(jihad)* against his baser self in pursuit of the right way that leads to God. Islam is the pursuit of that very path of submission. Hence, as the maker of his own destiny, *insan* also has the responsibility for it as an *insan*. Hence, this responsibility was incumbent on the whole of mankind and could be discharged only through *al-amr bi'l ma'ruf wa'l-nahi 'an al-munkar,* the most frequently cited appendages to which is *jihad* and *shahadat*.

Connotations of *jihad* and *shahadat* in Islamic discourse have varied with the contexts in which such discourse took shape. Literally, *jihad* denotes "effort," but in the Qur'an and Islamic legal texts it is popularly taken to signify "effort" in a strict sense—namely, armed struggle against unbelievers, an injunction stressed as "*jihad fi sabil Allah.*"[76] During the time of the Prophet, such struggles were waged against all those who denied and opposed the Prophet and his message, and posed a threat to the fledgling Islamic community. Subsequently, *jihads* waged by Islamic states could be shown as much to have been in the interests of promotion of the Islamic faith as it was to defend the Muslim state/s that emerged in the course of time. Many participants in such *jihads* considered such participation a religious duty and a pious deed. Many believe that those who die in a jihad would gain *shahadat* and would be rewarded with a place in Paradise.

There is, though, no clear and unanimous position on what would pass for *jihad fi sabil Allah*.[77] A large section of *Ithna 'Ashari* Shi'i thinkers, for instance, would agree on the aim of *jihad* to be "removal of barriers that prevent the divine message from being [peacefully] conveyed to people throughout the world, so that the right way can be clarified and presented to all. It is to be expected that if the liberating message of Islam is prevented from being spread peacefully, then *jihad* must be undertaken, [but only] in order to remove these obstacles necessary for the peaceful propagation of message among such peoples."[78]

A *shahid*, by inference, is a person who dies in "defense of the faith" (thereby testifying or bearing witness to *(shahada)* the faith with great willingness. A perfect martyr or *ash-shahidu al-Kamil* is one who has either been slain in a *jihad* or killed unjustly.[79] The Qur'an is replete with mentions of *shuhahda*; of particular significance is where the *shuhada* are spoken of with *nabiyun* (Prophets), *siddiqin* (confessors), and the *salihin* (righteous).[80] A special blessing is promised to those of the *shuhada* who died in *jihad fi sabil Allah*: "Count not those who are killed in the way of the Lord as dead, but living with their Lord."[81]

Shari'ati's notion of *jihad* conforms primarily to this position of an effort/struggle in defense of the true Islam, and the equitable order and *'adalat* (justice) it promised. He argued that the Prophet of Islam "was appointed to complete the movement which has existed throughout history in opposition to deception, falsehood, discord, hypocrisy, aristocracy and class differences ... Equality was declared for all: and with philosophical disputation as well as by waging a *jihad* against the economically powerful regime, social equity was upheld."[82] Upon his death the forces of *shirk* had resurfaced and staged a comeback via the Sunni institution of the Caliphate where they retained the form of Islam but discarded its essence.[83] Imam 'Ali tried to stem the tide of *shirk*, but failed because of the challenge of Mu'awiya who then went on to set up the Umayyad dynasty at Damascus. The deviation from the essence of the faith was marked by the turning away from the simplicity and austerity that marked the lives of the Prophet and 'Ali as the seductive nature of affluence began to corrupt the Islamic Ummah, to the extent that even the wife of Imam Hasan, Ju'da, poisoned the Imam in order to marry Yazid, the son of Mu'awiyah.[84]

By the time Hossein became the Imam of the Shi'i, the Umayyad dynasty was firmly in the saddle of the Islamic state, with the *Muhajirun*, *Mujahidun*, and *Ansar* of the first generation either intoxicated with material prosperity (thus, deviating from the Islamic way of life), or silenced (as was Abu Dhar) through persecution upon expressing dissent over the aberrations that had crept into Islam, or even in retreat from an "Islamic" order that caused them great dismay, but about which they could do nothing beyond nonparticipation. Even amidst this dismal scenario, Hossein dared to take the most difficult option—that of standing by and dying for his convictions. Shari'ati praises this decision to wage a *jihad,* the outcome of which was not only foregone, but also one about which Hossein himself was aware.

> A responsible leader, Imam Hossein sees that if he remains silent, Islam will change into a mere civil religion ... Neither can he remain silent, nor can he fight ... He cannot remain silent because he has a duty to fight against oppression. ... [H]e cannot fight because he has no army.[85]

Yet he chose to fight because it was his "responsibility *(mas'uliyat)* to fight against the subjugation of truth, the destruction of the rights of the people, annihilation of all values ... destruction of the message of the revolution."[86] As a result, for Shari'ati, the significance of the tragic defeat and massacre of Hossein at the battle of Karbala by the Umayyad forces led by Yazid and his followers does not lie in the tragedy of the occasion, but in what it signified. It signified *istizhar* (exposure) of those very evils which had began to pervade Islam.

> Thanks to this exposure, any Islamic and learned person who believed in his own faith and virtue was careful not to get close to the regimes, even though the regimes were "Islamic regimes" ... the fatal blow of martyrdom had affected the history of Islam so deeply that the social conscience, option, and ethics of Muslim societies would ... read the mark of negation that Hossein stamped on the forehead of every government.[87]

From this point, Shari'ati argues, began the practice of negative resistance to government by the Shi'i. Where *jihad* in the sense of active militant struggle against an oppressive government was not possible, the willingness to wage *jihad* in order to rob the government/ruler of its/his legitimacy was immensely significant. This, Shari'ati was suggesting, was the responsibility that was incumbent on all Muslims following from the religious requirement to Command the Good and Forbid Evil, because for Shari'ati Islam was not simply about praying and performing ritual functions. Rather it was about striving in path of God *(jihad fi sabil Allah)* to bring about a *jama'-ye betabaqati* (egalitarian society) and *'adalat* (justice).

Shari'ati was thus recommending to the people to assume the responsibility of maintaining a just order by themselves. The ruling class, by virtue of its own nature, was likely to engage in *istibdad* (despotism), underwrite a system of *istismar* (economic exploitation), and seek legitimacy in the name of some higher cause through *istihmar* (deception). If the people do not remain vigilant, a just political and societal order would never be attained. The people would thus have to be constantly mindful of the imperative of *'adalat* (justice), enjoin it upon others and forbid its violation. And if a situation comes to pass when such enjoining is not feasible, even then—in the manner of Hossein at Karbala—a stand had to be taken because it is worth taking a stand for justice and perishing in the process, rather than eke out a life in conditions of injustice.

## Repercussions of Arguing Revolution

For the better part of Shari'ati's stint at the *Hosseiniyeh-ye Ershad,* his obvious target was the *'ulema,* with capitalists and the political establishment identified as a part of an evil triad. Each of these groups had different responses to make. The industrial entrepreneurs by and large ignored him as too insignificant. The *bazaaris* were split among those who were mesmerized by his advocacy of social justice (despite its potentially negative repercussions for their interests) and those who prompted their social ally, the *'ulema,* to oppose his discourse. The traditionalist *'ulema* were Shari'ati's staunchest opponents from the very beginning of his career as a lay commentator on Islam, but their attacks were mostly either on a personal level or carping at the inadequacy of Shari'ati's Islamic scholarship. This (along with Shari'ati's well-pronounced differences with the Marxist and Tudeh traditions) in fact made the Shah's regime initially take a lenient approach toward him.

However, Shari'ati's discussion of *Tashai'yo 'Alavi wa Tashai'yo Safavi* entailed a degree of radicalization which neither the *'ulema* nor the Pahlavi regime could take casually. For a prominent cleric, Sheikh Qassem Eslami the talk itself was "the first act of treason in the world of Shi'ism." According to Ansari-Qomi, the lecture convinced the *'ulema* that not only was Shari'ati intent on destroying the basis of the faith, but that his teachings were actually growing deep roots in the society, so much so that it was becoming difficult to argue with Shari'ati's followers about his fallacious propositions. Those who meant to soothe the clergy suggested that before Shari'ati's advent in the public space, the young used to frequent discotheques, cabarets, and cafes. By weaning them away and drawing them to *Ershad*, and popularizing an Islamic discourse Shari'ati was actually serving the cause of Islam. To this Sheikh Qassem Eslami's rejoinder was representative of the majority of the *'ulema*: that before the advent of Shari'ati the youth engaged in *fisq* (sin), yet they had neither lost their faith, nor were hostile to it or its clergy. The argument was that sin was better than apostasy, and Shari'ati was training Muslims to become apostates. By October 1972, there were clerics and *tullab* (seminary students) who would "happily stick a knife into Shari'ati."[88]

It was, however, Morteza Motahhari who came up with perhaps the most substantive clerical response to Shari'ati. Having been a patron at one point of time, Motahhari had even come under criticism from the more traditionalist *'ulema* because of his support for Shari'ati.[89] As late as 1969, Motahhari even defended many of Shari'ati's assertions in private and among his friends in the *bazaar*; faced with the prospect that a *fatwa* might be issued against *Hosseiniyeh-ye Ershad,* Motahhari assured one of his clerical colleagues—Aqa Mirza Abol Hassan Rafi'i—that being a student of *fiqh* and philosophy he [Motahhari] would know when Islam was in danger; and that he was being very vigilant indeed.[90] Motahhari subsequently sought Shari'ati to clarify or modify some of his positions. It was only when Shari'ati failed to comply that Motahhari began to grow distant.

This coincided with Motahhari's own power struggle with Naser Minachi for the control of *Ershad,* and Motahhari began to think that Shari'ati had joined forces with Minachi against him. He accordingly launched a bid to heel the "uncontrollable and stubborn" Shari'ati by having him thrown out of the *Ershad* in 1970. The deadlock caused Shari'ati to stay out of *Ershad* between August 1970 and April 1971 while his credentials as a speaker on Islam were being disputed; the struggle eventually lost Motahhari his position at the *Ershad*, and led to the reinstatement of an even-more-radical Shari'ati.[91] In fact, when after the death of Shari'ati in 1977 his popularity seemed to grow as the demonstrators began taking to the streets against the Shah, Motahhari had to clarify his position vis-à-vis Shari'ati in a letter to Khomeini. He wrote:

> It is a matter of fact which is not deniable that the only issue which the different groups—from the regime's supporters to the communists, the *Munafiqin-i Khalq* [lit. "hypocrites of the people," a pun on the name *Mojahedin-e Khalq*] and some seemingly religious groups who are pro-Shari'ati—all share this same desire, that is to damage fundamentally the *'alim* and to remove this obstacle from the scene.... As a consequence of his [Shari'ati's] teachings, a cleric [*ahl-e ilm*] is, in the eyes of today's youth, worse than a security officer.[92]

From his days as a student at Qom, Motahhari had always advocated a comprehensive reform of the clerical establishment. However, he believed that reform should come from within the clerical system, through a leading *mujtahid*, and not from outside, through the secular intelligentsia. Clearly this was at cross-purposes with Shari'ati and his understanding of the role of *raushanfikr*. Motahhari criticized the very idea of *raushanfikr* as a faithful reproduction of the views of Shari'ati's teachers at Sorbonne—Louis Massignon and Georges Gurvitch—as also of Sartre.

> It is not enough that we mix some chosen elements of foreign philosophies, such as Marxism and existentialism or similar philosophies, with our philosophy and then disguise them with a superficial Islamic stratum in order to guide our revolt towards the path of Islam. We must collect the ethics, history, politics, economics and religion through perspectives, which are inspired by Islamic texts.[93]

Unlike other critics of Shari'ati from among the *'ulema*, Motahhari did not indulge in carping over how Shari'ati was contradicting particular aspects of Shi'i orthodoxy. However, because of the concerns caused in the *bazaar* by Shari'ati's redistributive agenda, Motahhari felt compelled to defend property as an integral feature of the Islamic order in order to propitiate his allies in the *bazaar*. He mounted defense of property by citing the fact that paying the *zakat* was a pillar of the faith, implying that it was the duty of a Muslim to acquire property so that *zakat* could be paid for the well-being of the community. In his bid to have Shari'ati modify his views, Motahhari had earlier suggested that a board of clerics be allowed to vet all the lectures delivered by lay preachers at the *Ershad*; this virtually questioned Shari'ati's Islamic credentials. Motahhari then reached for the jugular by attacking Shari'ati's methodology of harmonizing Islam with a modified version of historical materialism (without naming him).

> Does Islam accept the theory of historical materialism? Is the Quranic logic based on historical materialism regarding the interpretation and analysis of historical events? There are people who claim that historical materialism was put forward by the Qur'an at least a thousand years before Marx.... It has become a fashion among a group of contemporary Muslim writers to analyze history in Islamic phraseology from this [point of view], which is considered the mark of being a *raushanfikr*. But in our view, those who think in this way either do not correctly understand Islam, or historical materialism, or both.[94]

Motahhari however refrained from attacking Shari'ati directly, because he thought it "fortunate" that "a new class of [religious intellectuals] has developed—being educated in the modern western culture and simultaneously having interests in Islam and Islamic studies. They represent Islam with a modern style, which is normally welcomed by the young generation who are naturally Muslims but who have become attracted to the western culture."[95] Perhaps the strongest statement that he made was after Shari'ati's death in 1977—and even this reflected his ambivalent posture toward Shari'ati:

> Since his [Shari'ati's] culture and higher education were western and he had not found a suitable opportunity to study Islamic sciences sufficiently, he remained unaware of some of the indisputable facts of the Qur'an, *sunnat*, *ma'arif* [gnostic knowledge] and *fiqh*—although, he was gradually, with many endeavors, increasing his information in this regard—[but] he has made many mistakes on Islamic issues and even principles.[96]

The response of the state was, of course, much more direct and significant.[97] The SAVAK had kept an eye on Shari'ati from 1967 because there were those in that organization who could read between the lines of what he had to say. Nonetheless, the SAVAK put up with Shari'ati partly because he refrained from any direct exhortation against the state. Still more important was the fact that from the very beginning the SAVAK had been obsessed with the communist and Soviet threat, and was alarmed at the rate which the disaffected Iranian youth kept on opting for Marxist-revolutionary path to overturn the regime. The popularity of Shari'ati's Islamic discourse probably convinced many in the SAVAK that being a body of modern, polemical and radical ideas Shari'ati attracted the youth, but was not revolutionary enough to challenge the regime. This assessment changed rapidly in 1971–72 when *Ershad* was revealed to be "a revolutionary beehive" from where the *Mojahedin* drew its ideological inputs as much as recruits. Shari'ati's works, especially *Abu Dhar: Soshialist-e Khodaparast* (Abu Dhar: the God Worshipping Socialist) was found to be an essential reading for the *Mojahedin*. By the autumn of 1972, as the subversive nature of the discourse emanating from the *Ershad* became clear, the very act of attending it was considered a statement of antiregime sentiments. On November 17, 1972, *Ershad* was closed down. By July 1973, the SAVAK was convinced that Shari'ati had close ties with the *Mojahedin*, leading to the decision to arrest him. After some attempts at evasion, Shari'ati gave himself up in September 1973, whereupon he was put away at the Komiteh prison. His career as a demagogue well and truly ended at this point—but the force of his ideas kept inspiring the youth of Iran through clandestinely printed monographs, collections or even cyclostyled speeches.

# 6

# The Individual as an Agent of Change: *Khudsazi-ye Inqilabi*

The urban youth of Iran had found in Shari'ati a voice that was completely different from that of any other political figure or ideologue, speaking for or against the government at a time of great social and economic change. The regime was busy projecting itself as the successor to the great Persian empires—the Achaemenids, the Sassanids, the Safavids—and was promising further greatness if the people were to follow the lead of the Pahlavi establishment. The opposition (be it Khomeini, advocating Islamic government from exile in Iraq, or Islamic democrats like Bazargan) each were speaking in terms of an Islamic order where the people were to be guided by laws (under a system of clerical or democratically elected stewardship). Shari'ati broke the trend by talking not of systems, but of the individuals who would make up the society.

This was important, for it addressed a major limitation of Pahlavi politics. The language of politics of Iran in the Pahlavi era, of the regime and the opposition alike, was premised on the assumption of popular sovereignty. But a crucial question was never quite resolved with any degree of clarity. In practice, where would sovereignty lie? Would the state embody the people, or would there exist a social order distinct from the state where sovereignty lay? The problem was a tough one largely owing to the Pahlavi agenda of modernization, which created a small body of beneficiaries and a large body of disaffected. However, despite its professed modernist claims, and imputations of *gharbzadegi,* the Pahlavi regime never got around to systematically defining the role of the individual in transforming a "community" into a "people."

The relationship between "community" and the "individual" tends to be a crucial aspect of the discourse on community formation and behavior. Although this discourse regarding the character of communities has varied according to assumptions concerning their cultural/intellectual nature, the preoccupation with situating the "individual self" in the broader matrix of the "collective self" has proven to be a regular feature. In the case of Islam/Islamic cultures, it is widely believed, by Muslims and non-Muslims alike, that Islamic culture prioritizes collective values to such an extent that it results in a nearly total subordination of the individual to the *ummah*.[1] Such an assumption frequently ignores individualist positions on societal and political mechanisms taken by renowned Islamic scholars and thinkers down the ages, favoring instead other pronouncements that stress on primacy of collective values.[2]

Several such individualist assumptions played a major role in the opposition discourse that developed in late Pahlavi Iran. The Islamic political movements that were generated in response to Pahlavi rule were inspired by a diverse set of political positions, ranging from the doctrine of *Vilayat-e Faqih* (Rule of the Jurist, propagated by Ruhollah Khomeini), through the ideal of Islamic democracy of the *Nehzat-e Azadi-ye Iran* (Liberation Movement of Iran), to the ideas of 'Ali Shari'ati. Despite the claims of each of these political positions to be inspired by Islam, they cannot be fitted into a single "Islamic" paradigm. Khomeini's political vision was heavily conditioned by his own personal career trajectory as an Iranian *Ithna Ashari* Shi'i *'alim;* Bazargan's *Nehzat-e Azadi* was the intellectual inheritor of several of the strands that made up the *mashruteh* (constitutional) movement in early twentieth-century Iran; Shari'ati developed his position from Existentialism and Third Worldism of the 1960s as much as reformist Islam and Iranian nationalism of the Mosaddeq years. Many of these positions, however, at one level or the other were prepared to valorize the individual in keeping with the ideal of *javânmardi* (derived from *javân,* young, and *mard,* man), shorthand for a set of values that a quintessential Iranian male was hoped would follow.

'Ali Shari'ati was, however, the only major political thinker who used the cultural trope of *javânmardi* deliberately in order to bring the "individual" to the heart of political discourse in modern Iran. Shari'ati's political thinking was oriented toward the task of confronting the aggregative Pahlavi construct of the *mardom-e Iran (Iranian people)* with an alternative individualist construct—that of an *Irani (Iranian)*—where the individual would be rated at his/her own worth. The individual that Shari'ati conceived of was, prima facie, to be rooted in the values of Persian culture and Islam, but had to be open to all ideas regardless of where they came from, because the human condition was everywhere essentially the same. Accordingly, the true test of the individual lay not in his/her following one set of ideas and beliefs or the other, but in the extent to which the individual could fulfill his/her potentials.

The distinctive feature of Shari'ati's treatment of the human condition was that despite using common Shi'i idioms and terms of references, Shari'ati did not bind himself to only religious categories in assessing the worth of an individual. The individual that comes out through his works is a distinctly modern being, conversant with all the debates pertaining to the human condition—the charm of conservatism, the limits as much as emancipating potentials of liberalism, the predicament of modernity, the substance yet the lonesomeness of existentialism. Above all, Shari'ati envisages an individual who would be political through and through and would engage with his society and its problems, and would be the building block with which the *ummah*, that is, a just society, could be built.

### The Man of Integrity: Javânmardi in Modern Iranian Society

The term *javânmardi* (*javân*, young, *mard*, man) denotes an existential ethic derived from the idea of youth. It is the Persian form of the Arabic *fotowwat*, which comes from the root *fati* (young); it is taken to mean a "man of integrity." Despite the fact that it seems to be a constant factor in Iranian culture, the origin and evolution of the cultural trope of *javânmardi* remains to be properly documented.[3] The diverse range of personalities who are claimed to have conformed to the code of *javânmardi* makes it very difficult to narrow down on any particular set of attributes as the essence of the concept. While philosophers like Henri Corbin would argue that it is possible to identify such an essence behind the trope running across several ages, sociologists like Fariba Adelkhah would disagree. Adelkhah contends, that such lifestyles as of the *javânmard* are inseparable from material (therefore, temporal) considerations in which they emerged, and "far from being an invariable that can alone account for behavior, it is a dynamic combination within which individual activities and social changes are discernible."[4] The ethic of the *javânmard* helped the emergence of "an individuality of eminence" with a certain charisma, but the individual that "emerged" did not embody the same qualities across the ages.

It can be said with some certainty that the adaptation of the existential ethic of *javânmardi* in its modern form began sometime during Qajar rule in the nineteenth century. In the background were some elements of assertion of something like a "national" identity in the context of penetration of the economy of the kingdom of Persia by the British and the Russians. There were also elements of struggle against despotism and arbitrary rule, which eventually fed into the *mashruteh* movement. Similarly, it is difficult to overlook elements of social protest against tax collectors (widely perceived as corrupt) of a state that had begun to centralize, or even a form of social banditry in the notion of *fotowwat*.[5] In either case, the *javânmard* in modern Iran would seem to have emerged in opposition to the power and/or policies of the state, in defense of a cause rising above (although not necessarily opposed to) personal interests.

Confronting a regime that was as repressive as it was weak, people of Qajar Persia sought some sort of security in local personalities of some importance. Communities used to look upon their community leaders to represent their cause before the ruler, and such leaders were seen as *javânmard* if they could stand up against policies prejudicial to the interests of the concerned people. This willingness to mediate between official action and the expectations of the subjects (which risked alienating the ruler of an arbitrary regime, thereby jeopardizing personal standing, property, and even life) symbolized *mardanegi* ("valor befitting a true man") and a good deal of *shojâ'at* (courage). Community leaders from the *bazaar* trying to persuade the rulers, through deputations and protests (such as calling a general strike) to reverse government policies that ran against the interests of the subjects,[6] or replacement of some public official who fell out with the people[7]—all such activity would call for precisely such *mardanegi*. Such activity would be possible only if the person concerned were widely known *(sarshenâs)* and enjoyed a considerable degree of influence over, and support from, the local community.[8] Such influence, in turn, could flow from either one's personal social status (viz. that of a distinguished *'alim* such as during the Tobacco Protests of 1892) or one's ability to extend patronage to others (especially material support at times of economic hardship that characterized late nineteenth-century Persia). Hence, material generosity *(sekhâvat)* could prove to be crucial in the making of a *javânmard* since the late Qajar times, if not earlier.

It needs be appreciated, however, that values like *shojâ'at, mardanegi, sekhâvat*, etc. individually did not necessarily denote *javânmardi*, at least not till 1979.[9] It was essential for a *javânmard* to be, above all an *adam-e ijtema'i* (social being). He is expected to "do without (him)self" *(az khod gozashtan)*; He "is not overwhelmed by the good things of this world, he can give up his interests, he willingly 'does without' his wealth by letting others benefit by it."[10] The *javânmard* ethos was by its very nature a manner of assertion of the "self" where the key lay in overcoming the narrow confines of the "self"—that is, a *javânmard* must be humble. It allows him to get on the stage and build his life doing exemplary deeds to win attention from others, and acquire self-respect. However, neither the attention nor the self-respect can be set as goals to be achieved. The *javânmard* is expected to find his own fulfillment by allowing the society/community to benefit from the attributes of his being.

The trope of *javânmardi* became politically significant in the last five decades of Qajar rule in a situation when the government and a large segment of the society seemed to be at cross-purposes, and society sought to circumscribe the powers of the ruler. The success of the Mashruteh revolution of 1906–09 in setting up a constitutional regime marked a temporary victory of the people over the ruler. When Reza Khan Pahlavi dislodged the Qajars in 1925, and became the Shah, it was thought to have marked yet another triumph of the people because prima facie this ouster was legitimized by a popular referendum. Reza Shah, moreover, emerged as the most determined proponent of a modernization program that was deemed necessary to remove the weakness that seemed to characterize the Iranian state under Qajar rule, so much so that to some Iranians, he himself personified the ethic of *javânmardi*.

\* \* \*

Shari'ati's engagement with the trope of *javânmardi* took place from within the Sufi tradition. During 1963–68, a phase in Shari'ati's life when he was at his mystical and poetic best, he was torn by a dilemma. On the one hand, lay his sense of disorientation or even cultural shock after his return to Mashhad from Paris; his disappointment with his social environment and preoccupations and concerns of those who used to be close to him; and his weariness of organized political activity in Pahlavi Iran. On the other hand, Shari'ati's stint in Paris sharpened his sense of social responsibility, inspired as much by left-wing French intellectuals as by Third World activists and Algerian nationalists. Ironically as it may appear, this dilemma affected not so much Shari'ati's public persona as it did his private, Sufi, self.[11]

Some of Shari'ati's Sufi idols like Abu Yazid (Bayazid) al-Bastami and al-Hallaj strongly believed that concern for people distracted the pursuit of God.[12] Pursuit of inner peace was based on "pietistic devotion of the practitioner's entire life to the search and eventual communion with the Truth." Shari'ati saw the practice of this anti-social brand of Sufism as effectively collaborationist, a source of alienation, resignation and acquiescence. Later, as Shari'ati's radicalism reached a peak, he cited al-Bastami and al-Hallaj as examples of alienated Sufis.[13] He identified this variant of Sufism as a reactionary and collaborationist Islam that survives in collaboration with, and facilitates the existence of the triad of *zor, zar,* and *tazveer*.

Shari'ati was more at home with a second variant of Sufism that was characterized by heroism, aggressiveness, and a tendency to challenge the status quo.[14] He saw this variant as one that taught the individual the means of obtaining freedom from the shackles of religion, the ruling classes, and all other oppressive forces.[15] Shari'ati argued that this variant of Sufi thinking was responsible for repeated movements attacking repression, despotism, and "the decadence, aberration and hollowness of Islam." Sufism therefore had the potential to become a movement rebelling against a soulless Islam of "restrictions and obligations."[16]

Among the works that Shari'ati read around this time (1970s) were those of Sa'id Nafisi, who argued that Sufism in Iran was cultivated not only among the elite, but the same notions and principles were also propagated among the common people under the name of *fotowwat* or *javânmardi*. Such *fatiyan* (sing. *fata*) or *javânmardan* (sing. *javânmard*) were reputed for their selflessness in the name of just and noble causes. They helped the needy and the distressed, liberated those who were subjected to tyrannical rule, brought food to the hungry and provided the people with spiritual and moral guidance. In this way of understanding the essence of Sufism, the Sufi was no longer an introverted hermit, but a heroic fighter for just and honorable causes.[17]

The impact of this dimension of Sufism on Shari'ati was quite profound. He read into history the evidence of how individuals, working selflessly for others, have repeatedly tried to change the course of history, and doing so have fulfilled their human potentials more than the followers of academic Gnosticism unmindful of the human context ever could. This particular reading of Sufism underpins his entire notion of *khudsazi* (self-reconstruction).

### Reworking the "individual": "raushanfikr" as "javânmard"

On January 8, 1968, the 1956 Olympic middle-heavy freestyle wrestling gold medalist Gholamreza Takhti was found dead in suspicious circumstances. While the Iranian press reported the death as a suicide, regardless of the substance of such claim no one believed in it. This National Front activist admired for his chivalry was given a hero's burial. Takhti's death provided an ideal occasion for students across Iran to vent their antiregime feelings; it generated considerable activity in the Mashhad University, and fed into a meeting commemorating the foundation of the Iranian Peoples' Party. The meeting was held at the home of Mosaddeq Rashti, a student of the Faculty of Literature at the University, who was associated with the Takhti commemorations. 'Ali Shari'ati was one of the eleven people present at this meeting. In the course of the discussions, Shari'ati referred to his experiences in France and argued that "success in political struggle was only possible through a relentless educational campaign." He criticized the type of political struggle conducted in Iran and argued that the only alternative was to create a conducive militant environment in the universities.

"People," he said, "had to be compelled to think." He identified his own political vocation as posing problems and provoking contradictions in the minds of his students, and rejected the idea of any premature organized opposition activity at a time the state was riding so high.[18]

Shari'ati thus had defined for himself the role he sought the *raushanfikr* to play in society. His experience in France at the height of the Algerian struggle had convinced him that no substantive change can occur in a society without popular involvement, but, he felt, the people seldom realized that they could usher in any change. He resented the idea popular in Iran's Marxist circles that the force of *jabr-e tarikh* (historical determinism) would invariably usher in thoroughgoing social change in Iran once the conditions were ripe for a change. As he put it:

> Contemporary "intellectuals" generally believe that dialectical contradictions in any society necessarily moves the society forward toward freedom and revolution, and give birth to a new state of being. According to this logic, mere "poverty" or "class-differences" which symbolize the existence of social conflicts, inevitably lead to a dialectical contradiction, which in turn creates motion in the society. In reality, however, this is not more than a big illusion. *No society will be mobilized and obtain its freedom merely because of the existence of class-differences or tragic disparity between rich and poor*. Poverty and class conflict may exist in a society for thousands of years without causing any structural transformation. *Dialectic has no intrinsic motion*.[19] [Emphasis mine]

The *raushanfikr* that Shari'ati spoke of, therefore, had the responsibility to give intellectual and social direction to the masses of that particular society.[20] In other words, a *raushanfikr* had to be an *adam-e ijtema'i*. Shari'ati argued that an enlightened person "is not necessarily one who has inherited and continues the works of Galileo, Copernicus, Socrates, Aristotle and Ibn Sina," because they had insulated themselves from the problems afflicting their societies. Rather, the *raushanfikran* were similar to the prophets in being "aware and responsible individuals whose most important objective and responsibility is to bestow the great God-given gift of 'self-awareness' *(khud-âgâhi)* to the general public."[21]

\* \* \*

In Shari'ati's thinking, the role of the human "self" was pivotal to the whole understanding of Islam. Interpreting the allegory of creation in the Qur'an, Shari'ati argued that Islam acknowledges the ambivalent potentials of humanity: human beings were capable of fulfilling the nobler possibilities latent in their personality (represented by the life carried by God's breath in human soul); they were equally capable of yielding to the baser side of the human condition (symbolized by clay).[22] Man is thus the maker of his own destiny. To seek God, he has to wage a struggle *(jihad)* against his baser self in pursuit of the right way that leads to God. Islam is the pursuit of that very path of submission before the will of God. In the realm of this world, the *ummah* is the ideal that man has to attain in order to realize the will of God. Hence, as the maker of his own destiny, man also has the responsibility for it.

Shari'ati delved into the Islamic past to show how, down the ages, the selflessness of certain individuals had altered the course of history by assuming responsibility for creating a just order. He cited Prophet Muhammad as the exemplar *javânmard* in this respect. Despite being a habitual loner in early life, upon receiving revelation from Allah the Prophet ceased to be reclusive. He went instead, straight into the heart of the city of Mecca, and delivered his message atop the Safa Heights, opposite the Dar al-Nadwah (where the Meccan nobility used to gather) to denounce the false gods, and save the people. The choice of the venue was designed to carry his message to the largest number, and the message itself was one that was to ensure the people liberation from tyranny in the name of innumerable gods. Among all the prophets sent by God, as Shari'ati pointed out repeatedly, only Muhammad stayed on the side of *al-nas* and fought with established powers until he carved out a space for a just order—in a manner befitting a true *javânmard*.[23]

Imam 'Ali continued with this tradition of fighting for the oppressed masses, standing for "honesty, rectitude, truth and justice" at a time when Uthman, in his capacity as the *Khalifat al-Rasul* "like a magnetic pole, attracted all the counter-revolutionary agents." 'Ali became representative of the struggle in defense of the new set of values that Islam came to represent against the greed and worst elements of *jāhiliya* that Uthman set about upholding. In a vein clearly evocative of the struggle that the opposition to Pahlavi regime was waging, he valorized 'Ali as "the embodiment of Islam in an age in which an internecine struggle took place... between friend and pseudo-friend, or should we say, 'an internal enemy' who paid mere lip-service to the movement."[24] To Shari'ati, 'Ali was "a human being who in different and contrary scenes of life" behaved like a true *javânmard*—"a champion of sword, eloquence, wisdom, faithfulness, self-sacrifice, belief, truth, adoring, generosity, patience, piety, simplicity, justice and worship."[25]

Imam Hossein, however, was probably the one whom Shari'ati valorized the most. Not only did he personify the virtues of *shojâ'at* (valor), *fidakari* (selflessness) and *khod-agahi* (self-awareness) he also personified the value of action. The significance of the tragedy of Karbala was not simply the proof of Imam Hossein's *mardanegi* (manliness), but also the fact that when he went into the battle, he was alone. He could have given up— the way Iranian opposition activists and politicians had given up against the Pahlavi regime—and either made his peace with Yazid, or else he could have retreated into a limited private sphere without legitimizing the Umayyads, as his brother Imam Hasan had done. Instead he decided to fight for the cause of Islam, for an order which was just and equitable, to the point of self-extinction. Shari'ati argued, that the *istizhar* (exposure) of Umayyad inequity could not have been more forcefully driven in by any successful *jihad* as it was by Hossein's *shahadat*.[26]

The value of Hossein's action lay not in its success or failure, but in the act itself—because the act alone sufficed to spread awareness of the nobility of his cause and the evil that his adversaries stood for. The exposure of evil itself generated a sense of responsibility that inspired such self-effacement in the defense of Islam and the cause of the *ummah*—an act in the true tradition of *futuwwat*. This action, however stemmed from *considerations* about the ideal order. The *ummah* had to be aspired to *not because* mankind was so told by God, but because man *realized* it to be in the best interests of mankind. Thus, a consummate *javânmard* was a thinking man, a self-conscious man, and a socially responsible being—that is, a *raushanfikr*.

### The Question of Iranian Women: Why Was Fatima the Way She Was?

The trope of *javânmardi* has come under considerable criticism in postrevolutionary Iran. As a young Iranian academic, Fatemeh Sadeghi, puts it—the trope deals with the values, responsibilities, and concerns of *mard-e javân* (young man); what of the *zan-e javân* (young woman)?[27] A fair number of postrevolutionary Iranian academics have criticized Shari'ati rather harshly for his depiction and valorization of the Prophet's daughter Fatima Zahra as the embodiment of the ideals of Islamic womanhood without seriously engaging with the question of womanhood at all. While they accept that Shari'ati was more accommodative of the role of women than any other prerevolutionary religious thinker, lay or clerical, they also point out that by choosing figures like Fatima and Zainab as embodiments of the qualities of Muslim women he circumscribed their ambit of activities too narrowly.[28]

Shari'ati engaged with the question of the role of women in Islamic society at a crucial time. The Pahlavi regime had identified emancipation of women from their traditional Islamic roles as one the essential components of its modernization agenda. The educational opportunities made available to women equipped them to compete for participation in the civil society. By the end of the 1950s women were becoming visible in many vocations and activities. This major change in Iranian society was acknowledged by the enfranchisement of women during the White Revolution, and by increasing number of women appointees in various public offices, in the teeth of opposition from the traditional elements of society, especially the clergy. However, because of the resounding response in favor of emancipation during the 1960s, even the traditionalists swallowed the principle of emancipation and tried to circumscribe the limits of emancipation in accordance with Islamic *fiqh*, the principal architect of this revised position of the clergy was Morteza Motahhari. Motahhari's attempts at engaging this issue, however, came in the wake of Shari'ati's opening up of the debate with some highly charged discussions on the role of women in Islam at the *Hosseiniyah-ye Ershad*.

Of the 37 volumes of the collected works of Shari'ati, only one (volume 21, called *Zan* i.e., Woman) deal with the position of women directly. Of all the works on the theme, the most renowned was the talk he delivered in April 1971 at *Ershad*, which was later transcribed as *Fatima Fatima Ast* (Fatima is Fatima)—a text that is considered to "mesmerize" Islamic modernists even today. In it, Shari'ati contended that there are three visages of women in contemporary Islamic societies such as Iran: the traditional woman, the new woman modeled on European women, and the third is the visage of Fatima "which has no resemblance whatsoever to that of the traditional woman. The visage of the traditional woman, which has taken form in the minds of those loyal to religion in our society, is as far away from the face of Fatima as Fatima's face is from the modern woman."[29] The difference between the traditional and the modern Shari'ati ascribed to the reality of a changing society—the traditional woman strove to remain true to a stereotype inherited from an era when "values and social characteristics were incapable of change"; a modern woman "without having gone astray, without having been corrupted, creates a distance between herself and the traditional woman." By using the analogy of a mother and daughter, Shari'ati said that the traditional woman ("mother") "is pulled and preserved by habit." The modern woman ("daughter") on the other hand, "is just beginning the first days of the journey." He then added very perceptively, that the distance in terms of social time will diminish between the mother and the daughter. Their relationship would be exactly the same relationship that the mother had to the grandmother. "The change from the traditional type of mother to the new type of daughter is inevitable."[30]

Shari'ati attacked the traditionalists, especially the *'ulema*, for seeing the old as being synonymous with tradition, thus calling every change, including even change in dress or hair-do, *kufr* (infidelity). The woman in their view, must remain as she is today, conforming to social traditions that are centuries old. "They accept this view because it has become part of their way of life or because it suits their interests... They say, "Islam wanted it to be this way. Religion has taken this form. It should remain like this until Judgment Day"."³¹

Shari'ati then warned that "everything changes." "If we wish to keep the forms because of our own inexperience, the inconsiderate speed of time will run us over. We must realize that destruction is also a reality. The insistence upon preserving these forms will bear no fruit because society will never listen."³² Very clearly, Shari'ati was pointing out that the transformations in Iranian society and the changing features of womanhood was a product of historical movement; and the values and stereotypes that were being dismantled were products of a different societal order framed in a different context.

> When we equate religion and social traditions, we make Islam the guardian of declining forms of life and society. We confuse cultural and historical phenomena with inherited, superstitious beliefs. Time comes along, and as it moves in haste, it changes habits, forms of life, social relationships, historical phenomena and ancient cultural signs. We mistakenly believe the Islamic religion to be these social traditions.³³

He then went to warn those enamored of the stereotype of modern women of the west that the examples they had ahead of them were those that the capitalist system wanted them to emulate. The western/westernized media showcased concerns of material comfort, sexual freedom, and women's rights in such a way that encourages consumerism—but that was not the only face of the western woman. He complained how the media never highlights the case of those European women who have escaped the trap of consumerism and achieved something substantive in life by spreading awareness and knowledge in many different fields—from ornithology to physics, from philosophy to the politics of revolution. "The women in the west have progressed to the point of becoming the embodiment of an ideology of a country and place, of salvation, pride, and the honor of a generation."³⁴

Having analyzed how the visage of women change from the one to the other, Shari'ati then embarked on his discussion of Fatima. Interestingly, the discussion of Fatima covers only a fourth of the whole lecture, and strictly speaking even less because much of the discussion is taken up by Fatima's father, the Prophet, and her husband, 'Ali—the two principal male protagonists in her life. Shari'ati depicts Fatima as the dutiful daughter who held the charge of the Prophet's household, until the Prophet took Ayesha as his wife and Fatima could set up her own family with 'Ali—who thinks "only about *jihad*, God and people. He will return home with only empty hands." As in the Prophet's household, so in the house of the first Imam, Fatima was the pillar of support and the source of comfort, herself living a life of drudgery, hardship, and self-sacrifice.

The portrayal of Fatima as the dutiful daughter and the silently suffering wife fits so neatly with the patriarchal stereotype of womanhood that activists for women's rights in Iran today find little in Shari'ati to appeal to them. As Zeba Mir-Hosseini points out, of the 200 pages of the text, fewer than ten deals directly with the question of women in Islam. Even there, Shari'ati neither elaborates on the position of women in the *Shari'ah*, nor does he engage with the proponents of *Shari'ah*-centric discourse on women. "Instead he uses the occasion to elaborate his own interpretation of Shi'i history, to condemn those in power for distorting it, to denounce Iranian society as one of pseudo-Muslims whose ways have little resemblance to true Islam, and to blame clergy and intellectuals alike for not enlightening people on true Islam. Although he criticizes narrow interpretations of the Shari'ah, he remains imprecise and evasive himself."[35]

Confronted with this criticism of Shari'ati's position on the role of women, Shari'ati's defenders and apologists came up with an interesting set of responses. Nahid Tavassoli, who prefers to remember Shari'ati more as a friend than to think of him in his persona of a demagogue, saw a clear difference between what Shari'ati said at *Ershad*, and what he said in private conversations. Tavassoli remembers Shari'ati as a man who did not make any major distinction between the rights and responsibilities of men and women. His relationship with his wife, Pouran, his upbringing of his daughter, Suzan, and his conduct toward friends like Tavassoli bear this out very clearly. So why did he not challenge the traditional Islamic notions concerning the subordination of women? Tavassoli argued, that the *Hosseiniyah-ye Ershad* lectures were among the very few public gatherings where even the most traditional families would not hesitate to send their daughters. If Shari'ati were to bare his radical persona and beliefs in totality, the emancipating role *Ershad* had come to play among the women of the most conventional parts of the society would have been lost.[36]

Taqi Rehmani, a staunch disciple of Shari'ati hailing from a traditional background, argues that there was no such dichotomy in Shari'ati's public and private persona. Upon being asked why was Fatima chosen as the model for Muslim women to follow, and not, for instance, 'Ali, Rahmani's response was simply that Fatima was a woman, 'Ali was not—and Shari'ati appreciated the difference between the two without assigning one of these more value and the other less. "Men and women are equal but different."[37]

The response of Reza 'Alijani (who despite never having met Shari'ati considers him his intellectual mentor) was probably the most balanced. He agreed with Tavassoli that in the private sphere Shari'ati made no distinction between man and woman, but 'Alijani argues Shari'ati was careful enough to acknowledge it by endorsing the standard symbolisms in societal life. 'Alijani then goes on to suggest that despite such endorsements of standard symbolism, Shari'ati also legitimized the changing perceptions of the social role of modern Iranian women. 'Alijani believes, that after the White Revolution opened up opportunities for the economic independence of Iranian women, it was no longer easy for even the most traditional families in urban Iran to make the women behave as generations before them had done. Hence despite the Islamic Republic's championing of Motahhari's text on the role of Muslim women as the model of Iranian womanhood, that text really does not hold much water in postrevolutionary Iran.[38] By contrast, he points out, Shari'ati's lambasting of the stereotypes of the traditional Muslim womanhood gave even traditional families in prerevolutionary Iran some food for thought, and helped open up the discourse on women's rights in a Muslim society.[39]

However, neither the critics nor the apologists are interested in commenting on why was Shari'ati speaking of Fatima as a third visage, if she was simply a variation of the traditional woman? Also, why was it necessary to dedicate nearly a third of the talk to the questions faced by women in modern Iran as a prologue to his discussion of Fatima? For even by Shari'ati's own standards of digression this was excessive. A possible reason could have been the presence of a large number of women among his regular listeners—but then he need not have waited till April 1971 to address that particular constituency.

A more plausible answer is one that takes into account the timing of the delivery of the lecture. The lectures on womanhood came immediately after Shari'ati spoke on the responsibility of the *raushanfikr*, on 'Ali, and, most significantly, after the lectures on 'Ali's Shi'ism as against Safavid Shi'ism—but before the discussions veered toward Hossein. In other words, in Shari'ati's schema, the lecture on Fatima was integral to the making of his argument on Islam as a political ideology advocating resistance—as a *mazhhab-e aitraz* (religion of protest) where all the principal protagonists were engaged in some form of resistance to injustice. Fatima served this symbolic purpose well because she publicly protested when the succession of the Prophet was usurped by Abu Bakr, even when 'Ali kept quiet because of pragmatic considerations. So doing, in a virtual anticipation of Hossein, she challenged the legitimacy of the succession itself. Moreover she challenged the legitimacy of Abu Bakr not simply because her husband was deprived of succession, but because the successor did not represent the values and ideals of equity and justice that that the *ummah* of the Prophet had stood for till that time. She was punished for her opposition with illegal confiscation of her property; she eventually died a lonely death near her father's grave, rather than settle with an unjust ruler. Such a conduct was in the best traditions of *futuwwat / javânmardi*.

Moreover, what is taken to be an inordinately lengthy prologue on the condition of women actually encapsulates the main argument, which is presented behind the guise of a discussion on Fatima. Shari'ati's principal argument seems to have been that whatever societal demands might be made of *women* in particular contexts (tending the home and the hearth, looking after the father, the husband, and the children) the ultimate identity of a Muslim, man or woman, lay in resisting injustice. If the conditions are not right for direct confrontation, then the mere expression of difference or disagreement *(ikhtilaf)* would suffice, but that expression of opposition to injustice is essential as a part of the individual's *masu'liyat-e ijtema'i* (social responsibility) to spread awareness of injustice. So Zeba Mir-Hosseini is right in saying Shari'ati did not engage with the *position* of *women* in Muslim societies. His agenda was to engage with the *responsibilities* of (Muslim) *individuals,* men or women. In speaking of the western "women we cannot know" because of the selective portrayal of womanhood by the media, Shari'ati spoke of European and American activists who had discharged their social responsibility quite handsomely. The implication is clearly that unlike any of the traditionalist Muslim woman or her "westernized" daughter, such westerners, whom the clergy would mark out as "a disbeliever destined for hell," were cast in the mould of Fatima, the mold of a responsible individual.

### The Individual as a Driving Force

In speaking of exemplary feats of *khud-âgâhi* Shari'ati repeatedly referred to the exemplars as *waris-e Adam* (heir of Adam). This term was very deliberately loaded with multiple layers of significance. At the most literal level, all the protagonists of Islam were inheritors of a monotheistic tradition that began with Adam, hence anyone upholding the true faith was, after all, a *waris-e Adam*. At a slightly more intricate level, all the champions of Islam were inheritors of the charge of the Creation that Adam had boldly volunteered to accept, when all other of God's creations had turned it down. Adam might have been naïve in accepting the charge, but he set the standards by assuming responsibility for something he considered worth preserving. At the most intricate level, however, the term can be sheared of all the standard Islamic allegory to argue that the inheritance of Adam was not simply of monotheism (in the predominant sense of the term), or even of the charge of creation. The inheritance was, above all, of the *human* condition, and what it means to *be* a human being. Here the Sufi in Shari'ati had Shari'ati the existentialist as his interlocutor. The influences of a lifetime of exposure to the existentialism of Heidegger, Camus and above all Sartre made Shari'ati inquire into the human condition not simply in terms of God's (finest) creation; rather whether it had a meaning in *itself*.

The *raushanfikr* of 'Ali Shari'ati partially reworked the cultural trope of *javânmardi* in the context of late Pahlavi Iran, so much so that the *adam-e ijtema'i* was expected to be a thinking being. Far more important, imagining the *raushanfikr* as a *javânmard* Shari'ati highlighted the significance of the individual in the Islamic scheme of things. This in itself was nothing new. In fact in according centrality in sociopolitical dynamics to the individual, Shari'ati was conforming to the general trend in modern Islamic political thought (ranging from Jamal al-din Afghani, through Muhammad Iqbal to Anwar Ibrahim). The real worth of Shari'ati lay elsewhere. Conceptualizing the significance of the individual in terms of the hitherto metaphysical category of *tauheed*, he was able to harness the attributes of the "individual" as conceived by the school of "existentialism" to rework the potentials latent in the metaphysics of scholars like Ibn 'Arabi and Mullā Sadrā.

In Islamic philosophy, the individual has often been conceived with an inherent element of dynamism that frequently eludes the casual observer. In their preoccupation with studying the example of the *Insān al-kāmil* (the Perfect Man) that the Prophet was meant to be, most Muslim philosophers refrained from working out the attributes of that perfection. The twelfth-century Andalusian philosopher Ibn 'Arabi for the first time tried to address this issue, when he argued that God created the universe in order to be known, but this knowledge can be actualized only through human beings. Created in God's image, they possess the potential to know and to live all His Attributes. Those people who do so are the "perfect beings," commonly called the prophets and the *awliya' al-Khuda* (friends of God). "Becoming" human represents the unfolding of what people are, but from the human perspective, the course of this unfolding is not fixed. Freedom plays an important role in the process of becoming.[40]

The sixteenth-seventeenth-century Iranian philosopher, Mullā Sadrā synthesized the views of Ibn 'Arabi and others who followed him from within the Platonic tradition in Islamic philosophy to come up with his own concept of "Perfect Man" in the context of his doctrine of "transsubstantial motion" *(al-harakat al-jawhariyyah)*.[41] Claiming that existence cannot be static, Sadrā argued that existence moves continuously and successively through higher and higher forms of "evolutionary modes of being," culminating in the Perfect Man, without which the creation would have no meaning. Echoing Ibn 'Arabi and subsequent Muslim mystics, he defined this last stage of human perfection in terms of *khud-âgâhi* (self-awareness) and awareness of the existing relationship with the Divine Being. Mullā Sadrā thus proposed a more humanist vision of the world in perpetual progressive evolution toward perfection, and a more positive faith in man's spiritual ability to perfect itself.

Shari'ati's perspective of *tauheed* was an intellectual extension from ruminations about the Perfect Man and his awareness of his relationship with the Divine, which Shari'ati argued to be one of unity. He rejected the existentialist position that man's existence has no inherent purpose, that man himself ascribes meanings to his being. The doctrine of *tauheed* with the emergence of something akin to the "perfect man," which Shari'ati simply calls *Insan*, was an adequate raison d'être of the human condition. Shari'ati however gave the notion of "free will" a dimension that was altogether new in Islam, adapting the existentialist notion that man makes his choices freely and is completely responsible for the outcome of such choices, Shari'ati reworked the relation between *batini* and *zahiri* dimensions of Islam in an innovative manner.

As Colin Turner indicates, Shari'ati was able to identify the problem of excessive stress on the *zahiri* (external) aspects in the predominant discourse of Shi'i Islam in Iran. However, Turner suggests, that instead of advocating stress on the *batini* (internal) aspects like al-Ghazzali, Mullā Sadrā (or even Khomeini), he set out to prescribe a whole new set of values that were merely variations on the same theme. His means of removing the stultifying effects of externalism of the Safavid *fuqaha* on the masses was merely a *zahiri* variant of interpreting *Ithna Ashari* Shi'ism, albeit in a revolutionary manner.[42]

Shari'ati's position blended smoothly with the politics of the twentieth-century lay Islamists in Iran, which stemmed from a renewed emphasis on *'iman* as against *fiqh* (Islamic jurisprudence).[43] Lay Islamists argued that over the previous centuries the *zahiri* elements of the *farz al-'ain* had eclipsed the relative importance of *iman*, since belief was not easy to gauge but enforcement of external codes and regulations was easy. Thus even though Iranian society continued to adhere to Islamic rules and regulations over the ages, it was merely Muslim by practice, not a community of true Believers *(mominin)*. One reason behind this decline in belief *(iman)* was, indeed, the restriction of *'ilm* to archaic studies associated with Islam, without accounting for the changing world.[44] However, they meant to use this *'ilm* and apply it to the precepts of Islam, in a bid to understand Allah and his creation better.⁴⁵ Given such comprehension of the will of Allah, the *momin* becomes a *raushanfikr*.

In Shari'ati's interpretation of Shi'ism, and Islam in general, deeds spoke louder than words. It was not the Islam of an individual gaining knowledge of God, believing in Him, correcting himself and acting as an example for the salvation of others, which was the way Khomeini thought it should be. Shari'ati's Islam was a vehicle for collective political experience, where action is all-important, hence his reduction of key tenets of the faith to little more than political formulae on occasion.⁴⁶

However, Shari'ati did not play down faith *(iman)*. Nor is it that he assumed *iman* merely to be the basis of all action, and then concentrated solely on action. Shari'ati conceptualized *iman* differently. For Shari'ati, action in itself was not redeeming; it had to be exerted in the proper cause, which constituted the core of *iman*, that is, creating conditions for the fulfillment of human dignity and attainment of true human worth. In his words:

> Of course, "belief in God" must be the basis of enjoining good deeds upon others and forbidding evil... But in my opinion, God's main purpose in creating man was not that man should believe in God—since God is not in need of man's belief—but rather that man should struggle in the name of his fellow men to bring about that which is good and do away with that which is evil.⁴⁷

*Iman*, according to Shari'ati, was integral to activism for the cause of Islamic order, founded upon equity and justice. Failing to work toward this end denoted ignorance about, or unwillingness to assume the responsibilities of, "free will." This was why he was insistent in his attacks against the *'ulema*, marked by their Safavid brand of legalist Shi'ism, that they served to conceal the essence of 'Ali's Shi'ism *(tashayyo 'Alavi)*. This, he contended, robbed Islam of its vitality. He exhorted the *raushanfikr* to step forth and help the masses rediscover the essence of 'Ali's Shi'ism, so that they could strive to be aware of themselves, and thus restore Islam (and Iran) to their lost glory.

Shari'ati's doctrine was, therefore, a blend of the *zahiri* element of activism and the *batini* element of *iman*. It is only in becoming *(shudan)* that one could really be *(budan)*; internal "truth manifests only in action." This harmonious blend of the internal and external aspects of Islam produced a dynamic political ideology driven by the efforts of the individual (in the generic sense), with active resistance to unjust authority as its cardinal tenet.

The centrality accorded to the individual in Shari'ati's thought thus forms the nucleus of a counterhegemonic discourse that can be used to confront not only the statist Pahlavi ideology, but even a collectivist Islamic worldview, which constitutes one of the ideational points of reference of any Islamic order in popular imagination. In any given set up, if the ruling authority presumes to subordinate the interests of the individual (in the generic sense) in the name of collective interests (religious, national, societal) to the extent that it thwarts the (extremely vague) values of equity and justice, such an authority would be ipso facto "unjust." It becomes incumbent on the self-aware individual *(fard-e Khud-âgâh)* that is, a *raushanfikr*, then, to stand up like a *javânmard* against such an unjust order and usher in a change for the better.

### Situating Shari'ati's Discourse of Self in Islamic Modernity

The binary of "tradition" and "modernity" in the context of Islam is quite frequently supposed to revolve around their respective approaches to the human individual. Traditional Islam is popularly associated with an idea of primacy accorded to the *ummah,* where the individual supposedly does not have any overriding significance. Hence, the "traditionalists" emphasize on the primarily legalist approach to the issue of "being" for a Muslim. A Muslim individual, in order *to be* a Muslim individual has to conform to the practices of the faith and obey the regulations that bind the *ummah* together.[48]

On the other hand modernist Muslims, like Jamal al-din Afghani believed that unless Muslims dared to break out of the "traditionalist" logic of conformism, Islamic societies would continue to stagnate and would be overwhelmed by the material superiority and prosperity of the western world. But the nineteenth-century "modernist" Muslims had continued to think in terms of the community as central to the Islamic notion of order. If Muslim societies were backward, then it was necessary for them to be forced to shed their backwardness. Hence, the traditionalist urge to bind the Islamic collective with regulations was replaced by the modernist urge to bind the collective with the "new learning" of material sciences—the rhetoric of collective conformity to the straight path of Islamic laws was replaced by that of collective conformity to the path of Islamic values. The Islamic imagery as late as the turn of the twentieth century, thus, remained primarily one of a community that existed only as a collective identity. The individual had little independent existence.

Interestingly, one of the defining preoccupations of Islamic modernity was that revolving around the "individual self." The preoccupation was driven not simply by the need to accommodate some intellectual contradictions between "tradition" and "modernity," although that was the principal raison d'etre of "Islamic modernism." It was in nearly equal measure prompted by the need to go beyond "tradition" and "modernity" and establishing the category of "self" on an Islamic matrix. It is tempting to conclude that the "self" was an ideational category that was borrowed by the "Islamic modernists" from the west—this is possibly not entirely correct. Muhammad Iqbal (1873–1938) and 'Ali Shari'ati, the twin architects of the category of "self" in "Islamic modernism," valorized the "self" in a context where the twin forces of traditionalism and modernism had championed the collective identity over the individual.

Muhammad Iqbal's notion of the *khudi* (self) was the immediate point of reference for Shari'ati's notion of *khistan*. Iqbal believed that the Qur'an in its simple, forceful manner emphasized the individuality and uniqueness of man, and has a definite view of his destiny as a unity of life. It is in consequence of this view of man as a unique individuality that makes it impossible for one individual to bear the burden of another, and entitles him only to what is due to his own personal effort, that the Qur'an is led to reject the idea of redemption. Iqbal went on to suggest that human sensibilities of pleasure and pain, joy and sorrow are all personal to individuals; not even God could share in those.

> [T]he element of guidance and directive control in the ego's activity clearly shows that the ego is a free personal causality. He shares in the life and freedom of the Ultimate Ego who, by permitting the emergence of a finite ego, capable of private initiative, has limited this freedom of His own free will. This freedom of conscious behavior follows from the view of ego-activity which the Qur'an takes.[49]

In other words, Iqbal jettisoned the whole rationale for *taqlid* by arguing that blind emulation of jurists is not only not advisable for Muslims, but also actually opposed to the very will of Allah who gave man the capacity to forge his own destiny for himself. It was thus man's responsibility to engage in the task of forging his own self in such a manner that he could attain the highest possible stature in God's eyes. This concept of the autonomy of the *khistan* Shari'ati then went ahead to politicize.

Dismayed by the traditionalism of the *'ulema* and materialism of those Muslims who had succumbed to the temptations of westernization, Shari'ati (like Iqbal before him) called for an essentialization of what he identified as Islamic values, such as justice and equity. His idea of the "individual" was not inspired by the predominant understanding of the theory of "individualism" in the western liberal tradition—*fard-e khud-âgâh* was not an individual who pursued only gratification of personal interests. His/her self-awareness ipso facto drives him/her to engage with the society around him/her, very similar to the notion of the individual in the western "conservative" tradition. In Islamic modernism, this preference for engagement with the society around the individual constitutes the core of *being* an *insan* (human). For the existentialist in Shari'ati therefore, the problem of "being" was solved very simply (just as it had been for Iqbal)—the purpose of "being" is *insan shodan* (to become a human being). Reconciling this existentialism with Islam, both of Iqbal and Shari'ati contended that the purpose of Islam was to fulfill the potentials of *being* a human. But breaking with nearly all previous understandings of the human condition in Islam, Shari'ati followed Iqbal to argue in favor of the autonomy of the individual "self" vis-à-vis the community. It was not an autonomy of being *(budan)*, rather one of doing *(kardan)*. The "self" was to find its meaning and fulfillment only in working toward collective well-being, but it was to enjoy an autonomy in *determining* what constituted this well-being—and, most importantly, it had to defend this autonomy from the logic of conformism. Hence the emphasis on *ijtihad,* which, too, Shari'ati borrowed from Iqbal.

Iqbal and Shari'ati, needless to say, never met. Sharia'ti was only five years old when Iqbal passed away. But Shari'ati was a direct legatee of Allama Iqbal to the extent the notion of the "self" was concerned. Like a good legatee he built his own idea of *khistan* upon Iqbal's legacy by politicizing the notion of *khudi* with his own emphasis on the notion of *khud-âgâhi*. The *raushanfikr* of Shari'ati's thought was a direct extension of the conscious ego that Iqbal had portrayed in his *Asrar-e Khudi*. In fact, as Shari'ati had once put it, Iqbal personified the very essence of a *raushanfikr*:

> [Iqbal was] a reformer of Islamic society, who thinks about the conditions of human and Islamic society, a society in which he himself lives and for which he performs *jihad* (i.e. struggles nobly in the way of God) for the salvation, awareness, and liberation of Muslim people.... He struggles and strives and, at the same time, he is also a lover of Rumi. He journeys with him in his spiritual ascensions and burns from the lover's flames, anguishes, and spiritual anxieties. This great man does not become one-dimensional, does not disintegrate, does not become a one-sided or one-dimensional Muslim. He is a complete Muslim. Even though he loves Rumi, he is not obliterated by him.[50]

This notion of being at one with some other being/beings, yet retaining one's own autonomy, lies at the core of the Islamic modernist understanding of the individual. The sense of individuality, in turn, has proven to be the mainstay of Shari'ati's ideology of resistance in the modern Islamic world to the hegemonic discourse of the state and society alike—because the individual, in order to remain an individual has to engage in a perpetual act of *khudsazi-ye inqilabi* (building the self for revolution). Such championing of human initiative as a motive force for change—rather than any notion of historical inevitability determined by economic forces or even religion—appealed to a generation of urban Iranians more than anything else. Here lay the real charm of the revolutionary political Islam that Shari'ati was advocating. Islam as explicated by him did not constrict Muslim activity within an ossified jurisprudential structure; it emancipated. This was also the reason why two years after his death, when the Islamic revolution occurred, Shari'ati was immediately hailed as the ideologue of the revolution. And even when the Islamic Republic began to move toward Khomeini's doctrine of the *Vilayat-e Faqih,* Shari'ati could not be discarded altogether from the revolutionary baggage.

# 7

# The Ripples of a Revolution

'Ali Shari'ati was never allowed to speak in public in Iran after his imprisonment in 1973. Upon protests from Egyptian, Algerian, and other foreign academics he was let out of prison but kept under house arrest in 1975.[1] In May 1977 he left Iran for Belgium by means of a subterfuge.[2] By the time of his death in June 1977 he was already a legend among the urban Iranian youth, so much so that when the massive public demonstrations began against the Shah in 1977, posters of Shari'ati were held aloft by the demonstrators alongside those of Khomeini. By this time, in view of the popularity of Shari'ati's ideas among the youth, Morteza Motahhari had succeeded in modifying many visible differences that existed between the rhetoric of the clerical thinkers and that of Shari'ati. The additional fact that both Khomeini—the leading ideologue among the 'ulema—and Shari'ati—the lay ideologue—were raising several similar objections to the nature of the Pahlavi regime (and even of the 'ulema) made it easier to speak of a united front of political Islamists. The circle was complete when Mehdi Bazargan, along with his *Nehzat-e Azadi*, decided to accept the leadership of Khomeini. Once the opposition closed ranks, civil society followed its lead, to the point that the oil industry workers joined in the calls for the Shah to go. At that stage, the momentum developing against the Shah became virtually unstoppable.

When the Shah abdicated and the revolution began to take shape in the winter and the spring of 1979, there was yet to be a coherent or uniform Islamic ideology. Despite all the years of developing an Islamic language of political resistance, even as an Islamic Republic was proclaimed after a referendum on March 30–31, the protagonists of the revolution were not in agreement as to what specifically made the republic Islamic. Khomeini's declaration on the occasion of the proclamation of the Republic was vague about the Islamic character itself, even as it made hostility to the west or western models very obvious:

> I ask the government that, fearing neither East nor West and cultivating an independent outlook and will, it purge all remnants of the tyrannical regime, which left deep traces upon all the affairs of our country. It should transform our educational and judicial systems, as well as ministries and government offices that are now run on western lines or in slavish imitation of western models, and make them compatible to Islam, thus demonstrating to the world true social justice and true cultural, economic and political independence.[3]

Given the experience of the Pahlavi era, the revolutionaries—lay or clerical—were convinced of the inadequacy of the scheme of institutional checks devised by the *Mashruteh* revolution, hence the case for *mashru'eh* (government in accordance with the Shari'ah, requiring oversight by the *'ulema*) became stronger. But Khomeini and corevolutionaries "had only a vague notion of the government they would create to transform Iranian society."[4] It was only after seizure of power that the revolutionaries confronted the problem of state-building, undertaken by the provisional government of Mehdi Bazargan, named Prime Minister by Khomeini on February 11.[5]

The draft constitution proposed by the Bazargan government conceived of Iran as a republic on the Gaullist model with a strong presidency.[6] On social welfare and private property it did not differ much from the Pahlavi era. It guaranteed limited individual rights and freedoms like the 1906 constitution. It paid lip service to the idea of an Islamic state but did not enshrine any special privilege for the clergy, apart from the limited veto powers of the Council of Guardians to keep laws in conformity with Islam. There was no mention of the *Vilayat-e Faqih* and no special position for Khomeini. The draft was approved by the cabinet and the Revolutionary Council (including Motahhari and Akbar Hashmi-Rafsanjani), and Khomeini made only two changes (in part to bar women from Presidency and judgeships).[7] The secular opposition demanded that the draft be submitted to an elected Constituent Assembly, with powers to revise the draft: the government settled for a compromise—an Assembly of Experts was to be elected, authorized to amend and redraft the constitution.[8] The Islamic radicals, who made up the town revolutionary committees that played a significant role in the popular mobilizations of 1978–79, also were against this constitution. They prevailed in the election to the Assembly of Experts with the blessings of Khomeini, who was by that time alarmed at the manner in which the secular opposition was bent on completely secularizing the constitution.[9] Khomeini himself gave them the spur when on June 5, 1979 commenting on the anniversary of the 1963 uprising at *Faiziya Madraseh* in Qom, he laid the claim that only the *'ulema* had been consistently opposed to the Shah's oppression of the people, accordingly they should be in charge. He also warned that all those who had not stood against the Shah, this was to be their opportunity to stand for the people by standing for Islam.[10] The Assembly of Experts dominated by the radical Islamist clergy, meeting in August 1979, promptly rejected the draft constitution and prepared instead a constitution that introduced theocratic elements, which characterize the present system, absent in the first draft. The demand that Khomeini as *faqih* should be entrusted with supreme authority was also made around this time. "It quickly became clear to Khomeini and his lieutenants that there existed considerable support and no mass opposition to the constitution and that the constitution could serve to institutionalize both supremacy of the *faqih* and clerical rule."[11] It was only around this point that Khomeini's doctrine of *Vilayat-e Faqih* began to be pushed as the official revolutionary ideology.

Among the forces ranged in opposition to the doctrine of *Vilayat-e Faqih,* apart from the secular constitutionalists were the left-wing revolutionary outfits like the *Fedayan* and the *Mojahedin,* inspired by 'Ali Shari'ati. The *Mojahedin-e Khalq* embarked on a particularly violent resistance to the imposition of theocracy, and the Republic could suppress them only through a brutal campaign of counterinsurgency under the cover of national emergency during the Iran-Iraq war.[12] But some other Shari'ati enthusiasts were considerably swayed by the manner in which the Republic adopted many of the egalitarian components of Shari'ati's thinking, and especially his activist reading of *intezar*. Accordingly they decided to cast their lot with the regime, and helped in its manufacturing of *one* Islamic revolutionary ideology that could be presented before the world. Among such enthusiasts were a body of the *'ulema,* the *Jama'-ye Rouhaniyat-e Mobarez* (Society of the Combatant Clergy), advocating a redistributive economic policy.[13]

## Shaping a Revolutionary Ideology

Despite the institutionalization of Khomeini's principle of *Vilayat-e Faqih,* the Islamic revolutionary ideology was not altogether a simple adaptation of that doctrine. Revolutionary ideology evolved by means of a reflexive discourse shaped first by the debate on the constitution, and then by demands for regional autonomy made by the Azeris, the Kurds, the Baluchis, and Arabs, which required Islam to be projected as the tie that binds Iranians. The ideological posture was further strengthened by the radicalization of the political situation around the U.S. Embassy hostage crisis, and then finally the invasion of Iran by Saddam Hussein's Iraq. The language of political Islam, which had emerged as a language of political resistance to state authority thus began to be steadily appropriated by the state as the revolutionary regime began to congeal in the 1980s.

In the course of 1979, the *komiteh* (revolutionary committees in the cities dominated by the *'ulema*), and the sermons of the revolutionary clergy at mosques and in the media, successfully conveyed the image of "the revolution under siege" from within (i.e., from the secular opposition) and without (from the United States and Israel, two of the staunchest allies of the deposed Shah). They persuaded a large number of people that the danger of a Pahlavi return would persist so long as western influences remained strong in the country's institutions. Hence the revolution was not quite over with the departure of the Shah, it had merely begun. For the revolution to be consolidated, the Islamic (meaning, free-of-western-influence) character of the Republic had to be ensured. Since the *bazaaris* and many other Iranians feared that the United States would not give up its interests in Iran easily, their impression fitted with what the clerics told them, hence the resounding victory of hardliner clerics in the August 1979 elections. The idea that the U.S. Embassy was effectively "a den of spies" subverting the Republic was reinforced by Washington's decision to grant the Shah asylum. The seizure of the U.S. Embassy was prompted by a kind of "defensive reaction," thereby, ironically, ensuring continued U.S. hostility to the Republic. Prime Minister Mehdi Bazargan, who was in the middle of negotiations with the United States at that time, was taken by surprise at the news of the incident and promptly resigned. The United States understandably took umbrage at violation of its territory and broke off diplomatic ties. Given the turbulent domestic situation, and the tense diplomatic stand-off over the hostage crisis in the international arena, the Islamic regime appeared extremely vulnerable. Anticipating an easy victory, Saddam Hussein invaded Iran apparently to settle a long-standing territorial claim Iraq had on its neighbor. This helped the projection of the notion of "the revolution under threat" to come true. The U.S. hard line had already been seen as a proof of evil American designs on Iran, and Washington was labeled *Shaitan-e bozorg* (the Great Satan). Iraq's invasion was immediately denounced as a part of a conspiracy hatched by the Great Satan in conjunction with Zionist Israel—thus all "enemies" of the Islamic regime were painted with one brush.

A far greater problem had to be solved with reference to the war. Having instituted Islamic law as the law of the land, technically the regime could not shed the blood of fellow Muslims. The regime thus began to engage more consciously with the process of formulating an ideology, in order to mobilize the Iranian people to defend their land, and also establish its own legitimacy more firmly in the minds of the people. The war was, therefore, declared to be a *jihad fi sabil allah* (*jihad* for the cause of God)—waged in order to defend the Muslims and the Islamic way of life against a combination of threats.[14] Montazeri later divided *jihad* into *jihad-e ibtida'i* (initiative *jihad*) and *jihad-e difa'i* (defensive *jihad*), and labeled the war against Iraq as a *jihad-e difa'i*.[15] The war against Iraq was further defended as one against *bughat* (dissenters), which required it to be fought lest it deceived other Muslims. Khomeini defended this war citing the war 'Ali fought against the Umayyad opponents. Almost taking a leaf out of Shari'ati's exhortations on 'Ali, Khomeini proclaimed: "*They wanted ['Ali's enemies] to turn Islam to the same things that existed during the jahiliya but under cover of Islam* ... When we are in such a situation ... it is necessary and an Islamic duty that we defend Islam ... This war is not between Iran and Iraq, it is a war between Islam and *kufr*."[16] [Emphasis mine]

The essentialization of the revolutionary regime as Islamic and opponents of the regime (domestic and foreign) as *kufr* (unbelievers) was premised primarily upon the distinction between *iman* and Islam championed by many Muslim modernists, Shari'ati being one of the most vocal. From the mid-1960s, Shari'ati had spoken of *shirk* as a range of activities that hinder justice, which he argued to be the essence of Islam. In a Muslim society where *shirk* prevails, Islam has to be defended by the *mominin* until the *ummah* (understood by Shari'ati as a just order) is attained. Till then society witnesses a conflict between *tabaqeh-ye qabeel* (the ruling class or oppressors) and *tabaqeh-ye habeel* (the people, or the oppressed). Khomeini in his pronouncements on politics from around the mid-1970s used a similar frame of reference derived from the Qur'an: that society was divided into the *mustakbirin* (lit. arrogant)/*zalimin* (oppressors) and the *mustazafin* (lit. disinherited)/*mazlumin* (oppressed). At that stage, since both the thinkers were speaking out against the inequities of the Pahlavi order, both those rhetorical positions were (correctly) understood to refer to roughly the same kind of dispensation of power in a society. Upon the outbreak of war, Khomeini and many other protagonists of the revolution drew a logical extension to the argument—that having ousted the iniquitous Pahlavi order the Islamic Republic was, ipso facto, an embodiment of the interests and concerns of the *mustazafin,* that is, it now had attained the status of *ummah*. Thus, whoever was opposed to the Islamic regime was, by definition guilty of *istikbar* (arrogance), which was said to be also an expression of *kufr* (or *shirk,* as Shari'ati would have put it). Saddam Hussein was alternately denounced as *Kafir, munafiq* and *taghut* (lit. idolater)—glossing over the technically different connotation that each carried[17]—in order to mobilize the masses *and* defend the legitimacy of the Islamic Republic *as* an *Islamic regime*.[18]

In an assertion of arguments similar to Shari'ati, 'Ali Khamenei (who later succeeded Khomeini as the *Rahbar* upon his death) spoke in detail about the activism that was latent in the Shi'i notion of *intezar* addressing a gathering in 1981. He argued that since the revolution was in the interests of the oppressed people of the world crushing materialist expectations, and the Islamic Republic was fighting against the great powers of the world, the revolution had thereby brought forward the reappearance of the Imam, since the revolution was fulfilling the Imam Mahdi's purpose of restoring justice to the world. *Intezar,* therefore, was expectation of the rule of the Qur'an and Islam—and the Islamic regime had the task of installing justice because the *mustazafin* were unable to do it by themselves. Every step taken to promote the continuity of the revolution thus hastens the return of the Mahdi.[19]

To the considerable discomfort of the Islamic regime, however, the attempt to create an ideological monolith did not fully succeed. As Asef Bayat argues, although Iran witnessed a social revolution that put "Islamists" in power, the social revolution itself did not have the particular Islamic character that was subsequently imposed on the people. Thus, the Islamization of public life attempted by the authorities in the Islamic Republic was flowing from the top downwards, and was sought to be resisted by the people once the crisis posed by the Iraq war was over.[20] Several challenges have been mounted by various intellectuals against the so-called revolutionary ideology in general, and the principle of *Vilayat-e Faqih* in particular, reflecting the growing disquiet over the manner in which the Republic works. These challenges have proven crucial to the making of the dynamic and continuing debate on the meaning of the Islamic Revolution in Iran nearly three decades after the departure of the Shah.

## The Struggle Within

There are two major components to the challenge mounted against the Islamic revolutionary ideology in the Islamic Republic from those using the language of Islamic politics. On the one hand is the position first adopted by Ayatollah Kazim Shari'atmadari, later endorsed by Ayatollah Hussain 'Ali Montazeri, which questions the principle of *Vilayat-e Faqih* itself from within the discursive space of Shi'i jurisprudence, suggesting that the *'ulema* should play no direct role in politics. On the other hand is the more intricate question of what constitutes the *Islamic* element in the revolutionary ideology—raised by lay and clerical critiques alike.

Shari'atmadari following a long tradition among the Shi'i *'ulema* preferred to stay aloof from the machinations of politics.[21] As early as the turbulent days of September 1979, when the principle of *Vilayat-e Faqih* was being instituted, Shari'atmadari voiced his agreement with the secular nationalists and Islamic democrats alike that a new constitution and political system should be created by a broad-based, elected constituent assembly in which the *'ulema would not* be involved.[22] Shari'atmadari's problem with the doctrine, which Ayatollah Taleqani also seemed to have shared, was the exalted status it conferred upon one individual *faqih* (jurist) who was to hold the office of the *Rahbar,* the highest executive and juridical authority in the country.[23]

Indeed, Khomeini seldom involved himself with the quotidian aspects of governance in the Islamic Republic, but whenever he intervened he did so by virtue of his position as the *Rahbar*. Such conduct of the office, by implication reduced all other *marja'-e taqlid* to a subordinate position, even though some of them (like Ayatollahs Golpayagani and Shari'atmadari) were reputed to have better credentials as *faqih* than Khomeini. The problem came to a crisis point when the issue of succession to Khomeini began to be considered in the late 1980s, because none of the other *marja'-ye taqlid* had the political skills which the post required. Accordingly, *marjai'yyat* (ability to function as a source of emulation for the faithful) was discarded as a precondition for the appointment of *Rahbar*, facilitating the rise of 'Ali Khamenei, Khomeini's disciple and the President of the Republic, to the post of *Rahbar* despite him being merely a *Hojjat al-Islam* (a mid-level cleric).[24]

Khamenei's elevation to the office of *Rahbar* in 1989 evoked fresh criticism of the doctrine of *Vilayat-e Faqih* from several prominent *fuqaha,* who complained that the office was being transformed into an unelected but all-powerful executive—and in so doing, it was threatening the functional autonomy from the state that the Shi'i *'ulema* had enjoyed for quite some time. The office of the *Rahbar,* they charged, was being abused to enforce an authoritarian system in the name of Shi'ism. The most well-known protagonist of this critique of the *Vilayat-e Faqih* was, ironically, one of the architects of the doctrine itself: Ayatollah Hussein 'Ali Montazeri.[25] He was initially slated to succeed Khomeini, but his gradual disenchantment with the system had caused his removal from that perch. In 1994, responding to attempts of Khamenei's associates in Qom to have him declared a *marja,'* Montazeri categorically condemned such attempts as a subversion of the autonomy of the *'ulema* (and therefore, of religion) by the state— the very offence that Muhammad Reza Shah had committed. Montazeri went on to contend that Khamenei's interpretation of the doctrine, saying that the *Rahbar* is not bound by the laws of the land, "contradicts religious principles."²⁶ Despite Montazeri being put under house arrest and kept *incommunicado* after this outburst, the debate he opened up on the office of the *Rahbar* has continued. Although outright questioning of the doctrine itself remains a crime in the Islamic Republic, efforts to rework the meaning of *Vilayat-e Faqih* have gathered momentum. Clerical critics of the doctrine (such as Montazeri and Sayyid Muhammad Khatami) persist in their attempts to circumscribe the powers of the office by emphasizing the compatibility of the notion of *Vilayat-e Faqih* with the idea of accountability of the *Rahbar* before the people he is supposed to lead.

\* \* \*

While the debate on the doctrine of *Vilayat-e Faqih* seems to revolve primarily around the institution of the *Rahbar,* a more substantive and intricate set of questions have been raised about the very *Islamic* character of the Republic. These questions, raised by lay and clerical thinkers alike, do not accept the institutionalization of *'ulema* in the saddles of power as adequate justification for calling it Islamic, and seek instead to measure the attainments of the Islamic Republic against what the opponents of the Shah had set out to achieve in 1979.

Perhaps the most prominent among such thinkers is the lay philosopher Hossein Dabbagh, who is better known by his pen-name of Abdolkarim Soroush (b. 1945). A student of the prestigious 'Alavi secondary school in Tehran, Soroush had his first university degree in pharmacology in Tehran; in the mid-1970s Soroush went to England for a Masters in analytical chemistry at the University of London, followed by several years of research in the philosophy of science. Around this time, Soroush was attracted to attempts to produce political interpretations of religious texts by thinkers like Bazargan, Motahhari and most of all Shari'ati. Courtesy his reputation as a formidable critic of Iranian leftist and Marxist discourse, he was appointed the Director of the Islamic Culture Group of the *Tarbiat-e Modarres* (Teacher's Training College) in Tehran after 1979. He was later appointed a high-ranking member of the Advisory Council of the Cultural Revolution, which was responsible for the purge of Iranian universities in the 1980s. Soroush's apologists, however, contend that he was appointed to the council *after* the purges and restriction of free speech among the academia, and that in fact he was instrumental in the subsequent relaxation of controls. In the late 1980s and early 1990s his investigations into the process of change in the interpretation of texts made him a considerable number of enemies in the ruling establishment. At present there is a ban on his teaching, writing and speaking in public in Iran.²⁷

Having been associated with the Islamic Republic in its earlier years and trusted by Khomeini himself, Soroush has turned out to be arguably the most high profile intellectual dissident in the Islamic Republic. Inspired by 'Ali Shari'ati's lectures at *Ershad* in the late 1960s, Soroush believes the reconciliation of changes in the modern world with the notion of immutability of Islam requires neither "revival" nor "reconstruction" of Islam itself. Soroush argues that in order to meet the challenges of modernity, Muslims should not seek to change their religion; rather they need to reconcile their own understanding of religion with changes in the outside world.[28] Almost taking a leaf out of Shari'ati's *Ravish-e Shenakht-e Islami,* he argues that *ma'rifat-e dini* (religious knowledge), in which the *'ulema* specialize, is "only one among many sources of human knowledge, and should not be confused with religion itself." This implies that when a particular position is taken to be "Islamic" or "un-Islamic," such assessment merely indicates what the commentator *understands* to be Islamic; the nature of such deductions are largely shaped by the methodology adopted. Soroush however cautions that even the methodology adopted cannot predetermine the outcome of any investigation of the meaning of Islam, because religious knowledge changes and evolves over time, as more comprehensive understandings replace previous, more limited ones. All interpretations, therefore, are bound by the era in which an *'alim* lives, and the degree of advancement that the religious and natural sciences have made in that particular era—virtually echoing Shari'ati's opinion on the matter.[29]

Soroush appreciates the role played by Islamic ideology as formulated by people like Shari'ati in galvanizing the opposition to the Shah in the run-up to the revolution, but he refuses to accord ideologies the status of religion.[30] He defines ideology as a social and political instrument used to determine and direct public behavior situating itself in opposition to other such instruments. Necessarily such instruments tend to be reductionist in nature. Soroush contends that ideologies tend to reduce the complexity of religion to a fixed ideological worldview—as, for instance, Shari'ati posited Islam as a plank of justice in opposition to injustice and inequity. Such reductionist approach to Islam necessarily vitiates one's understanding of the complexity of the faith. Soroush believes, religion is "more comprehensive than ideology," and supports aspirations to an understanding that includes and exceeds the values enshrined in ideology. He goes on to argue that the Iranians had resorted to Islamic ideology against the Shah because the state had ceased to be *'adl* (just), and they sought to establish instead an *ijtema'-ye dini* (religious society) which they hoped would establish *'adalat* (justice). But the Islamic Republic, claiming to uphold the one "genuine" Islamic order and suppressing all other possibilities of interpretation, was content to turn the religion of Islam into an ideology—and therefore can be said to have forfeited the initial agenda of establishing a *ijtema'-ye dini* (religious society) by founding an *hukumat-e ideolozhi* (ideological order). He puts the distinction clearly as follows:

> In an ideological society, the government ideologizes the society, whereas in religious societies, the society makes the government religious. In an ideological society, an official interpretation, an official interpretation of ideology governs, but in a religious society, [there are] prevailing interpretations but no official interpretations. In an ideological society, the task of [formulation of] ideology is relegated to the ideologues. In a religious society, however, the issue of religion is too great to be relegated to the official interpreters alone. In a religious society, no personality and no *fatwa* is beyond criticism. And no understanding of religion as religion is considered the final or most complete understanding.[31]

Soroush's concept of *ijtema'-ye dini* (religious society) is remarkably similar to Shari'ati's notion of *ummah*. Shari'ati contended the notion of *'adalat* is integral to Islam, so much so that an order that is not just is *ipso facto* un-Islamic; and Shari'ati understood justice primarily in terms of an order that would establish equity, facilitate the process of *insan shudan* (lit. becoming human, i.e. help human beings fulfill their human potential). Soroush says nearly as much when he comments on what he understands to be religion and religious society:

> [J]ustice is at once a prerequisite for and a requirement of religious rules. A rule that is not just is not religious. Justice, in turn, aims to fulfill needs, attain rights, and eliminate discrimination and inequity. Thus *'adalat* (justice) and *hoquq-e bashar* (human rights) are intimately connected... [T]he effort to restrain and restrict power is closely related to the establishment of justice and human rights.... [T]he right and acceptable religion should, inevitably, be just.[32]

Despite his reservations about confusing religion with ideology, therefore, Soroush himself does not seem to have risen above identifying the essence of religion as a normative category. Further making a connection that Shari'ati never did in as many words, Soroush maintains that the essence of a religious society is analogous to the democratic ideal.

> Religion [in itself] and religious understanding [what we think of as religion] rely on... rational precepts. Once the status of reason, particularly the dynamic collective reason, is established; once the theoretical, practical and historical advances of humanity are applied to the understanding and acceptance of religion; once extra-religious factors find an echo within the religious domain; and finally, once religion is rationalized, then the way to

epistemological pluralism—the centerpiece of democratic action—will be paved.

> Sober and willing—not fearful and compulsory—practice of religion is the hallmark of a religious society. It is only from such a society that the religious government is born. Such religiosity guarantees both the religious and democratic character of the government.... [This] sensibility permits the transformation and variation of religious understanding. The acknowledgement of such varieties of understanding and interpretation will, in turn, introduce flexibility and tolerance to the relationship of the ruling and the ruled, confirm rights for the subjects, and introduce restraints on the behavior of the rulers. As a result, the society will become more democratic, humane, reasonable and fair ... the result will be religious democracy.[33]

Soroush's insinuations are fairly clear. The Islamic Republic has devised an ideological order, but has failed to promote the development of a *religious society* that the Islamic Revolution was supposed to usher in. Hardliner elements associated with the regime contended that Islam, acknowledging as it does that only God is sovereign, is incompatible with democracy because of its assumption of popular sovereignty.[34] Soroush argues such a contention confuses Islam with *fiqh* (jurisprudence), and observes that "the *shari'ah* is not synonymous with the entirety of religion." He then goes on to underline what he considers to be the yardsticks against which the failure of the Republic in attaining democracy, therefore religious society, can be measured:

> Democracy comprises of a method of restricting power of the rulers and rationalizing their deliberations and policies, so that they will be less vulnerable to error and corruption, more open to exhortation, moderation, and consultation; and so that violence and revolution will not become necessary. Separation of powers, universal compulsory education, freedom and autonomy of the press, freedom of expression, consultative assemblies on various levels of decision-making, political parties, elections and parliaments are all methods of attaining and securing democracy. Conversely, a nation that is illiterate, unfamiliar with its rights, and unable to attain them, in other words, a nation deprived of the right to criticize and choose, will be unable to achieve democracy.[35]

Soroush's critique was tantamount to a challenge to the Islamic "self" that the revolutionary regime had sought to construct. It was considered intimidating enough for the Republic to impose major restrictions on Soroush's activities and movements in the country for the better part of the decade of the 1990s, causing him to live in virtually self-imposed exile. The regime's discomfort, however, only grew further when one of the candidates for the

Presidency of the Republic, Sayyid Muhammad Khatami voiced a similar critique of the revolutionary establishment, challenging its conceptions of the "other" in a manner that ultimately reworked the ideas of the "self."

\* \* \*

Like Soroush, Sayyid Muhammad Khatami too was an "insider" of the Islamic revolution who later became disenchanted with the totalitarian color that the regime gradually acquired. Khatami (b. 1943) was the eldest son an open-minded and immensely popular prayer leader of Yazd, Ayatollah Ruhollah Khatami.[36] In 1961 Muhammad Khatami went to the *Hawzeh-ye 'Ilmiyeh* in Qom to study theology, where he became a student of Ruhollah Khomeini. While studying philosophy at the Esfahan University for his Bachelor's degree, he developed a deep interest in western philosophy, and particularly western political philosophy. It was also during this period that he joined the left-wing students association at the University and became exposed to the ideologies of the Islamic left. He was particularly drawn to the ideas of Shari'ati, whose works he continued to read long after he left the university and returned to Qom to resume his studies in *ijtihad*. Khatami then went to Tehran University for his master's degree in philosophy at a time when Shari'ati was at the height of his popularity in 1970.[37] Thereafter, Khatami returned to Qom once again to finish his doctoral study in philosophy. In 1978 he was appointed director of the Hamburg Islamic Centre. In 1980 he returned to Iran and was elected to the Majlis as a member of the *Jame'eh-ye Rouhaniyat-e Mobarez* (Society of Combatant Clergy). After a brief stint as the director of the *Keyhan* publishing house, he became the minister of Islamic Guidance in 1982. Over the next few years, even as he defended the autocratic policies of the regime, his misgivings grew about state repression. By 1987, even before the end of the Iran-Iraq war, Khatami began to call for a more open cultural regime. Hardliners opposed Khatami's program for the liberalization of the cultural regime but could not dislodge him because of the support he enjoyed from Khomeini. After Khomeini's death, President Rafsanjani continued to back Khatami till the pressure became intense, and Khatami had to resign in 1992.[38] He was then appointed the head of Iran's National Library and continued to function as cultural advisor to Rafsanjani. In the five years that followed, Khatami produced a series of books where he questioned many aspects of the official revolutionary ideology. In 1997, he ran for the post of President and won the elections by a landslide, ushering in what many Iranians called the Thermidor of the Islamic Revolution.[39]

Central to Khatami's ideas is the relationship between *din* (religion) and *tamaddun* (civilization). Khatami, like Soroush, distinguished between *din khudash* (religion itself) and *tafsir-ha-ye gunagun-e din* (many different interpretations of religion). Interpretations of religion are invariably subjective, addressing "specific needs and dilemmas of a community in a particular time and place."[40] Following the general drift of Shari'ati's lectures on the *Tarikh-e Tamaddun* (History of Civilizations), Khatami observes that civilizations emerge from such different interpretations. By contrast, he thinks, religion itself is objective, and has an eternal life that transcends civilization. He expresses his conviction that civilizations are neither monolithic nor self-contained, rather that "the give-and-take among civilizations is the norm of history." Indeed " 'new' civilizations are never new in true sense, for they always feed on the work of previous civilizations, appropriating and digesting all that fits their needs, dispensing with all that does not."[41] Accordingly, civilizations tend to engage in a dialogue with each other, each benefiting from advances made by other civilizations. However, Khatami cautions, such *guft-o-gu-ye tamaddun-ha* ("dialogue of civilizations") has to be carried out with an awareness of religion itself, because such awareness enables adaptation of experiences of other civilizations into one's own; on the other hand, lack of such awareness simply leads to the abandoning of one's own values in pursuit of those of another. Khatami contends that it is the duty of *raushanfikran-e dini* (religious intellectuals) to perform this crucial task of engaging in the "dialogue of civilizations."[42] He believes, three such *raushanfikran-e dini*—'Ali Shari'ati, Jalal Al-e Ahmad and Ruhollah Khomeni—helped create a new Islamic civilization in modern Iran by endowing it with "dynamism, relevance and ability to provide answers to the people's problems."[43]

Khatami emphasizes on the fact that the *raushanfikran-e dini* are *independent*—that is, they are not constricted by any inhibitions or any inadequacies that might prevent a meaningful comprehension of the ideas of some other civilization. This has important repercussions on Khatami's argument. Because Khatami believes that each civilization is the distinctive product of independent-minded *raushanfikran-e dini* using cultural codes and signs to achieve a wide range of cultural, economic and political ends, he opposes the very notion of clerical hegemony without actually debunking the *Vilayat-e Faqih*. In an innovative manner, he refutes the idea of clerical hegemony *using* Khomeini. Khomeini is supposed to have often warned his followers that "until the clergy are active in every sphere, they will not realize that religious authority and knowledge are not enough." Khatami cites this to contend that because clerics have inadequate knowledge of issues extrinsic to Islam, reliance on "current religious leadership is necessary but not sufficient."[44] Echoing Shari'ati's position, Khatami argues the *raushanfikran-e dini* must forge a "new vision" to respond to challenges of the new era. In postrevolutionary Iran, their first task is to "understand *real* Islam" that is essential to the forging of such a new vision that would then create a new civilization.⁴⁵ Such new "religious intellectuals" *might* hail from among the *'ulema* (as, clearly, Khatami himself does), but not necessarily so. In a major break with the official revolutionary ideology Khatami goes on to argue that it is not necessary that the religious intellectuals be associated with the state. With the emergence of a new era of global communications, Khatami argues, the state needs to rethink its policies in order to capture the imagination of the people (especially the youth). He recommends the development of a climate in which the young freely develop a *Jahanbini-ye Islami* (Islamic vision) without any guidance of the establishment—that is, the disenchanted can be re-enchanted only when in the compulsion of an official dogma is removed.⁴⁶

When Khatami as the Minister for Islamic Culture and Guidance had tried to bring about such an opening up of the Republic's cultural climate, his hardliner opponents had accused him of yielding to pressures of western powers and globalization. Hence, he was careful enough to couch this entire position in an apparently nativist discourse. He identifies the "west" as *digar-e falsufi wa akhlaqi-ye ma* (our philosophical and moral "other") and cautions that the "west" continues to propagate a worldview that lures its prey into subjugation, and that in order to overcome it Iranians need to reinforce their own identity and values to resist such subjugation.⁴⁷ Khatami then goes on to disentangle his position from the standard xenophobic discourse of the Republic by dismissing the idea that the "west" is a monolithic entity. He points out that the terms *bakhtar* or *gharb* (west) have been and continue to be used as a *political* shorthand for colonial and neocolonial forces of America and Europe, and that such colonial and neocolonial ambitions have oftentimes carried a cultural baggage. Khatami goes on to observe, that such a monolithic depiction of the "west" fails to understand its complexity. He believes that the charm and appeal of western civilization cannot be dismissed by calling it *farsudeh wa salkhordeh* (worn out and senile), because quite clearly it "maintains tremendous political, economic, military, social and technological power."⁴⁸ Indeed, the "East" has gained considerably from the "west." Western civilization "rests on the idea of liberty or freedom ... [and these are] the most cherished values for humans of all ages."⁴⁹ Khatami admits that the west looks at human beings and freedom from a monodimensional perspective, almost echoing Shari'ati when he said that for the "west" man was essentially an *adam-e eqtesadi* (economic man). But, alluding to the familiar Islamist charge that western notions of freedom subordinate the moral imperatives of the community to the material needs of the individual, Khatami exhorts Iranians to create a new civilization that can "absorb the positive aspects of the western civilization and [have] the wisdom to recognize the negative aspects."⁵⁰

In order to forge that new vision, a synthesis of the two civilizations, Khatami advocates abandoning the nativist ideology of the revolution. The approach of intellectuals in the Republic has to be, he contends:

> different from a rigidly *political* appraisal of the west. Those who cannot separate the *political West from the non-political West* are acting against the interests of the nation and Islamic Revolution, even though they may be doing so inadvertently. Here introspection, rationality, and objectivity will be effective, not harsh words and violence.⁵¹

Khatami, however, is mindful of the fact that "closed-minded and dogmatic persons" can use the excuse of the bogey of the west to stage a witch-hunt. "Anyone can mount an attack on thoughts different from his... with the excuse of defending the interests of the system, the revolution and religion." He is also averse to the option of restrictions to be imposed by the state that "closed-minded and dogmatic persons" seemed to favor:

> [I]n today's world... the global broadcast of mass-communicated electronic images... is under no government control. How can we prevent dynamic and curious minds from accessing what they desire?⁵²

Khatami warns that "while confronting the opponent in the name of rejecting the west and defending religion, if we step on freedom we will have caused a great catastrophe."⁵³ He therefore suggests that the Islamic Republic needs "accountability and discipline"; at the same time it requires "a cultural strategy that will make our people immune... to... the cultural onslaught of the west." By definition such a strategy had to rely on a "dialogue between civilizations," not insulating the republic with a narrow-minded interpretation of Islam. "An active, evolving society must be in contact and communication with different, sometimes opposing views, to be able to equip itself with a more powerful, attractive and effective thought than that of the opponent."⁵⁴

Khatami, clearly, uses Shari'ati's motif of *bazgusht beh khistan* (return to the self) and call for *tajaddud-e Islami* (Islamic renaissance) in speaking of the need to *create* a "new vision" in accordance with the values of Islam. The "return" to Islamic essence is to be staged by "advancing" toward a new order that promotes the interests of Muslims. As a member of the left-wing formation *Jam'eh-ye Rowhaniyat-e Mobarez* (JRM, Society of the Combatant Clergy) inspired by the socialist strands in Shari'ati's thinking, Khatami's politics had often favored a regulated economy. By the time he finished his ministerial stint under the Rafsanjani presidency in 1992, however, he veered away from the idea of a regulated economy, presumably because it failed to promote social justice. Those members of the JRM who shared this disenchantment with the Republic's failure in the realm of social justice and its repressive policies followed Khatami's lead in forming the *Majma'-ye Rowhaniyun-e Mobarez* (MRM, Association of the Combatant Clergymen) in the early 1990s with an agenda of working toward a more open and equitable society. The agenda was to a large extent analogous to of Shari'ati's notion of *ummah*, but Khatami was careful to reach his conclusion through the ideas of Khomeini.[55] Invoking Khomeini's utilitarianism, Khatami said in an interview published in the hardliner paper *Jomhuri-ye Islami* in February 1997 "the most important... [problem] is the preservation of the system and our Islamic values.... The Imam... exerted great efforts for the revolution to flourish... What is a priority is that this system should be preserved, improved and strengthened... It should be made strong and stable."[56] He argued that he formulates his program with that aim in mind, on the basis of his own understanding of priorities and needs of the society, but "the people have the *natural right*... to vote for the [program they consider] the best." Khatami then goes on to say that "in an ideal society everyone is a leader... [and that, such a view] is not inconsistent with the need for the presence of the immaculate Imam as the pivot of society.... [Yet] all talents are not equal in society, and important duties are handed to people who have a higher degree of knowledge... [for] experts should serve the people... Ruling [of the *faqih*] should serve the people and not vice versa."[57] Khatami's argument that significance of the *'ulema* is proportionate to the expertise they bring to society indicates a functional appreciation of the *'ulema* in his notion of an Islamic society. An *'alim* cannot claim a "higher degree of knowledge" in his scheme of things. In this as in Khatami's notion of an Islamic society (where every individual has the right *and* the responsibility to make the best choice as a member the community) there is an intrinsic similarity with Shari'ati's vision of the *ummah* with its responsible and conscious individual.

In perhaps the most original of his works, *Az Donya-ye Shahr ta Shahr-e Donya* (From the World of the City to the City of the World), Khatami laid down the blueprint of his vision. He argued a new order based on *chand-arzeshi* (pluralism) is taking shape in the world. The challenge for Islamic societies—he contends—is to join this world while rediscovering "the essence of our identity." The "rediscovery of the essence" (like Shari'ati's "return" to the "self") was to take place by creating "a new Islamic civilization," at the core of which lay the realization of "Islamic civil society." In such a civil society, he believes, the real danger was that one tendency may be labeled Islamic while another be denounced as heresy, even though both might be equally valid positions from the viewpoint of society. Khatami accordingly places the old argument of the need for the *'ulema* to stay away from politics in a new form. He recommended that the *'ulema* should stay aloof from the mundane activities of government, thereby remaining free from the unwanted negative consequences of being too close to power. Such proximity, Khatami warned, would distract them from their cardinal function of providing spiritual guidance to society.[58]

In 1997, after eight years of tussle between a right-wing *Majlis* and a pragmatist President Rafsanjani, a left- and center-left reformist coalition, known as the *Dovvom-e Khordad* movement helped Khatami to win the presidential election by a landslide. In his inaugural address as President on August 4, 1997, praising the far-reaching contributions of Khomeini in the making of the Islamic Revolution, Khatami declared that the President's mandate was to institutionalize the rule of law and the constitution. This, he maintained, was the only way to ensure the "continuity of the revolution, dynamism of the system and power and dignity of the people of Iran." While such aims would be achieved by a government that was "duty-bound to base its programs and policies on the *essence* of Islam," Khatami additionally promised to discharge the obligations that the law required of him by upholding the freedom of individuals and the rights of the nation by means of constitutionally guaranteed liberties, strengthening the institutions of civil society. After noting that the *Rahbar* ('Ali Khamenei) would "guide and assist" in the performance of such duties, Khatami asserts categorically that "the legitimacy of the government stems from the people's vote ... the Islamic government is the servant of the people and *not* their master."[59] Clearly, Khatami's agenda was to establish society/people at the helm, rather than the state.

Despite beginning with a great promise, Khatami the President proved much less effective than Khatami the intellectual, partly because the hard-line right-wing Islamist and conservative clerical establishment closed ranks against Khatami and the reformists to counter the threat posed by his ideas and his program. Nonetheless, the kind of revisionist agenda that Khatami managed to put in the forefront of Iranian politics continues to play a major role years after his departure from office in 2005.

\* \* \*

Ayatollahs Shari'atmadari and Montazeri, Sayyid Muhammad Khatami, and Abdolkarim Soroush are only a handful among the many votaries of social and political reform in post-Khomeini Iran who have used the language of *Islamic* politics to question the official establishment in the Islamic Republic. Their interrogations into the Islamic character of the regime have tended to reopen the kind of political discourse in Iran that makes a distinction between the state and society, quite similar to the discourse that obtained for the better part of the Pahlavi period. This is perhaps not as ironical as it may otherwise seem. The language of political Islam that was developed in Iran during the third-quarter of the twentieth century was Islamic in form but revolutionary in content. The key to success of the revolution lay not in the language used to mobilize the nation against the Pahlavi regime, rather in the promise of a revolution—or to play with the phrase coined by Hamid Dabashi, it was not the "theology" that caused the revolution, rather the "discontent" that had been essentialized by means of the "theology." It might be argued that after a period of "abnormal" politics during the Iran-Iraq war, Iran has returned to yet another round of politics where state activity has generated considerable discontent, and society is resuming its interrogation of the limits of state authority. The difference with any other period of Iranian history in the past two centuries is that, because of a change in the character of the parameters of legitimate political discourse, both the ruling establishment and the voices of discontent are using the language of political Islam.

The ambience of intellectual freedom that Khatami introduced also seems to have influenced renewal of interest in Shari'ati. Fresh compilations of Shari'ati's works have been brought by at least 20 different publishing concerns since 1997, as against about six or seven before that date. Many of these have gone for several reprints. During the first term under President Ahmedinejad, as the conservative and hardliners in the Iranian establishment began to clamp down on left-wing dissidence, Shari'ati's popularity seems to have grown by leaps and bounds. Many in the left-wing and center-left in Iranian politics and academia today (such as Morhad Saghefi, Kaveh Ehsani, and Reza 'Alijani) continue to engage with the ideas of Shari'ati.

## 1979 and the Polyvalence of Political Islam

Islamic revolutionary ideology relied primarily on the essentialization of Islam that characterized the language of political Islam shaped in the late Pahlavi era. It was premised upon resistance to the western economic stranglehold over, and transformation of, Muslim societies in the modern world. Indeed, the success of the revolution, almost in tandem with the Nicaraguan revolution of 1979, seemed likely to kindle a rebirth of the Third World movement of the 1960s, and the essence of Islam was seen to be like a variation of the Liberation Theology—an understanding which went quite a distance in highlighting the polyvalence of Islam.

In many ways, 1979 represents a noticeable change in the very meaning of Islamic politics. Till then most Islamic movements revolved around the demands of an Islamic state, which was taken to mean an order where the *shari'ah* formed the basis of all laws. The dominant Islamist discourse in the world as late as the 1960s tended to be characterized by assertion of the superiority and relevance of the *shari'ah* as the only body of laws suitable for Muslims in the modern world. Thus for every "Islamic" movement that aimed at gaining political power, a *signifier* of Islamic politics was understood to be ready and available.

The Islamic Revolution in its early stages professed to introduce a distinctly modern set of standards as the essence of Islamic law—primarily, justice and equality. These went on to reinforce intellectual trends that had already begun to circulate around the Muslim world.[60] The defining attribute of these new intellectual trends in the Muslim world in the last quarter of a century is the change in the nature of the Islamic discourse where the pivot is beginning to shift from the state to the society.

The discursive shift is largely owing to growth in awareness of intellectual and political currents in the broader world. The generation that grew up after the Second World War, some of whom were either educated or exiled in Europe or America, was attracted to Third World and "social liberation" movements. Simultaneously, their exposures to western culture encouraged them to take a fresh look at Islam, which was often taken as a signifier of their identity by the westerners. By the 1960s many among this generation of Muslim thinkers began to cast Islam in the mould of an ideology of social liberation. The success of one such ideologue—Muammar Qaddafi in Libya—caused the authoritarian regimes of Syria, Saudi Arabia, Tunisia, Jordan, et cetera, to restrict the scope of such votaries of political Islam.[61]

Moreover, in the late 1960s, and particularly in the 1970s, a new generation of Muslim/Islamic scholars began to cultivate new intellectual trends at the universities of Cairo, Damascus, Zaytouna, Beirut, et cetera. The resultant shift in choice of the institutional apparatus for education proved significant. Although al-Azhar remained the preferred destination for students from all over the Muslim world coming to study Sunni jurisprudence, Cairo, Damascus and Zaytouna developed impressive faculties on Islamic theology and philosophy as well as sociology, politics and the natural sciences. This served to fracture the façade of Islamic monovalence created by the assumption of centrality of *shari'ah* in Muslim societies. A number of Muslim thinkers from all across the Muslim world who went for their higher studies at Islamic or modern centers of learning in the Arab countries (or Europe) returned with the same kind of conclusion that people like 'Ali Shari'ati and Jalal Al-e Ahmad had reached with their own exposure to the Third World and social liberation movements—that Islam could be understood and interpreted in a wide number of approaches, of which *legalism was only one*.

Faced with repression from authoritarian regimes, this new generation of Muslim thinkers has been responding by attempts to turn Islam into a veritable social movement, challenging the state from within the bounds of its own laws. 1979 marked an important milestone in this respect. As the Islamic Republic forged an official revolutionary ideology, despite the impression of an ideological monolith that Tehran wanted to convey, various agenda were reflected willy-nilly. An advocate of rule by *shari'ah* could find as much endorsement of his cause as could a constitutionalist; a nationalist could take solace as much as a universalist; a socialist could notice reflection of his own concerns of equity and social justice, just as a property owner could be assured that Islam safeguarded and encouraged property. With such an "official" vindication of the notion of polyvalence of Islam, Islamic activism began to develop a new momentum in the Muslim world.

The 1980s marked the beginning of this new age of Islam activism, of which militant Islamic activities are only one fringe manifestation. With a lowering of the toleration threshold of most of the authoritarian regimes in the Arab world after 1979, open political dissidence was met with the full force of repression. As Asef Bayat argues, despite the severe repression of the Hosni Mubarak regime from the 1980s, civil society in Egypt began to be *Islamized* with the penetration of the Islamists (such as of the *Ikhwan*) in public offices, civil society organizations like social, cultural, and professional associations, NGOs, print and electronic media, et cetera.[62] The process of *Islamization* could not be stopped because there was no frontal attack on the authority of the state, but the steady advances made by the Islamists were readily discernible. Bayat for instance shows that the health centers, educational and other public services run by Islamists in accordance with *Islamic* principles amounted virtually to a parallel authority in the relatively poorer southern part of the city of Cairo.[63] This model of civil society organizations working among the underclass—corresponding to the stated purpose of organizations like the *bonyad-e mustazafin* in the Islamic Republic—resulted in the creation of a virtual social security net for a large segment of the people.[64] Such activities were depicted as being in consonance with the Islamic notion of *al-fitr* (charitable works). The success of Islamic social movement in Egypt has encouraged similar experiments in other parts of the Arab world as well, which has been adopted in Palestine (particularly the Gaza Strip) and Lebanon with some success. The steady ascendancy of the Hizb al-Tahrir in Central Asia and the Tabligh-e Jama'at in South Asia is also generally attributed to a similar approach.

One of the fundamental changes in the world of Islam that could be seen in the 1980s was, therefore, an activism that contested the traditional literalism. The rise of literacy levels around the Muslim world had already ensured closer interrogation of the practices of the faith around the Muslim world; the example of the Islamic Revolution gave this tendency a further boost. The result was, as a cultural anthropologist, Dale Eickelman puts it, "an Islamic Reformation."[65] Increasingly, a new generation of Muslims began to take the position that it is not enough to fast and pray. "Muslims must explain their beliefs."[66]

It is probably simplistic and incorrect to assume that such major assertions in the realm of popular politics since 1979 can be directly or indirectly related to the Islamic Revolution. The revolution did not bring about any total shift in the political priorities of a generation of Muslims by presenting an alternative political structure to follow, unlike what the Bolshevik Revolution of 1917 did to a generation of socialists. Nor has it offered, unlike the Bolsheviks, to vigorously export its revolutionary ideology overseas, if only to secure its own gains. But it certainly has helped change the Muslim world by establishing the possibility of success by following Islamic political ideology. Unlike at any other time in the modern era, Muslims are beginning to dare to challenge the modern state with a political baggage and language that is critical about, inter alia, the disorienting role westernization plays in nonwestern societies. Significantly, such baggage and language are essentially modern, speaking about the *social* basis of political power, even though many of their outward forms appear to hark back at a premodern era.

# Conclusion

The language of political Islam that was devised in late Pahlavi Iran was not opposed to modernity itself, only to its "westernizing" variant. From the late Qajar times, the challenge before Iran was indeed to create a modern state, where the government is entrusted with the responsibility of defending the interests of its people against external threats and promoting their general well-being. The 1906 revolution established the principle of popular sovereignty—despite disagreements among advocates of *mashrutiyyat* (following western models) and those of *mashru'eh* (instituting rule by the *shari'ah*), both essentially agreed that the executive authority should be mindful of the needs and aspirations of the subjects. Even the advent of Reza Shah was meant to serve the interests of the people—thus, the language of politics in Iran was decidedly modern since the 1906 revolution.

"Islamist" critiques of the Pahlavi "modernization" agenda developed by people like Al-e Ahmad and even more by 'Ali Shari'ati were not critiques of the phenomenon of modernity, rather the manner in which Iran was being westernized. The objection that Al-e Ahmad and Shari'ati raised to the Pahlavi modernization project was similar to the Marxian critique of western capitalism—that it alienates a larger number of people than it benefits. The Pahlavi agenda of economic modernization played such an alienating role in Iranian society because the benefits of economic modernization did not filter down to many sections of the society. As Shari'ati explained, the basic idea underlying community formation of any type has do with the need to be together, so that collective interests could be served, and in serving the collective interest alone the human individual stands to benefit, being a part of the collective. Consciously devising an argument similar to Rousseau's principle of the General Will, Shari'ati contended that a regime that serves the interests of a handful of people and deprives the rest cannot be the repository of popular sovereignty. The critique was essentially "modern" because it did not challenge the basis of "political modernity"; rather it held the authorities to task for not being "modern."

The critique was simultaneously Islamic because it pertained to concerns of Muslims in a Muslim society. Like many other critics of the

Pahlavis, Shari'ati freely borrowed concepts from the western intellectual tradition to address issues concerning Muslims—thus, ideas were not Islamic or un-Islamic because of their origins, rather because of their applicability to the situation in the Muslim world. Hence, mindless emulation of the west, *gharbzadegi*, was un-Islamic not because it concerned practices that originated in the west, rather because it was proving harmful for Iranian Muslims. As a counterpoint to *gharbzadegi*, therefore, Shari'ati came up with a Utopian vision of social order that was devised with Islamic idioms, but most importantly, it served to underwrite the principle of popular sovereignty.

\* \* \*

The most significant component of Shari'ati's critique that went to lay the basis of the revolutionary ideology was his advocacy of assumption of responsibility by the people. In the context of Iran, where the dominant "reading" of *Ithna 'Ashari* Shi'ism tended to favor quietism, Shari'ati made the case that the essence of Shi'ism, and indeed of Islam, lay in activism in defense of justice and equity. So arguing, Shari'ati threw a major challenge not only to the "traditional" Islamist position, but also the "modernist" position, which required the people to be subservient to the government, because the government would be promoting the interests of the state. Shari'ati's argument was that should the government abdicate that responsibility then the people would have to assume responsibility for removal of such a government.

Even though this argument was distinctly Rousseaunian, Shari'ati used the concept of *jihad* to argue that such a reading of popular sovereignty was not only compatible with Islam, but actually central to it. As is true for most other essentializations, this argument had to be premised upon the further contention that Islam had been systematically and consistently subverted—or as Shari'ati claimed, "inverted." This helped him make a case that would be acceptable to even the most traditional-minded Muslims—that Islam was always *purported* to empower the people; if this had never been realized in the course of Islamic history, then it was precisely because no one had assumed the responsibility of realizing that *purpose* that was central to Islam. Dialectics (of good and evil, right and wrong), as Shari'ati was fond of saying, has no intrinsic motion.

As Shari'ati explicated it, the idea of assuming responsibility to determine the course of history is not Islamic *because* Islam endorses it; rather Islam endorses it *because* it promotes the general well-being of mankind. To put it differently, Islam is not concerned with the well-being of Muslims alone, rather "true" Muslims adhere to "true" Islam *because* it promotes the well-being of mankind. Hence, the essence of Islam is fully compatible with the general applicability that the theory of popular sovereignty is supposed to have. This was the reason why secular democrats, Islamic democrats, and theologians could rally behind one banner of opposition to the Shah, because everyone seemed to agree that the Shah had abused his authority to exercise sovereignty on behalf of the Iranian people. In 1977–79, the opposition may not have agreed on what form the state should acquire in order to uphold popular sovereignty, but all were agreed that the Pahlavi monarchy was not to be trusted to do that.

\* \* \*

In the turmoil of the revolution of 1979, and the manner in which the *'ulema* succeeded in putting their stamp on the revolution, the Islamic political discourse that emerged in late Pahlavi Iran was passed off as the whole, although it was just a fragment. The revolutionary *'ulema* appropriated the discourse of popular responsibility by deploying more identifiably Islamic symbols—presenting Islamic jurisprudence and jurists as the indispensable custodian of the rights of Muslims. By advocating such an argument, the clerical establishment appropriated the role of the sole legitimate representative of the people in accordance with Islam—any opposition to the Islamic regime was thus both un-Islamic and antipeople. The legitimating factor in the Islamic Republic thus remained the abstract category of collective (national/Islamic) interest, as it used to be under the Pahlavis. This circumscribed the potentials of genuine popular sovereignty that the Islamic political discourse promised to fulfill through the mediation of 'Ali Shari'ati.

Unlike his clerical opponents, Shari'ati did not engage with Muslims merely as an aggregative category. A Muslim, for him, was the prototype of what a human individual had to be. Nor was his notion of a human individual akin to that of his secular westernized compatriots, who saw the modern individual as a unit that did not require any sociocultural props to establish its identity. For Shari'ati, a "true" Muslim was the prototype of a human individual who was conscious of his/her historical context, aware of his/her position within the society he/she lived in, and above all willing to assume the responsibility of spreading such awareness and self-consciousness *(khud-agahi)* among the rest of the people. The aim in spreading such awareness was not to secure any narrow personal gain for oneself; rather to help the society achieve its fullest potential as an aggregate of individuals. In other words, the collective found its meaning only as an aggregation of individuals who had attained their fullest potentials *as* human beings.

The basic difference between Shari'ati and other contemporary Iranian intellectuals lay in the fact that Shari'ati's vision of the *ummah* as a just order was an Islamic version of societal democracy, as against political democracy that characterizes much of the modern political thinking about the state. He sympathized with the cause of the constitutionalists not because constitutionalism was an end in itself, rather because it was merely a necessary condition for attaining the end of a just order. An order where every individual would be allowed to attain his/her fullest potential without any external constraints being imposed on him/her by virtue of membership in that order. According to Shari'ati's concept of popular sovereignty, then, an order that imposes restrictions (symbolized by *zor, zar, tazveer*) on an individual's freedom in the name of greater good has not attained the level of perfection; it is unjust—and it is the responsibility of individuals to mobilize the collective body and struggle till that level of a just order is attained. Thus, *jihad* is meant to be waged protesting against injustice, in defense of an Islamic order, and Islamic order is one that liberates the individual by allowing him/her to flourish *as* a human being. Shari'ati was indeed, as Ervand Abrahamian calls him, "the ideologue of protest."

\* \* \*

The language of Islamic politics that emerged in late Pahlavi Iran was one geared toward protest against an unjust order that had established its legitimacy as the harbinger of modernity. This conforms to the general pattern of emergence of political Islam nearly everywhere—confronted with the absolutist logic of power of the modern state in the name of the people, votaries of political Islam respond with the absolutist logic of a higher order, that is, God. Political Islam is, thus, essentially a critique of the totalitarian possibilities that are integral to the notion of popular sovereignty in modern political thinking. The charm of 1979 lies in the very fact that it was the first such challenge that succeeded, encouraging many other challenges in the name of Islam against the might of the modern state. Egypt under Hosni Mubarak is a very good instance of this, where the civil society has been Islamized to an extent that the secularist state appears almost an anomaly.

This does not mean that all challenges in the name of Islam necessarily envisage an order that is ipso facto more just than the order that will be replaced. Nor does it mean that an order that comes into being confronting a despotic order would not become despotic in its turn. The Islamic Republic, in many ways, betrays such a tendency occasionally. The more significant development, however, is that the resistance to such a despotic tendency too has come from practitioners of political Islam, like former President Khatami, as much as secularists. Elsewhere, the Islamic monarchy of Saudi Arabia has come under attack from practitioners of political Islam (of whom bin Laden is only the most extremist fringe). One can multiply such instances of tension in the politics of the Muslim world.

Clearly, political Islam is not a program that comes to fruition once an Islamic state is established; it is a language of politics that envisages resistance as much as order. Therefore, it is perhaps premature to assume that political Islam has failed, as Olivier Roy has done.[1] The jury is still out.

# Appendix I

# Shi'ism—A Brief Sketch of the Early Years

Shi'ism is supposed to have originated in ca. 632, when at the death of the Prophet Muhammad, his father-in-law Abu Bakr was elected as the leader of the Islamic *ummah* as the *Khalifat al-Rasul* (Deputy of the Prophet), overriding the claims of the Prophet's cousin and son-in-law, 'Ali ibn Abi Talib. The issue of succession was disputed among the *muhajiruns* ("emigrants" who left on *hijrat* with the Prophet from Mecca) and the *ansarun* ("associates" from Medina), as a result of which the Prophet's father-in-law Abu Bakr was ordained the *Khalifah*, denying 'Ali his right of succession. Those who refused to accept Abu Bakr as the *Khalifah* were thenceforth known as Shi'i (partisans). Those who had supported the cause of Abu Bakr did so citing a tradition *(sunnah)* of the Prophet, hence they came to be known as the Sunni. The partisans *(shi'i)* of 'Ali believed that the Prophet wanted 'Ali to take over the mantle of leadership after him, and that the Prophet had been grooming 'Ali to that end.

The Shi'i believe that the Qur'an is susceptible of a literal reading, as also a deeper exoteric reading. They argue that divine inspiration had made the Prophet capable of such exoteric reading because of his *masoumiyat* (infallibility), which was inherited by 'Ali and that part of his family line that arose from the Prophet's daughter Fatima. Denying succession to the line of the Prophet, thus, was tantamount to denying divinely inspired infallible guidance in leadership of the community. The Shi'i accordingly refused to acknowledge the legitimacy of the political order of the *Khalifat* (Caliphate), and came up with their own notion of infallible social, religious, and political *Imamat* (Leadership), with 'Ali being acknowledged as the first Imam.

Shi'i discontent subsided in 655 when the third *Khalifa*, Uthman ibn Affan was murdered and succession passed over to 'Ali. However, 'Ali's tenure as the *Khalifa* did not last for long. 'Ali encountered two challenges to his authority, nominally upon his failure to find and prosecute Uthman's assassin. The first challenge came from a coalition headed by Aisha, widow of the Prophet and daughter of Abu Bakr, which 'Ali beat back at the Battle of the Camels. A more significant challenge was mounted by the powerful governor of Syria and nephew of Uthman, Mu'awiyah. When the Prophet was preaching his message, the house of Abu Sufyan in Mecca opposed him. Abu Sufyan's son Mu'awiyah and grandson Yazid led the forces of Mecca against the army of Islam and were trounced at the battles of Badr and Khandaq. Thereupon the house of Abu Sufyan crossed over to join the ranks of the faithful, and during the reigns of Abu Bakr, Umar and Uthman swept over Syria, where Mu'awiyah was appointed the military governor. When the Caliphate passed to 'Ali, Mu'awiyah contested his succession and eventually claimed the Caliphate for himself. 'Ali opened negotiations with Mu'awiyah with the hope of regaining his allegiance but Mu'awiyah insisted on autonomy for Levant under his rule. Mu'awiyah mobilized his forces and refused to pay homage to 'Ali on the pretext that he was not represented in his election. In 657, accordingly, 'Ali met the forces of Mu'awiyah at the field of Siffin, where the two armies spent encamped more than 100 days, most of the time being spent in abortive negotiations. After a week of combat came the *laylat al-harir* (the night of clamor), when, as his army was on the point of being routed, Mu'awiyah's soldiers hoisted *mushaf* (either parchments inscribed with verses of the Qur'an, or complete copies of it) on their spearheads, seeking arbitration. 'Ali settled for arbitration to prevent two Muslim armies fighting each other, thus allowing Mu'awiyah to leave Siffin unmolested, retain charge of Damascus, and eventually extend his authority over Egypt. A segment among 'Ali's own supporters, however, believed 'Ali had betrayed the cause of Islam by settling with Mu'awiyah; they rejected the compromise and broke with 'Ali, thus being called the *Kharijiyah* (seceders), causing the first split among the Shi'i. In 661, the *Kharijiyah* assassinated 'Ali, upon which Mu'awiyah successfully claimed the *Khalifat*, moved its capital to Damascus, and founded the Umayyad dynasty.

Although most of the Muslims chose to follow Mu'awiyah, the party (Shi'i) of 'Ali maintained that the succession to 'Ali should pass to the direct descendants of the Prophet , through his daughter Fatima and her husband, 'Ali. The Shi'i at Kufa in Iraq openly refused to swear allegiance to Mu'awiyah and pledged their loyalty instead to 'Ali's elder son, Hassan, as the second Imam. Even as Mu'awiyah tried to negotiate with Hassan, he raised a huge army and eventually marched against Hassan, whose forces he met at the field of Sabat. On the eve of an encounter, as Hassan was voicing his unwillingness to shed the blood of fellow Muslims, a section of his men took umbrage at the prospect of a compromise and assaulted and injured Hassan badly. Mu'awiyah was also keen on avoiding bloodshed, and proposed fresh terms, and a badly wounded Hassan found it prudent to settle for a compromise. According to Sunni scholars, Hassan ibn 'Ali stipulated that Mu'awiyah should follow the Qur'an and the Sunnah, allowing a *shura* for the Caliphate to be held after his death, and refrain from any acts of revenge against Hasan's followers. According to Shi'i scholars, Hasan further stipulated that the Caliphate should be returned to him after Mu'awiyah's death, if he was still alive, and in case he died before that then the Caliphate should be given to his younger brother Hossein ibn 'Ali. Mu'awiyah is supposed later to have had Hassan poisoned to death (arguably by Hassan's wife, who then married Yazid), to pave the way for the succession of Yazid, the son of Mu'awiyah.

In 680, the succession dispute reopened with the death of Mu'awiyah and the succession of Yazid to the Caliphate. Hassan having died by this time, Hossein was proclaimed the Imam by the people of Kufa. Persuaded by his followers' refusal to accept Yazid's succession, Imam Hossein tried to mobilize forces of opposition to Yazid. When popular support failed to materialize, Hossein and his small band of followers were slaughtered by Yazid's forces at the battle of Karbala on the *'ashura* (tenth day) of Muharram. The memory of this tragedy, the *shahadat* (martyrdom) of the Shi'i, continues to guide the paradigm of suffering and protest that characterizes Shi'ism. For the Shi'i, the original injustice that had denied 'Ali the succession to the Prophet was repeated at Karbala.

Of the four sons of Imam Hossein, only one—'Ali ibn Hussain (supposedly the grandson of King Yazdegerd)—survived the massacre at Karbala because he was too ill to go to battle. Hailed as the fourth Imam by his followers, despite being in confinement at Medina and Damascus, he became a natural rallying point of the Shi'i in the resistance to the Umayyads. He was succeeded to the *Imamat* by Muhammad ibn 'Ali Baqir, who like his father before him, remained content disseminating "truths about Islam."

The second major split occurred among the Shi'i in the seventh century. Partly owing to Imam Baqir's quiescence in the face of Umayyad misrule, a section of the Shi'i refused to acknowledge his *Imamat,* and acknowledged Zayd ibn 'Ali as the Imam instead. They became known as the Zaidi Shi'i, characterized by their position that any descendant of 'Ali can become the Imam, and that the duty to "enjoin the good and forbid the evil" was incumbent on all Muslims at all times. The Zaidi faction rebelled against both the Umayyads and Abbasids and was able to find a Zaidi state in Tabaristan, on the Caspian. Another Zaidi state was founded in Yemen, where it lasted till the civil war in 1963.

The sixth Imam, Ja'far ibn Muhammad, known as al-Sadiq, was probably the first to contribute toward the evolution of the Shi'i *fiqh*. His *Imamat* over the Shi'i coincided with an era of uncertainty in the Caliphate, as the opposition against the Umayyads became formidable and central authority weakened to allow major regional assertion. In the political vacuum thus generated, Imam Jafar al-Sadiq laid the basis of Shi'i jurisprudence in a manner that the Shi'i could refer to questions of law without referring to Sunni *mazahib* or the laws of state. Upon the replacement of the Umayyad dynasty by the Abbsids, severe restrictions were placed upon the Imam, and he was supposedly poisoned to death by the Abbasid Caliph al-Mansur.

The third major split among the Shi'i took place over the issue of succession to Imam Ja'far al-Sadiq. A majority of the Shi'i believe that the younger son of the sixth Imam, Musa ibn Ja'far, was the rightful seventh Imam, who spent the better part of his life in hiding before being captured during *Hajj*, and was then imprisoned in Basra and Baghdad. He was eventually supposedly poisoned to death in prison.

Some among the Shi'i, however, believe that the succession to the sixth Imam belonged to his elder son, Ismail, who died in 760 even before his father. Followers of Ismail, known as the Ismaili Shi'i, have in turn gone through several splits. A large number of Ismailis believe that Imamate had come to an end with the death of Ismail, the Seventh Imam (hence the name Sevener Shi'i); others believe the Imam did not die; he is in seclusion and will return at the End of Days to identify his loyal followers and take them to heaven. The early Ismailis evolved as a revolutionary missionary movement that would frequently assassinate Sunni leaders and rulers and seize power. Ismaili groups were very active in Syria, Palestine, southern Iraq, and India. They set up a power base in Bahrain, and more significantly the Fatimid state in Egypt in 969. The Fatimid rule proved pivotal to Shi'i missionary activities; one such mission occasioned the rise of the Druze community in southern Lebanon. Upon the fall of the Fatimids in 1171, the Nizari Ismailis began a major campaign of violence under Hassan Sabah and his Hashishin movement against the remnants of the Abbasid dynasty, till they were driven underground by the Mongols in 1258. A later descendent of Hassan Sabah married a daughter of the Shah of Persia, receiving the honorary title of Aga Khan, which remains the honorific by which the leader of the Nizari Ismailis is known even today.

A large segment of the Shi'i, however, believes that the line of the Imams continued beyond the seventh into Imam Rida/Reza, a contemporary of Haroun al-Rashid and his two sons. It is said that Caliph al-Mamoun had once offered to declare Imam Reza as his successor to the Caliphate—thereby hoping both to stem the growing disaffection of the Shi'i against the Abbasids and also to undermine the saintly reputation of the Imams by involving them in matters of this world. Imam Reza is supposed to have initially turned this down, but accepted upon further persuasion. The consequent increase in the ranks of Shi'i prompted the Caliph to renege on his offer, and have Imam Reza poisoned to death. Imam Reza lies buried in Tus, which later became known as Mashhad.

The ninth, tenth, and eleventh Imams continued to keep the Shi'i cause alive despite persistent Abbasid persecution. The persecution peaked during the years of the eleventh Imam, because it was widely believed among the Shi'i that the son of the eleventh Imam would be the Imam Mehdi, who would usher in a rule where justice and order would prevail. Upon the death of the eleventh Imam, therefore, the Caliph's forces were sent looking for the child, Muhammad ibn Hassan 'Ali.

Muhammad ibn Hassan 'Ali was, however, never found, because upon becoming the twelfth Imam he went into occultation *(ghaibat)*. The Twelfth Imam appeared supposedly only before his deputies during 872–939, and then disappeared completely and is supposed to return only at the End of Days. The period when he appeared only before his deputies is known as the *ghaibat al-asghar* (lesser occultation), and the period thereafter is known as *ghaibat al-akbar* (greater occultation). A segment among the Shi'i believes that the line of the Imams ended with the twelfth, hence the name *Ithna 'Ashari* (Arabic for Twelve). It was the *Ithna 'Ashari* that eventually constituted the majority among the Shi'i when the Safavid dynasty in the sixteenth century began to promote the order as the official religion of the Persian Empire.

The *Ithna 'Ashari* Shi'i believe that the Twelfth Imam, Muhammad ibn Hasan— usually referred to by his titles *Imam-e 'Asr* (Imam of the Period) and *Sahib al-Zaman* (Lord of the Age). He is also called *al-Montazeri* (the one who is awaited). The Twelfth Imam went into hiding by Divine command in 872 at the age of four, maintaining contact with the faithful through his deputies *(na'ib)*. The period between 872 and 939, when he maintained indirect contact with his people through four deputies consecutively, is known as *ghaibat-i sughra* (lesser occultation). Upon the death of the fourth of his deputies, the Imam passed into *ghaibat-i kubra* (greater occultation), which will continue till God grants the Imam the permission to manifest himself.

A dominant position in the *Ithna 'Ashari* tradition since the Safavid era argues that even though all political authority till the coming of the Imam Mahdi is ipso facto illegitimate, it is not desirable for the Shi'i to resist existing temporal authorities lest there be social anarchy and chaos that would make it difficult for Muslims to carry on with their daily lives. During the *ghaibat,* therefore, the *'ulema* were assigned the authority to guide the faithful regarding proper conduct (classifying all activity under the fivefold classification of *wajib, mandub, murakkas, makruh,* and *haraam*) so that the *usul al-din* (fundamental obligations of the faith) can continue to be fulfilled in preparation for the return of the Mahdi. Till the return of the Mahdi, the Shi'i have to practice *taqiyya* (dissimulation, concealment of beliefs) so that the illegitimate political authorities cannot persecute them—that is, the Shi'i would have to resort to *intezar* (waiting). The doctrine of *intezar* is pivotal to Ithna 'Ashari Shi'ism, as "return" of the Vanished Imam signifies the ultimate realization of God's will on earth.

# Appendix II

# Selected Works/Lectures of 'Ali Shari'Ati

The following table lists most of the major works/lectures of 'Ali Shari'ati, chronologically arranged as best as possible, although allowing for some inaccuracies where contrary reports exist as to exactly when a lecture was delivered. It does not include some of the pieces that are attributed to Shari'ati, which he may or may not have written, but had he written these, that would certainly have been done under duress. It also does not include those writings of Shari'ati that cannot be dated properly.

| Year | Essays/Books | Lecture | Place |
|------|--------------|---------|-------|
| 1954 | *Namuneh-ha-ye 'Ali Ikhlaqi dar Islam na dar bahamdun* (trans.) | | |
| 1955 | *Tarikh-e takameel-e Falsafeh Abu Dharr Ghafaree* (trans.) | | |
| 1958 | *Muqadama chap-e dovvom Abu Dharr Ghafaree* | | |
| 1959 | *Dar Naqad wa Adab*(trans.) *Niyaish* (trans.) *Salman-e Pak* (trans.) | | |
| 1960 | *Kitab-e Khushbeeni wa badbeeni* | | |
| 1961 | *She'r Cheest?* | | |

(Continued)

| Year | Essays/Books | Lecture | Place |
|---|---|---|---|
| 1963 | Wasiyatnameh-ye Frantz Fanon | | |
| 1965 | Rahnama-ye Khurasan | | |
| 1966 | | Umanism dar 'Arab wa Sharq | Adabiat, Mashhad[1] |
| 1966–67 | | Islamshenasi | " |
| 1967 | | Ma'aref Islami<br>Mazhhab 'Dar'i wa Hunar 'Pinjra'i | |
| 1967–69 | Maktab-e Ta'alim wa Tarbiat-e Islami<br>Guftagu-ha-ye Tanhai Nauroz | Barrasi Pareh-ai az Waqi'a Sadr-e Islam | |
| 1968 | | Existensialism | Daneshgah-e Melli[2] |
| | Kavir<br>Tashai'yo: Miyadgah-e Ruh-e Sami wa Ruh-e Ariyai<br>Totem-parasti | | |
| | | Insan wa Islam<br>Chahar Zandan-e Islam<br>Tarikh-e Tamaddun (1&2) | P.U. Abadan[3]<br>" |
| | | Tamaddun Cheest? | Adabiat, Mashhad |
| 1968 | | Bahes kulli raje' be Tamaddun wa Farhang | " |
| | | Makatib Tarikh wa Raweesh-e Shenakht-e Aan | " |
| | | Hadsei Shegarf dar Tarikh | " |
| | | Khasusiat-e Qarn-e Mo'asr | " |
| | | Jahanbini wa Maheet | " |
| | | Giraesh-ha-ye Siyasi dar Qarn-e Mo'asr | " |
| | | Masleh-ye Khudyabi | " |

| Year | Col 1 | Col 2 | Col 3 |
|---|---|---|---|
| | | *Weizhgihayi Tamaddun-e Imroz* | " |
| | | *Rawish-e Shenakht-e Islam* | Ershad |
| | | *'Ali, Haqeeqati barguneh-i Asatir* | " |
| 1969 | | *Ummat wa Imamat* | Ershad |
| | | *Tamaddun wa Tajaddud* | " |
| | | *Nighai beh Tarikh-e Ferda* | " |
| | | *'Hunar'garezi az 'Aanche hast'* | Adabiat, Mashhad |
| | | *Tarikh-e Iran ta Islam-e Safavi* | " |
| | | *'Ali Tanha Ast* | Ershad |
| | | *'Ali, hayat-e barwarash pas az marg* | " |
| | | *Metodolzhy-ye 'Ilm* | Madraseh-ye Bazargani |
| | | *Insan-e Tamam* | Ershad |
| | | *Sukhani dar baraye Kitab* | Adabiat, Mashhad |
| | | *Insan wa Tarikh* | Fani, Tehran |
| | | *Sukhanrani-ha-ye Safr-e Hajj-e Awwal* | Medina |
| | *Habut* | *Medina, Shahr-e Hijrat* | " |
| | *Idiyulozhy (1 & 3)* | *Tamaddun Nateejeh-ye Mintaq-e Muhajirat* | " |
| | *Jahanbini basteh wa Jahanbini-ye baz* | *Nejat Nasl-e Jawan* | " |
| | *Hijrat zameensazi-ye Jahanbini-ye baz* | *Hijrat, Ummat wa Imamat* | Mecca |
| | *Jamehshenasi Scientisti* | *Tahlili Az Minask-e Hajj* | 'Orfat |
| | *Darwinism dar Tabdeel Anwa' Tamaddunha beh Ekdigar* | *Islam-e Muhammad Yahiya Kunandeh Din-e Ibrahim* | Mani |
| | *Doniya-ye Sevvom Khud beh Zaban Amadeh Ast* | *Ismail-at ra Qorbani Kun* | Mani |
| | *Talqi Mazhhab az deed-e raushanfikr waqe'been wa raushanfikr-e Muqallad* | *Vesaiyat wa Showra* | Mani |
| | *Az Hijrat ta Wafat* | *Che Bayyad Kard?* | Mecca |
| | | *'Abarti wa Hakayeti* | Mashhad |

(Continued)

| Year | Essays/Books | Lecture | Place |
|------|--------------|---------|-------|
|  |  | *Mi'ad ba Ibrahim* | Ershad |
|  |  | *Hijrat wa Tamaddun* | Ershad |
|  |  | *Makhrut-e Jamehshenasi-ye Farhangi* | P.U. Abadan |
|  |  | *Insan bekhud* | Adabiat, Tehran |
|  |  | *Ischolastik-e Jadid* | Sane'ti Sharif |
|  |  | *Nigahi beh Weizhgehai Qaron-e Qadeem, Wasati wa Qaron-e Jadid* | Adabiat, Mashhad |
| 1970 |  | *Tarikh wa Arzish-e Aan dar Islam* | Ershad |
|  |  | *Falsafeh-ye Niyaish* | ” |
|  |  | *Iqbal, Masleh-e Qarn-e Akhir* | Ershad |
|  |  | *Hussain, Waris-e Adam* | ” |
|  |  | *Mazhab 'Aliyeh Mazhab* | ” |
|  |  | *Raushanfikr wa Masuliyat-e Oo dar Jame'h* | ” |
|  |  | *Resheh-ha-ye Iqtisadi Renaissance* | Madraseh-ye Bazargani |
|  |  | *Tauheed wa Shirk* | Mecca |
|  |  | *Mumalik-e Hamjoar* | ” |
|  |  | *Beenash Tarikh-e Shi'i* | Masjid al-Jawad |
|  |  | *Honar dar Intezar Mo'awad* | Mashhad University |
|  |  | *Falsafeh-ye Tarikh az Deedgah-e Islam* | Ershad |
|  |  | *Bahes-e 'Amumi raje' beh Jahanbeeni wa Farhang* | Ferdowsi High School |
|  |  | *Chera Asateer Roh-e Hamae Tamaddunha-ye Duniya Ast?* | ” |
| 1971 |  | *Tarikh wa Shenakht-e Adian* (14 lessons) | Ershad |
|  |  | *Istandard-ha-ye salbat dar Ta'alim wa Tarbiat* | Ershad |
|  |  | *Fatima Fatima Ast* | ” |

|      |                                   |                                      |                                        |
| ---- | --------------------------------- | ------------------------------------ | -------------------------------------- |
|      |                                   | *Marg, Paighami beh Zindegan*        | ”                                      |
|      | *Hajj*                            | *Mashin dar Asarat Mashinism*        | ”                                      |
|      |                                   | *Intezar, Mazhhab-e Aitraz*          | ”                                      |
|      |                                   | *Pedar, Madar, Ma Mutahmeem*         | ”                                      |
|      |                                   | *Tashaiy'o Alavi wa Tashaiy'o Safavi* | ”                                     |
|      |                                   | *Maso'uliyat-e Shi'i budan*          | ”                                      |
|      |                                   | *Che niyazi ast beh 'Ali?*           | ”                                      |
|      | *Tashaiy'o Surkh wa Tashaiy'o Siyah* | *Che bayied Kard?*                 | ”                                      |
|      |                                   | *Arey, Inchunin bud, beradar!*       | ”                                      |
|      |                                   | *Jahanbini*                          | P.U. Abadan                            |
|      |                                   | *Az Kuja Aghaz Kuneem*               | Sana'ti Sharif                         |
|      | *'Ali, beniyanguzar-e Wahdat*     | *Islamshenasi* (6 lectures)          | Ershad                                 |
|      |                                   | *Pas az Shahadat*                    | Masjid-e Narmak                        |
|      |                                   | *Bazgusht beh Kheishtan*             | Ershad                                 |
|      | *Sukhanrani Safr-e Hajj*          | *Niyazhai Insan-e Imroz*             | J.I. Ahvaz                             |
| 1971 | *Hajj Buzurgtar Buzurgtar az Hajj, Shahadat* | *Wazeh Agahi Tabaqati*    | ”                                      |
|      | *Bazgusht beh Kudam Kheish?*      |                                      |                                        |
|      | *Bazgusht beh Kheish*             |                                      |                                        |
|      |                                   | *Farhang wa Idiulozih*               | Danishsarai, Tehran                    |
|      |                                   | *Shi'i, Ek Hizb-e Tamam*             | Ershad                                 |
| 1972 |                                   | *Islamshenasi* (18 lectures)         | Ershad                                 |
|      |                                   | *Chahar Zindan-e Insan*              | Madraseh-ye Aliyeh Dukhtaran[4]        |
|      |                                   | *Intezar, Asr-e Hazir az Zan-e Musalman* | Ershad                             |
|      |                                   | *Ekbar Digar Abu Dharr*              | ”                                      |
|      |                                   | *Qarn-e Ma Dar Justaju-ye 'Ali*      | ”                                      |

(Continued)

| Year | Essays/Books | Lecture | Place |
|---|---|---|---|
| | | *Naqsh-e Inqilabi yad o yadawran dar Tarikh-e Tashaiy'o* | " |
| | | *Khudagahi wa Istihmar* | " |
| | | *Shahadat* | " |
| | | *Perwan-e 'Ali wa Ranjhaesh* | " |
| | | *Payyam-e Omid beh Raushanfikr-e Masoul (Tafsir-e Surah al-Rum)* | " |
| | | *Muqaddameh-ai bar Konfarans-e Hussain al-Amin* | |
| | | *Sir Sayyid Ahmed Khan* | Isfahan |
| | | *Khuda Hafiz, Shahr-e Shahdat* | Mashhad |
| 1976 | *Khudsazi-ye Inqilabi* *Horr* *Hijab* *Insan-e Azad Azadi-ye Insan* *Ma wa Iqbal* | | |

*Notes*: [1] Faculty of Literature, University of Mashhad;
[2] National University;
[3] Petroleum University, Abadan;
[4] Girls' High School. Tehran.
*Sources*: Rahnema (1998); Reza Alijani (2000b).

# Glossary of Arabic and Persian Terms

| | |
|---|---|
| *'adl* | just, fair |
| *'adalat* | justice |
| *'adalatkhaneh* | (lit. house of justice), law court |
| *adam-e ijtema'i* | (lit. social man) social being, one who is concerned with his/her social situation |
| *adam-e eqtesadi* | lit. economic man |
| *ahadith* | (sing. *hadith*) traditions: for the Sunnis, traditions of the Prophet; for the Shi'i traditions of the Prophet and the Imams |
| *akhir-e zaman* | (lit. End of Days) the time when God will call His creation to account for its conduct and preside over it in judgment |
| *akhund* | (lit. one who reads) cleric, popular preacher |
| *al-amr bi'l-ma'ruf wa'l- nahy 'an al-munkar* | (lit. enjoin what is known [to be Good] and Forbidding the Evil) the Islamic requirement to command what is good and forbid what is evil |
| *'ashura* | (lit. Tenth) the tenth day of the month of Muharram, the day when Imam Hossein was martyred with his followers by Yazid's forces at Karbala |
| *asr-e bidari* | (lit. Age of Awakening) the period in Iranian history associated with introduction of western learning and exposure to the ideas of the west |
| *awadi-ye geraftanha* | confusion of (less important with more important) issues |
| *bakhtar* | the west |
| *bashariyat* | humanity |
| *batini* | (lit. internal) the intrinsic aspects of the faith, which emphasizes faith in God, rather than mere conformity to the extrinsic *faraz al-'ain* |
| *bazaar* | the market; in the context of Iran, the physical space where wholesale and commercial exchanges are carried out. The traditional *bazaar* is invariably a sprawling area at the heart of the old city, where rows of shops offering similar merchandise are grouped together. |
| *bazaari* | merchant operating in a *bazaar* |

| | |
|---|---|
| *bi'da* | heretical innovation |
| *budan* | being |
| *chand-arzeshi* | pluralism |
| *chand-khudai* | polytheism |
| *daulat* | state |
| *faqih* | (pl. *fuqaha*) jurist |
| *faradh al-'ain* | (lit. primary obligations) the five obligations of *kalimah* (asserting the unity of God), *salaat* (prayer), *Hajj* (pilgrimage to Mecca), *rozeh* (daytime fast during Ramadhan), and *zakat* (alms for the community's poor) |
| *fasad al-zaman* | (lit. troubles of the age) the doctrine that it is better to endure a cruel and oppressive ruler than engage in rebellious anarchy, because anarchy jeopardizes the faithful discharge of *faraz al-'ain* |
| *fiqh* | Islamic jurisprudence |
| *ghaibat* | occultation |
| *gharbzadegi* | (lit. struck by the west) a state of intoxication/fascination with the west |
| Hosseiniyeh | a place where the tale of the suffering of the Prophet and his family, particularly that of Imam Hossein, is recounted by lay or clerical preachers |
| *hamwatani* | compatriot |
| *hijab* | veil, worn by women to cover their hair |
| *ijtihad* | independent legal reasoning, using which a true and faithful Muslim can deduce legal positions on matters that have not been categorically ruled upon in the Qur'an or the *ahadith* |
| *'ilm* | (lit. science) learning |
| Imamat | (lit. Leadership) the Shi'i doctrine whereby legitimate authority of the *ummah* is vested in the Prophet and the 12 Imams who followed him |
| *iman* | faith |
| Inqilab | revolution |
| *intezar* | (lit. waiting) the Shi'i doctrine of enduring illegitimate authority while waiting for the return of the Imam Mehdi |
| *'irfan* | Gnosticism, the mystical tradition of learning in Islam |
| *istibdad* | despotism, political oppression |
| *istihmar* | deception by the clergy |
| *isti'mar* | colonialism, exploitation |
| *istismar* | exploitation |
| *istizhar* | exposure |
| Ithna 'Ashari | (lit. Twelver), those among the Shi'i who believe that there were 12 Imams, of whom the Twelfth is in hiding and will return at the End of Days. |
| *jahiliyya* | (lit. ignorance) the age of darkness before the advent of Islam |

| | |
|---|---|
| *javânmardi* | the values and code of conduct befitting an Iranian of some social standing |
| *jihad* | (lit. struggle) any kind of struggle waged in defense of Islam, ranging from struggle with the evil latent/dominant in oneself (greater jihad or *jihad al-akbar*) to struggle with some external force that threatens the faith (lesser *jihad* or *jihad al-asghar*) |
| *khariji* | foreigner, outsider |
| *Khilafat* | Caliphate, the political order that emerged in the Muslim world after the death of the Prophet |
| *khud-agahi* | self-awareness |
| *khudi/khistan* | Self |
| *madraseh* | Islamic seminary, high school |
| *Majlis* | (lit. Assembly) the Iranian Parliament |
| *maktab* | traditional primary school |
| *mardanegi* | "valor befitting a true man" |
| *mardom* | people |
| *marja'-ye taqlid* | "Source of Emulation," a Shi'i Ayatollah whose legal injunctions are to be followed in his lifetime |
| *mashru'eh* | in Iranian politics, the position that the *shari'ah* is the source of all laws |
| *mashruteh* | constitutional |
| *mashruteh-khwahi* | constitutionalist |
| *mas'uliyat* | accountability |
| *masoum* | infallible, impeccable; the Shi'i use this term to refer to the Prophet, the 12 Imams, and Fatima, the Prophet's daughter (*chahardah-e masoum* or the Fourteen Impeccable), to indicate their divine inspiration that makes them infallible |
| *mellat* | people, nation |
| *melliyat* | nationality |
| *mujtahid* | a person (usually, but not necessarily, an 'alim) capable of *ijtihad* |
| *mulk* | country/kingdom |
| *mumalik/mamlikat* | kingdom |
| *mumin* | faithful, someone who has true *iman* |
| *munafiq* | (pl. *munafiqun*) hypocrites |
| *mustadhafin* | (lit. disinherited), the oppressed (people) |
| *mustakbirin* | (lit. arrogant) the oppressors |
| *nizam-e jaded* | (lit. the new order) the drive toward modernization of the Qajar state |
| *nizamiyyat* | order, government |
| *qanun* | laws |
| *raushanfikr* | (lit. the enlightened thinker) the enlightened; intellectual; intelligentsia |

| | |
|---|---|
| *rouhaniyat* | clergy, spiritual classes |
| *sarshenâs* | widely known, well known |
| *sekhâvat* | material generosity |
| *shahadat* | martyrdom |
| *shahid* | (lit. witness) martyr, someone who bears witness to the truth of the faith by asserting the willingness to embrace death in its defense |
| *shari'ah* | (lit. path) compendium of Islamic laws |
| *shirk* | (lit. association) the association of other beings in the divinity of Allah; idolatry |
| *shojâ'at* | courage |
| *showra* | consultation |
| *shudan* | becoming |
| *tabaqeh* | class |
| *taghut* | (lit. an idol mentioned in the Qur'an), idolatry, illegitimate |
| *tajaddud* | modernity |
| *talib* | (pl. *tullab*) student |
| *tauheed* | (lit. unity) unity of God |
| *tazveer* | (lit. deception) deception by the clergy |
| *'ulema* | (sing. *'alim*) (lit. learned man) one who has *'ilm*; clergy |
| *ummah* | (lit. community) the community of Muslims |
| *'urf* | laws made by the state for smooth governance, independent of (but in conformity with) the *shari'ah* |
| *Vilayat-e Faqih* | (lit. Rule by the Jurist) Khomeini's doctrine of political authority being vested in the learned jurist |
| *visayat* | (lit. trusteeship) the Shi'i doctrine of political authority being held in trust on behalf of the Imams |
| *wahdat al-wujud* | (lit. Unity of Being) the mystical concept of the cosmic unity of the Divine where the creation and the Creator are integral to each other |
| *watan* | homeland, country |
| *wataniyyat* | nationalism |
| *wujud* | existence, being |
| *zahiri* | (lit. external) the intellectual position that emphasizes the extrinsic aspects of the faith, such as the *faradh al-'ain* |
| *zar* | (lit. force) political oppression |
| *zor* | (lit. gold) economic exploitation |

# Notes

### Introduction

1. Political Islam denotes an intellectual category in which Islam functions less as a religion and more as a political ideology that lays down certain specific objectives for those in pursuit of it. The category (of political Islam) might range from a puritan dispensation of order, stressing upon the literal implementation of the *shari'ah* in a tribal monarchical framework (as in Sa'udi Arabia), to a parliamentary democracy. What makes such widely divergent political formulations Islamic is the pursuit of certain values or forms of social order *identified* as Islamic, and thought worthy of preservation as such.
2. See, for instance, Esposito (1999); Roy (1996); Schulze (2000).
3. For the purpose of this work, the terms "sign," "signifier," and "referent" are used as in the discipline of linguistics. A *sign* "is an abstract object, it is not to be confused with whatever it is a sign of." A *sign* therefore indicates to a *signified*, which can be a particular object, which in turn corresponds to an idea in the mind, which is called a *referent*. The act of *signifying* is taken to be establishing a link between the *sign* or the *signifier, signified,* and the *referent*. In terms of this particular work, Islam is neither the *signifier*, nor the *signified*—but the *referent*. Particular ideas, laws, or practices associated with Islam are merely the signifiers for the referent, and the categories of "laws," "values," "practices," "ideas," "philosophy" are the signified. For a discussion on the use of these terms in the sense that is done here, see Sturrock (1993), pp. 1–32.
4. The rehabilitation, however, would seem to be cosmetic. When I tried to track down followers of Shari'ati in Iran in 2004 and 2006, I was told that a large number of them lost their lives in a systematic domestic purge behind the cover of the instability of the Iran-Iraq war. A fairly large number of the remaining found it convenient to leave Iran seeking better opportunities abroad as their own country became less hospitable. A fair number of them, however, have stayed back and keep in touch with each other through formal and informal channels—such as the 'Ali Shari'ati Foundation, the *Hosseiniyah-ye Ershad*, et cetera.
5. Muhammad Faiyyaz Bakhsh, a student of Shari'ati, in conversation with the author, June 2006.
6. See, for instance, Akhavi (1980); Keddie (1981); Abrahamian (1982); Haikal (1983); Irfani (1983); Milani (1988); Taheri (1983); Madani (1991).

7. See, for instance, Irfani (1983).
8. Nikkie Keddie actually calls it the "February Revolution of 1979." See Keddie (1981), p. 258.
9. See Haikal (1983); Madani (1991).
10. Schirazi (1997).
11. See Chapter 7.
12. See Moore (1966).
13. See Gurr (1970), Johnson (1966), Tilly (1969).
14. See Skocpol (1994).
15. Sewell (1994).
16. See, for instance, Foucault (1990).
17. Skocpol (1994), pp. 240–57.
18. See Keddie (1981).
19. Abrahamian (1982).
20. Abrahamian (1993).
21. Katouzian (1981).
22. Parsa (1989); see also Parsa (2000).
23. Akhavi (1980).
24. Arjomand (1988).
25. Moaddel (1992).
26. Algar (2001).
27. Dabashi (1993).
28. Boroujerdi (1996).
29. Mirsepassi (2000).
30. Martin (2000).
31. The *faraz al-'ain* are reciting the *kalimah* (assertion of the belief in the unity of God and the prophethood of the Prophet), offering the *salaah* (prayers), observing the *rozeh* (daytime fast during the month of *Ramadhan*), paying the *zakaat* (a share of one's earning for distribution among less fortunate members of the community), and *Hajj* (pilgrimage to Mecca at least once in life during the month specified for *Hajj*).
32. Islam is supposed to classify human activity into *wajib* (correct), *mandub* (encouraged), *murakkhas* (indifferent), *makruh* (discouraged), and *haraam* (prohibited). The *shari'ah* is the corpus of legal injunctions classifying human activity into these five heads. Sunni *shari'ah* derives such laws from the Qur'an, the *ahadith* (traditions of the Prophet), *ijma* (social consensus), *qiyas* (analogy), and *ijtihad* (independent legal reasoning); the Shi'i *ahadith* includes traditions of both the Prophet and the Imams.
33. Even the Qur'an is supposed to have had seven authorized readings approved by the Prophet himself, till the third *Khalifa*, Uthman, suppressed the other six in order to prevent confusion. See Moussalli (2001), p. 47.
34. Raymond (2001).
35. Dabashi (1993); Abrahamian (1993).
36. Brumberg (2001).
37. Bernard Lewis, for instance, is confident enough to assert that he knows "what went wrong" with Islam—assuming something did—and that there is

an alternative trajectory that Islam could have taken in order to go right. See Lewis (2001).
38. See, for instance, Esposito (2008); Skinner (2005).
39. This, for instance, is the approach taken by Olivier Roy. As he puts it himself: "When Bin Laden says that *jihad is fard 'ayn* [*sic*] (a personal religious duty), we have no intention to look at what the Koran [*sic*] (or Ibn Hanbal) says on that issue: it suffices to look at the present debate among Muslims to assess the meaning of such a statement (and its political consequences)." The problem with such an approach is that the reader (and indeed, even the author) might take a fringe element like Usama bin Laden not simply as a Muslim voice, but as *the* voice of *Islam*. From such a premise it is only a short leap to reach the conclusion that a clash is impending between the Christian and Muslim civilizations, "because Osama says so." See Roy (1996), ix.
40. For a detailed exposition of this problem, see Skinner (2002), pp. 92–102.
41. See Austin (1962), pp. 94–98.
42. For a comprehensive understanding of the speech-act approach, see Austin (1962); Searle (1975, 1976, 1989).
43. See Derrida (1976), pp. 6–73.
44. See Austin (1962); Searle (1989).
45. For a detailed treatment of the significance of the study of context in helping determine the meaning of a text, see Searle (1978), pp. 207–24; Skinner (2002), pp. 62–89.
46. Rahnema (1998).
47. Shari'at-Razavi (2004 a & b).

## Chapter 1

1. See, for instance, Akhavi (1980); Keddie (1981); Abrahamian (1982); Arjomand (1988).
2. For an exhaustive account of Anglo-Russian rivalry over Persia, see Kazemzadeh (1968), pp. 3–100. See also Ramazani (1966).
3. For an exhaustive treatment of the Tobacco Protests, see Keddie (1966 a). See also Akhavi (1980); Arjomand (1988); Moaddel (1986), pp. 519–56; Moaddel (1994), pp. 1–20. For a discussion of the response of the *bazaar*s from all over Iran to the policy of concessions, see Martin (2005).
4. A useful portrayal of some of the leading persons of the Qajar ruling elite, such as Amir Kabir and Taqi Khan Farahani, and their approach to the issue is available in Parvez Afshari's biographical accounts of the Qajar period. See Afshari (1994).
5. For an account of the modernist intelligentsia, see Adamiyyat (1976).
6. The term *watan* in Farsi was used to denote principally "homeland" in the sense of land of origin, and only after 1870 did it begin to be used to denote the sense of fatherland or *patrie*. This began effectively in 1870, when the reigning Qajar, Naser al-din Shah, impressed by the freedom of press prevalent in France, invited Baron Louis de Norman to bring out a French journal in Iran

called *Le Patrie*. The libertarian posture of the paper proved so forthright that it was suppressed after the very first edition, yet the coinage of the term *patrie* and its translation as *watan* immediately caught on. See Mowlana (1963), p. 262.

7. For the emergence of the concept of *watan* in the public sphere of Iran, see Tavakoli-Targhi (2001), 113–22.
8. For a sense of the shared experience of the *bazaari*s and the intelligentsia, see Farsani (2005), pp. 53–55.
9. This shift is evident, for instance, in the most trenchantly critical newspaper, *Habl al-Matin*. Following the standard practice of Iranian newspapers from the 1870s, the newspaper carried news about the court and the capital in the first two pages, and then the following pages were devoted to the various *ayalat* and *vilayat* (provinces). From mid-1892 reports constantly carried the term *melli* (nation) to refer to the people of the various provinces, and to the subjects of the Shah generally.
10. Born of Armenian parentage in New Julfa, outside Esfahan, Malkum Khan had advocated major structural reforms as a Minister to Nasir al-din Shah that cost him his job in the 1870s. After a second abortive stint at reforming the Qajar apparatus from within, Malkum Khan made the first cogent case for constitutionalism in Persia in the 1890s. For a detailed biography of Malkum Khan, see Algar (1973).
11. For a detailed treatment of the shift, see Adamiyyat and Natiq (1977). See also Martin (2005), pp. 168–94.
12. For a detailed contemporary account of the struggle over the constitution and the civil war, see Kirmani (2004), pp. 404–527. For a slightly later account, see Kasravi (2005), pp. 699–72. A more recent account could be had from Martin (1989), pp. 65–87.
13. Cited in Kirmani (2004), p. 516.
14. Ibid., p. 516.
15. See Adamiyat (1972), pp. 65–91.
16. The most intransigent votary of this position was Shaikh Fazlallah Nouri, who, having previously resisted royal despotism, broke ranks with the constitutionalists after 1907 to make common cause with the royalists. He was among the five top royalists to be executed after the constitutionalists prevailed in the civil war. For a good account of the struggle between votaries of *mashruteh* and *mashru'eh*, see Kasravi (2005), pp. 375–465. For a historical perspective, see Martin (1989), pp. 113–38.
17. Ibid., pp. 127–38.
18. The term *tajaddud* derives from *jadid* (new). It is distinct from the term *tajdid*, which means renewal, restoration, or resumption of something from the past. *Tajaddud* connotes on the one hand revival, and on the other, something new, innovation, invention, or modernity—therefore speaking of a break from the past, either retaining some links with the past or effecting a total break. The people of Iran looked on the changes that were collectively labeled *tajaddud* in the light of something as altogether new with reference to state and society under the Qajars. This has to be differentiated from the notion of

*nizam-e jadid*, for any change in any existing dispensations could be labeled as such. *Tajaddud*, by contrast, refers to specific changes in almost every aspect of Iranian life, which marked a sharp disjunction from the immediate past, if not from the past altogether. The chief point at issue in Iran in the matter of *tajaddud* was whether or not the desired changes were a total break from the past. There were those who wanted to embrace desired changes after localizing their roots and the context—that is, they claimed that the "new" elements were not actually new, that they essentially existed sometime in the past, and only needed "revival." Others claimed that the "new" elements were altogether new, and these had to be embraced as such because the historical conjuncture was also new.

19. Jamal al-din Asadabadi (1826–97) was among the earliest thinkers to raise the alarm against colonial penetration in Muslim societies. Educated in traditional Shi'i institutions, Afghani travelled to India in 1857 in pursuit of modern sciences. The suppression of the great uprising of that year by the British impressed upon Afghani two things—that imperialism, having conquered India, was threatening West Asia, and that the only effective means of stopping this imperialist onslaught was immediate adoption of western technology by the Muslim peoples. Failing to motivate rulers of Afghanistan, Egypt, and the Ottomans apart from that of Persia to this end, Afghani set about spreading awareness about imperialism, religious dogmatism, and inefficient despotism among the people. For a detailed account of the work of Afghani, see Keddie (1968). For a detailed biographical account, see Keddie (1972).
20. For an account of the reorganization of Iran's finances, and the problems faced during this period by the American team assigned with the task, see Shuster (1912).
21. Abrahamian (1982), pp. 111–14.
22. For a detailed account of the almost interminable conflict among the constitutionalists on this issue, see Kasravi (2005), 373–465.
23. For a brief indication of the contemporary positions on the contribution of Reza Khan to the stabilization of Iran after the Great War, see Katouzian, in Cronin (2000 a), pp. 19–25.
24. Abrahamian (1981), pp. 121–22.
25. For a comprehensive treatment of the intellectual discourse on modernity in early twentieth-century Iran, see Mirsepassi (2000), pp. 55–64.
26. Cronin (1997).
27. It is an interesting comment on the modernization of the military, however, that the bulk of the fighting in the 1920s to pacify insurgent regional and tribal forces continued to be done not by the regular troops, but by irregular tribal levies (as in Qajar times) raised and disbanded as the occasion required. Cronin (2000), p. 41.
28. For a sympathetic account of the modernization of the Iranian bureaucracy see, Wilber (1975). For a slightly critical account, see Katouzian (1981), pp. 111–17.

29. Chehabi (1997), p. 237.
30. See Wilber (1975); also Katouzian (1981), p. 116.
31. For an account of Reza Shah's policy toward Iran's tribes, see Bayat (2000), pp. 213–19; see also Cronin (2000 b), pp. 241–68; Tapper (2000), pp. 220–39. For an account of the impact of sedentarization and subjugation on tribal life in Iran, see Bradfurd (1981), pp. 123–37; Barker (1981), pp. 139–57; Garthwaite (1981), pp. 159–72.
32. In 1922, Reza Khan had been instrumental in the appointment of Dr. Arthur Millspaugh of the U.S. State Department as the Treasurer-General of Iran, in a bid to check British influence in the country's economy. Britain, however, successfully neutralized any incipient interest that the United States might have had, and Millspaugh began to be sympathetic toward the British. As such, Millspaugh obstructed Reza Shah's program for modernization to such an extent that Reza Shah began to refer to him as Dr. Pool-neest (Dr. No-Money). Finally in 1928, when Millspaugh's contract came to an end, the mood in the country being firmly against foreign stakes in the country's economy, there was no consideration whatsoever of its renewal. The Shah is supposed to have told Millspaugh that there can be only one Shah in Iran, and it was to be Reza Shah. For an account of the Millspaugh mission, see Millspaugh (1946). On termination of capitulations to foreign powers, see Zirinsky (2000), pp. 81–98.
33. In 1901, Sultan Muzaffar al-din Shah had sold the monopoly of oil exploration in central and southern Iran to an Englishman called D'Arcy. This monopoly constituted the cornerstone of the Anglo-Persian Oil Corporation. In 1931, this sale was abrogated and the contract was renegotiated, leading to a new contract in 1933. Under the new contract, the geographical area under the APOC was reduced, but covered all the fields and proven reserves under exploitation. A slightly favorable revenue mechanism was also worked out by which Reza Shah increased the state's share of revenue by around 25 percent—from 16 percent to 20 percent of all proceeds.
34. Abrahamian (1981), pp. 146–47.
35. For an account of Pahlavi education policy, see Menashri (1992); Matthee (2000), pp. 123–45.
36. Afshar (1925), pp. 5–6.
37. Abrahamian (1981), p. 128.
38. For a brief account of how Reza Shah was influenced by the Kemalist project, see Marashi (2000), pp. 98–119.
39. Ahmad Kasravi (1890–1946) was one of the intellectual giants of twentieth-century Iran. Despite coming from a very traditionalist family and having his education in a seminary, Kasravi became a very strong supporter of the *Mashruteh* movement, and went on to produce perhaps the most analytically sophisticated contemporary account of the *Mashruteh* revolution. After the constitutionalist position weakened, Kasravi became a great champion of the secularist, territorial nationalist vision that dominated the intellectual landscape of Pahlavi Iran. In 1946, he was assassinated by the hardliner Islamist outfit Fidayan-e Islam.

40. Kasravi (1942).
41. The Shi'i *'ulema* in Iran were intricately connected with the communities they lived amidst. The *'ulema* dispensed justice and registered documents on behalf of the state, over and above their usual function of keeping the people mindful of their faith by recounting the foundational legends of *Ithna 'Ashari* Shi'ism (viz., those of 'Ali, battle of Karbala), and appraising them of the prescriptions and proscriptions of the faith. The people in return financially supported the *'ulema* establishment by providing the wherewithal for the payment of stipends for students aspiring to become *'alim*. The higher echelons of the *'ulema* also frequently married into landowning and great merchant families. Thus, clergy-*bazaar* ties were not only functional but also relational.
42. In their capacity as custodians of *Ithna 'Ashari* Shi'i legal tradition from the Safavid times, the *'ulema* were entrusted with not simply the judicial functions of the state but also the roles of notary and registrar for any official transaction. The fee for such services often proved crucial for the livelihood of minor *'alim* in small towns and villages or even in big cities. Reza Shah divested the *'ulema* of such functions progressively from the late 1920s.
43. See Next Chapter.
44. Abrahamian (1981), pp. 126–30.
45. British Minster in Tehran to the Foreign Office, "Annual Report for 1941," India Office/L/P&S/12-3472A.
46. The literature on this period is quite exhaustive. Brief accounts of the decade can be seen in Abrahamian (1981), pp. 169–224; Daneshvar (1996), pp. 10–31; Haikal (1983); Moaddel (1993), pp. 29–44; Katouzian (1981), pp. 144–80.
47. The *Hizb-e Tudeh-ye Iran* (Party of the Iranian Masses) was set up after the abdication of Reza Shah in 1941. The founding fathers were mostly Marxist by persuasion, who by and large chose to follow Moscow, yet refrained from calling themselves communists. Their initial agenda was uncompromisingly democratic in its tone and content, yet they never trusted the other democratic movements of Iran. Muhammad Reza Shah repeatedly tried to smash the Tudeh on account of its persistent opposition, and for all practical purposes achieved this aim by the late 1960s. For a brief account of the Tudeh, see Abrahamian (1981), pp. 155–62, 281-84; also Abrahamian (1970), pp. 291–316.
48. Azeris were never very keen supporters of the centralization undertaken by the Pahlavis. So they seized the opportunity provided by weak central authority after the ouster of Reza Shah to struggle for political space. Moscow was, therefore, merely promoting an already existing secessionist tendency.
49. The fear was so widespread that a rumor circulated even in Iranian Azerbaijan—traditionally a leftist bastion—that "wife-sharing" was just round the corner. The all pervasiveness of such fears go a long way to account for how the regime managed to persuade a wide cross-section of Iranian society to be complicit with political repression that peaked on the eve of the revolution.
50. For an insider account of the National Front, see Bazargan (1984).
51. Katouzian (1981), pp. 160–85; Moaddel (1993), pp. 41–44. See next chapter.

52. Halliday (1979), p. 138.
53. For an account of American involvement with the Shah, see Heikal (1983), pp. 13–64.
54. Katouzian (1981), pp. 223–25.
55. For a sympathetic account of the White Revolution, see Amuzegar (1991). For a more critical account see Abrahamian (1981), pp. 426–35: Daneshvar (1996), pp. 63–67; Katouzian (1981), pp. 223–75. Moaddel (1993), pp. 65–84. For a contemporary account see Firoozi (1974), pp. 328–43. For a sense of the politics around the making of the economic policies of the White Revolution, see Nasr (2000), pp. 97–122.
56. Katouzian (1981), pp. 225–26.
57. Halliday (1979), p. 143.
58. Ibid., pp. 147–67.
59. See Katouzian (1981), pp. 234–75; Bayat (1997), pp. 81–83.
60. Parsa (1989), pp. 62–90.
61. Tavakoli-Targhi (2001), pp. 77–95.
62. Quite a number of Muslims profess that the Qur'an (the Book, containing revelations from God to the Prophet Muhammad), the *ahadith* (reports of the sayings or deeds of the Prophet transmitted by his companions), and the *Shari'ah* (lit. the path, corpus of Islamic law) together hold all answers for all human situations for all times. Anything new and completely beyond the scope of these three is *bid'a* (innovation), which, according to a Prophetic *hadith*, is "misguidance," and "misguidance originates in hell." There continues to be a considerable debate about whether the warning is to be read literally, but on numerous occasions in the history of Islamic societies, attempts were made to block new things and ideas in the name of this *hadith*, not necessarily for religious considerations.
63. For a sense of the arguments that emerged in Iran during the nineteenth century and flourished in the early twentieth century, see Tavakoli-Targhi (2001), pp. 96–112.
64. Moaddel (1993), p. 61.
65. For arguments echoing the ideological positions of the revolutionary *'ulema* favoring political activism, see Ezzati (1981); Madani (1991). For a more critical account, see Akhavi (1980); Arjomand (1988).
66. Akhavi (1980), pp. 37–40.
67. For a discussion on the cardinal templates of Islamic historiography, see Robinson (2003). For a sense of application of these templates to the history of Iran, see Tavakoli-Targhi (2001), pp. 78–86.
68. For a sense of the secularist consensus during Pahlavi times, and how it influenced the reading of the history of Qajar times, see Ravandi (1975).
69. Nabavi (2003), p. 5.
70. Pahlavi was one of a group of Middle Iranian languages—that is, those that evolved between the period of Avesta and the rise of Islam. It was spoken between third and tenth centuries A.D. and was used as the official

language of the Sassanids and continued till it was replaced by the Islamized Dari/Darbari (Courtly) Persian in the mid-ninth century. See Tavakoli-Targhi (2001), pp. 22–25.
71. The Pahlavi regime in Iran found the name Persia "unsuitable" because of its association with all Muslim dynasties that had ruled in the region, generally having their powerbase in the Fars region, where Esfahan is located. However, it was subsequently shown that the term dated back to the age of Cyrus when Persia was at its apogee and that the Greek texts referred to the land as "Perse." In 1959, Muhammad Reza declared the two names would be used interchangeably, as per the advice of the Ehsan Yarshater committee, which advised that the renaming of the country was an unnecessary measure.
72. For a detailed treatment of the question, see Sanasarian (1982).
73. Moaddel (1993), pp. 52–59.
74. Chehabi (1990), pp 110–28; Moaddel (1993), pp. 44–49.
75. Abrahamian (1981), p. 421.
76. Muhammad Reza gave Boroujerdi a free hand because all through the 1950s Boroujerdi advocated a conservative position on the role of the *'ulema*—that the *'ulema* should not intervene in the political sphere. See Akhavi (1980), p. 63; Martin (2000), pp. 56–59.
77. Akhavi (1980), p. 99; Martin (2000), p. 60.
78. Akhavi (1980), pp. 105–10.
79. Chehabi (1990), pp. 169–74.
80. For a discussion of the debates around the role of Shi'ism in Iranian politics, and some of the principal protagonists of the debate, see Keddie (1983 a). For a discussion revolving exclusively around protagonists, see Dabashi (1993).
81. A dominant interpretation of *Ithna 'Ashari Shi'ism* holds that all matters of social reality are affected by considerations of religious law, and only those versed in religious law are authorized to engage in *ijtihad*. In absence of the infallible Imams and pending the return of the Vanished Imam, a guide (or guides) would be available for every generation to give guidance to the faithful. Such individuals are the *marja'-ye taqlid* (source of emulation), following whose injunctions and practices an individual Shi'i is supposed to adhere to the straight path. Such adherence to the rulings of a *marja,'* though, end with his death, whereupon allegiance has to be given to some other *marja.'* If at a given time, there exist more than one *marja,'* allegiance can be offered to any one of them. There is a tradition among the *Ithna 'Ashari Shi'i* that periodically a "rejuvenator" emerges among the *'ulema*, who almost single-handedly revitalizes the faith. Such a figure is called the *Ayatollah-ye Ozma* (i.e., the Grand Ayatollah, or the Supreme *Marja'*), head and shoulders above the other *marja.'* In the twentieth century, Ayatollah Boroujerdi was recognized as being one such. For a discussion of the issue of *marja'yyat*, see Akhavi (1980), pp. 10–11; Moussavi (1994), pp. 279–99. For an instance of the complications in the post-Khomeini era, see Gieling (1997), pp. 777–87.
82. Martin (2000), pp. 60–64.
83. Ibid., 63.

84. Khomeini was rounded up with many of his supporters, and for the first time ever in the history of the Pahlavi regime a high-ranking Ayatollah actually faced the prospect of execution. Although intervention by several high-ranking *'ulema*, led by Ayatollahs Shari'atmadari and Hadi Milani, made the Shah spare Khomeini's life, he had to go into exile. Ibid., p. 64.
85. Ibid., pp. 69–74.
86. Turner (2000), pp. 21–22.
87. Among the lay Islamist political movements in the post-Mosaddeq era, the *Nehzat-e Azadi-ye Iran* (Liberation Movement of Iran) was the most formidable. Led by Bazargan, it held together many of the splinter outfits that emerged after the disintegration of the constitutionalist umbrella of the *Jeb'eh-ye Melli* (National Front) in the 1950s. The Liberation Movement played the crucial role of keeping the Islamic constitutionalist option alive through the 1960s and 1970s. Even though the Liberation Movement later rallied behind the banner of Khomeini in 1977–79, such alliances were prompted by considerations of mass mobilization. See Chehabi (1990).

## Chapter 2

1. In their pathbreaking work on the political economy of the mass media Edward Herman and Noam Chomsky had spoken of how an underlying elite consensus largely structures all facets of the news carried by mass media. Such news then in its turn becomes instrumental in devising "public opinion." Although the theory was devised with instances drawn from mass media in the later half of the twentieth century, the theory has interesting resonances for general understanding of aggregative principles like "national interest," "public interest," etc. See Herman and Chomsky (1988).
2. Intellectual nativism refers to a position that calls for "resurgence, reinstatement or continuation of native or indigenous cultural customs, beliefs and values." Nativism rests on resisting acculturation, privileging one's own "authentic" ethnic/cultural identity, and has proven a powerful instrument of asserting autonomy from the intellectual hegemony of the west in the postcolonial Third World. In the case of Iran, this cultural reflex was influenced by the desire to establish the distance between the state and the society, in a bid to challenge the regime. For a reasonably comprehensive treatment of the phenomenon in modern Iran, see Boroujerdi (1996).
3. For a sense of how the language of Islamic political thinking has accommodated the various compulsions associated with the experiences of the modern world, see Enayat (2001); Esposito and Voll (2001).
4. For a very detailed treatment of the life of Mosaddeq, see Rouhani 1987. For a brief sketch on the early life of Mosaddeq, see Daneshvar (1996), pp. 11–12, Mottahedeh (1985), pp. 116–18.
5. Mosaddeq's thesis, "the Will in Muslim Law (Shi'i sect) Preceded by an Introduction on the Sources of Muslim Law" was an interesting exercise because he

virtually devised his own terminology of French equivalents of concepts from Islamic Law in a manner that would make his arguments clear to any lawyer trained in the European tradition.
6. The Shi'i accept the Qur'an and the *ahadith* (traditions) of the Prophet and the 12 Imams as the primary sources of law. The most important derivative sources of law according to the Shi'i were *ijma* (societal consensus) and *'aql* (reason). The role of *ijiihad/'aql* remains particularly contentious among Sunni and Shi'i alike. For several centuries the orthodox position among the Sunni jurists tended to have been that the "door of *ijtihad*" had been closed in the twelfth century; it was only in the late nineteenth and early twentieth century that Sunni modernists refuted this position. The Shi'i by contrast never "closed" the door of *ijtihad*, but the issue of its significance as a source of law occasioned several debates, the most significant one being the *Usuli*-Akhbari debate between the sixteenth and eighteenth century. The *Usuli* school believed, that each Shi'i faithful could interpret the Qur'an and the *ahadith* of the Prophet and the Imams, and thus did not need the *'ulema* to deduce new laws from those sources. The *Akhbari* school argued that every Shi'i needed the guidance of a living *mujtahid* (one capable of *ijtihad*) as a *marja'-ye taqleed* (source of emulation). The debate was thus not about whether "reasoning" should be a derivative source of law, rather about what kind of reasoning and agency would make such deductions valid and legitimate. For a discussion on the principle of *taqleed* and *ijtihad*, see Hallaq (2001), pp. 86–120. For an understanding of the position from the standpoint of the *Ithna 'Ashari* Shi'i see Cole (1983).
7. Mottahedeh (1985), pp. 118–19.
8. Ibid., pp. 19–20.
9. For a sense of his political ideas see Mosaddeq (1979).
10. Mosaddeq's works of this period were, *Iran wa Kapitulashyun-ye Haquq beh ghair-iranian* [Iran and the Capitulation of Rights to non-Iranians] (1914); *Haquq-e Madani dar Iran* [Civil Rights in Iran] (1914) and *Qawanin va Usul-e Mali dar Mumalik-e baganeh* [the Laws and Principles of Property in Other Lands] (1926).
11. Mottahedeh (1985), p. 121.
12. Daneshvar (1996), p. 12.
13. Abrahamian (1982), pp. 268–69.
14. For an exposition of the principle of "negative equilibrium" see Kayastovan (1948–50); see also Rouhani (1987).
15. Cited in Astawan (1978).
16. The National Front comprised originally of four political formations: Iran Party (*Hizb-e Iran*) represented primarily secular, educated urban professionals, calling for national sovereignty, strengthening of constitutional monarchy, ouster of landed aristocracy and promotion of social liberalism; Toiler's Party (*Hizb-e Zehmatkeshan*) principally a breakaway faction of the Tudeh Party that favored constitutional monarchy, abolition of social privileges, and resistance against all sorts of imperialism (including Soviet imperialism), respectful of

Islam and advocating class harmony rather than class struggle; the National Party (*Hizb-e Mellat-e Iran*) was primarily a body of urban, secular educated high school and university students who were fervently antiroyalist, anticapitalist, anticommunist, anticlerical, and even anti-Semitic; Society of Muslim Warriors (*Jam'eh-ye Mujahidin-e Islam*), led by Ayatollah Kashani, represented mostly the *bazaaris*, seminary students and small shopkeepers, i.e, the traditional middle classes of urban Iran. Because of the nature of its social composition, the Front represented both *bazaaris* favoring private property and salaried professionals favoring social ownership, those favoring association of religion in public life and also those favoring dissociation. They were all bound by their opposition to the increasingly powerful court-military complex.

17. *Ittila'at*, June 20, 1950.
18. Between 1901 and 1933, APOC made a profit of £200 million, while Tehran received only £10 million of the £32 million due by the contract. During 1916–20, payment of royalties and arrears were suspended. Despite the much vaunted renegotiation by Reza Shah in 1933, APOC made a 500 percent profit from the domestic sale of petroleum products in Iran—hampering, if not preventing, establishing manufacturing industries based on oil. The price at which oil was sold to Iran by the APOC/AIOC compelled Tehran to look for cheaper oil from USSR. In 1948, the Company's net revenue amounted to £61 million, and UK treasury received £28 million in income tax alone, whereas Iran received only £9 million.
19. For accounts of Mosaddeq's years as Premier, see Abrahamian (1982), pp. 267–80. Daneshvar (1996), pp. 10–35: Moaddel (1993), pp. 36–44.
20. In the elections for the seventeenth *Majlis*, for instance, Mosaddeq stopped the electoral process as soon as 79 deputies (the minimum to form a parliamentary quorum) were returned to the parliament, with 30 from the National Front.
21. Abrahamian (1982), p. 274.
22. Ayatollah Sayyed Abu al-Qasem Kashani (1882–1962), the son of a Tehrani Ayatollah, had his higher education at Najaf, where he became a *mujtahid* at the exceptionally young age of 25. He played a noticeable role in the anti-British struggle (1918–20) in Mesopotamia at the end of the Great War, and was jailed in, and exiled from, Iran due to his pro-German activities during the Second World War. Upon his return from exile, Kashani joined forces with the National Front in the campaign for nationalisation of the oil industry. His desertion of Mosaddeq proved crucial to the success of the 1953 coup.
23. Abrahamian (1982), pp. 274–80.
24. For a sketch of Al-e Ahmad's life, see Dabashi (1993), pp. 42–46.
25. Khalil Maleki was a social democrat educated in Germany, who was one of the four dozen Marxists arrested in a crackdown on radicals in 1937, and released after Reza Shah's abdication in 1941. Hailing from an Azeri family, he grew up in Arak and then Tehran. Al-e Ahmad considered Maleki as his political and intellectual mentor.
26. Al-e Ahmad (1978a).
27. See, Dabashi 1993, pp. 47–49.

28. Ibid., p. 57.
29. Al-e Ahmad (1993e).
30. Al-e Ahmad (1960), p. 45.
31. Essentially a report prepared for the Commission on the Aim of Iranian Education within the Ministry of Education in 1961, the Commission dared not publish the piece because of its overtly critical view of the regime. When Al-e Ahmad published the book on his own initiative, it turned out to be an intellectual bombshell.
32. Al-e Ahmad (1993 a), p. 34.
33. Hence the most common translation of the term, westoxication. There are several other renderings of the term viz. "weststruckness," occidentosis, "plagued by the west," "western-mania," Euromania, xenomania, westititis, etc. It denotes a state of intellectual stupor which leaves a person feeling too numb to think by himself, almost as if he has been "struck" by or intoxicated with something.
34. Al-e Ahmad (1993a), p. 31.
35. See for instance, Dabashi (1993), p. 264; Boroujerdi (1996), pp. 67–71.
36. Al-e Ahmad (1978b), pp. 200–01.
37. Al-e Ahmad (1993a), pp. 53–54.
38. Al-e Ahmad (1978a) (vol. 2), p. 149.
39. Zamani-nia (1983) (v. I), p. 108.
40. Ibid., p. 110.
41. Ibid., p. 135.
42. Al-e Ahmad (1993a), p. 111.
43. Al-e Ahmad (1978a) (vol. 2), p. 11.
44. Ibid., p. 13.
45. See Al-e Ahmad (1993b).
46. *Keyhan*, August 26, 1979.
47. Al-e Ahmad (1984), p. 52.
48. See for instance Madani (1991); Bakhshayishi (1985).
49. See Moin (1999); Taheri (1983).
50. The terms Islamic Gnosticism and mystical philosophy (in the sense of love of divine wisdom) are normally used to denote '*irfan*, even though these fail to convey the full connotation of the term). For a detailed treatment of the term '*irfan* and its evolution within the rubric of Islamic philosophy, see Netton (1994); Fakhry (2004).
51. These lectures gained him disciples who remained with him all through the Pahlavi era, and helped him forge his resistance movement against the regime—namely, Montazeri, 'Ali Khamenei, Akbar Hashmi Rafsanjani, Morteza Motahhari—long after he had to discontinue the course on '*irfan* under pressure from the '*ulema* of Qom.
52. Martin (2000), pp. 110–12.
53. An *Ayatollah-ye Ozma* emerges by means of a consensus of the faithful; followed by acknowledgment of the other *marja*'s, or else the acknowledgment from the state/secular authority. However, if there is no clear consensus on any

particular candidate, the secular authority gains the priority to acknowledge any one of these contenders. Upon the death of Boroujerdi, such a situation had come into being—Ayatollahs Golpaigani, Shari'atmadari, Najafi Mara'shi and Khomeini were frontrunners for the succession, proximate to each other in age, following and ability. Unlike the other contenders, the strength of Khomeini's candidature lay not in his qualifications as a jurist, but in his political activism—the very reason for which the Shah was determined to not accord him the status of Ayatollah-e Ozma. See Martin (2000), pp. 56–59.

54. Interestingly, no one outside the *'ulema* circles and some sections of the *bazaar* seemed to know much about Khomeini, so much so that the *Keyhaan* newspaper had to commission a journalist to find out about him once the cycle of mass demonstrations began in 1977.
55. See Appendix I.
56. The five pillars of the faith are the five obligatory requirements (*faradh al-'ain*) for Muslims—reading the *kalimeh*, offering *namaaz/salaat* five times a day, going on Hajj at least once in a lifetime, keeping the daytime fast (*rozeh*) during the month of Ramdhan, and paying the zakat (alms tax).
57. Khomeini, *Sahifeh-ye Noor* (Vol. 1), p. 166. Cited Dabashi (1993), p. 452.
58. Ibid., p. 166.
59. Khomeini (1985), p. 80.
60. Vali amr "one who holds authority," referring to Qur'an 4:59: "O you who believe! Obey God and obey the Messenger of God and those who hold authority (vali amr) among you."
61. Mullah Naraqi (d. circa. 1831) had argued that after the Prophet and the Imams, the only legitimate rule could be that of a *faqih* (qualified jurist). He argued that the *faqih* had authority over all matters that the Prophet had—that is, *vilayat-e 'amma* (governance) and *vilayat-e khassa* (special cases of trusteeship). Especially he singled out the spheres where the Prophet and the Imams had exercised authority, and in matters connected to the *shari'ah* or religion, where the *fuqaha* were perceived as having an agreed and substantiated view. Ansari (d. 1864), a student of Naraqi believed guardianship to be of two types. First, that where the guardian might act independently constituting absolute authority over the people—this was a prerogative of the Prophet and the Imams. Second, that which was based on permission and confined to guardianship over those Muslims who were unable to administer their own affairs. That is to say, the *fuqaha* had residual executive authority over only a certain aspects of lives of Muslims.
62. Khomeini (1985), pp. 30, 41–42.
63. Ibid., p. 56.
64. Ibid., p. 60.
65. Ibid., p. 63.
66. Ibid., p. 28.
67. Ibid., p. 28.
68. Ibid., p. 34
69. Ibid., p. 94.

70. Ibid., pp. 109–15.
71. Dabashi (1993), p. 409.
72. Abrahamian (1993).
73. Martin (2000), pp. 127–28.
74. Shaul Bakhash argues that after the ouster of the Shah, Khomeini was not much inclined to bring in place a regime even remotely resembling his supposed ideal as envisaged in the *Hokumat-e Islami*. The radical *'ulema* virtually forced institutionalisation of the ideas during the autumn of 1979, and Khomeini decided to sail along with them. See Bakhash (1984), pp. 70–81. Baqer Moin, Amir Taheri and Hamid Dabashi seem to believe Khomeini and his followers knew exactly what they wanted all along; that they played along with secularists and democrats till early 1979 and then grabbed power riding a popular tide to establish a regime dominated by the *'ulema*. See, Moin (1999), pp. 203–22; Taheri (1983), pp. 18–19; Dabashi (1993), p. 415.
75. In the *'irfan* tradition, Muslim thinkers like Abu al-Kindi (d. 886), Abu Nasr al-Farabi (d. 950), Abu 'Ali ibn Sina (d. 1037) and Muhyi al-din ibn al-'Arabi used platonic concepts of the ideal world and the real world to bring out the difference between *Islam* (submission before God) and *Iman* (faith in God). In this tradition *'ilm* is given the same standing as *sophia* (wisdom) in Plato, and the best ruler is one who has knowledge of reality (which stood for wisdom in the Platonic system). This emphasis on *batini* (internal) attributes of faith made Khomeini argue that the just *faqih* could be the best possible ruler, because he could see beyond appearances into reality. This strand of thinking remained a constant factor in Khomeini's politics—while he wavered between tolerating monarchy (*Kashf al-Asrar*), through full-fledged rule by the *fuqaha* (*Hokumat-e Islami*) to the theocratic democracy of the Islamic Republic, Khomeini never suggested that the *'ulema* need refrain from politics.

## Chapter 3

1. Mehdi Bazargan (1907–1995) was a prominent academic, longtime pro-democracy activist, and head of Iran's interim government in 1979. Educated in thermodynamics and engineering at the École Centrale des Arts et Manufactures in Paris, he became the head of the first engineering department of Tehran University in the late 1940s. In 1951, during the Mosaddeq era Bazargan served as the first Iranian head of the National Iranian Oil Company. After the fall of the Mosaddeq government, he cofounded the Liberation Movement of Iran, a party similar in program to Mosaddeq's National Front. He was jailed several times by the Shah for political reasons. In February 1979, after the revolution forced the Shah to leave Iran, Bazargan was appointed Prime Minister of Iran by the Ayatollah Khomeini, but later resigned in the wake of the US embassy takeover in 1979 and lived in Iran till his death.
2. See Linz (1975); Sugar (1971); Parla and Davidson (2004).
3. For a brief treatment of Muhammad Taqi's life see Rahnema (1998), p. 11.

4. In 1945, during the Premiership of Qavam al-Saltaneh, the education portfolio was given to a Tudeh member Fereidun Keshavarz. This enabled the Tudeh to lure a number of teachers to its cause, by extending the incentive of rapid promotion and salary increase. The activities of several such newly converted Tudeh teachers gained such an intensity that Muhammad Taqi decided to increase the number of classes per week from 10 to 22, with no extra pay.
5. Safavieh, an intimate friend of Shari'ati believes Muhammad Taqi wanted his son to follow his footsteps, and his being a teacher at the *tarbiat-e Modarres* may have made it easy for his son to be enrolled. Shari'ati's own account however cited family's financial hardships as the main consideration for starting to teach at an early age (see Rahnema 1998, p. 39). Shari'ati later went on to finish his high school diploma in 1954.
6. Set up in 1944 as the *Nehzat-e Jahani-ye Khodaparastan-e Sosialist* the MGWS maintained that Islam was an internationalist idea capable of providing solution for all oppressed peoples. The ideology of the movement was laid out to be socialism as an economic system, social justice as its social agenda and monotheism as its philosophical foundation. Socialism based on the absence of private property was believed to be the primary premise of social justice, which in turn was understood to be the essence of justice in Islam. The movement thus saw socialism as ipso facto inherent in Islam, and thus compatible to Iran's social psyche and culture.
7. Shari'at-Razvi (2004a), pp. 15–19.
8. The NRM in Mashhad was composed of three main cells *(jaleseh)*—one comprising of the bazaaris; one of the state bureaucrats; the third (and the largest) *jalseh* was founded and managed by Shari'ati and comprised of students. In course of NRM meetings, Shari'ati began playing with ideas that later came to be known as the Median School of Islam. Ibid., p. 25.
9. Rahnema (1998), p. 71.
10. For Shari'ati's period at the Mashhad University, see Shari'at-Razvi (2004a); Rahnema (1998), pp. 69–87.
11. This segment is based primarily on Shari'at-Razvi (2004a).
12. Rahnema (1998), pp. 84–85.
13. Shari'ati had some tough time trying to persuade his father about the prudence of the match. Taqi Shari'ati had settled his son's marriage with one of 'Ali's cousins, which was quite normal for a reputed Khorasani clerical family. Socially, it was desirable that the wife would be a practising Muslim, which in Mashhad meant she had to be veiled. Because of Puran's free spirited demeanour and her refusal to wear the veil before or after the marriage, Taqi Shari'ati was opposed to the match for over a year. But 'Ali's argument that piety and purity were not related eventually won his father over.
14. See Algar (1979), pp. 21–25.
15. Rahnema (1998), p. 128.
16. In those days, foreign students at Sorbonne could either opt for a *doctorat d'état* (as French students were obliged to do) or *doctorat d'Université* (open only to foreigners). *Doctorat d'état* was more rigorous, required a voluminous

dissertation. Shari'ati, looking for the shortest way to his doctorate, settled for correcting, commenting and translating into French a Persian text at the National Library in Paris, *Fazayel al-Balkh* (The Merits of Balkh) written by Safi al-din Balkhi.
17. For an account of Shari'ati's political activities in Paris, see Shari'at-Razvi (2004b), pp. 55–82; Rahnema (1998), pp. 89–97.
18. Rahnema (1998), pp. 193–225; Algar (1979), p. 26; Akhavi (1980), p. 145.
19. Rahnema (1998), pp. 228–45; Akhavi (1980), pp 143–44.
20. Rahnema (1998), pp. 244–60; Akhavi (1980), pp. 144–45.
21. See Chapter 7.
22. For an account of the positions of the *Jama'* and the *Majma,'* see Moslem (2002), pp. 50, 112.
23. An interesting manifestation of this binary was seen on June 19, 2006 on the occasion of the twenty-ninth anniversary of Shari'ati's death. A state-run television channel screened a very long documentary on Shari'ati, detailing his life and then his pronouncements on Islamic order—the tapes of his lectures that were played out had been completely expunged of anything even mildly critical of the *'ulema*. By contrast, in a gathering held on the same day at the *Hosseiniyeh-ye Ershad* speakers like Shari'ati's daughter Susan Shari'ati and scholars like Reza 'Alijani used Shari'ati's works to make a very powerful case for social democracy *and* societal democracy in the Islamic Republic.
24. For a detailed account of how both the votaries of clerical dominance and its opponents in the Republic are deploying Khomeini, see Brumberg (2001).
25. While some of the upper echelons of the *'ulema* came from landed aristocratic families, a far larger share of the *'ulema* came from smaller landed families from the various provinces who preferred to bring their family property under *awqaf* (sing. *waqf*) to keep it safe from depredation by the Shah or the tribes. Such *waqf* foundations were central to the foundation and administration of educational institutions like the *madraseh*s and *maktabs* where members of the families making the endowment would be guaranteed a berth. Additionally, a section of the *'ulema* were entrusted with the functions of both notary and judiciary till the late 1920s. In this manner landed wealth, public service and offices of profit secured the *'ulema* a degree of social respectability that was valued greatly in Iranian society. For detailed treatments of the social composition of the Shi'i *'ulema* in Iran, see Arjomand (1987) and (1988); see also Akhavi (1980); Fischer (1980).
26. Obvious reason for the decline of traditional learning needs emphasising— traditional learning had little relevance for the modern society and economy that was being brought into existence by Reza Shah. Previously, a large segment of the people joined the *madraseh* in order to have some education with an eye to eventual gainful employment; by the early 1930s, they preferred to head for the western-type schools (state-run and private). Additionally, many poor Iranians used to join the ranks of the clergy to avoid being drafted into the military by the local warlords. The Law on Military Conscription of 1925 (agreeing to exempt the *tullab* only after a lay civilian board of examiners

evaluated the merits of any claim for exemption) narrowed down the prospects of dodging the draft. For an exhaustive treatment of the impact of Pahlavi interventionism on the Shi'i *'ulema,* see Akhavi (1980), pp. 37–59. For a survey of the varying numbers of *madraseh* and *tullab* during the Pahlavi period see Appendices I and II of the same book.

27. 'Ashura is the tenth day of Muharram, the day when Imam Hossein died at the field of Karbala battling the forces of Yazid with only 72 faithful followers. On the tenth of Muharram the Shi'i take out *ta'aziyeh* (processions) bearing the colors of the house of Quraish, in a gesture of solidarity with the cause of the Imam, frequently accompanied with self-flagellation with sharp blades, in order to feel the pain of the Imam who laid down his life for his faith.

    *Rowzehkhwani* is a very popular Shi'i tradition in Iran. A *rowzehkhwan* is a preacher and teller of edifying stories, who generally begins with a sermon and then moves on to the sufferings of the family of the Prophet, particularly Hossein. The narration of stories is done in the trope of lamentation, which is intended to move the entire audience to a point where it weeps without restraint, creating a spiritual and emotional bond with the sufferers, which would hold the Shi'i faithful together. A *rowzehkhwani* is usually arranged by individual (or group) initiative, generally held in someone's residential quarters, with separate seating arrangement behind a curtain for the women. By the very nature of the practice, *rowzehkhwani*s are arranged by men of means and influence in a community. In the context of urban Iran, the *bazaar* is the most consistent patrons of the practice.

28. The figures on Iran's education system in this section are derived from reports of Ministry of Education, as cited Sadiq (1959), p. 478; Abrahamian (1982), pp. 144–45, 431, 432; Akhavi (1980), appendix 1, p. 187; Katouzian (1981), p. 207.

29. Al-e Ahmad (1978b), pp. 149–50.

30. Rahnema (1998), p. 12.

31. Mirsepassi (2000), p. 62.

32. An elaborate set of festivities were held at the ancient city of Persepolis near Shiraz during October 12–16, 1971 observing the 2,500th anniversary of the founding of monarchy in Iran by Cyrus the Great. The celebrations were intended to demonstrate Iran's long and magnificent history and to showcase its contemporary advancements under the administration of Mohammad Reza Pahlavi. On the last day the Shah inaugurated the Shahyad Tower (later renamed the Azadi Tower after the Iranian revolution) in Tehran to commemorate the event. Official estimate for the expenditure on the event was said to be as high as $17 million, while Ansari, one of the organizers, puts it at $22 million. Unofficial estimates have put the tab as high as $200 million.

33. Parsa (1989), p. 218.

34. "It is the belief that Allah is One, without partner in His dominions and His Actions (al-*Ruboobiyyah*), One without similitude in His essence [sic] and attributes (al-*Asma'a wa al-Sifaat*) and One without rival in His divinity and in Worship *(Uloohiyyah 'Ibaadah).* These three aspects form the basis for the

categories into which the science of *tauheed* has been traditionally divided. The three overlap and are inseparable to such a degree that whoever omits any one aspect has failed to complete the requirements of *tauheed*. The omission of any one of the abovementioned aspects of tauheed is referred as *shirk*." www.allahuakbar.net/aqeedah/tawheed.html (accessed on May 14, 2007).

35. Nasr (2006), pp. 65–67.
36. Ibid., p. 74.
37. Ibid., pp. 75–77.
38. Muhammad Abduh (1849–1905), a disciple of al-Afghani, was a pivotal figure in modern Islamic learning. Appointed Mufti of Egypt by the Khedive Ismail, Abduh was the architect of the reform of al-Azhar University in the closing years of the nineteenth century.
39. Sayyid Qutb (1906–66), was educated in an old centre of traditional learning in Egypt, the *Dar al-Ulum*. By profession an educationist, Qutb was a major ideologue of the *Ikhwan*. His thinking marks a noticeable shift from *an* Islamic alternative to *the* Islamic imperative, for which all Muslims were obligated to live and die. Such a conclusion, removing all alternate avenues of negotiation, appealed to the more radical militant components of the *Ikhwan*, and other militant outfits.
40. In conversations with the author, Tehran, June 2006. The positions of Taqi Rahmani and Reza 'Alijani can also be gleaned from their extensive writings on Shari'ati. See for instance, Rahmani (2004, 2005); 'Alijani (2000 a, b and c).
41. Kavir is the name of the vast desert to the southwest of Khorasan. Shari'ati's hometown of Mazinan was situated right on the rim of the Kavir desert, and from the days of his childhood, the desert seemed to captivate Shari'ati in all its vastness. When Shari'ati began with his mystical writings, he turned the desert into a parable for the greatness of God, "a mysterious nowhere land where the here and the hereafter stand face to face." Rahnema believes that Shari'ati's *kaviriyat* was similar to the *shathiyat* (ecstatic words of a Sufi). As *shathiyat* is associated with drowning the faculty of reason with the overflow of emotions, some thinkers consider *shathiyat* amounts to *kufr* (disbelief), even though it is meant by the Sufis as an affirmation of *iman* (faith).
42. Rahnema (1998), p. 147.
43. Shari'ati (2001c), p. 4.
44. Shari'ati (2004b), p. 28.
45. Ibid., p. 28.
46. Ibid., p. 202.
47. The course became so popular that he was later to present this course, and elaborate it much further in Ershad in 1971–72.
48. Shari'ati, *Islamshenasi* (1971a), p. 67.
49. Ibid., pp. 48–49.
50. Ibid., pp. 55–56.
51. Ibid., p. 56.
52. Ibid., pp. 57–58.
53. Ibid., p. 56.

54. Ibid., 68.
55. Shari'ati (1971a), pp. 69–70.
56. Shari'ati based the parable of Cain and Able not only on the cryptic narrative in the Qur'an (5: 30–34) which does not even mention them by their names, but also on the traditions that emerged amplifying and explaining the Qur'anic account for the dispute between the two. It is said that both Cain and Abel had a twin sister each, and Adam decided that each should marry the twin of the other. Cain considered his twin to be more beautiful, hence he wanted to marry her himself. Some commentators considered this tale of primordial incest distasteful, hence they said that the proposed brides were jinns, not twins.
57. Shari'ati (1971a), p. 70.
58. Ibid., p. 71.
59. Ibid., p. 72.
60. Ibid., pp. 82–83.
61. Ibid., pp. 84.
62. For a good exposition of this particular understanding of the Sufi variety, see Shah (1971).
63. Shari'ati (1971a), p. 88.
64. Ibid., p. 85.
65. The phrase Ummah Wahida (the "One Community") in the Qur'an refers to the entire Islamic world unified. The Quran says: "You [Muslims] are the best nation brought out for Mankind, commanding what is righteous (Ma'ruf—lit. 'recognized [as good]') and forbidding what is wrong (Munkar—lit. 'unrecognized [as good]')" [3:110].
66. Enayat (2001).
67. Rashid Rida (1865–1935) was a close disciple of Abduh who carried on with Abduh's task of reforming Islam in the Arab world. Subsequently however he gave the Salafiya movement in Egypt a conservative turn. He firmly believed that implementation of the *shari'ah* required Islamic government. He left a deep impact on Hasan al-Banna, the founder of the *Ikhwan*.
68. Muhammad Iqbal (1873–1938), probably the greatest Urdu poet of the twentieth century, was born in Sialkot, in what is now Pakistan. Having once been a proponent of territorial nationalism *(wataniyyat)* Iqbal later became convinced of the inanity of western materialist culture and the perniciousness of nationalism. He began to champion the cause of resuscitation of Islam in India, arguing that the trappings of the *Shari'ah* had ossified Islam. He became a powerful advocate of *ijtihad* and provided a very individualistic reading of the Islamic understanding of "self" *(khudi)*.
69. Maulana Maududi (1903–79) was brought up within a traditionalist milieu in central India. Till the partition of India in 1947, Maududi opposed the principle of Muslim nationalism and the demand for a Pakistan because he considered nationalism an un-Islamic import from the west. He advocated a gradual societal, rather than a violent political, revolution. To this end he sat up the Jama'at-e Islami in 1941. Maududi emphasized the universalism and

comprehensiveness of the Islamic way of life. He considered the *shari'ah* as the complete scheme of life, and an all embracing social order. His understanding of the Shari'ah as *the* blueprint of *the* Islamic order has been accused of laying the basis of a totalitarianism of (Islamic) law.

70. Shari'ati (1971a), p. 97.
71. Ibid., p. 98.

## Chapter 4

1. Muhammad Fayyaz Bakhsh, in conversation with the author, Tehran, June 2006.
2. For a general treatment of this phase of Shari'ati's life, see Shari'at-Razvi (2004b), pp. 83–137; Rahnema (1998), pp. 176–209.
3. On his dealings with the SAVAK, see Shari'at-Razvi (2004b), pp. 138–46; Rahnema (1998), pp. 210–25; see also 'Alijani (2003), pp. 41–90.
4. "We offered the Trust to the Heavens, the earth, and the mountains, but they refused to carry it and were afraid of it, but man carried it. He has indeed been unjust and ignorant" (33:72).
5. Enayat (2001), p. 38.
6. See Musavi-Lari (1996), pp. 141–48; Tabatabai (1989), pp. 174–76.
7. Enayat (2001), p. 38.
8. "Ummat wa Imamat," in Shari'ati (2004a), pp. 390–91.
9. Ibid., p. 383.
10. Ibid., pp. 448–84.
11. The Shi'i believe that Imam 'Ali and all his descendants through his wife Fatima, the Prophet's daughter, had inherited not only the political authority of the Prophet, but also his *Masoumiyyat* (infallibility). By contesting *Imamat* and establishing an Arab kingship, the Khilafat had deprived the Muslim *ummah* of the shining example of the divinely inspired Imams. Accordingly, the Shi'i considered all political authority to be illegitimate. See Appendix I.
12. See, for instance, "Tashai'o surkh wa tashai'o siyah," in Shari'ati (2004g).
13. See "Shahadat," in Shari'ati (2004c).
14. Shari'ati (1979b), pp. 8–9.
15. "Tashai'o 'alavi wa tashai'o safavi," in Shari'ati (2004g), p. 129.
16. Shari'ati (1979b), p. 4.
17. Ibid., p. 5.
18. Ibid., p. 6.
19. "'Ali, heyat-e barwarsh pas az marg," in Shari'ati (2004a), pp. 303–54.
20. Ibid., pp. 342–43.
21. "Surah al-Rum," Shari'ati (1987b), p. 88.
22. "Shahadat," Shari'ati (2004c), p. 111.
23. Ibid., 112–13.
24. Ibid., p. 114.
25. Ibid., p. 155.

26. Bilal was owned by Umayyad ibn Khallaf, a prominent Meccan. When Bilal joined the ranks of Muhammad's followers, he was brutally tortured—yet he refused to recant. He was saved by Abu Bakr, later the first of the Sunni Caliphs, who purchased and manumitted Bilal. Later Bilal became the first person to give the call to prayer *(adhaan/azaan)* in Medina.
27. Shari'ati (1981), p. 43.
28. Ibid., p. 43.
29. Ibid., pp. 25–6.
30. Ibid., p. 27.
31. Ibid., p. 28.
32. Idid., p. 18.
33. Ibid., p. 17.
34. Ibid., p. 22.
35. Shari'ati (1989a), p. 29.
36. Ibid., p. 30.
37. Ibid., pp. 30–31.
38. Ibid., pp. 32–33.
39. Ibid., pp. 34.
40. For an account of Akbari's critique, see Rahnema (1998), pp. 201–04.
41. The fact that two of his most provocative talks at the Hosseiniyah-ye Ershad were called *Az kuja aghaz kuneem* (Where do we begin?) and *Che Bayied Kard?* (What is to be done?) shows that he was at least familiar with the names of some Lenin's most famous works.
42. Rahnema (1998), p. 205.
43. Ibid., pp. 207–09.
44. For a detailed discussion of this phase, see 'Alijani (2003), pp. 46–60. See also Rahnema (1998), pp. 216–17.
45. Parsa (1989), p. 63.
46. Ibid., pp. 63–64.

## Chapter 5

1. In fact, one of the reasons why Khomeini became the embodiment of resistance to the Shah's regime in 1979 was that, among all who entered the political fray, *he* alone had never relented in his opposition from 1963 onward.
2. Nabavi (2003), p. 67.
3. Jalal Al-e Ahmad discussed this sense of alarm in the group of essays that was later published as *Dar Khidmat va Khiyanat-e Raushanfikran* (On the Service and Betrayal of Intellectuals).
4. Morteza Motahhari (1920–80) came from Fariman near Mashhad. Son of a well-known *'alim,* Motahhari went to Qom for his higher studies in 1937, having Boroujerdi, 'Allama Tabatabai, and Khomeini among his teachers. Motahhari is supposed to have been the closest of all Khomeini's students. In 1952, having failed to introduce a radical reform program as a teacher in the *Madraseh-ye Faiziyah,* Motahhari left Qom disheartened with clerical

conservatism and settled down in Tehran. In 1954 Motahhari started teaching in the faculty of theology at Tehran University, where many leading figures of the revolution, such as Baheshti and Bahonar, became his students. Following Khomeini's exile, Motahhari remained continually in touch with Khomeini and was his sole designated representative in Iran for the collection and disbursement of religious dues paid to Khomeini by his followers. For a detailed treatment of Motahhari's life and contribution, see Davari (2005).

5. Nabavi (2003), pp. 70–71.
6. For a discussion of the debate in Iran on the role of intellectuals in society see Nabavi (2003), pp. 70–76.
7. The name of the institution indicated its dual character—*Hosseiniyeh* is simply a religious location where the Shi'i faithful congregated to mourn the martyrdom of Imam Hossein, of which there are hundreds all over the country; *Ershad* denotes guidance, implying an enlightened rupture with the past. In traditional *Hosseiniyeh*s believers relived the martyrdom of Hossein and soothed themselves by shedding tears over an event that happened 13 centuries back. By contrast *Ershad* sought to guide the people back to the source of their faith, interpret its historical evolution, and explain its meaning and role in the modern world.
8. For a detailed account of the foundation of the *Hosseiniyeh-ye Ershad*, see Minachi (2005); Rahnema (1998), pp. 226–30.
9. Fakreddin Hejazi, whom Motahhari had introduced at the *Ershad*, attracted such large crowds that the clergy began to look upon him as a dangerous rival. They pressurized Motahhari to terminate Hejazi's association with the *Ershad*, and Motahhari used it as an issue in the power struggle against the Minachi-Homayun duo. For Motahhari's side of the story, see Davari (2005); for Minachi's side of the story see Minachi (2005).
10. For an account of Shari'ati's experience at *Ershad*, see Shari'at-Razvi (2004b), pp. 147–58.
11. In conversation with the author in Tehran, June 2006. Khanum Tavassoli is a writer, journalist, and women's rights activist, associated with the journal *Nafa.*' Her husband is now retired.
12. Shari'ati (1981), p. 12.
13. Ibid., p. 12.
14. Ibid., p. 13.
15. Ibid., p. 7.
16. By way of examples Shari'ati made a revealing statement of his own political preferences. He referred to Sattar Khan Tabrizi—a valiant hero of the *Mashruteh* revolution who fought Qajar attempts at counterrevolution—as a *raushanfikr* but not an intellectual; Allamah Muhammad Qazvini, an anti-*Mashruteh* cleric, as an intellectual but not a *raushanfikr*; and 'Ali Akbar Dehkhoda—scholar, philologist, poet, journalist, and an advocate of constitutionalist government as both a *raushanfikr* and an intellectual.
17. Shari'ati (1981), p. 5.
18. Ibid., pp. 7–8.

19. Ibid., p. 11.
20. Ibid., pp. 16–7.
21. In this context he referred to a popular idea of the 1940s that the real reason behind a high rate of illiteracy was the unscientific nature of Persian written in the Perso-Arabic alphabet. Shari'ati compared this argument as similar to saying that the real reason behind Iran's backwardness is the presence of potholes in the streets. But potholes exist because nobody attends to these; similarly illiteracy exists because nobody wants to address the problem—that is, the real reason was lost behind manifestation of the problem. Ibid., p. 18.
22. Shari'ati (1981), p. 32.
23. Ibid., p. 32.
24. Ibid., p. 32.
25. Ibid., p. 32.
26. Ibid., p. 33.
27. Ibid., pp. 33–34.
28. Ibid., p. 35.
29. Ibid., p. 11.
30. Shari'ati (1989a), p. 11.
31. Ibid., p. 12.
32. Ibid., pp. 22–23.
33. Ibid., pp. 25–26.
34. "Tauhid o shirk," in Shari'ati (2003b), pp. 42–43.
35. See Appendix I.
36. *Jahiliya* (lit. ignorance) refers to "the dark ages" when mankind had become ignorant of God, and carried out practices that amounted to a negation of the will of God. Islam (submission, to the will of God) was revealed as the path to bring mankind back to the straight path that leads to God.
37. Shari'ati (1989a), p. 8.
38. Ibid., p. 10.
39. "Intezar—Mazhab-e aitraz," in Shari'ati (2004c), p. 247.
40. "Tashai'yo surkh wa tashai'yo siyah," in Shari'ati (1999), p. 5.
41. Ibid., p. 5.
42. Ibid., p. 5.
43. Ibid., pp. 5–6.
44. Ibid., p. 8.
45. Ibid., p. 10.
46. The Shu'ubiyyah movement took place in the eleventh-twentieth centuries, opposing Arab predominance in the Persian political structure. The movement had little intellectual impact in the Muslim world outside Persia, because it highlighted the significance of ethnic and racial ties, which Islam does not acknowledge.
47. *Ajam* literally means "deaf"—this term was used by the Arabs to refer to the Iranians, implying the Iranians were "deaf" to the revelation of God.
48. "Tashai'yo 'Alavi wa Tashi'yo Safavi," in Shari'ati (1999), p. 113.
49. Ibid., p. 92. He showed that if the *hadith* were authentic, then Imam Hossein had got married to Shahrbano at the age of 15, but their son (later Imam Sajjad,

one of the few to have survived the massacre at Karbala) was born 20 years later, of which there was a slim possibility had Hossein married that young.
50. Ibid., 50.
51. Ibid., p. 233.
52. Ibid., p. 133.
53. Ibid., pp. 215–16.
54. Ibid., pp. 232–63.
55. Ibid., pp. 219–24.
56. Ibid., pp. 120–24.
57. Tabatabai (1989), pp. 210–12.
58. The question of the *walayah* (authority) of the Imam in absentia was particularly contentious. Apart from the *usul al-din*, nothing was more absolute for the *Ithna 'Ashari* Shi'i than the *walayah*. Hence, during the *ghaibat* continuity of the *walayah* was of primary importance. This led to the position that during the *ghaibat* of the Vanished Imam, the community had to rely on the most learned among the *'ulema*, who were not *masoum* (infallible) themselves, but were by virtue of their piety and learning capable of helping the faithful to stay on the path to God. See Akhavi (1980), p. 7.
59. There exists a major debate on the implications of this position. One school of thought suggests that this position implies quietism—that the Shi'i are supposed to bear all the injustices of the temporal rulers lest any opposition results in anarchy, thus undermining the observance of the minimum requirements of the faith. In mid-twentieth-century Iran, this positioned was championed among others by the Ayatollah Ozma, Sayyid Hassan Borujerdi. Another school suggests that while ordinarily the Shi'i are supposed to be quietist, on occasions when the basic conditions themselves of observing the faith are under threat the faithful have to rally in defense of the faith behind the custodians of the faith, *the 'ulema*—this was the position of Ayatollah Shirazi over the Tobacco Protests of 1892. Ruhollah Khomeini took the latter argument several steps farther by suggesting that the *'ulema* being the custodians of the faith, had to initiate defense of the faith whenever Islam was in danger. See ibid., pp. 6–22.
60. Surah, 2: 34–38.
61. This particular Sufi reading of the "self" is derived primarily from the arguments of Ibn al-'Arabi, the most influential theoretician of the principle of *wahdat al-wujud*. See Netton (1994), pp. 269–88, and Nasr and Leaman (2001), pp. 497–510. For a more comprehensive treatment of the Sufi notion of "self" and "return" see Shah (1971); Lings (1993); Nasr (2000); Fakhry (2004).
62. Shari'ati (1999), p. 232.
63. "*Intezar*—mazhhab-e aitraz," Shari'ati (2004c), p. 244.
64. Ibid., pp. 246–48
65. Ibid., pp. 248–49.
66. Ibid., pp. 256–57.
67. Ibid., pp. 258.
68. Ibid., pp. 260–61.
69. Ibid., pp. 277–78.

70. The Mujahidin-e Khalq was a group of radically inclined graduates of Tehran University who had broken away from the *Nehzat-e Azadi* (Freedom Movement) after the uprising of 1963, and come to form a series of discusision cells to study the Alegrian, Cuban, and Vietnamese revolutions in preparation for their own revolutionary struggle. Some of them even went to Palestine to receive guerrilla training.
71. Parsa (1989), pp. 200–01. For a detailed treatment of the Mujahidin-e Khalq, see Abrahamian (1989).
72. Ahmad Reza'i was one of the six graduates of Tehran University who left the *Nehzat-e Azadi* to found the militant Marxist-Islamist *Sazman-e Mojahedin-e Khalq* in 1965. The organization began its military operations in August 1971 (aimed at disrupting the 2,500-year anniversary of the monarchy) by bombing Tehran electrical works. After a botched plane hijack attempt, nine Mojahedin were arrested. One of them gave information under torture that led to the arrest of 66 others, including Reza'i. Reza'i committed suicide in February 1972 to deny the regime the opportunity to pass a sentence of death upon him.
73. For an exhaustive treatment of the doctrine, see Cook (2000).
74. The first systematically activist interpretation of this doctrine was formulated by Ayatollah Khomeini in rationalizing the *Vilayat-e Faqih*. He argued that since the *'ulema* know what is right from what is wrong, it is incumbent on them to take up the responsibility of guiding the uninitiated in this direction. It follows that the *'ulema* have to be associated with government in one way or another.
75. Shariati, *Insan wa Islam*, www.shariati.com/farsi/insanwaislam.html (accessed on May 23, 2003).
76. Gieling (1999), p. 40.
77. For a detailed discussion, see El-Fadl (2001).
78. Sobhani (2001), p. 17.
79. In addition to these two categories, the status of *shahid* is given to anyone who dies in such a manner as to excite the sympathy or pity of mankind—although such persons are not entitled to the ritual purification and burial processes to which the *ash-shuhada al-kamil* are entitled.
80. Surah 4:71.
81. Surah 3:163.
82. "Shahadat," in Shari'ati (2004c), p. 118.
83. Ibid., pp. 119–20.
84. Ibid., p. 122.
85. Ibid., pp 138–39.
86. Ibid., p. 139.
87. Ibid., p. 154.
88. For a detailed treatment of the clergy's responses to Shari'ati see Rahnema (1998), p. 268.
89. Davari (2005), p. 44.
90. Rahnema (1998), p. 240.
91. Ibid., pp. 252–59.

92. Cited Davari (2005), p. 44.
93. Ibid., p. 46.
94. Motahhari (1985), p. 102
95. Cited, Davari (2005), p. 45.
96. Motahhari, in a joint letter with Bazargan, 23 Azar, 1356/14 December, 1977), cited ibid., p. 46.
97. This section relies heavily on 'Alijani (2003).

## Chapter 6

1. One of the principal reasons for such an assumption is the considerable emphasis the Qur'an and the Prophet are supposed to have laid on the ordering of Islamic society as the *khayra ummatin* (the best community), bound as it was by the laws of Allah and destined to be *as-shuhada 'ala'n-nas* ("a witness for the whole of humanity") [2: 143]. For a very brief exposition of the significance of the *ummah* in Islam see Esposito (1998), pp. 28–30; Ansari (2001), pp. 43–46.
2. The category of "individualist" is deployed in its broader connotation of a set of values which accords primacy to the human individual, rather than the generic aggregative unit of the "community" in the general arena of social conduct. It does *not* refer to the narrower connotation of the term that evolved out of the western intellectual tradition with definite economic, social and political implications.
3. The debate about the historical origin of *fotowwat* has proven quite intractable. Louis Massignon and Hamid Hamid believe the idea goes back to pre-Islamic times. Others speak of a direct relationship between Islam and *fotowwat*. See Adelkhah (1999), p. 33.
4. Ibid., p. 4.
5. Ibid., p. 34. See also Floor (1981), pp. 83–93.
6. There were several such protests all over Persia, carried out at the local level, led by local merchants or other prominent personalities. The most effective one, though, were the tobacco protests of 1892–94.
7. Such as the demand which occasioned the outbreak of the *mashruteh* revolution in 1905.
8. It remains crucial in the Islamic Republic even today for a *javânmard* to "have a back" *(posht dashtan)*, that is, support from people who stood behind him. See Adelkhah (1999), pp. 40, 60–67.
9. Adelkhah's field study indicate that the economic crisis occasioned by the Iran-Iraq war afflicting the Islamic Republic is probably transforming the popular notion of *javânmardi*, to an extent by depoliticising it, and confining it to the virtue of generosity alone. See Ibid., p. 31.
10. Ibid., p. 45.
11. Rahnema (1998), pp. 144–60.

12. Persian mystics Abu Yazid al-Bistami (d. 874) and Mansur al-Hallaj (d. 922) believed that God dwelt in the hearts of the believers, and the only way to attain that knowledge was to extinguish all consciousness of the human self. See, Fakhry (2004), pp. 241–48.
13. Shari'ati (1971a), p. 279.
14. Shari'ati (1999), p. 45.
15. Shari'ati (1991), p. 655.
16. Shari'ati (1999), p. 158.
17. Rahnema (1998), p. 158
18. Ibid., p. 210. Shari'ati's associations with Mossadeq Rashti eventually brought the attention of the SAVAK onto him in March 1968—ever since then he remained high on the watchlist of SAVAK.
19. Shari'ati (1981), p. 30.
20. Ibid., p. 31.
21. Ibid., p. 9.
22. Shari'ati, *Insan wa Islam,* www.Shari'ati.com/farsi/insanwaislam/html (accessed on May 23, 2003).
23. Shari'ati (1981), pp. 16–30.
24. Ibid., p. 16.
25. Shari'ati n.d.c, p. 27.
26. "Shahadat," Shari'ati (2004c), p. 167.
27. In conversation with the author in Beirut, December 2005.
28. See for instance, Mir-Hosseini (1999).
29. Shari'ati (1980), p. 57.
30. Ibid., p. 60.
31. Ibid., p. 61.
32. Ibid., p. 62.
33. Ibid.
34. Ibid., p. 84.
35. Mir-Hosseini (1999), p. 214.
36. In conversation with the author in Tehran, June 2006.
37. Ibid.
38. Motahhari addressed the issue of women's responsibilities in Muslim societies in the course of the debate on Iranian Civil Law in the mid-1970s. He published a series of articles in the magazine *Zan-e Roz*. This was later published as *Nizam-e Huquq-e Zan dar Islam,* and became the definitive official text on women's issues in the Islamic Republic. See Motahhari (1991).
39. In conversation with the author in Tehran, June 2006.
40. See, Chittick (2001), pp. 497–509.
41. For a discussion of the doctrine, see, Nasr's essay on Mullā Sadrā in Nasr and Leaman (2001), pp. 648–50.
42. Turner (2000), p. 237.
43. The Qur'an clearly distinguishes between adherences to the *farz al-'ain* (five practices obligatory upon any Muslim), which are the "external conditions" *(al-wajh al-zahiri),* and genuine belief *(iman),* which is the "internal

condition" *(al-wajh al-batini)*. Adherence to the external conditions collectively constitutes *Islam,* that is, submission before the will of God; this is distinct from having genuine and unflinching faith in Allah, which constitutes *iman*. This distinction manifests in the classification of the ummah into *Muslim,* those who adhere to the obligations of submission *(Islam),* and *Momin,* those who have faith *(iman)* in their heart. The Qur'an gives greater significance to *Momins,* because personal choice prompted their abject submission before God. See for instance, *Suratu 'l-Hujurat* (Chapter of the Inner Chambers), verse 14:

> The desert Arabs say: "We believe." Say: "Ye do not believe: only say that 'We have submitted', for not yet has faith entered your hearts."

44. Both iman and Islam involve a conscious choice—hence the Qur'an lays great emphasis on reason *(aql)* and knowledge *('ilm)*. Here, *'ilm* is not understood in the narrow sense of knowledge about Allah relating to the Qur'an, Shari'a, Hadith, or even the fiqh. *'Ilm* also includes spiritual knowledge *('ilm al-ladunni),* wisdom *(hikma),* gnosis *('irfan),* thought *(tafakkur),* science *('ulum),* the science of history *('ilm al-tarikh),* the science of ethics and morality *('ilm al-akhlaq)*. *'Ilm* denotes the certainty of knowledge regarding God and his signs, and *iman* signifies belief in the incumbency such knowledge necessitates. There can be *'ilm* without *iman,* but there cannot be *iman* without *'ilm*. *'Ilm,* therefore, goes way beyond the limited confines of *fiqh,* and the *'ulema* wield command over only one aspect of it.
45. The desire to associate *'ilm* received from the western civilization with Islamic worldview stemmed essentially from the way Imam Jafar al-Sadiq understood *iman*. The Imam held that *iman* constituted of conviction of the heart *(aqida),* confession of faith by the tongue *(iqrar)* and observance of the principal obligations *(farz al-'ain)*.
46. Turner (2000), pp. 236–37.
47. "Shi'i: yek hizb-e tamam," in Shari'ati (2004c), pp. 35–36.
48. The priority accorded to the binding force of religious regulations in 'traditionalism' is reflected in the fact that the term *Mazhab* (originally, school of law) has come to be used almost interchangeably with religion.
49. Iqbal, "The Human Ego: His Freedom and Immortality," The Reconstruction of Religious Thought in Islam (Iqbal Cyber Library, Iqbal Academy, Lahore, http://www.iqbalcyberlibrary.net/reconstructionofreligious thought/humanego3.html).

    > If ye do well to your own behalf will ye do well: and if ye do evil against yourselves will ye do it. (17:7)

50. Shari'ati, "Muhammad Iqbal: A Manifestation of Self-reconstruction and Reformation," www.shariati.com/english/mawaiqbal/khudsazi.html.

## Chapter 7

1. In March 1975 Shari'ati was released in suspicious circumstances. According to Nasir Minachi, Shari'ati was told by Aqa Hosseinzadeh that his release was due to the pressure brought to bear on the Shah by influential figures in the Algerian government, such as the Foreign Minister Abdel-Aziz Bouteflika, who had been associated with Shari'ati in France during 1960–62. The account is chronologically tenable because the Shah travelled to Algeria during March 5–8, 1975; Shari'ati was released on March 25. A second argument coming from the official chronicler of the Khomeini movement, Aqa Sayyid Hossein Rowhani, argues that Shari'ati had made a deal to be released from prison. Using "classified" SAVAK reports, Rowhani argues that in prison Shari'ati realized how his lectures had motivated the Mojahedin to launch a campaign of terror. Repentant, Shari'ati is said to have written two works—*Insan, Marxism wa Islam* (Man, Marxism, and Islam) and *Bazgusht be Khish* (Return to Oneself)—that denounce Marxism as a western infliction on Iran and vulgar economism. The first was published in the form of a book; the latter was serialized in *Keyhan* in 33 parts during April 22-June 22, 1976. If these works were indeed written by Shari'ati, then they involve a number of volte-faces that are difficult to reconcile. Shari'ati's followers argue the Pahlavi regime had these concoctions published in Shari'ati's name, but they fail to explain why he never publicly denied having written them. See Rahnema (1998), pp. 337–49.
2. The SAVAK had impounded Shari'ati's original passport, which was in the name of 'Ali Shari'ati. Applying for a fresh passport under the name 'Ali Mazinani, Shari'ati managed to leave Iran without the SAVAK knowing about it till after he had left. Rahnema (1998), pp. 363–65.
3. Khomeini's declaration from Qom, April 1, 1979, cited in Khomeini (1985), p. 267.
4. Bakhash (1984), p. 3. Khomeini's treatise on *hokumat-e Islami* lacked any discussion on the institutions of the Islamic state. He merely assigned to the government the traditional duties of protecting Islam, defending the frontiers, administering justice, and collecting taxes. A legislature would not be needed since all laws were laid down by the Qur'an and Islamic traditions and Islamic traditions unencumbered by appeals courts, bureaucracy and western laws.
5. Bazargan's government was basically a cabinet of engineers, lawyers, educators, doctors and former civil servants—professional middle class and at the center of Iran's political spectrum. The members were invariably close associates of Bazargan in the opposition to the Shah—either at the Nehzat-e Azadi, or at the Islamic Society of Engineers, or men like Naser Minachi—Shari'ati's principal patron at the Ershad.
6. For a brief account on the draft constitution proposed by the Bazargan government, see Bakhash (1984), pp. 72–81; Schirazi (1997), pp. 22–24.
7. Bakhash (1984), p. 74; Schirazi (1997), pp. 24–27.
8. Akbar Hashmi Rafsanjani, anticipating the outcome of the August elections is supposed to have told Bani-Sadr: "Who do you think will be elected to a

Constituent Assembly? A fistful of ignorant and fanatic fundamentalists who will do such damage that you will regret ever having convened them." Cited in Bakhash (1984), p. 75.
9. Schirazi (1997), p. 27.
10. Address to the *'ulema,* June 5, 1979, cited in Khomeini (1985), pp. 268–74.
11. Bakhash (1984), p. 82.
12. For an authoritative treatment of the *Mojahedin,* see Abrahamian (1989).
13. Moslem (2002), p. 50.
14. Gieling (1999), p. 44.
15. *Jihad-e ibtida'i* is a *farz-e kifaya* (secondary obligation), that is, an obligation when no one else undertakes it, but optional if even one has already undertaken it. This is unlike a defensive *jihad* which is a *fardh al-'ain* (primary obligation), which is mandatory for all Muslims. See Gieling (1999), p. 44.
16. *Ittila'at,* 17/1/64 (April 1985).
17. A *kafir* is a person guilty of *kufr* (concealing)—that is, someone who conceals the truth about God and does not believe in the Revelation. A *munafiq* is a person who professes to believe in Islam, but actually does not. *Taghut* (derived from the Arabic for idol) represents those forces which "transgress the laws prescribed by God," and "claims the prerogative of divinity for himself." In Islamic law, it is obligatory to wage *jihad* against an authority that is *taghut*; a *kafir* can be spared if he does not challenge the Islamic way of life, but *jihad* is necessary if he disturbs it; a *munafiq,* being at least nominally a Muslim cannot be killed, hence with him a *jihad ba zaban* (verbal *jihad*) has to be waged.
18. For an exhaustive treatment of the issue doctrinal discourse on the war, see Gieling (1999), pp. 74–105.
19. Cited in Ibid., p. 124.
20. Bayat's position is that the Islamic Revolution reflects the agenda as defined by a handful of Iranians, and not a demand emanating from the society in general. He points out that Iran did not experience any kind of "social movement" with an Islamic character, rather only a political movement speaking an Islamic language. Bayat (2007), pp. 16–48.
21. Ayatollah Shari'atmadari was one the most important jurists in Iran after the death of Boroujerdi with credentials as *faqih* better than Khomeini. In 1982, when a plot to overthrow the government was uncovered, several of the conspirators were said to have been in contact with Shari'atmadari. Despite highly contentious evidence of Shari'atmadari's complicity in the plot, in a move unprecedented in the history of Shi'ism, the government prevailed upon 17 seminary teachers to strip Shari'atmadari of the rank of Ayatollah.
22. Abdo and Lyons (1997), p. 30.
23. Ibid., p. 31.
24. Gieling (1997), pp. 777–87.
25. For a very comprehensive account of the critique of *Vilayat-e Faqih* by Montazeri, see Abdo (2001), pp. 9–24.

26. "Montazeri on State's Road to Destruction," *Keyhan*, October 10, 1994, FBIS-NES-96-231, October 10, 1994.
27. For a brief biographical sketch of Soroush's life, see Vakili (2001), pp. 152–53.
28. Soroush, "Qabz va bast dar mizan-e naqd va bahs," *Kiyan*, 1, 2 (1995), p. 9, cited in Vakili (2001), p. 153.
29. For a detailed exposition of Soroush's ideas on interpretation of religious texts and the formation of religious knowledge, see Soroush (1990).
30. Soroush has written extensively on Shari'ati's influence as a thinker. See for instance Soroush (2006). See also, "Duktur Shari'ati va baz-sazi-ye fikr-i dini," in Soroush (1994).
31. Soroush, "Farbih-tar az idiolozi" cited in Vakili (2001), p. 158.
32. Soroush (2000), pp. 132–33.
33. Ibid., p. 133.
34. Soroush's essay on "Tolerance and Governance" was in response to one such critique, Hamid Paydar, in particular his essay in "The Paradox of Islam and Democracy," *Kiyan*, no. 19.
35. Soroush (2000), p. 134.
36. For a brief life sketch of Ayatollah Ruhollah Khatami, see Abdo and Lyons (1997), p. 77.
37. Brumberg (2001), p. 196.
38. In his last months as Minister for Culture and Islamic guidance, Khatami was attacked by his clerical opponents for refusing to censor foreign music video and films beamed through satellite television channels. Clerical Majlis deputies argued that such films and videos are "agents of corruption and fornication." Khatami tried in vain to explain that "if there is a dispute against a piece of film or music, we cannot declare films or music as inadmissible and thereby spoil the issue." "Culture, Islamic Guidance Minister on Policies," broadcast May 3, 1992, FBIS-NES-92-105, June 1, 1992.
39. See for instance, Wells (1999), pp. 27–39.
40. Khatami (1993), p. 11
41. Ibid., pp. 1–2.
42. For a detailed exposition of the theory, see Khatami (2001).
43. Khatami (1993), p. 26.
44. Ibid., pp. 40, 42.
45. Ibid., pp. 50, 55–56.
46. Ibid., p. 48.
47. Ibid., p. 15.
48. Ibid., p. 13.
49. Ibid., p. 15.
50. Ibid., p. 19.
51. Ibid.
52. Ibid., p. 46.
53. Ibid., p. 17.
54. Ibid., pp. 47–48.
55. Daniel Brumberg makes the argument that almost anyone trying to push an agenda of either reaction or reform from within the establishment tend to

legitimise their agenda by citing Khomeini. Thereby, Brumberg argues, Islamic Republic in the 1990s is redefining what Khomeini and the Islamic revolution stands for. See Brumberg (2001), pp. 185–229.
56. Cited in ibid., p. 220.
57. Cited in ibid., p. 221.
58. See Khatami (1994).
59. "Inaugural Speech by President Khatami, 4th August 1997," www.persia.org/khatami/speech.html.
60. See for instance, Esposito and Voll (2001); Ajami (1999).
61. For the implications of Qaddafi's rise to power for, and impact on, authoritarian regimes in the West Asia and North Africa, see Owen (1992), pp. 39–55.
62. Bayat calls this process "Islamization without an Islamic state." He notices a "decline of the core" that is, militant wing of the *Ikhwan* and militant outfits like *al-Jama'a al-Islamiyya*, accompanied by the rise of a "fragmented" Islamic space. For a sociological analysis of this phenomenon, see, Bayat (2007), pp. 136–51. For a narrative treatment see Abdo (2006), pp. 70–106.
63. Bayat (2007), pp. 137–66.
64. *Bonyad-e Mostaza'fin* (Foundation of the Disinherited) was a revolutionary organization set up in 1979. It took over the considerable assets of the Pahlavi Foundation, which was one of a string of organizations set up by the Pahlavis to deposit their wealth. The *Bonyad* was set up with an agenda of charitable activities and public service, but like its pre-revolutionary counterpart it has been alleged to be mired in corrupt and illegitimate practices. Egypt, by comparison seems to have fared better.
65. Eickelman (1998), pp. 80–89.
66. An Omani police official, cited ibid., p. 81.

## Conclusion

1. See Roy (1996).

# Select Bibliography

Abbot, John (1977) *The Iranians: How They Live and Work* (London and Vancouver, BC: David and Charles).
Abdi, Kamyar (2001) "Nationalism, Politics and the Development of Archaeology in Iran," *American Journal of Archaeology*, vol. 105, no. 1 (January), pp. 51–76.
Abdo, Geneive (2001) "Rethinking the Islamic Republic: A 'Conversation' with Ayatollah Hossein Ali Montazeri," *The Middle East Journal*, vol. 55, no. 1 (Winter), pp. 9–24.
——(2006) *No God but God: Egypt and the Triumph of Islam* (Oxford: Oxford University Press).
Abdo, Geneive and Jonathan Lyons (1997) *Answering Only to God: Faith and Freedom in Twenty-First Century Iran* (New York: Henry Holt).
Abedi, Mehdi and Gary Legenhausen (eds.) (1986) *Jihad and Shahadat: Struggle and Martyrdom in Islam* (*Essays and Addresses by Ayatullah Muhammad Taleqani, Ayatullah Murtada Mutahhari, Dr. 'Ali Shari'ati*) (Houston, TX: Institute for Research and Islamic Studies).
Abrahamian, Ervand (1968) "The Crowd in Iranian Politics," *Past and Present*, vol. 41 (December), pp. 184–210.
——(1970) "Communism and Communalism in Iran: The Tudeh and the Firqeh-i Dimukrat," *International Journal of Middle East Studies*, vol. 1, no. 4 (October), pp. 291–316.
——(1974) "Oriental Despotism: The Case of Qajar Iran," *International Journal of Middle East Studies*, vol. 5, no. 1, pp. 3–31.
——(1978) "The Political Challenge," *MERIP Reports*, July-August, pp. 3–8.
——(1979a) "Iran in Revolution: The Opposition Forces," *MERIP Reports*, no. 75/76 (March/April), pp. 3–8.
——(1979b) "The Causes of the Constitutional Revolution," *International Journal of Middle East Studies*, vol. 10, no. 3 (August), pp. 381–414.
——(1980) "Structural Causes of the Iranian Revolution," *MERIP Reports*, no. 87, *Iran's Revolution: The Rural Dimension* (May), pp. 21–26.
——(1982) *Iran Between Two Revolutions* (Princeton, NJ: Princeton University Press).
——(1989) *Radical Islam: The Iranian Mojahedin* (London: I.B. Tauris).
——(1993) *Khomeinism: Essays on the Islamic Republic* (Berkeley, CA: University of California).
Adamiyyat, Faridun (1972) *Fikr-e Demukrasi Ijtema'i dar Nahzat-e Mashrutiyat-e Iran* (Tehran: Intesharat-e Payam).

——(1976) *Ideoluzhy-e Nihzat-e Mashrutiyat-e Iran*, vol. I. (Tehran: Amir Kabir).
Adamiyyat, Faridun and Homa Natiq (1977) *Afkar-e Ijtima'i va Siyasi va Iqtisadi dar Asar-e Muntashir-nashudeh-ye Dauran-e Qajar* (Tehran: Agah).
Adelkhah, Fariba (1999) *Being Modern in Iran* (translated from the French by Jonathan Derrick) (London: C. Hurst & Co.).
Afary, Janet (1991) "Peasant Rebellions during the Constitutional Revolution 1906–09," *International Journal of Middle East Studies*, vol. 23, no. 2 (May), pp. 137–61.
Afshar, Haleh (1985) *Iran in Turmoil* (London: Macmillan).
Afshar, M. (1925) "Awwaleen khwahish-e ma: Ittehad-e Melli-ye Iran," *Ayandeh*, I (June), pp. 5–6.
Afshari, Mohammed Reza (1983) "The Pishivaran and Merchants in Precapitalist Iranian Society: An Essay on the Background and the Causes of the Constitutional Revolution," *International Journal of Middle East Studies*, vol. 15, no. 2 (May), pp 133–55.
Afshari, Parvez (1994) *Sadr-e 'Azam-ha-ye Silsila-ye Qajariyeh* (Tehran: Mosaseh-ye chap o intesharat-e wizarat-e amwar-e kharijeh).
Aghajanian, Akbar (1983) "Ethnic Equality in Iran: An Overview," *International Journal of Middle East Studies*, vol. 15, no. 2 (May), pp. 211–24.
——(1991) "Population Change in Iran: A Stalled Demographic Transition?," *Population and Development Review*, vol. 17, no. 4 (December), pp. 703–15.
Ajami, Fouad (1999) *The Arab Predicament: Arab Political Thought and Practice since 1967* (Cambridge: Cambridge University Press).
Akhavi, Shahrough (1980) *Religion and Politics in Contemporary Iran: Clergy-State Relations in the Pahlavi Period* (Albany, NY: SUNY Press).
——(1983) "Ideology and Praxis of the Iranian Revolution," *Comparative Studies in Society and History*, vol. 25, no. 2, pp. 195–221.
——(1992) "The Clergy's Concepts of Rule in Egypt and Iran," *Annals of American Academy of Political and Social Sciences*, vol. 524 (November), pp. 92–119.
Al-e Ahmad, Jalal (1960) *Kharg: Dorr-e Yatim Khalij* (Tehran: Amir Kabir).
——(1977) *Bazgasht az Shoravi* (translation of Andre Gide's work on his return from the Soviet Union) (Tehran: Amir Kabir).
——(1978a) *Dar Khidmat wa Khianat-e Raushanfikran* (2 vols) (Tehran: Kharazami).
——(1978b) *Kar-nameh-ye seh saleh* (Tehran: Ravaq).
——(1984) *Safar beh Vilayat-e Israyil* (Tehran: Ravaq).
——(1992) *Nafreen-e Zameen* (Tehran: Intesharat-e Firdaus).
——(1993a) *Gharbzadegi* (Tehran: Intesharat-e Firdaus,).
——(1993b) *Khasi dar Meqat* (Tehran: Intesharat-e Firdaus).
——(1993c) *Mudeir-e Madraseh* (Tehran: Intesharat-e Firdaus).
——(1993d) *Panj Dastan* (Tehran: Intesharat-e Firdaus).
——(1993e) *Urazan* (Tehran: Intesharat-e Firdaus).
——(2003) *Nun wa al-Qalm* (Isfahan: Nashr-e Khurram).
Algar, Hamid (1973) *Mirza Malkum Khan* (Berkeley, CA and Los Angeles, CA: University of California Press).

——(1979) "Introduction," in 'Ali Shari'ati *On the Sociology of Islam* (Lectures, translated by Hamid Algar) (Berkeley, CA: Mizan Press).
——(2001) *Roots of the Islamic Revolution in Iran* (New York: Islamic Publications International).
'Alijani, Reza (2000a) *Naugirayi dini: nigahi az darun* (Tehran: Intesharat-e Insan).
——(2000b) *Shari'ati-shenasi* (I), *zamaneh, zindagi wa armanha* (Tehran: Nashr-e Shadgan, 1380/2000).
——(2000c) *Shari'ati-shenasi* (II), *Islah-ye Inqilabi* (Tehran: Yadawran, 1380/2000).
——(2001) *Shari'ati-shenasi* (III) *Baz saf-ha Ishtibah nishawad* (Tehran: Yadawran, 1381/2001).
——(2002) *Shari'ati: Rah ya be-raheh* (Tehran: Intesharat-e Qalm).
——(2003) *Shari'ati wa SAVAK: muravari-ye tahleel-e bar seh jeld asnad-e savak darbaraye doctor Shari'ati* (Tehran: Intesharat-e Kavir).
——(2005) *Bad-fehmi-ye ek tawajieh namuwaffaq: bar rasi tahlili-inteqadi nazrieh " 'Ummat-Imamat"-e Doktor 'Ali Shari'ati* (Tehran: Intesharat-e Kavir).
Alterman, Jon (2000) "Egypt: Stable but for How Long?," *The Washington Quarterly* vol. 23, no. 4, (Autumn), pp. 107–17.
Amuzegar, Jahangir (1991) *The Dynamics of the Iranian Revolution: The Pahlavi's Triumph and Tragedy* (New York: State University of New York Press).
Ansari, M.T. (ed.) (2001) *Secularism, Islam and Modernity: Selected Essays of Alam Khundmiri* (New Delhi: Sage Publications).
Arjomand, Said Amir (1987) *The Shadow of God and the Hidden Imam: Religion, Political Order and Social Change in Shi'ite Iran from the Beginning to 1890* (Chicago, IL: University of Chicago Press).
——(1988) *The Turban for the Crown: The Islamic Revolution in Iran* (New York: Oxford University Press).
——(2002) "The Reform Movement and the Debate on Modernity and Tradition in Contemporary Iran," *International Journal of Middle East Studies,* vol. 34, no. 4 (November), pp. 719–31.
Ashkuri, Hussain Yusufi (1993) *Mi'ad ba 'Ali: Yaadawareh-ye shanzhdahumin salgard-e shahadat-e doctor 'Ali Shari'ati* (Tehran: Nashr-e Tafkir).
Astawan, H.K. (1978) *Siyasat-ha-ye mo'vazan'ai man'efi,* vol. II (Tehran: n.p.), pp. 74–75.
Austin, John L. (1962) *How to Do Things with Words, the William James Lectures Delivered at Harvard University in 1955.* Ed. J. O. Urmson (Oxford: Clarendon).
Aysha, Imad al-din (2006) "Foucault's Iran and Islamic Identity Politics: Beyond Civilizational Clashes, External and Internal," *International Studies Perspectives,* vol. 7, pp. 377–94.
Ayubi, Nazih (1992) "State Islam and Communal Plurality," *Annals of American Academy of Political and Social Sciences,* vol. 524 (November), pp. 79–91.
Bakhash, Shaul (1981) "Center-Periphery Relations in Nineteenth Century Iran," *Iranian Studies,* 14 (Spring-Winter) 29–51.

——(1984) *Reign of the Ayatollahs: Iran and the Islamic Revolution* (New York: Basic Books).
Bakhshayishi, Aqiqi (1985) *Ten Decades of Ulama's Struggle* (Tehran: Islamic Propagation Organisation).
Barker, Paul (1981) "Tent Schools of the Qashqa'i: A Paradox of Local Initiative and State Control," in Michael E. Bonine and Nikkie Keddie (eds.), *Modern Iran: The Dialectics of Continuity and Change* (Albany, NY: State University of New York), pp. 139–57.
Bayat, Asef (1997) *Street Politics: Poor People's Movements in Iran* (New York: Columbia University Press).
——(2007) *Making Islam Democratic: Social Movements and the Post-Islamist Turn* (Stanford, CA: Stanford University Press).
Bayat, Kaveh (2000) "Riza Shah and the Tribes: An Overview," in Cronin (ed.), *The Making of Modern Iran: State and Society under Riza Shah* (London: Routledge Curzon), pp. 213–19.
Bazargan, Mehdi (1984) *Inqilab-e Iran Dar do Harikat* (Tehran: Mazaheri).
Behdad, Sohrab (1989) "Winners and Losers of the Iranian Revolution: A Study in Income Distribution," *International Journal of Middle East Studies*, vol. 21, no. 3 (August), pp. 327–58.
Black, Antony (1999) *The History of Islamic Political Thought: From the Prophet to the Present* (Edinburgh: Edinburgh University Press).
Bonakdarian, Mansour (1995) "Iranian Constitutional Exiles and British Foreign Policy Dissenters, 1908–9," *International Journal of Middle East Studies*, vol. 27, no. 2 (August), pp. 175–91.
Bonine, Michael E. and Nikkie Keddie (eds.) (1981) *Modern Iran: The Dialectics of Continuity and Change* (Albany, NY: State University of New York).
Boroujerdi, Mehrzad (1996) *Iranian Intellectuals and the West: The Tormented Triumph of Nativism* (New York: Syracuse University Press).
Bradfurd, Daniel A. (1981) "Size and Success: Komachi Adaptation to a Changing Iran," in Michael E. Bonine and Nikkie Keddie (eds.), *Modern Iran: The Dialectics of Continuity and Change* (Albany, NY: State University of New York), pp. 123–37.
Brumberg, Daniel (2001) *Reinventing Khomeini: The Struggle for Reform in Iran* (Chicago, IL and London: Chicago University Press).
Chehabi, H.E. (1990) *Iranian Politics and Religious Modernism: The Liberation Movement of Iran under the Shah and Khomeini* (London: I.B. Tauris).
Chehabi, H.E. (1997) "Ardabil Becomes a Province: Center-Periphery Relations in Iran," *International Journal of Middle East Studies*, vol. 29, no. 2 (May) pp. 235–53.
Chittick, William C. (2001) "Ibn 'Arabi," in Nasr and Leaman (eds.), *History of Islamic Philosophy*, 2 vols. (Qom: Ansariyan Publications).
Cole, Juan R. (1983) "Imami Jurisprudence and the Role of the 'Ulama: Mortaza Ansari on Emulating the Supreme Exemplar," in Nikkie R. Keddie (ed.), *Religion and Politics in Iran* (New Haven, CT and London: Yale University Press).
——(1992) "Iranian Millenarianism and Democratic Thought in the 19th century," *International Journal of Middle East Studies*, vol. 24, no. 1 (February), pp. 1–26.

Cook, Michael (2000) *Commanding Right and Forbidding Wrong in Islamic Thought* (Cambridge: Cambridge University Press).
Cronin, Stephanie (1997) *The Army and the Creation of the Pahlavi State in Iran, 1921–26* (London and New York: I.B. Tauris).
——(ed.) (2000a) *The Making of Modern Iran: State and Society under Riza Shah* (London: Routledge Curzon).
——(2000b) "Riza Shah and the Disintegration of Bakhtiyari Power in Iran, 1921–34," in Cronin (ed.), *The Making of Modern Iran: State and Society under Riza Shah* (London: Routledge Curzon).
Curzon, G. (1892) *Persia and the Persian Question*, vols I & II (London: Longmans, Green & Co.)
Dabashi, Hamid (1983) "'Ali Shari'ati's Islam: Revolutionary Uses of Faith in a Post-traditional Society," *The Islamic Quarterly*, vol. 27, no. 4, pp. 203–22.
——(1993) *Theology of Discontent: The Ideological Foundation of the Islamic Revolution of Iran* (New York: New York University Press).
Daneshvar, Parviz (1996) *Revolution in Iran* (New York: St. Martin's Press).
Davari, Mahmood T. (2005) *The Political Thought of Ayatullah Murtaza Mutahhari: An Iranian Theoretician of the Islamic State* (New York: RoutledgeCurzon).
Davidson, Charles R. (2000) "Reform and Repression in Mubarak's Egypt," *The Fletcher Forum of World Affairs*, vol. 24, no. 2 (Fall), pp. 75–93.
Derrida, Jacques (1976) *On Grammatology* (translated by G.C. Spivak) (Baltimore, MD: Johns Hopkins University Press).
Dorraj, Manouchehr (1990) *From Zarathustra to Khomeini: Populism and Dissent in Iran* (Boulder, CO and London: Lynne Riener).
Eickelman, Dale (1998) "Inside the Islamic Reformation," *Wilson Quarterly* (Winter), vol. 21, no. 1, pp. 80–89.
El-Fadl, Khaled Abou (2001) *Rebellion and Violence in Islamic Law* (Cambridge: Cambridge University Press).
Eliash, Joseph (1979) "Misconceptions Regarding the Juridical Status of the Iranian 'Ulema,'" *International Journal of Middle East Studies*, vol. 10, no. 1 (February), pp. 9–25.
Enayat, Hamid (2001) *Modern Islamic Political Thought* (Kuala Lumpur: Islamic Book Trust).
Esposito, John L. (1991) *Islam and Politics* (Syracuse, NY: Syracuse University Press).
——(1998) *Islam: The Straight Path* (Oxford and New York: Oxford University Press).
——(1999) *The Islamic Threat: Myth or Reality* (New York and Oxford: Oxford University Press).
Esposito, John L. and Dalia Mogahed (2008) *Who Speaks for Islam: What a Billion Muslims Really Think* (New York: Gallup Press).
Esposito, John L. and John O. Voll (2001) *Makers of Contemporary Islam* (Oxford: Oxford University Press).
Ettehadieh (Nezam-Mafi) Mansoureh (ed.) (1998) *Inja Tehran ast: Majmu'eh Maqalat darbareh-ye Tehran 1269-1344 h.q.* (Tehran: Nashr-e Tarikh-e Iran).

Ezzati, Abu'l Fazl (1981) *The Revolutionary Islam and the Islamic Revolution* (Tehran: Ministry of Islamic Guidance).

Faghfoory, Mohammad H. (1987) "The 'Ulema State Relations in Iran: 1921–41," *International Journal of Middle East Studies*, vol. 19, no. 4 (November), pp. 413–32.

Fakhry, Majid (2004) *A History of Islamic Philosophy* (New York: Columbia University Press).

Farsani, Sahila Turabi (2005) *Tujjar, Mashrutiyat wa Daulat-e Modern* (Tehran: Nashr-e Tarikh-e Iran).

Fathi, Asghar (1979) "The Role of Rebels in the Constitutional Movement in Iran," *International Journal of Middle East Studies*, vol. 10, no. 1 (February), pp. 55–56.

Firoozi, Ferydoon (1974) "The Iranian Budgets: 1964-70," *International Journal of Middle East Studies*, vol.5, no. 3 (June), pp. 328–43.

Fischer, Michael M.J. (1980) *Iran: From Religious Dispute to Revolution* (Cambridge, MA and London: Harvard University Press).

Floor, William M. (1980) "The Revolutionary Character of the Iranian Ulema: Wishful Thinking or Reality," *International Journal of Middle East Studies*, vol. 12, no. 4 (December), pp. 501–24.

——(1981) "The Political Role of the Lutis in Iran," in M.E. Bonine and N.R. Keddie (eds.), *Modern Iran: The Dialectics of Continuity and Change* (Albany, NY: State University of New York), pp. 83–93.

Foran, John (1991) "The Strengths and Weaknesses of Iran's Populist Alliances: A Class Analysis of the Constitutional Revolution of 1905–11," *Theory and Society*, vol. 20, no. 6 (December), pp. 795–823.

——(ed.) (1994) *A Century of Revolution: Social Movements in Iran* (Minneapolis, MN: University of Minnesota Press).

Foucault, Michel (1990) "Iran: The Spirit of a World Without Spirit," in Foucault and Lawrence Kritzman (eds.), *Politics, Philosophy and Culture: Interviews and Other Writings, 1977–82* (London: Routledge), pp. 211–24.

Garthwaite, Gene R. (1981) "Khans and Kings: The Dialectics of Power in Bakhtiyari History," in Michael E. Bonine and Nikkie Keddie (eds.), *Modern Iran: The Dialectics of Continuity and Change* (Albany, NY: State University of New York), pp. 159–72.

Gasiorowski, Mark J. (1987) "The 1953 Coup in Iran," *International Journal of Middle East Studies*, vol. 19, no. 3 (August), pp. 261–86.

Gastil, Raymond (1958) "Middle-Class Impediments to Iranian Modernization," *The Public Opinion*, vol. 22, no. 3 (August), pp. 325–49.

Gesink, Indira Falk (2003) " 'Chaos on the Earth': Subjectice Truths versus Communal Unity in Islamic Law and the Rise of Militant Islam," *American Historical Review* (June) vol. 108. no. 3, pp. 710–33.

Gieling, Saskia (1997) "The Marja'iya in Iran and the Nomination of Khamenei in December 1994," *Middle Eastern Studies*, vol. 33, no. 4 (October), pp. 777–87.

——(1999) *Religion and War in Revolutionary Iran* (London and New York: I.B. Tauris).

Greenstein, Fred J. and Nelson W. Polsby (eds.) (1975) *Handbook of Political Science*, vol. 3. Macropolitical Theory (Reading, MA: Addison-Wesley Educational Publishers).
Gurr, Ted Robert (1970) *Why Men Rebel* (New Jersey, NJ: Princeton University Press).
Habermas, Jürgen (1989) *Structural Transformation of the Public Sphere: An Inquiry into a Category of Bourgeois Society* (translated by Thomas Burger and Frederick Lawrence) (Harvard: MIT Press).
Haikal, Mohammad (1983) *The Return of the Ayatollah: The Iranian Revolution from Mossadeq to Khomeini* (London: Andre Deutsch).
Hallaq, Wael B. (2001) *Authority, Continuity and Change in Islamic Law* (Cambridge: Cambridge University Press).
Halliday, Fred (1979) *Iran: Dictatorship and Development* (Harmondsworth: Penguin).
Hanson, Brad (1983) "The 'Westoxication' of Iran: Depiction and Reactions of Behrangi, Al-e Ahmad and Shari'ati," *International Journal of Middle East Studies*, vol. 15, no. 1 (February), pp. 1–23.
Herman, Edward and Noam Chomsky (1988) *Manufacturing Consent: The Political Economy of the Mass Media* (New York: Random House).
Hiro, Dilip (1990) *The Longest War: The Iran-Iraq Military Conflict* (London: Paladin Grafton Books).
Irfani, Suroosh (1983) *Iran's Islamic Revolution: Popular Revolution or Religious Dictatorship?* (London: Zed Books).
Issawi, Charles (1971) *The Economic History of Iran, 1800–1914* (Chicago, IL: University of Chicago Press).
Jazayeri, Mohammad Ali (1973) "Ahmad Kasravi and the Controversy over Persian Poetry 1: Kasravi's Analysis of Persian Poetry," *International Journal of Middle East Studies*, vol. 4, no. 2 (August), pp. 190–203.
Johnson, Chalmers (1966) *Revolutionary Change* (Boston, MA: Little Brown).
——(1981) "Ahmad Kasravi and the Controversy over Persian Poetry 2: The Debate on Persian Poetry between Kasravi and his Opponents," *International Journal of Middle East Studies*, vol. 13, no. 3 (August), pp. 311–27.
Kasravi, Ahmad (1942) "Dar baraye Reza Shah Pahlavi," *Parcham*, 23–25 June.
——(2005) *Tarikh-e Mashruteh-ye Iran* (Tehran: Intesharat-e Nigah).
Katouzian, Homa (1981) *The Political Economy of Modern Iran* (London and New York: Macmillan and New York University Press).
——(1983) "The Aridisolatic Society: A Model of Long-Term Social and Economic Development in Iran," *International Journal of Middle East Studies*, vol. 15, no. 2 (May), pp. 259–81.
——(2000) "Riza Shah's Political Legitimacy and Social Base," in Stephanie Cronin (ed.), *The Making of Modern Iran: State and Society under Riza Shah* (London: Routledge Curzon).
——(2003a) *Iranian History and Politics: The Dialectic of State and Society* (London: Routledge Curzon).

——(2003b) "Legitimacy and Succession in Iranian History," *Comparative Studies of South Asia, Africa and the Middle East*, vol. 23, no. 1& 2, pp. 225–39.
Kayastovan, Hossein (1948-50) *Siasat Movazaneh nanfi dar Majlis Chahardahom*, vol. I&2 (Tehran: n.p.).
Kaye, John William (1856) *The Life and Correspondence of Major-General Sir John Malcolm, GCB, Late Envoy to Persia, and Governor of Bombay, from Unpublished Letters and Journals* (London: Smith, Elder & Co.).
Kazemzadeh, Firuz (1968) *Russia and Britain in Persia, 1886–1914: A Study in Imperialism* (New Haven, CT and London: Yale University Press).
Keddie, Nikkie R. (1966a) *Religion and Rebellion in Iran: The Tobacco Protest of 1891-92* (London: Cass).
——(1966b) "Origins of the Religious-Radical Alliance in Iran," *Past and Present*, vol. 34 (July), pp. 70–80.
——(1968) *An Islamic Response to Imperialism: Political and Religious Writings of Sayyid Jamal al-din 'al-Afghani'* (Berkeley, CA and Los Angeles, CA: University of California Press).
——(1971) "The Iranian Power-Structure and Social Change 1800–1969: An Overview," *International Journal of Middle East Studies*, vol. 2, no. 1 (May), pp. 3–20.
——(1972) *Sayyid Jamal al-din 'al-Afghani': A Political Biography* (Berkeley, CA and Los Angeles, CA: University of California Press).
——(1981) *Roots of Revolution: An Interpretative History of Modern Iran* (New Haven, CT and London: Yale University Press).
——(ed.) (1983a) *Religion and Politics in Iran* (New Haven, CT and London: Yale University Press).
——(1983b) "Iranian Revolutions in Comparative Perspective," *American Historical Review*, vol. 88, pp. 579–88.
Khatami, Sayyid Muhammad (1993) *Beem-e Mowj* (Tehran: Intesharat-e Sorat-e javan).
——(1994) *Az Donya-ye Shahr ta Shahr-e Donya: Seyri dar andisheh-ye siyasi-ye gharb* (Tehran: Intesharat-e Ney).
——(2001) *Goft-o-go-ye tamaddun-ha* (Tehran: Tarh-e Nau).
Khomeini, Ruhollah (1984) *Resaleh-ye Towzieh al-Masael* (*Clarification of Questions*, translated by J. Borujerdi) (Boulder, CO and London: Westview Press).
——(1985) *Islam and Revolution: Writings and Declarations of Imam Khomeini* [1967–79] (translated and annotated by Hamid Algar) (London: Routledge and Kegan-Paul).
——(1992) *The Last Message: The Political and Divine Will of His Holiness Imam Khomeini* (Tehran: Imam Khomeini Cultural Institute).
——(n.d.) *The 'Ashura Uprising* (*in the Words and Messages of Imam Khomeini*) (Tehran: Institute for Compilation and Publication of the Works of Khomeini, Department of International Affairs).
Kirmani, Nazim al-Islam (2004) *Tarkih-e Bidari-ye Iran* (Tehran: Amir Kabir).
Ladjevardi, Habib (1983) "The Origins of US Support for an Autocratic Iran," *International Journal of Middle East Studies*, vol. 15, no. 2 (May), pp. 225–39.

Lambton, Ann (1988) "Persian Society under the Qajars," Ann K.S. Lambton, Qajar Persia (Austin: University of Texas Press), pp. 87–107. Lapidus, Ira (2002) *A History of Islamic Societies* (Cambridge: Cambridge University Press).

Laqmani, Ahmed (2002) *Allameh Tabatabai* (Tehran: Shirkat Chap wa nashr bin al-Melal).

Lee, Robert D. (1997) *Overcoming Tradition and Modernity: The Search for Islamic Authenticity* (Boulder, CO: Westview Press).

Lewis, Bernard (2001) *What Went Wrong: Western Impact and Middle-Eastern Response* (Oxford: Oxford University Press).

Lings, M. (1993) *What is Sufism?* (Cambridge: Cambridge University Press).

Linz, Juan J. (1975) "Totalitarian and Authoritarian Regimes," in Fred J. Greenstein and Nelson W. Polsby (eds.), *Handbook of Political Science*, vol. 3. *Macropolitical Theory* (Reading, MA: Addison-Wesley Educational Publishers).

Madani, Jalal al-Dine (1991) *The Islamic Revolution of Iran* (Tehran: International Publishing Corporation).

Majd, Mohammad Goli (2000) "Small Landowners and Land Distribution in Iran, 1962–71," *International Journal of Middle East Studies*, vol. 32, no. 1 (February), pp. 123–53.

Manouchehri, 'Abbas (2004) *Shari'ati, Hermeneutic reha'i wa 'irfan-e madani* (Tehran: Mu'asesah-ye tahqiqat wa tawasa'eh-ye 'ulum-e insani).

Marashi, Afshin (2000) "Performing the Nation: The Shah's Official State Visit to Kemalist Turkey, June to July 1934," in Cronin (ed.), *The Making of Modern Iran: State and Society under Riza Shah* (London: Routledge Curzon), pp. 98–119.

Martin, Vanessa (1989) *Islam and Modernism: The Iranian Revolution of 1906* (London: I.B. Tauris).

——(1993) "Religion and State in Khumaini's Kashf al-Asrar," *Bulletin of the School of Oriental and African Studies*, University of London, vol. 56, no. 1, pp. 34–45.

——(2000) *Creating an Islamic State: Khomeini and the Making of a New Iran* (London: I.B. Tauris).

——(2005) *The Qajar Pact: Bargaining, Protest and the State in 19th Century Persia* (London and New York: I.B. Tauris).

Masroori, Cyrus (2000) "European Thought in 19th Century Iran: David Hume and Others," *Journal of the History of Idea*, vol. 61, no. 4 (October), pp. 657–74.

Matthee, Rudi (2000) "Transforming Dangerous Nomads into Useful Artisans, Technicians, Agriculturalists: Education in the Reza Shah Period," in Cronin (ed.), *The Making of Modern Iran: State and Society under Riza Shah* (London: Routledge Curzon), pp. 123–45.

Menashri, David (1992) *Education and the Making of Modern Iran* (New York and London: Ithaca).

Milani, Mohsen M. (1988) *The Making of Iran's Islamic Revolution: From Monarchy to Islamic Revolution* (Boulder, CO and London: Westview Press).

Millspaugh, Arthur (1946) *Americans in Persia* (Washington, D.C.: Brookings Institution).

Minachi, Naser (2005) *Tarikhcheh-e Hosseiniyeh-ye Ershad: Majmu'eh masahibeh-ha, dafa'yat wa khatirat-e Naser Minachi* (Tehran: Intesharat Hosseiniyeh Ershad).

Mir-Hosseini, Ziba (1999) *The Religious Debate in Contemporary Iran* (Princeton, NJ: Princeton University Press).

Mirsepassi, 'Ali (2000) *Intellectual Discourse on the Politics of Modernisation: Negotiating Modernity in Iran* (Cambridge: Cambridge University Press).

Mirsepassi-Ashtiani, Ali (1994) "The Crisis of Secular Politics and the Rise of Political Islam in Iran," *Social Text*, no. 38 (Spring), pp. 51–84.

Moaddel, Mansoor (1986) "The Shi'i 'Ulema and the State in Iran," *Theory and Society*, vol. 15, no. 4 (July), pp. 519–56.

——(1992) "Ideology as an Episodic Discourse: The Case of Iran," *American Sociological Review*, vol. 57 (June) pp. 353–79.

——(1993) *Class, Politics and Ideology in the Iranian Revolution* (New York: Columbia University Press).

——(1994) "Shi'i Political Discourse and Class Mobilisation in the Tobacco Movement of 1890–92," in John Foran (ed.), *A Century of Revolution* (Minneapolis, MN: University of Minnesota Press).

Moin, Baqer (1999) *Khomeini: Life of the Ayatollah* (London: I.B. Tauris).

Moore, Barrington, Jr. (1966) *Social Origins of Dictatorship and Democracy: Lord and Peasant in the Making of the Modern World* (Boston, MA: Beacon Press).

Morier, J. (2001) *Second Journey through Persia, Armenia and Asia Minor* (London: Richard Bentley, 1818; reprinted New Delhi: Asian Educational Services).

Moslem, Mehdi (2002) *Factional Politics in Post-Khomeini Iran* (New York: Syracuse).

Mosaddeq, Muhammad (1979) *Khaterat va ta'alomat* (Tehran: Intesharaat-e 'Ilmi).

Motahhari, Morteza (1985) *Jame' wa Tarikh* (Tehran: n.p.).

——(1991) *The Rights of Women in Islam* (Tehran: World Organisation for Islamic Services).

——(2003) *Piramun Inqilab-e Islami* (Tehran and Qom: Intesharat-e Sadra).

——(2004) *Andisheh-ye Motahhari* (vols. 13-15) (Tehran: Tahqeeq-e tause'-ye sada).

Mottahedeh, Roy (1985) *The Mantle of the Prophet: Religion and Politics in Iran* (New York: Simon and Schuster).

Moussalli, Ahmed (2001) *The Islamic Quest for Democracy, Pluralism and Human Rights* (Gainesville, FL: University Press of Florida).

Moussavi, A. Kazemi (1994) "The Institutionalisation of Marja'-i Taqlid in the Nineteenth Century Shi'ite Community," *The Muslim World*, vol. 83, no. 3–4, pp. 279–99.

Mozaffari, Mehdi (1991) "Why the Bazaar Rebels," *Journal of Peace Research*, vol. 28, no. 4, pp. 377–91.

Musavi-Lari, Sayyid Mujtaba (1996) *Imamate and Leadership: Lessons on Islamic Doctrine*, Book Four (translated by Hamid Algar) (Qom: Foundation for the Propagation of Islamic Culture in the World).

Nabavi, Negin (2003) *Intellectuals and the State in Iran: Politics, Discourse and the Dilemma of Authenticity* (Gainesville, FL: Florida University Press).

Nasr, Seyyed Hossein (2000) *Ideals and Realities of Islam* (Chicago, IL: Kazi Publications).
——(2006) *Islamic Philosophy from Its Origins to the Present: Philosophy in the Land of Prophecy* (New York: SUNY).
Nasr, Seyyed Hossein and Oliver Leaman (eds.) (2001) *History of Islamic Philosophy*, 2 vols. (Qom: Ansariyan Publications).
Nasr, Vali (2000) "Politics within the late-Pahlavi State: The Ministry of Economy and Industrial Policy," *International Journal of Middle East Studies*, vol. 32, no. 1 (February), pp. 97–122.
Nasri, Abdollah (2003) *Haasil-e 'Umr: Seir-e Andisheh-ha-ye Ustad Motahhari* (Tehran: Dafter-e Nashr-e Farhang-e Islami).
Netton, Ian Richard (1994) *Allah Transcendent: Studies in the Structure and Semiotics of Islamic Philosophy, Theology and Cosmology* (Richmond, VA: Curzon Press).
Owen, Roger (1992) *State, Power and Politics in the Making of the Modern Middle East* (New York: Routledge).
Parla, Taha and Andrew Davidson (2004) *Corporatist Ideology in Kemalist Turkey: Progress or Order* (Syracuse, NY: Syracuse University Press).
Parsa, Misagh (1988) "Theories of Collective Action," *Sociological Forum* vol. 3, no. 1 (Winter), pp. 44–71.
——(1989) *The Social Origins of the Islamic Revolution* (New Brunswick, NJ and London: Rutgers University Press).
——(2000) *States, Ideologies and Social Revolutions: A Comparative Analysis of Iran, Nicaragua and Philipines* (Cambridge: Cambridge University Press).
Qane'irad, Muhammad Ameen (2001) *Tabarshenasi-ye 'Aqlaniyat-e Modern: Qira'eti post-modern az andisheh-ye Doktor 'Ali Shari'ati* (Tehran: Naqad Farhang).
Rahmani, Taqi (2001) *Talash dar rah-e taweel ma'na dar hasti* (Tehran: Intesharat-e Qalm).
——(2004) *Shari'ati naqad-e sunnat, qudrat, madaniyyat* (Tehran: Nashr Samdieh).
——(2005) *Raushanfikran Mazhhabi wa 'Aql-e Modern* (Tehran: Intesharat-e Qalm).
Rahnema, Ali (1998) *An Islamic Utopian: A Political Biography of Ali Shari'ati* (London and New York: I.B. Tauris).
Rahnema, Saeed and Sohrab Behdad (1995) *Iran after the Revolution: Crisis of an Islamic State* (London and New York: I.B. Tauris).
Rajaee, Farhang (1983) *Islamic Values and Worldview: Khomeyni on Man: The State and International Politics*, vol. XIII (Lanham, MD and London: University Press of America).
——(2004) *Mushkileh-ye howiet Iranian-e Imroz: Ifayi-ye Naqsh dar asr ek Tamaddun wa chand Farhang* (Tehran: Nashr Ney).
Ramazani, Ruhollah (1966) *The Foreign Policy of Iran: A Developing Nation in World Affairs 1500–1941* (Charlottesville, VA: University Press of Virginia).
——(1974) "Iran's White Revolution: A Study in Political Development," *International Journal of Middle East Studies*, vol. 5, no. 2 (April), pp. 124–39.

Ravandi, Morteza (1975) *Tarikh-e Ijtema'i-ye Iran,* several volumes (Tehran: Amir Kabir, 1355/1975).
Raymond, Eric S. (2001) *The Cathedral and the Bazaar: Musings on Linux and Open Source by an Accidental Revolutionary* (Cambridge, MA; O'Reilly Media).
Roberson, B.A. (2002) *Shaping the Current Islamic Reformation* (London and Portland, OR: Frank Cass).
Robinson, Chase (2003) *Islamic Historiography* (Cambridge: Cambridge University Press).
Rouhani, Fuad (1987) *The Political Biography of Mossadegh in the Context of the Iranian National Movement* (London: Iranian National Movement).
Roy, Olivier (1996) *The Failure of Political Islam* (Cambridge, MA: Harvard University Press).
Sadiq, Isa (1959) *Tarikh-e Farhang-e Iran* (Tehran: Tehran University Press).
Safa, Reza F. (1996) *Inside Islam: Exposing and Reaching the World of Islam,* (Chennai, Frontline).
Said, Edward (1997) *Covering Islam: How the Media and the Experts Determine How We See the Rest of the World* (London: Vintage).
Salehi-Esfahani, Djavad (1989) "The Political Economy of Credit Subsidy in Iran, 1973–78," *International Journal of Middle East Studies,* vol. 21, no. 3 (August), pp. 359–79.
Sanasarian, Eliz (1982) *The Women's Rights Movement in Iran* (New York: Praeger).
Savory, Roger M. (1972) "The Principle of Homeostasis Considered in Relation to Political Events in Iran in the 1960s," *International Journal of Middle East Studies,* vol. 3, no. 3 (July), pp. 282–302.
Schirazi, Asghar (1997) *The Constitution of Iran: Politics and State in the Islamic Republic* (London: I.B. Tauris).
Schulze, Reinhard (2000) *A Modern History of the Islamic World* (translated by Azizeh Azodi) (London: I.B. Tauris).
Schwartz, Stephen (2002) *The Two Faces of Islam: Saudi Fundamentalism and Its Role in Terrorism* (New York: Anchor Books).
Searle, John R. (1978) "Literal Meaning," *Erkenntnis* (1975–), vol. 13, no. 1; *Philosophy of Language* (July, 1978), pp. 207–24, http://www.jstor.org/stable/20010627 (accessed August 16, 2010).
——(1976) "A Classification of Illocutionary Acts," *Language in Society,* vol. 5, no. 1 (April), pp. 1–23, http://www.jstor.org/stable/4166848 (accessed August 16, 2010).
——(1989) "How Performatives Work," *Linguistics and Philosophy,* vol. 12, no. 5 (October), pp. 535–58, http://www.jstor.org/stable/25001359 (accessed August 16, 2010).
Sewell, William H., Jr. (1994) "Ideologies and Social Revolutions: Reflections on the French Case," in Theda Skocpol (ed.), *Social Revolutions in the Modern World* (Cambridge: Cambridge University Press), pp. 169–98.
Shah, Idris (1971) *The Sufis* (New York: Anchor Books).
Shari'ati, 'Ali (1971a) *Islamshenasi* (I) (Tehran: Ershad).

——(1971b) *Islamshenasi* (II) (Tehran: Ershad).
——(1971c) *Islamshenasi* (III) (Tehran: Ershad).
——(1977) *Hajj* (Tehran: Ershad).
——(1979a) *On the Sociology of Islam* (Lectures, translated by Hamid Algar) (Berkeley, CA: Mizan Press).
——(1979b) *Arey, Inchonin bud, beradar!* (Tehran: Hamdami Foundation).
——(1980) *Fatima Fatima Ast* (Tehran: 'Ali Shari'ati Foundation).
——(1981) *Az Kuja Aghaz Kuneem* (Tehran: Chapkash).
——(1987a) *Insan, Marxism wa Islam* (Tehran: Al-Huda).
——(1987b) *What Is to Be Done: The Enlightened Thinkers and an Islamic Renaissance* (translated and edited by Farhang Rajaee) (Houston, TX: Institute for Research in Islamic Studies).
——(1989a) *Che Bayied Kard*? (Tehran: Chapkash).
——(1989b) *Zan* (Woman) (Tehran: Chapkash).
——(1990) *Abu Zar* (Tehran: Intesharat-e Al-ham).
——(1991) *Miyad beh Ibrahim* (Tehran: Intesharat-e Mona).
——(1999) *Tashai'yo 'Alavi wa Tashai'yo Safavi* (Tehran: Intesharat-e Chapkhash).
——(2001a) *Bazgusht* (Tehran: Intesharat-e Al-ham).
——(2001b) *Khudsazi-ye Inqilabi* (Tehran: Intesharat-e Al-ham).
——(2001c) *Guftoguha-ye tanha'i* (Tehran: Intesharat-e Agha).
——(2001d) *Ma Va Iqbal* (Tehran: Intesharat-e Al-ham).
——(2001e) *Tarikh-e Shenakht-e Islami* (I) (Tehran: Shirkat-e Intesharat-e Qalm).
——(2001f) *Tarikh-e Shenakht-e Islami* (II) (Tehran: Shirkat-e Intesharat-e Qalm).
——(2002) *Ravish-e Shenakht-e Islami* (Tehran: Intesharat-e Chapkhash).
——(2003a) *Islamshenasi* (Tehran: Intesharat-e Chapkhash).
——(2003b) *Jahanbini wa Idiulozhy* (Tehran: Shirkat-e Sahami Inteshar).
——(2004a) *'Ali* (Tehran: Amoon Sanduq pasti).
——(2004b) *Habot dar Kavir* (Tehran: Intesharat-e Chapkhash).
——(2004c) *Hossein Waris-e Adam* (Tehran: Shirkat-e Intesharat-e Qalm).
——(2004d) *Insan-e Bekhud* (Tehran: Shirkat-e Intesharat-e Qalm).
——(2004e) *Nameh-ha* (Tehran: Intesharat-e Chapkhash).
——(2004f) *Shi'i* (Tehran: Intesharat al-Ham).
——(2004g) *Tarikh-e Tamaddun* (I) (Tehran: Shirkat-e Intesharat-e Qalm).
——(2004h) *Tarikh-e Tamaddun* (II) (Tehran: Shirkat-e Intesharat-e Qalm).
——(2005) *Hunar* (Tehran: Intesharat-e Chapkhash).
——(n.d.a) *Islam: Maktab-e Mobarez* (Tehran: Abu Dhar).
——(n.d.b) *Visayat wa Showra* (translated by 'Ali Akbar Ghassemy) (New Delhi: Iran Culture House).
——(n.d.c) *The Visage of Muhammad* (translated by Abdul Aziz Sachedina) (Tehran: Committee for International Propagation of the Islamic Revolution).
Shari'at-Razvi, Pouran (2004a) *Tarhi az ek Zindagi: naqad-ha wa nazar-ha*, vol. I (Tehran: Intehsarat-e Chapkhash wa Bonyad-e Farhangi Doktor 'Ali Shari'ati).
——(2004b) *Tarhi az ek Zindagi: naqad-ha wa nazar-ha*, vol. II (Tehran: Intehsarat-e Chapkhash wa Bonyad-e Farhangi Doktor 'Ali Shari'ati).

Sheikholislami, R. (1971) "The Sale of Offices in Qajar Iran, 1858-96," *Iranian Studies*, vol. 4 (Spring-Summer), pp. 104–18.
Shuster, William Morgan, (1912), *The Strangling of Persia*, (New York and London: Century Company,)
Skinner, Patricia (2005) *Islam: The Facts: What a Muslim Really Thinks and Feels* (Lulu.com).
Skinner, Quentin (2002) *Visions of Politics: Regarding Method*, vol. I (Cambridge: Cambridge University Press).
Skocpol, Theda (1994) *Social Revolutions in the Modern World* (Cambridge: Cambridge University Press).
Sobhani, Ayatollah Ja'far (2001) *Doctrines of Shi'i Islam: A Compendium of Imami Beliefs and Practices* (translated and edited by Reza Shah-Kazemi) (London: I.B.Tauris).
Soroush, Abdolkarim (1990) *Qabz va bast-e tiorik-e shari'at* (Tehran: Muassassah-ye Farhangi-ye Sirat).
——(1994) *Qisseh-ye arbab-e ma'refat* (Tehran: Muassesseh-ye Farhangi Sirat).
——(2000) *Reason, Freedom and Democracy in Islam* (Oxford: Oxford University Press).
——(2006) *Az Shari'ati: Majmu'eh arbab ma'refat* vol. 3 (Tehran: Muassesseh-ye Farhangi Sirat).
Sturrock, John (1993) *Structuralism* (London: Fontana).
Sugar, Peter F. (ed.) (1971) *Native Fascism in the Successor States: 1918-45* (Santa Barbara, CA: ABC-Clio).
Tabatabai, Allama Sayyid Muhammad Hussain (1989) *Shi'a* (translated by Sayyid Hossein Nasr) (Qom: Ansariyan).
Tabatabai, Sayyid Javad (2003) *Dar Aamad-e Tarikh-e Andesha-ye siayasi dar Iran* (Tehran: Intesharat-e Kavir).
Taheri, Amir (1983) *The Spirit of Allah: Khomeini and the Islamic Revolution* (London: Hutchinson).
Tapper, Richard (2000) "The Case of the Shahsaven," in Cronin (ed.), *The Making of Modern Iran: State and Society under Riza Shah* (London: Routledge Curzon), pp. 220–39.
Tavakoli-Targhi, Mohammad (2001) *Refashioning Iran: Orientalism, Occidentalism and Historiography* (New York: Palgrave).
Tilly, Charles (1969) "Does Modernization Breed Revolution," *Comparative Politics*, vol. 5, pp. 425–47.
Tripp, Charles (2006) *Islam and the Moral Economy: The Challenge of Capitalism* (Cambridge: Cambridge University Press).
Turner, Colin (2000) *Islam without Allah? The Rise of Religious Externalism in Safavid Iran* (Richmond: Curzon Press).
Vakili, Valla (2001) "Abdolkarim Soroush and Critical Discourse in Iran," in John L. Esposito, and John O. Voll (eds.), *Makers of Contemporary Islam* (Oxford: Oxford University Press).
Wells, Mathew (1999) "Thermidor in the Islamic Republic of Iran: The Rise of Muhammad Khatami," *British Journal of Middle Eastern Studies*, vol. 26, no. 1 (May), pp. 27–39.

Wilber, D. (1975) *Reza Shah Pahlavi: The Resurrection and Reconstruction of Iran* (New York: The Exposition Press).
Yaqub, Ahmed Hussein, *The Conception of the Sahaba's Ultimate Decency and Political Authority in Islam* [Nazariyat al-'adalat al-sahabeh wa al-Marja'ieh al-siasieh fi al-Islam] (Qom: Ansariyan Publications, 1420/1999).
Yazdi, Hussein (2001) *Azadi az Andisheh-ha-ye Ustad Motahhari* (Tehran and Qom: Intesharat-e Sadra, 1381/2001).
Zamani-Nia (ed.) (1983) *Farhang-e Jalal Al-e Ahmad* (two volumes) (Tehran: Pasargad).
Zarin-Kob, Abd al-Hussein (1998) *Rozgaran: Tarikh-e Iran az Aaghaz ta Saqot-e Saltanat-e Pahlavi* (Tehran: Intesharat-e sokhan).
Zirinsky, Michael (2000) "Riza Shah's Abrogation of Capitulations 1927–28," in Cronin (ed.), *The Making of Modern Iran: State and Society under Riza Shah* (London: Routledge Curzon), pp. 81–98.

## Newspapers, News Agencies

Ayandeh
*Habl al-Matin* (1892–1908)
*Iran-e Ma* (1943–47)
*Iran-e Nau* (1909–11, 1945–46)
*Ittela'at* (1945–79)
*Kayhan* (1949–54, 1960–79)
*Parcham* (1942–43)
*BBC Summary of World Broadcasts* (1961–79) [Reading]
Foreign Broadcasting Information Service (1965–79) [Washington]
*New York Times*
*The Observer*
*The Times*

## Research Monographs

Manoochehri, Abbas (1988) *Praxis of a Revolutionary Faith: 'Ali Shari'ati and Islamic Renaissance* (Unpublished Ph.D. Thesis, Faculty of Graduate School, University of Missouri-Columbia).
Mowlana, Hamid (1963) *Journalism in Iran: A History and Interpretation,* 2 vols. (Unpublished Ph.D. Thesis in Journalism, Northwestern University, Illinois).

# Index

Abduh, Muhammad, 84, 95, 131, 237, 238
Abel, parable of Cain and, 90–2, 94, 96, 104, 105, 179, 238
Adam, 87, 90, 140, 166–7, 238
Al-e Ahmad, Jalal, 2, 12–13, 18, 19, 49, 56, 64, 71, 81, 114, 115, 122, 125, 130, 187, 194, 197, 230, 231, 240
  early life, 57
  critique of industrialism, 58–60, 62
  *gharbzadegi*, 49, 59–61, 63, 81, 114, 115, 126
  on Israel, 63
  and Tudeh, 57–8, 61
  and National Front, 58
  and the 'west', 59, 60, 62
  and role of the *'ulema*, 62
'Ali (ibn Abi Talib), Imam, 3, 67, 90, 97, 101–2, 105, 108, 133, 134, 135, 137, 138, 146, 160, 163–4, 165, 169, 179, 203–4, 225, 239
*al-amr bi'l-ma'ruf wa'l- nahy 'an al-munkar* (commanding right and forbidding wrong), 64, 69, 144–5
Anglo-Iranian Oil Company (AIOC), 28, 35, 54, 230
Anglo-Persian Oil Company, *see* Anglo-Iranian Oil Company (AIOC)
Al-'Arabi, ibn, 84, 167–8, 233, 243
Asadabadi, Jamal al-din (al-Afghani), 25, 131, 167, 223, 170

Ayatollah-ye Ozma (Grand Ayatollah), 41, 42, 65, 227, 231–2, 243
Azerbaijan, 26, 35, 57, 75, 225

Bani-Sadr, Abolhasan, 10, 43, 248
*Batini*, 43, 168–9, 233, 247
*bazaar*, 19, 32, 40, 55–6, 71, 73, 82, 124, 149, 150, 156, 221, 225
*bazaaris*, 19, 23, 31–2, 35, 40, 72, 79, 81, 82, 124, 129, 148, 178, 222, 230, 234, 236
Bazargan, Mehdi, 3, 7, 10, 43, 73, 78, 81, 99, 122, 124, 130, 153, 154, 175, 176, 178, 182, 228, 233, 245, 248
Behbahani, Ayatollah, 41
Berque, Jacques, 77, 86, 90
Boroujerdi, Ayatollah, 41–2, 65, 80, 227, 232, 240, 249
Britain, 22, 25, 26, 28, 32, 34, 35, 51, 52, 53, 54, 61, 62, 155, 223, 224, 230
Buddha, 92, 105

Cain, parable of Abel and, 90–2, 94, 96, 104, 105, 238
cathedral and the *bazaar*, 14–15, 16, 18
CIA, 35, 36, 56
communism, 2, 33, 35, 36, 48, 52, 53, 55, 56, 58, 61, 75, 80, 89, 118, 149, 151, 225, 230
Confucius, 92, 105
Constitutional (*Mashruteh*) Revolution (1906), 6, 10, 21, 23–4, 25, 26, 31, 43, 49, 50, 51, 52, 64, 80, 154, 155, 176

constitutionalists (*mashruteh-khwahi*), 10, 12, 25–7, 31, 43, 48, 52, 55, 56, 73, 177, 200, 222, 224, 228
constitutionalism (*Mashrutiyat*), 19, 23, 49, 66, 197

D'Arcy concession, 31, 224
Dehkhoda, 'Ali Akbar, 38, 39, 80, 241

Eslami, Sheikh Qassem, 148–9

Fanon, Franz, 77, 130
*faradh al-'ain* (five obligations), 13, 43, 232
Fatima, 3, 101, 102, 135, 161, 162, 163–6, 203, 204, 239
*Fedayan-e Khalq-e Iran*, 65, 144, 177

Gandhi, 61, 130
*ghaibat* (Occultation), 66, 138–40, 143, 206–7, 243
*gharbzadegi*, 49, 59–61, 63, 81, 114, 115, 126, 129, 153, 198
Gilan, 26
Golpayagani, Ayatollah, 42, 181
Gurvitch, George, 77, 150

Hedayat, Sadeq, 80
*hijab*, 40, 42, 44, 80
Hossein (ibn 'Ali), Imam, 3, 17, 69, 135, 137, 146–8, 160–1, 165, 204–5, 236, 241, 242–3
*Hosseiniyeh-ye Ershad*, 3, 78, 82, 101, 102, 119, 122, 123, 124, 141, 144, 148–51, 162, 164, 183, 219, 235, 237, 240, 241, 248
Hussein, Saddam, 178, 179

*iman*, 43, 168, 169, 179, 233, 237, 246, 247
intellectuals/intelligentsia, Iranian, 11–12, 122
  lay Islamists, 43, 123
  modernist, (*monavver al-fikr*), 22, 23, 24, 123

secular modernists, 38, 39, 62
  *see also* Raushanfikr
*intezaar*, *see* Shari'ati
Iqbal, Allama Muhammad, 95, 131, 167, 171–2, 238
Iran
  Islamic Revolution of, (1979), 1, 3, 4, 5, 7, 8, 9, 10, 12, 13, 19, 64, 71, 122, 173, 175–7, 178, 179–80, 183, 195
  Islamic Republic of, 3, 4, 5, 10, 19, 99, 175–7, 180, 182, 185, 191
  and modernity, 12, 43
  modernization of, 5–6
  nationalist discourse in, 22–3, 30, 37–8, 44, 57
  renaming, 39–40
  as a rentier state, 8
  war with Iraq, 177–8, 179, 186, 192
Islam, 13–14, 15, 16
  concept of state in, 66, 94–6
  political, 1–2, 3, 6, 9, 19, 20, 41, 43, 49, 192–5, 197, 198–201
  polyvalence of, 15, 193–5
*istibdad*, 3, 22, 93, 94, 104, 105, 108, 148
*istihmar*, 22, 93, 94, 105, 106, 148
*isti'mar*, 22
*istismar*, 93, 94, 105, 106, 108, 112, 113, 129, 148

Jafar al-Sadiq, Imam (Sixth), 145
*Jama'-e Rowhaniyat-e Mobarez* (Association of Combatant Clergy), 2, 79, 177
Jesus, 92
*jihad*, 3, 20, 134, 144, 145–6, 179, 198
  *see also* Shari'ati

Karbala, 17, 41, 135, 147–8, 160, 205, 225, 236, 243
Kashani, Aytollah, 55–6, 64, 65, 76, 230
Kasravi, Ahmad, 31, 38, 44, 57, 65, 75, 80, 128, 224, 225
Khamenei, 'Ali, 42, 63, 180, 181, 182, 191, 231

Khatami, Sayyid Muhammad, 79, 182, 186–91, 192, 201, 250
Khomeini, Ayatollah, 2, 3, 5, 7, 9, 11, 12, 18, 19, 49, 99–100, 109, 122, 130, 154, 175–7, 179, 180, 181, 186, 187, 190
  early life, 64–5
  at Qom, 64–5
  Islamic governance (*hokumat-e Islami*), 65, 68, 69, 70, 71
  in exile, 65
  *Kashf al-Asrar*, 65, 68
  Nature of authority, 66–7
  return from exile, 4
  leadership of the Islamic Revolution, 4
  on trap of materialism, 68–9
  opposition to the Shah, 42–3, 65, 71–2
  radicalism of, 41, 68
  resistance against unjust ruler, 69–70
  *Vilayat-e Faqih*, his idea of, 10, 48, 67–8, 69–70, 71, 173
  *visayat* (Trust), his idea of, 66, 68
Khomeinism, 7–8

Lao Tse, 92, 105

*Ma'jma-ye Rowhaniyun-e Mobarez* (Society of the Combatant Clergy), 79, 190
Maleki, Khalil, 57, 122
Malkum Khan, 23, 222
Mani, 89
Mansur, Hasan 'Ali, Premier, 54, 109
*marja'-e taqlid,* 181, 227, 229, 231
Mashhad, 22, 41, 74, 75, 76, 78, 81, 82, 86, 87, 88, 89, 94, 100, 101, 103, 116, 117, 118, 119, 124, 129, 140, 144, 157, 158, 206, 234, 240
*Mashru'eh*, 24, 25, 65, 66, 80, 176, 197, 222
*Mashruteh* Revolution (1906), *see* Constitutional (*Mashruteh*) Revolution (1906)

Massignon, Louis, 77, 85, 107, 139, 150, 245
Maududi, Maulana, 93, 238–9
*mellat* (nation), 22, 23, 24, 25, 26, 33–4, 35, 36, 42, 43, 44, 125
Minachi Moqadam, Nasser, 78, 124, 149, 241, 248
Modarres, Sayyid Hasan, 64
modernity, discourse of, 6, 11, 12, 25, 27, 44, 45
*Mojahedin-e Khalq*, Sazman-e, 2, 5, 78–9, 144, 149, 151, 177, 244, 248
Montazeri, Ayatollah, 42, 179, 180, 181, 182, 191, 206, 231
Mosaddeq, Muhammad, 7, 9, 19, 32, 35, 41, 49–52, 61, 71, 73, 99, 100, 158, 228, 229, 230, 233
  early years, 50
  and the *bazaar*, 55–6
  constitutionalism, 52, 53–5
  views on jurisprudence (Shi'i), 50–1
  Muhammad Reza Shah, 52–3
  nationalism, 52
  and National Front (*Jeb'eh-ye Melli*), 52–5
  negative equilibrium, 52–3
  and Oil Nationalism, 35, 54–6
  and political Islam, 49–50
  appointed Premier, 54
  ouster, 56
Motahhari, Morteza, 3, 41, 42, 71, 78, 99, 122, 124, 130, 149–51, 162, 175, 176, 182, 231, 240–1, 246
Mu'awiyah, 133, 135, 146, 204–5
Muhammad Reza Shah, 3, 47, 52, 53, 67, 99, 122, 123, 181, 225, 227
  abdication, 175
  accession, 34
  economy under, 36–7, 42
  and Mosaddeq, 52–3
  ouster of, 8, 9
  and the USA, 35–6
  and the White Revolution, 36, 42
  policy on secularization, 40–2, 80, 82

Muhammad, the Prophet, 13, 50, 66, 67, 68, 92, 97, 101, 102, 107–8, 115, 133, 134, 135, 137, 138, 142, 145, 146, 160, 161, 163, 164, 165, 166, 167, 203, 204, 220, 226, 229, 232, 236, 239, 240, 245

National Front (*Jeb'eh-ye Melli*), 35, 53–6, 58, 61, 158
nativism, 11–12, 48, 49, 63, 130, 188, 189, 228
*nizam-e jadid*, 25, 26, 223
*Nehzat-e Azadi-ye Iran* (Freedom Movement of Iran), 5, 124, 151, 175

oil prices crisis (1970s), 8

Pahlavis, 25, 33, 35, 47, 179
   centralization under, 27–8
   economy under, 6, 28, 36–7, 119
   modernization of Iran under, 6, 7, 8, 9, 11–12, 36, 73, 197
   nation-building under, 27–31, 39, 42, 44, 73–4, 153–4
   opposition to, 2, 4, 6, 7, 9, 11, 12, 31–3, 37, 48, 197
   as a rentier regime, 8, 48
   secularization under, 6, 32, 34, 39–40, 44
   state-building project, 1, 37–8, 47–8
   and the USA, 35–6, 56, 109
Pishevari, Sayyid Ja'far, 57

the Qajars, 9, 21, 22, 23, 25, 27, 33, 99, 116, 155, 156, 157, 197, 221, 222–3, 226, 241
Qavam, Ahmad Qavam, 53, 234
*Qayamat*, 66, 70, 139
Qur'an, 10, 14, 15, 70, 75, 86, 87, 88, 90, 93, 101, 107, 115, 131, 133, 134, 135, 141, 145, 146, 150, 151, 159, 171, 180, 203, 204, 220, 226, 229, 232, 238, 245, 246, 247, 248
Qutb, Sayyid, 84, 94, 237

Rafsanjani, Akbar Hashmi, 42, 176, 186, 190, 191, 231, 248
*Raushanfikr*, 3, 20, 123, 126–32, 150, 158–9, 161, 165, 167, 172
   *see also* Shari'ati
Razmara, General, 54
Reza Shah, 26, 27, 34, 47, 51–2, 80, 99, 157, 197
   abdication, 34
   and AIOC, 28
   centralization under, 27–8
   economic reforms, 28
   educational reforms, 28–9
   and nation-building project, 27–31
   opposition to, 31–3
   secularization under, 32, 39–40
   and socialists, 33
   subjugation of tribes, 28
Rezai, Ahmed, 144
Rida, Rashid, 95, 238
*rowzehkhwani*, 80, 82, 123, 236
Russia, 22, 25, 26, 27, 48, 155
   *see also* Soviet Union (USSR)

Sadra, Mullah, 84, 86, 87, 167
Sa'id, Muhammad, 53
Sartre, Jean-Paul, 58, 77, 111, 123, 128, 150, 167
SAVAK (*Sazman-e Amniyyat wa Ittela'at-e Keshvar*, National Security and Information Organization), 36, 82, 100, 101, 109, 118, 144, 151, 239, 246, 248
*shahadat*, 3, 20, 144, 145, 146, 161, 205
   *see also* Shari'ati
*shahid*, 145, 146, 244
*shari'ah*, 1, 10, 13, 14, 15, 24, 54, 66, 69, 95–6, 176, 185, 193, 194, 197
Shari'ati, 'Ali, 1, 3, 12, 16, 17, 18, 19, 20, 43, 45, 72, 73–4, 84, 177, 179, 182, 187, 190, 192, 197–200
   accommodation by Islamic Republic, 2, 79

*al-amr bi'l-ma'ruf wa'l- nahy 'an al-munkar* (commanding right and forbidding wrong), 144–5
anticlericalism, 2, 13
audience of, 116–17, 124–5
death, 1, 175
early years, 74–5
existentialism, influence of, 117, 150, 154, 155, 167, 168, 171–2
on history, 89, 90–2
at *Hosseiniyeh-ye Ershad*, 16, 78, 101, 102, 119, 122, 123, 124, 141, 144, 148–51, 162, 164, 183
*ijtihad*, 140
on *Imamat*/Imamate, 3, 20, 101, 102–3, 108, 115, 136, 138, 142, 143, 144, 203, 205
*iman*, 169–70
notion of *intezar*, 3, 139, 141–4, 177, 180
Iqbal and, 171–2
on Islamic order, 2, 94, 106–9
*javânmardi*, 154–7, 159–61, 166, 167
on *jihad*, 134, 144, 145, 146–8, 160, 161, 198, 200
leftist criticism of, 117–18
and Marxism, 89, 91, 92–3, 104, 117–18, 129, 130, 150, 159
influence of Massignon on, 77, 85, 107, 139, 150
during the Mosaddeq era, 76
and Motahhari, 78, 124, 149–51, 175
critique of modernity, 112–13, 125–6
*munafiq*, 133–4
critique of political order, 103–6, 121
critique of Pahlavi order, 2–3, 111–16, 119
in Paris, 77–8, 157
in prison, 78, 151, 175
and Puran Shari'at-Razavi, 76–7
on *raushanfikr*, 126–32, 150, 158–9, 161, 165, 167, 172
and SAVAK, 101, 109, 118, 144, 150
on Safavid Shi'ism, 137–8
on *shahadat*, 144, 147, 161
on Shi'ism, 134–7, 139
on *shirk*, 90–2, 93–4, 100, 132, 134, 135, 136, 144, 146, 179
on *showra*, 102
and socialists, 89
impact of Sufism on, 84–5, 139, 140, 157–8, 167
on *tauheed*, 73, 85–8, 92, 93–4, 100, 143, 144, 167, 168
*tazveer*, 93, 103, 104, 105, 112, 114, 115, 128, 131, 132, 133, 134, 137, 138, 140, 143, 144, 157, 200
and Third Worldism, 156, 157
on tradition and modernity, 109–11
*'ulema*'s criticism of, 118, 148–51
critique of the *'ulema*, 114–16, 134, 138, 140–1, 148
*ummah*, 96–7, 101–3, 108–9, 134, 135, 144, 146, 155, 160, 161, 166, 179, 184, 190, 200
at the University of Mashhad, 76, 78, 82, 88–8, 100, 101, 116, 118
on *visayat*, 103
on women, 161–6
*zar*, 93, 103, 104, 105, 106, 112, 113, 115, 128, 133, 137, 143, 144, 157, 200
*zor*, 93, 103, 104, 105, 106, 112, 113, 115, 128, 133, 137, 143, 144, 157, 200
Shari'ati, Muhammad Taqi, 74–5, 124
Shari'at-Razavi, Puran, 18, 76
Shari'atmadari, Ayatollah Kazim, 42, 180, 181, 191, 228, 232, 249
*Shirk*, 87, 89, 90, 91, 92, 93, 94, 100, 133, 134, 135, 136, 144, 146, 179, 237
Shi'ism, *Ithna 'Ashari*, 3, 16, 24, 39, 41, 42, 49, 50, 61, 65, 66, 67, 82, 90, 101, 102, 134, 135, 139, 144–5, 146, 154, 168, 198, 203–7, 225, 227, 229, 243
Siahkal, 132, 144
Skinner, Quentin, 16–17

socialism, 32, 57, 58, 61, 72, 75, 89, 90, 234
Socialists, 33, 34
Soroush, Abdolkarim, 182–6
Soviet Union (USSR), 34, 35, 52, 53, 57, 59, 61, 225, 230

*ta'aziyeh*, 80, 82, 236
Takhti, Gholamreza, 158
Taleqani, Ayatollah, Sayyid Muhammad, 3, 41, 62, 181
*tauheed*, 3, 19, 73, 83–4, 90, 92, 144, 167
  see also Shari'ati
Tehran, 3, 16, 22, 28, 29, 35, 41, 50, 57, 72, 76, 78, 81, 88, 89, 94, 100, 103, 116, 118, 119, 124, 125, 182, 186, 194, 230, 233, 236, 241, 244
Third World, 7, 36, 77, 78, 111, 112, 113, 130, 154, 157, 192, 193, 194, 228
Tobacco protests, 22, 23, 61, 64, 156, 221, 243, 245
Tudeh party, 33, 35, 36, 40, 41, 48, 53, 57–8, 61, 73
Twelfth Imam (Vanished Imam), 50, 62, 66, 67, 138, 139, 140, 141, 143, 145, 206–7, 227, 243

'ulema, 2, 3, 4, 5–6, 7–8, 9–10, 12–13, 23, 24, 32, 35, 37, 39, 40–1, 42–3, 62, 63, 64, 65, 66, 67, 69, 70, 72, 73, 80, 82, 89, 95, 101, 117, 118, 122, 123, 134, 137, 138, 140, 141, 143, 148, 149, 150, 162, 169, 171, 175, 176, 177, 178, 180, 181, 182, 183, 188, 190, 191, 225, 226, 227, 228, 229, 231, 232, 233, 235, 236, 243, 244, 249
Umayyads, 105, 133, 135–6, 146, 147, 161, 179, 204, 205
*ummah*, 3, 20, 24, 70, 94–6, 101–3, 108, 109, 134, 135, 144, 146, 154, 155, 160, 161, 166, 170, 184, 190, 200, 203, 238, 239, 245, 247
U.S.A, 5, 34, 35–6, 42, 53, 109, 178

Viet Cong, 61
*Vilayat-e Faqih*, 10, 78, 99, 122, 151, 173, 176, 180, 181, 182, 187
  see also Khomeini
*visayat* (Trust), 66, 68, 103

*wahdat al-wujud*, 83–4, 86, 140, 243
White Revolution, 36, 42, 64, 109, 111, 118
World War I (the Great War), 34
World War II, 33, 34, 53

Yazid, 69, 133, 146, 147, 161, 204–5, 236

*zahiri*, 43, 85, 168–9, 246
Zoroaster, 38, 89, 90, 92, 105

GPSR Compliance
The European Union's (EU) General Product Safety Regulation (GPSR) is a set of rules that requires consumer products to be safe and our obligations to ensure this.

If you have any concerns about our products, you can contact us on

ProductSafety@springernature.com

In case Publisher is established outside the EU, the EU authorized representative is:

Springer Nature Customer Service Center GmbH
Europaplatz 3
69115 Heidelberg, Germany

www.ingramcontent.com/pod-product-compliance
Lightning Source LLC
LaVergne TN
LVHW011805060526
838200LV00053B/3675